KINGS
OF
COCAINE

INSIDE THE MEDELLÍN CARTEL –
AN ASTONISHING TRUE
STORY OF MURDER, MONEY, AND
INTERNATIONAL CORRUPTION

GUY GUGLIOTTA AND
JEFF LEEN

SIMON AND SCHUSTER
NEW YORK   LONDON   TORONTO   SYDNEY   TOKYO

Simon and Schuster
Simon & Schuster Building
Rockefeller Center
1230 Avenue of the Americas
New York, New York 10020

SIMON AND SCHUSTER and colophon are registered trademarks of Simon & Schuster Inc.

Designed by Barbara M. Bachman

Manufactured in the United States of America

10 9 8 7 6 5 4 3 2 1

Library of Congress Cataloging-in-Publication Data
Gugliotta, Guy.
  Kings of cocaine: an astonishing true story of murder, money, and international corruption/
Guy Gugliotta and Jeff Leen.
    p. cm.
  Bibliography: p.
  Includes index.
  1. Medellin Cartel. 2. Narcotics, Control of—Colombia.
3. Narcotics, Control of—United States. I. Leen, Jeff.
II. Title.
HV5840.C7G84 1989   88-36756
363.4′5′09861—dc19   CIP
ISBN 0-671-64957-4

CONTENTS

En la vida se presentan dos o tres
ocasiones de ser héroe, pero casi
todos los días se presenta la ocasión
de no ser cobarde.

In our lives we have two or three
opportunities to be a hero, but almost
every day we have the opportunity
not to be a coward.

—FAREWELL MESSAGE FROM
AN OFFICER IN THE COLOMBIAN
ANTINARCOTICS POLICE TO
A FRIEND FROM THE U.S. DEA, 1986

1.

DADELAND

On a hot July day in 1979, a white Ford parcel delivery truck rolled into the parking lot of the Dadeland Mall, the largest shopping center in south Florida. If anyone had looked closely at the truck, he would have noticed that the signs on its sides did not match. The left side read "Happy Time Complete Party Supply," while the right side read "Happy Time Complete Supply Party." The signs were crudely stenciled in red paint. There was a telephone number underneath, but if anyone had called it, he would not have learned anything about party supplies.

The truck drove toward the southwest corner of the mall, where a Crown Liquors store was tucked between a Cozzoli's Deli and Mr. John's, a beauty salon. Dadeland was a showcase of subtropical suburban living. Spread over fifty acres, it sat on a small canal in Kendall, a vast bedroom community that every weekday sent an army of white-collar workers ten miles north into downtown Miami. Kendall was a place of manicured lawns and ranch-style homes, not quite up to the luxurious Spanish architecture of Coral Gables, but as all-American as things got in Dade County.

The white truck had come to Dadeland for a rendezvous with German Jimenez Panesso, a man who was going to make a purchase at Crown Liquors. Jimenez was one of the top cocaine dealers in Miami. The men in the white truck were also cocaine dealers. Like Jimenez, they were Colombian. The truck stopped at the curb near the liquor store, as if to make a delivery. The motor kept running.

About 2:20 P.M. Jimenez and his twenty-two-year-old bodyguard, Juan Carlos Hernandez, pulled into the Dadeland parking lot in a new white Mercedes-Benz sedan. They left a loaded 9-mm Browning automatic pistol on the floor in the backseat and walked unarmed into Crown Liquors.

Inside they asked clerk Thomas Capozzi for a bottle of Chivas Regal. Capozzi pointed to a shelf on the right. Hernandez went to fetch the bottle for his boss. Just then, two men walked from the white truck into the liquor store. One leveled a silenced .380 Beretta automatic handgun at Jimenez and opened fire. The other joined in with an Ingram MAC-10 machine pistol. The shooters sprayed Jimenez and Hernandez, shattering bottles on the shelves. Hernandez died where he stood, falling on his back, the quart of Scotch unbroken on the floor next to his left elbow. Jimenez dropped face up as he tried to run out the door, part of his head blown away by four or five .45-caliber slugs from the MAC-10. Capozzi, wounded by a stray bullet that hit his right shoulder and tore through his chest, staggered out of the store. The bullets went through cases of liquor and wine and the store's ceiling. The man with the MAC-10 emptied his thirty-round clip and reloaded.

Morgan Perkins, an eighteen-year-old stock boy eating lunch in the backroom, heard the commotion and came out front. He saw a man in a white shirt and dark pants shooting up the store. Perkins fell to the floor behind the counter, crawled to the front door, bolted into the parking lot, and scrambled under a parked car.

Next door in Cozzoli's, people heard the noise, and somebody yelled, "Skylab is falling." Everybody laughed. A woman and her son finished their lunch, walked out, and saw glass all over the sidewalk. They heard the gunfire. The boy ran ahead into the parking lot and spotted Capozzi, the wounded clerk. "Somebody's hit in the parking lot!" the boy yelled.

The woman ran back to Cozzoli's, but by then the owners had locked the door. "They're shooting! Call the police!" she yelled.

The woman ran to Mr. John's on the other side of the liquor store. The beauty salon customers had heard the slugs hitting the liquor store walls and thought it was just teenagers making noise. Then it dawned. "Call the police," the salon manager yelled to his receptionist. "Dial 911."

After firing more than sixty times, the killers stopped. They dropped the MAC-10 inside the liquor store, ran outside, and jumped into the cab of the white truck. Another man in the cab spied Perkins hiding under a car and fired a .30-caliber carbine at him. Perkins took bullets in both feet. "Why are they shooting at me?" he screamed. "I didn't do anything." To cover their getaway, the men in the cab indiscriminately blasted the mall parking lot with their weapons. They got so excited, they shot out their own rearview mirror. The bullets tore holes into parked cars and shattered plate-glass store windows. One shot ruptured a car's fuel tank, spilling gasoline into the parking lot. Another bullet whizzed by the ear of a pedestrian. The white truck finally disappeared around the Jordan Marsh store at the south end of the mall. The shooting was over in less than three minutes.

THE call came on a crackle of static into the Dade County Public Safety Department's homicide squadroom: a machine-gunning involving Latin males at the Dadeland Mall. It was 2:35 P.M., July 11, 1979.

Oh, shit, here we go again, thought Detective Al Singleton. Latins with machine guns meant Colombians and homicides. Here's another number two for the shelf, he thought. A "number two" was an unsolved homicide.

There was a cocaine war going on, and Colombians had been turning up dead in Miami and surrounding Dade County for months. The department had put together an eighteen-man squad to work on twenty-four Latin drug homicides dating back to November. The cases rarely got solved. The squad was called the Special Homicide Investigation Team—the S.H.I.T. squad.

Singleton was a regular homicide detective, not part of the S.H.I.T. squad. His own squad was not in line to handle the shooting at Dadeland. But it looked like one of those cases where a lot of people were needed to assist. So Singleton got into his light blue unmarked Plymouth Satellite and went west on the Dolphin Expressway.

Singleton's route bisected the populated part of the county. As he drove, he left behind Miami's budding skyline and headed to the flatter suburbs of southwest Dade. At thirty, Singleton was a jug-eared, rail-thin ex-marine who was just getting confident in his job after little more than a year in homicide. He wore a blue three-piece suit, summerweight, to deal with Miami in July.

Nobody in law enforcement had any clear idea why there was a cocaine war going on, least of all Singleton. The operative theory involved a rivalry between the Colombian cocaine factions. Others thought some of the killings were between the Colombians and the Cubans they were easing out. For years the balance of power between the Cuban middlemen and their Colombian suppliers had kept things on an even keel. Colombians bought the coca leaf in Bolivia and Peru, processed it into powder in their own country, and shipped it north. Then the Colombians decided to cut out the middlemen and in 1976 started to take over the cocaine distribution in Miami. Longtime Colombian traffickers came south in force from their traditional strong-hold in Jackson Heights in Queens. Illegal aliens—an estimated twenty thousand of them—poured in from Colombia. Within three years, four or five Colombian groups controlled nearly all of the Miami trade.

The business was getting out of hand by the late 1970s. The country's tastes were changing from marijuana to cocaine, and surging demand sent the price sky high: a kilogram (2.2 pounds) of cocaine, the standard unit of measure in the trade, sold for $51,000 in Miami, up from $34,000 just a year earlier. And there were more kilos coming in than ever before. South Florida was a smuggler's paradise. Miami was closer to Barranquilla, Colombia, than to Chicago, and Florida had 8,246 miles of shoreline to patrol.

By 1979 Miami was a boom town and cocaine was its currency, filling its banks with laundered cash and its nightclubs with Latin men in champagne booths watched over by other men with bulges in their suits. There was a fever in the air, a surface tension with a mean edge.

SHOOT-OUT AT THE COCAINE CORRAL, blared a front-page story stripped across the top of the newspaper Al Singleton had read that weekend. *The Miami Herald* detailed a series of drug executions the likes of which the locals had never seen. Colombians were dying in all sorts of interesting ways: stuffed in a cardboard box and dumped in the Everglades; delivered DOA to an emergency room in a white Cadillac; wrapped in plastic and dumped in a canal in Coral Gables; machine-gunned to death while sitting in noontime traffic. "It's Dodge City all over again," said a federal prosecutor. "A replay of Chicago in the 1920s," a county coroner called it. Colombians crowded the Dade County morgue—Dead County, the Colombians called it. "The Colombians are like Dixie Cups," said the coroner. "Use them once and throw them away." The story ended with a detective predicting, "It's just a question of who else is unlucky enough to get in the way."

Some of the dead were on the bad side of a bad debt; others were the creditors themselves, fallen to debtors with itchy fingers, figuring they'd do unto others before they got done themselves. The dead told no tales, but neither did the living, those the cops were lucky enough to catch. They had fake IDs, fake passports, or names like Jorge LNU —last name unknown. To identify people, the cops had taken to showing around a "book of faces"—personal photographs of uniden-tified Colombians collected at murder scenes.

The weapon of choice was the Ingram MAC-10. The Military Ar-mament Corporation Model 10 was a compact, box-shaped, little black killing machine that could send big .45-caliber slugs through a car body at the rate of a thousand per minute. Cops had taken to calling it the "Miami chopper."

Such a weapon figured prominently in the most notorious of the drug killings that Al Singleton and his fellow detectives were having such a difficult time solving. Less than three months before the Dadeland shooting, a balding man leaned out of a shiny black Audi 5000 and squeezed off a burst from his silenced MAC-10 at a pursuing white Pontiac Grand Prix. The Grand Prix had chased the Audi in broad daylight for nearly ten miles down the Florida Turnpike and U.S. 1 while the occupants of the two cars traded fire. When the cars finally stopped, the balding man jumped out of the Audi, took a stance behind a concrete pole and continued firing at the men in the Grand Prix, who fired back over the hood of a car filled with teenagers. Somehow no one was hit.

The Audi was found abandoned. Police opened the trunk and stared at the body of a Colombian. He had two Florida driver's licenses, both valid. The one that called him Jaime Arturo Suescun turned out to be correct. His mouth was taped shut, his feet were bound, and his hands were cuffed behind his back. A taut rope looped from the handcuffs to his blood-encrusted neck. An autopsy later revealed that he had died from asphyxiation. Next to him were Ziploc bags containing twenty kilos of white powder, which turned out to be milk sugar, a popular ingredient used to cut cocaine.

Police arrested two Colombians in what came to be known as "the turnpike shoot-out." One was the balding gunman, whose nickname was El Loco. Murder charges for the body in the trunk failed to stick, so the Colombians ended up charged with attempted murder for shooting at the Grand Prix. Less than a month after the shooting, El Loco's bond was reduced from $500,000 to $100,000. A satchel bearing $105,000 was delivered to a Miami bail bonding agency. Within two hours, El Loco walked out of jail and vanished. That sort of thing was getting typical.

AL Singleton turned south at the Palmetto Expressway. He arrived at the Dadeland Mall parking lot about twenty-five minutes after the radio call into the squadroom. Singleton parked quite a ways from the mass of cars arranged around the mall's southwest corner. It was the caution of a good detective: he didn't want to run over a piece of evidence in the parking lot.

Three coconut palm trees grew out of the lot in front of the stores where the green-and-white county police cars gathered. Gawkers pressed forward, and the uniforms kept them back with the yellow nylon rope that demarcated murder scenes. Singleton stayed outside the rope, careful not to disturb the scene. The lead detective appeared and told Singleton that the suspects had abandoned a white getaway truck in back of the mall. He dispatched Singleton to "process" the truck. Scene and body processing was Singleton's specialty.

Singleton drove to the rear of the mall and parked beside the truck. A television crew was already filming the scene. Singleton took out a yellow legal pad and began recording in meticulous detail what he saw.

The truck sat near a bridge spanning a canal that separated the shopping center from a residential neighborhood. The killers had apparently fled across the footbridge into suburbia. The truck was a white 1979 Ford on an Econoline chassis. The driver's door was open. The keys were in the ignition, and the motor was still running. The inside was done up in red shag carpet. The odometer had 108.2 miles on it. Singleton saw sunglasses and a blue police-issue bulletproof vest on the front seat. A sawed-off .30-caliber carbine lay on the passenger seat next to a .357 Magnum and another revolver. On the floor, a MAC-10 rested between the driver and passenger seats not far from a 9-mm Browning automatic pistol and another .30-caliber carbine. Very seldom do killers leave murder weapons at the scene. Here he had six. Singleton had never seen anything like it.

He drew a diagram and carefully noted the position of the weapons. Later, back at the station, he removed the weapons from the front of the cab and found that every gun had been fired. Like bandits in a cowboy movie.

When Singleton looked in the rear of the truck, he saw six more bulletproof vests hanging like smoked hams from the ceiling. The side panels were reinforced with quarter-inch stainless-steel plates. Whoever was inside the truck could look out small windows of one-way reflective plastic taped above the armor plating. In the truck's rear cargo doors, two circular holes stared out, each big enough to accommodate the muzzle of a gun. A pump shotgun, a .380 silenced Beretta, another 9-mm Browning, and homemade shotgun shells were ditched in the rear of the truck. By evening, everyone was calling it "the war wagon."

Even in the middle of a cocaine war averaging one murder a week —Jimenez and Hernandez were the thirty-seventh and thirty-eighth drug homicide victims of 1979—Dadeland was unique. Colombian hitmen had carried out brazen machine-gun assassinations in broad daylight before. But at Dadeland the Colombians turned their weapons on innocent bystanders for the first time. And then there was the war wagon. The police looked at it and got a very real chill. The killers had planned to escape, even if it meant blasting through a ring of police. The police decided to do something very out of character: they opened up the truck for inspection by a newspaper reporter, Edna Buchanan, the stellar crime writer from *The Miami Herald*. It went against the book to let a journalist get so close to a vital piece of evidence in an open homicide investigation, but the homicide chief wanted the uniform cops to know what they were up against.

Al Singleton had always carried a .38-caliber Model 19 blue-steel Smith & Wesson, standard issue for county police. After Dadeland he went out and bought a fourteen-shot 9-mm Browning automatic.

The Dadeland shoot-out was national news, introducing "cocaine cowboys" into the language. More than any other single incident, it shaped a Wild West image of Miami that would later surface on *Miami Vice* and in innumerable national magazine stories.

Dadeland did little to clarify Miami's cocaine war. Since Jimenez was hit in the face, it took several days to identify him as a thirty-seven-year-old Colombian drug fugitive wanted in New York. ("I started counting the bullet holes in them and gave up," said a county coroner. "They looked like Swiss cheese.") Jimenez was said to be either the Number-1 or Number-2 man in one of the Colombian rings running the cocaine trade in Miami. His death was believed to be retaliation for the killing of Jaime Suescun, the body found in the trunk of the Audi in the turnpike shoot-out. Suescun was another alleged kingpin, and his killing was thought to be revenge for the murder of Jimenez's fifty-year-old maid, who was found strangled in a field on Easter, a week before the turnpike shoot-out. She had apparently died after witnessing a forty-kilo drug rip-off by Suescun at one of Jimenez's stash houses. This theory was strengthened by the fact that Suescun died exactly as the maid had: both were strangled and hogtied. To top it off, the Audi bearing Suescun's body was registered to Jimenez. And El Loco, the balding gunman, was known to be Jimenez's close friend.

As the investigators dug deeper it got even more complicated. It turned out that one of the people Jimenez supplied with cocaine was Suescun's boss, one Carlos Panello Ramirez. The theory went that Panello feared Jimenez's wrath after his man Suescun killed Jimenez's maid during the forty-kilo rip-off. So Panello decided to go after Jimenez before Jimenez came after him. But Panello feared Jimenez and needed an ally. He found such a person in another Jimenez customer, Griselda Blanco de Trujillo, a Colombian woman known variously as "the Godmother of cocaine" and the "Black Widow." Cocaine is a credit business. The wholesaler fronts the drug to the distributor, and the debt is paid when the money comes in. Blanco owed Jimenez a lot of money for cocaine, and she had a habit of paying her debts with bullets. Blanco's chief hitman was Miguel "Paco" Sepulveda. And it turned out that Paco was upset because Jimenez was sleeping with his girlfriend. An afternoon of violence that would terrorize Miami for years to come was born out of the theft of forty kilos of cocaine and a sexual indiscretion.

Though they soon had plenty of suspects, the detectives investigating the Dadeland shoot-out had no arrests to show for it. Everyone was a fugitive: Paco, El Loco, Panello, and Blanco. After Al Singleton and the other detectives had looked at things long enough, all sorts of leads appeared, though what the detectives ended up with only got harder and harder to follow. The ex-wife of El Loco, for instance, turned out to be Griselda Blanco's bookkeeper. There were interesting connections all over the place. But what did they add up to?

THE NEW BREED

Dadeland and the turnpike shoot-out served sudden and terrifying notice of the ascension of a new breed of criminal. The Colombian cocaine traffickers brought to Miami a stark savagery that U.S. lawmen had never before encountered. Before the Colombians, Miami's drug culture had been populated by slick high-rollers, hip young professionals, casual thrill seekers, and leftover flower children. Now, the age of Aquarius was over.

The Colombians would transform Miami into the cocaine Casablanca of the 1980s. Metropolitan Dade County would become for a time the murder capital of the nation, and south Florida would see an unprecedented federal police effort against drug smuggling. By the end of the decade any cocaine seizure under a ton barely rated a mention in *The Miami Herald*'s local news pages.

Supplied by these Colombian traffickers, cocaine would grasp America in the late twentieth century like no drug had before it. Nearly one hundred years earlier, Dr. Sigmund Freud had proclaimed the drug an aphrodisiac and answer to morphine addiction, touching off a thirty-year cocaine frenzy in the United States that ended with the nation's first comprehensive drug law, the Harrison Act of 1914.

The lesson was forgotten in the 1970s. At first cocaine was fashionable, an antidote to the dull, marijuana-soaked seventies, a chic statement, "like flying to Paris for breakfast," Robert Sabbag wrote in *Snowblind* in 1976. In the beginning, it dusted jet-set parties with its seductive sparkle and pulled movie stars like Richard Pryor and Richard Dreyfuss under its destructive sway. "God's way of saying you've got too much money," the joke went. Later, as greater amounts poured in, it strung out sports stars like Hollywood Thomas Henderson of the Dallas Cowboys and infiltrated the thrill-seeking habits of upper- and middle-class youth, who danced in clubs to the incessant inner drumming provided by a "blast of blow." In the 1980s, best-selling books like *Bright Lights, Big City* and *Less than Zero* would chronicle a generation wasting itself on "Bolivian marching powder." Finally, "crack" and "rock" would creep into the nation's ghettos, addicting the poor and spreading misery into the most miserable places. By 1988 six million Americans would use cocaine regularly, and at least three of them would die every day. Cocaine would become the first drug to be declared a threat to America's national security.

In 1979, however, little of this was obvious. It was difficult, if not impossible, for Al Singleton and his colleagues to know that they were witnessing the growing pains of a business that was changing from a modest smuggler's sideline into a multibillion-dollar international industry. But by the time Singleton drove into the Dadeland parking lot, most of the amateurs had been weeded out.

IN the end, only a handful of Colombians would remain at the top of the heap. These few would become the kings of cocaine. They would be tested constantly—by rival traffickers, by police, even by governments. But they would always survive, and most of the time they would prevail. They would become famous, ranked among the most successful, the richest, and certainly the deadliest criminals on earth. Together they would be known as the Medellín cartel.

There were four of them: Pablo Escobar Gaviria, El Padrino— "Godfather"—who exchanged a modestly successful career as a hired gun, kidnapper, and car thief for a chance to make millions as a cocaine trafficker; Jorge Luis Ochoa Vasquez, El Gordo—"the Fat Man"—a soft-spoken, lower-middle-class kid who wanted a better life for his family and found it in cocaine; Carlos Lehder Rivas, "Joe Lehder," a wise guy who loved the Beatles and dreamed of building the world's biggest cocaine transportation network; Jose Gonzalo Rodriguez Gacha, "the Mexican," who used the proceeds from cocaine to buy soccer teams, horses, and vast tracts of land in the jungle.

By the middle of the 1980s these four would control more than 50 percent of the cocaine coming into the United States, as much as fifty metric tons each year. They would have hundreds—perhaps thousands—of employees: *campesino* peasants to grow coca and process it; airplane pilots to carry the drug; distributors to market it in the United States; lawyers to handle the requisite legal problems; bagmen to offer bribes and launder money; hired killers to eliminate enemies.

They would keep their own organizations separate, but increasingly they would cooperate on large deals and make common policy. In the mid-1980s the Medellín cartel would earn an estimated $2 billion per year—tax free.

In 1979 the future lords of cocaine had already reached the top rung of their profession, but to U.S. law enforcement they were four names among many. It was difficult to see the linkages, if linkages existed at all.

Still, the police noticed that Colombian traffickers shared many traits. Most were young—in their twenties or thirties. Most had little education, and many spoke no English at all. A lot of them looked grubby and almost sick—pasty-faced chain-smokers with pitted complexions.

And yet they had immense success. They were cunning, close-mouthed, and creative, utterly single-minded, and willing to do absolutely anything to get what they wanted.

THE first Colombian cocaine trafficker that U.S. law enforcement studied in any detail was Griselda Blanco de Trujillo, a former whore who had moved most of her operation to Miami from the Colombian neighborhood in Jackson Heights, Queens, in the mid-1970s. A federal grand jury in Brooklyn had indicted her in 1974 in a 150-kilo cocaine smuggling case, and by 1979, at the age of thirty-six, she was the best-known cocaine smuggler in the United States. Police and criminals knew her as "the Godmother," "the Black Widow," "Bety," La Gaga ("the Stutterer"), and Muñeca ("Dollface").

She was suspected as a prime mover in the Dadeland debacle and had a fearsome reputation both in Miami and New York. Three different husbands, all of them traffickers, had died in the drug wars—this was her "Black Widow" persona.

Blanco was short, about five feet two inches tall, big-hipped, and attractive. She had dark, coffee-colored eyes, fair skin, and a round, full face with deeply dimpled cheeks that gave her a vaguely chipmunkish appearance—"Dollface." She had a speech impediment—La Gaga—and spent a lot of time on her appearance, favoring fancy headgear: hats, turbans, wigs. And like many drug traffickers, she also had a fondness for hand jewelry and claimed that her favorite diamond once belonged to Eva Perón. The flamboyance was part of her "Godmother" image, and in some ways it was her favorite. She named one of her sons Michael Corleone Sepulveda, in homage to the character in *The Godfather*.

By the mid-1970s the DEA estimated Blanco had several hundred people on her payroll. She liked to work with other widows and with women in general and was said to have developed her own line of women's underwear, complete with secret pockets suitable for carrying a kilo or two of cocaine through Miami customs. Her chief Miami distributor was a childhood girlfriend.

For heavy work she had her own gang, known as Los Pistoleros. Full membership, it was said, was acquired by killing someone and cutting off a piece of the victim—an ear or a finger—as proof the deed was done. One prominent gang member had the habit of taping shut the eyes and mouths of his victims, draining their blood into a bathtub, and folding the corpses into empty boxes intended for televisions or stereos. Another *pistolero* earned renown by murdering Blanco's enemies with a machine pistol from the passenger's seat of a speeding motorcycle. This technique was so admired that it became the trademark of Colombia's cocaine killers.

ALTHOUGH Blanco had been born in Cartagena, on Colombia's Caribbean coast, and had started her career in Jackson Heights, she, like most of the other young Colombian cocaine dealers, claimed the Andean city of Medellín as her hometown. By 1979 U.S. newspapers were calling Medellín the "Wall Street of Cocaine."

But most U.S. narcotics cops didn't know where Medellín was, let alone what it signified. Yet understanding Medellín was crucial to understanding cocaine.

At first glance the city offered few clues. Tourist brochures called it the "City of Eternal Spring" or the "Orchid City"—a fast-growing, mountain metropolis of 1.2 million people sprawled across a mile-high river valley amid the pine forests of north-central Colombia's Antioquia province. The brochures were right as far as they went. Medellín, the capital of Antioquia province and the second-largest city in Colombia after Bogotá, was as pretty a place as a person could find in South America. In 1979 it had a bustling downtown with new skyscrapers adding a touch of glass-and-steel elegance to the stately colonial neighborhoods that framed the city's burgeoning industrial sprawl. Medellín had three university campuses, a botanical garden, dozens of parks, and many tree-lined boulevards. Picturesque winding roads crisscrossed the suburban hills where gentry had built large country homes and weekend chalets. Small farmers lived in neat white stucco cottages with red trim and flowerboxes overhanging the verandas. Mean temperature year round was 72 degrees Fahrenheit. It rained a lot, but Medellín offered plenty of gorgeous mountain sunshine to compensate.

The men and women of Medellín called themselves *paisas,* after the tough, resourceful, adventurous Antioquian "countrymen" of myth. Outwardly modest, they were an aggressive, ambitious people, hard workers with hard heads who coveted money and social position. Anyone in Medellín—rich or poor—could win prestige if he had enough guts, brains, and vision to be a success.

IN Spanish colonial times Medellín was isolated, squalid, short of social grace, and unpleasant for those colonists from Bogotá and elsewhere who preferred a richer, more refined life. The *paisa,* an in-bred, pale-faced, miserly, loquacious lout who gobbled his words with a peculiar accent, became the butt of jokes. Bogotanos found *paisas* incredibly crude.

By the mid-twentieth century, however, the joke was on the rest of Colombia. The *paisas* were creative businessmen, risk-takers not afraid of travel or bold ventures. Parents encouraged sons to leave home at an early age: "If you succeed, send money," went an old *paisa* saying. "If you fail, don't come home."

And it paid off. Medellín started as Colombia's colonial mining center, added coffee in the nineteenth century, and became the center of national industry in the twentieth. By 1979 Medellín was a rich, attractive, arrogant city. Now the *paisas* talked only half in jest about seceding from Colombia and forming their own country. If Bogotá's rich intellectual tradition had won it a reputation as "the Athens of South America," Medellín was its Sparta, a place to respect, but also a place to watch very carefully.

BESIDES mining, coffee, and industry, Medellín also had a reputation as a smuggling center, earned in the nineteenth century by itinerant *paisa* peddlers who sold notions to rural housewives. By the middle of the twentieth century the list of available goods had lengthened, and the techniques for transporting them had changed, but the nature of the business remained largely the same. Perfectly respectable men—and some not so respectable—made a living bootlegging liquor and cigarettes by ship from the United States and airlifting television sets, stereos, and radios from the duty-free ports of the Panama Canal Zone.

This was where Colombia's cocaine industry took root. The leaves of the coca bush had been chewed as a stimulant by the Indians of South America's high Andes for two-thousand years, but it was only in the latter part of the nineteenth century that enterprising chemists in Europe began to treat relatively large quantities of the leaf and create the first cocaine. Before 1973 the modern, criminal cocaine trade was a cottage industry based in Chile and controlled by a few refiners who bought coca leaf and paste from Peru and Bolivia, transformed it into cocaine in Chilean laboratories, and sent it north to the United States, often using Colombian smugglers as middlemen. U.S. demand was limited to those rich and sophisticated few who wanted something with more kick than marijuana but fewer unpleasant side effects than heroin. The Chileans made a lush living from cocaine, but the market was relatively small.

This began to change in September 1973, when Chilean army General Augusto Pinochet Ugarte overthrew elected Marxist President Salvador Allende Gossens. Pinochet's police jailed or deported dozens of drug traffickers. At the end of Pinochet's first year, seventy-three of them were in jail in Chile, another twenty bosses had been sent to the United States, and the Chilean cocaine business was finished.

The trade moved to Colombia, which had the smuggling know-how, and, like Chile, easy access to the coca leaf producers in Peru and Bolivia. Chileans brought the technology north but shortly disappeared. Within two years the Colombians had eliminated virtually all the foreigners. A few years later they brought the same philosophy to Miami.

FROM the beginning, Colombian cocaine production was headquartered within the triangle bounded by the three great Andean cities of Bogotá, Medellín, and Cali, but almost immediately Medellín was dominant. At first this was not easy to see. Law enforcement both in Colombia and in the United States concerned itself primarily with the multiton loads of Colombian marijuana that were leaving from the Caribbean ports of Barranquilla, Santa Marta, and Rio Hacha. The coastal marijuana smugglers had little to do with cocaine, and cocaine, it seemed, had little to do with stateside drug abuse. The U.S. Bureau of Narcotics and Dangerous Drugs and its successor organization, the Drug Enforcement Administration, or DEA, maintained an office in the U.S. embassy in Bogotá, but its agents were concerned mostly with marijuana. The Bogotá DEA bureau made only occasional forays to Medellín, mostly to observe and harass Griselda Blanco.

Eyes opened for the first time November 22, 1975, when police at Cali airport stopped and seized a small airplane that tried to sneak in for a landing in the radar clutter of an Avianca Airlines commercial jet. The six hundred kilos of cocaine found in the plane's cargo bay marked the biggest seizure in history up to that time and suggested that the cottage industry that Colombia had inherited from Chile was a cottage industry no more.

Police arrested the pilot and co-pilot of the plane. The seizure touched off a vendetta among Colombia's traffickers, the first of the cocaine wars that would periodically shake the nation. The reasons for the war were not clear. The results, however, were: forty people were killed in one weekend. What was unusual was that all the murders were committed in Medellín, not Cali. Regardless of whose cocaine was seized, it appeared that cocaine policy originated in Medellín.

THE "Medellín massacre" tarnished the "Orchid City's" carefully cultivated image. Law enforcement's attention focused on the city's working-class satellite suburbs and the new, slum neighborhoods in the north end. This was the cradle of the cocaine industry. Here people carried guns, knives, and whatever else could get them an advantage in the day-to-day struggle to stay alive. By 1979 north Medellín was as dangerous a place as any in Latin America, breeding ground for the hard-bitten, cold-eyed hustlers who were laying waste to Miami. North Medellín was where the teenaged Griselda Blanco, just up from Cartagena, learned how to become a pickpocket.

The idea was to get rich, move south into a villa or mansion like the rest of *paisa* aristocracy, then buy a chalet in the Andean woods for weekends and a cattle ranch—a *finca*—for vacations. Drug money could thus transform a north Medellín mugger into a respected, conservative, Catholic businessman or -woman almost overnight. In Medellín, Griselda Blanco owned two houses, drove her own automobile, and lived like any well-to-do Medellín señora. If outsiders thought that was scandalous and unseemly, then outsiders could go to hell. In Medellín people minded their own business and took care of their own.

The lords of cocaine in the mid-1970s were older men, mostly *paisa* smugglers who had added drugs to their portfolios when the opportunity arose. Most of them were already well established, fairly well-to-do, and even respectable by the time they started to dabble in drugs.

But they were being supplanted by the younger traffickers who had started in the late 1960s and early 1970s with nothing going for them but ambition and intelligence. Many had been introduced to crime by the older smugglers, but few, even in their earliest days, had ever sold radios or filter cigarettes. They dealt cocaine, and only cocaine.

In studying Griselda Blanco, the DEA and the Metro-Dade police began to learn a lot about the Colombians who were making Miami the center of the cocaine trade. But the trouble with Blanco as a model was that she was never more than a middle-level trafficker. Much later experts would refer to her as a classic "floater." She had some cocaine labs in Colombia, a distribution network in the States, some muscle in both places, and enough money to get more. Still, she always moved around the edges of the industry. By focusing on Blanco, U.S. law enforcement tended to overlook or underrate far bigger and more dangerous traffickers who at the time were unindicted and unknown, including a young man from Medellín who by the mid-1970s had quietly become one of the most important cocaine traffickers in the world.

His name was Pablo Escobar. As late as 1976 the Colombian Department of Administrative Security (DAS), the Colombian equivalent of the FBI, described Escobar as a "mule"—a petty criminal who earned an occasional grubstake by transporting a kilo or two of cocaine for a much larger trafficker.

And Escobar looked like nothing. He was a short, plumpish man, five feet, six inches tall, maybe 160 pounds. He had hazel eyes, full cheeks, and black, curly hair that he combed to one side. He was light-complected and periodically affected a wispy mustache that barely changed his appearance. He had a totally forgettable face.

Escobar was born December 1, 1949, in Rionegro, a town of green, piney woods twenty-five miles east of Medellín, but he grew up in Envigado, a tough, blue-collar Medellín suburb that would become legendary as a font of cocaine bosses. Escobar's mother was a schoolteacher, and his father was a small farmer of some means. Later, paid image makers would extol their boss's humble beginnings, but Escobar was not nearly as underprivileged as he pretended. He was a working-class kid who graduated from high school, no small accomplishment in Envigado. His parents and his community gave him as much as any *paisa* was supposed to need to get ahead. It was up to Escobar to make something of himself. He didn't lose any time.

He began his criminal career in adolescence, stealing headstones from local graveyards, shaving off the inscriptions, and reselling the blank slabs to bereaved relatives at bargain prices. Associates and enemies would come to describe him as an undereducated but spectacularly smart man, a quick learner with a brilliant business mind. Outwardly, of course, his demeanor was strictly *paisa*: he was soft-spoken, modest, unfailingly polite, painfully formal.

After high school Escobar went to work as a bodyguard/enforcer for a middle-aged smuggler who bootlegged stereo equipment from the Panama Canal Zone. Escobar handled security at the Medellín airport and pestered his boss about moving up in the business. He rose rapidly, helped along by two million pesos ($100,000) he made kidnapping and ransoming a Medellín industrialist in the early 1970s.

Escobar's first known arrest occurred September 5, 1974, when Medellín police picked him up for stealing a Renault. Nearly two years later, DAS arrested him and five others for transporting thirty-nine kilos of cocaine through downtown Medellín in the spare tire of a pickup truck. The young prisoners tried unsuccessfully to offer $15,000 in bribes. The arrest marked Escobar's first drug bust; the seizure was the biggest in the city that year.

Escobar stayed in prison for only three months, walking out when his arrest order was mysteriously revoked. Two and a half months later police picked him up again, but he was freed on bail in less than two months. Over the years, nine separate judges handled the case. At some point the documents just seemed to disappear. One judge said a telephone caller told her that Escobar and his friends were discussing ways she might be murdered. They favored a simulated traffic accident. The caller also said the gang planned to kill the DAS agent who arrested Escobar. The judge immediately reported the threat and handed the case to another judge. Five years later, gunmen murdered Escobar's arresting officer on a Medellín street.

This was the last facet of the Escobar persona. The quiet young Envigado businessman was a stone killer.

ESCOBAR was one of the first of the younger generation to take up cocaine trafficking. One of the last was Jorge Luis Ochoa Vasquez. Ochoa was born in Cali but raised in Envigado. He was two months older than Escobar and knew him from childhood.

Ochoa was the second of three sons of Fabio Ochoa Restrepo and Margot Vasquez. The Ochoas were an old Antioquia family known primarily for their expertise in the care and breeding of livestock. Fabio Ochoa, a grotesquely fat man with a fondness for felt hats, held a reputation as one of the province's finest trainers of Andean *cabal-*

los de paso—walking horses. Margot would claim much later that in 1963 Jorge accompanied the first Colombian walking horse ever exported to Miami.

Despite this facade, the Ochoas were not gentry. In the mid-1960s, to make ends meet, Fabio opened Las Margaritas, a family restaurant specializing in red beans, *arepa* corn muffins, *sancocho* chicken stew, and other *paisa* specialties. The whole family worked long, hard hours at the restaurant to make it a success. Jorge; his older brother, Juan David; his younger brother, Fabio; and their sisters all bused tables, cooked, and waitressed from the moment they got home from school in the afternoon until the early hours of the following day. One of the legends that later circulated in Medellín held that Jorge led his brothers into drug trafficking because he was tired of watching his mother and sisters working themselves to death at Las Margaritas.

The Ochoa brothers were introduced to the cocaine business by their uncle, Fabio Restrepo Ochoa, one of the old-time *paisa* pioneer smugglers. All three brothers eventually became deeply involved in cocaine, but Jorge dominated the "Ochoa clan" from the beginning. Yet he was an improbable criminal, quiet to the point of reclusiveness, mild-mannered, family-oriented, and temperate in his personal habits. Except for an occasional glass of white wine, he did not drink. He did not smoke. Cocaine was out of the question. He did not permit the word to be uttered in his presence.

Like his father and the other Ochoa men, Jorge had a tendency to get fat, and his weight yo-yoed with the direction of his personal fortunes. He was big-framed, a shade under six feet tall, and often carried more than two hundred pounds. Like Escobar, he was nondescript in appearance, a pale-faced Antioqueño. And like Escobar, he occasionally sported a mustache.

Ochoa thought cocaine was a harmless vice. If people could afford it, they could use it. And if that made Jorge Ochoa rich, all the better. Ochoa, more than any of the other young traffickers, was a *paisa* businessman.

Ochoa went to Miami in the mid-1970s as manager of the Sea-8 Trading Co., an import-export business. He lived in a modest apartment in Kendall. His real job, however, was distributing cocaine along the East Coast for his uncle.

In late 1977, Fabio Restrepo bragged to a DEA informant that he was smuggling up to one hundred kilos of cocaine a week into the United States. On October 12 of the same year, Restrepo gave the informant a suitcase filled with twenty-seven kilos of cocaine and asked him to deliver it to his nephew Jorge in Miami. The informant told the DEA, and the DEA set a trap for Jorge at the Dadeland Twin Theatres, a group of movie houses just across the street from the liquor store where German Jimenez Panesso and Juan Carlos Hernandez would die two years later.

As the cocaine was exchanged in the theater parking lot, the DEA swooped in and arrested nine Colombians, including Jorge Ochoa's sister and brother-in-law. Jorge alone escaped. He sat on a motorcycle when the trap was sprung and sped off before he could be caught. It was the beginning of a pattern. Over the years, Jorge Ochoa would demonstrate an uncanny ability to evade justice.

After that close call, Ochoa left Miami, never to return. His younger brother, Fabio, barely out of his teens, had to be sent in to handle the family's U.S. distribution. And shortly after Jorge returned to Medellín, his uncle Fabio was murdered. The DEA asked its field office in Bogotá to find out what happened.

"Jorge Ochoa is currently residing in Medellín, although he keeps a home in Barranquilla, and it has been learned that Ochoa has inherited the trafficking organization of the departed Restrepo," came the reply from Colombia on July 31, 1978. "It is speculated that Ochoa ordered the murder of Restrepo to install himself as the undisputed head of the organization. Several sources of information have related that Ochoa has become one of the most powerful traffickers in Medellín and the northern coast of Colombia, and is continuing to introduce between one hundred and two hundred kilos of cocaine into the U.S. by several unknown methods."

BY the mid-1970s Escobar, Ochoa, and other young Medellín traffickers had positioned themselves as leaders within Colombia's rapidly expanding cocaine trade. Escobar's group was known on the street as Los Pablos. Jorge and his brothers were El Clan Ochoa. But their business was still relatively small. What they needed was a reliable method of shipping large quantities of cocaine to the United States and a reliable method of distribution.

Escobar had no experience with the United States, and Ochoa's brief sojourn had almost ended in arrest. They needed someone—a Colombian—who understood how the United States worked, who understood how to manipulate the gringos.

They needed an interpreter.

THE DREAM OF DANBURY

In the spring of 1974, Carlos Enrique Lehder Rivas sat in the Federal Correctional Institution at Danbury, Connecticut, planning what to do with the rest of his life. He had plenty of time. Arrested in Miami the year before for smuggling marijuana, he had been sentenced to serve four years. Danbury was a minimum security prison that housed mainly white-collar criminals, drug dealers, and political activists. Along with Lehder, its inmates included G. Gordon Liddy of Watergate fame, Howard Hughes hoax biographer Clifford Irving, and the Berrigan brothers, two priests arrested for their protests against the Vietnam War.

At twenty-five Carlos Lehder had done little to distinguish himself. His criminal résumé showed that in addition to smuggling pot, he had sometimes shipped stolen cars to South America. He was born September 7, 1949, in Armenia, Colombia, to Wilhelm Lehder, a tall, courtly German engineer and his Colombian wife, Helena Rivas. Wilhelm Lehder had emigrated to Colombia in 1922 and opened a construction business. Carlos was the youngest of four children, three boys and a girl. His parents divorced when he was four. His mother charged wife beating; his father countered with adultery. Carlos spent his childhood with his mother in Armenia, one of the hubs of the Colombian coffee industry, then when he was fifteen he moved with his mother to the United States. He grew up to be short—five feet six inches tall and 135 pounds—but handsome, with thick dark hair, boyish features, and penetrating eyes. People who knew him then said he was somewhat quiet but very ambitious, a smart, respectful hustler. His criminal career had an unspectacular beginning. He was arrested for the first time in 1972 for unauthorized use of a motor vehicle in Mineola, New York. The next year he was charged in Detroit with interstate transportation of stolen vehicles. He posted bond and fled to Miami, where he was subsequently arrested for possession of 237 pounds of marijuana and sent to Danbury.

AT Danbury's Massachusetts House, the vast orientation unit for new prisoners, Lehder found himself bunked next to George Jung, also a convicted marijuana dealer serving four years. The product of an upper-middle-class family in Weymouth, Massachusetts, Jung had attended the University of Tennessee on a football scholarship, but his career as a flanker ended when he tore cartilage in his knee. He ended up at Long Beach (California) City College, where he studied advertising and started smoking marijuana. In the late 1960s, Jung joined Students for a Democratic Society and marched for peace in Los Angeles, San Francisco, and Boston. Jung and a boyhood friend hit on the idea that marijuana purchased cheap in California could be sold for a lot more money at campuses back east. The business took off. The friend was a pilot, and they were able to buy an airplane and fly down to Mexico for marijuana. Soon they were moving thousands of pounds, and George Jung was making $200,000 a year. Three years later Jung was caught in Chicago when a connection—the manager of the Playboy Club—informed on him. Jung jumped bond, lived on the lam for more than a year, and eventually returned to Cape Cod, where he sold marijuana out of his parents' house. His mother turned him in.

George Jung liked Carlos Lehder right away. Lehder spoke perfect English and seemed very intelligent and well mannered. He did not seem street smart, more like a roommate in college. Outwardly, the two men appeared to be opposites. While Jung was a shaggy ex-student radical, Lehder wore his hair very short and kept his khaki prison uniform spotless. But Lehder had something, Jung thought, a special charisma. Soon the two inmates were talking about their crimes. Jung, seven years older, was by far the more experienced criminal, moving tons of marijuana easily while Lehder had been struggling to unload a few hundred pounds. Lehder's interest piqued when Jung told of flying marijuana out of Mexico. Lehder asked if he knew anything about cocaine. Jung didn't know much; he had tried it a few times, and that was all. Cocaine was easier to smuggle than marijuana, Lehder said, because it was less bulky. And it was far more profitable. Cocaine could be bought for as little as $2,000 a kilo in Colombia and sold for as much as $55,000 in the United States. And now, in the disillusioning shadow of Watergate and Vietnam, people were just naturally going to want a new high. Lehder himself thought cocaine was poison, good only for gaining money and power. Jung wanted the money, but Lehder wanted the power, too. He dreamed of running his own country. He talked constantly of revolution, and he revered Ernesto "Che" Guevara, the matinee idol of the revolutionary left. Lehder also admired John Lennon and Adolf Hitler. Jung, a son of the Woodstock nation whose own tastes ran to Bob Dylan, could understand Che and Lennon, but Hitler was too much.

Drawn by their common interests in radical politics and drug smuggling, Lehder and Jung spent every day together. Because he had been to college, Jung became an assistant in the prison school, teaching inmate dropouts. Lehder, who had never finished high school, attended the prison school and quickly got his general education diploma. His grades were high, and he was asked to join the school to teach Hispanic inmates. Lehder was obsessed with learning. He was always sitting on his bunk with four or five books, usually provided by Jung, who considered himself well read and something of an authority on pop psychology. Jung gave Lehder *The Prince* by Machiavelli, Plato's *Republic,* Nietzsche, Hemingway's *For Whom the Bell Tolls,* Herman Hesse, and Carl Jung's *The Archetypes of the Collective Unconscious.*

To fend off the tedium of prison, Lehder and Jung dreamed incessantly of smuggling cocaine. Lehder said he could get an unlimited amount in Colombia from Pablo Escobar. Jung said he could market the drug in the States through his old marijuana network. Jung, who had kicked around Haight-Asbury and the rest of the San Francisco psychedelic scene, knew plenty of people in the movie and record industries, stars and the like, who craved getting high. "I figured that if the record industry and the movie industry were interested in it, they could promote the product through the greatest advertising medium there was," Jung said years later. "I saw what they did with marijuana in the 1960s."

Besides their connections, the two men had something equally important: the kind of inspiration that serves as a pivot for history. They were the first to recognize that the methods of marijuana smuggling could be married to cocaine.

In 1974, cocaine was still coming to the United States a few kilos at a time hidden in luggage or on the bodies of smugglers who were known as mules. Marijuana, by contrast, was picked up by American smuggler pilots who arrived at clandestine airstrips in northern Colombia and carted off hundreds of kilos in their small private aircraft. Lehder and Jung did not see why private aircraft couldn't be used to carry hundreds of kilos of cocaine. They could make millions providing an air transport service for the cocaine producers, who would be encouraged to pool their several small loads into one big load. Carlos Lehder was in a unique position to bring this about. Unlike Griselda Blanco or the young Pablo Escobar, Lehder was as comfortable in the United States as he was in Colombia, if not more so. He could be the cultural bridge between the Colombian cocaine producers and the pilots and distributors in the United States. And he had a knack for seducing people, a special skill for getting others to do his bidding. The force of his will and vision attracted weaker men, especially American criminals like George Jung. No other Colombian had this ability. And Carlos Lehder needed George Jung; on his own he barely had the ability to move even a couple of kilos of cocaine.

Lehder and Jung lifted weights together and spent a lot of time in the prison library looking at maps and plotting out possible smuggling routes into the United States. They were planning to go through Mexico, where Jung had been so successful smuggling marijuana. From a doctor in Danbury for Medicare fraud they learned about Belize, which had no extradition treaty. Belize gave Lehder the idea of creating a sanctuary for drug smugglers. From an imprisoned banker they learned about money laundering through offshore banks. Lehder would always refer to Danbury as his "college."

IN the spring of 1975, Jung was paroled. He gave Lehder his parents' address and told him to get in touch after Carlos was back in Colombia. As an illegal alien, Lehder would be deported upon his release.

Nearly a year later, Lehder sent Jung a telegram with a message to call Autos Lehder, his car dealership in Medellín. "Come on down, the weather is beautiful," Lehder told him. It was the prearranged signal that Lehder had lined up his cocaine contacts.

Jung said his parole conditions didn't allow him to leave the country. So he sent his childhood friend and fellow marijuana smuggler, Frank Shea.

As soon as he reached Medellín, Shea phoned George Jung in Massachusetts and told him he was at Autos Lehder, looking at the "snow" at that very moment.

"We've really hit the jackpot this time," Shea gushed. "We've really put it together."

Autos Lehder was known by police as an occasional fence for hot cars from the United States, but it did legitimate business as well, enough to give Lehder a front in the straight world. In addition, Lehder had the basic credentials to be successful in Medellín. He had intelligence and guile, traits that could be more highly valued than money and social position. And he knew some important people, like Pablo Escobar.

Still, Lehder was never altogether at home in Medellín. His hometown of Armenia was in Quindio province, about 180 miles to the south. He was an outsider, and outsiders, particularly those looking for the criminal big time, ordinarily did not prosper in Medellín. The rising young traffickers like Escobar did not view Lehder with the same kind of awe as his American friends, though they were impressed with his ingenuity. Lehder was not a *paisa,* and the *paisas* of Medellín would never quite trust this flashy half-German who loved Nazis. To them Lehder came across as a handsome swaggerer with a quick line; in short, a bit shallow. Women found him enormously attractive, but men ran things in Medellín.

WHEN Frank Shea arrived in Medellín in February 1976, Carlos Lehder was a long way from his dream of transporting hundreds of kilos of cocaine by airplane. Instead he had been slowly building his stake by shipping a couple of kilos at a time in specially modified suitcases. In April Lehder called Massachusetts and gave Jung his instructions. He should find two women and send them on an all-expenses-paid vacation to the Caribbean island of Antigua. The women should bring along some luggage.

"Don't tell them anything," Lehder said. "We'll explain everything when they get there."

Jung thought Betsy Strautman, the woman he lived with, and Shea's girlfriend, Winny Polly, would be perfect for the job. He tracked them down at a local schoolyard where they were watching Betsy's nine-year-old daughter play softball.

"Would you be interested in a free Caribbean vacation?" Jung asked.

"When?" asked Betsy.

"Now."

WINNY Polly and Betsy Strautman bought four hard-shell plastic Samsonite suitcases for the trip. Jung paid for their airline tickets, gave them spending money, and sent them on their way, telling them as little as possible. The two women called Jung when they arrived in Antigua and said they had linked up with Carlos Lehder and Frank

Shea. They were having a wonderful time. Betsy didn't tell Jung that she had slept with Carlos's friend, Cesar Toban. Winny was so smitten with Carlos that she found it difficult to speak in his presence. But Carlos wasn't interested. A few days later the women called Jung and said they were coming home.

The luggage the women carried through Customs at Boston's Logan Airport was not the same as what they took to Antigua. After delivering the suitcases, the women immediately flew back to Antigua on Lehder's orders. When he was alone, Jung opened one of the suitcases, removing an aluminum lip that secured a fiberglass false bottom. Beneath the fiberglass were two kilos of cocaine, flattened and taped onto the suitcase's outer shell. Made in Medellín, the compartment was virtually undetectable.

Several days later, the women returned with more suitcases and a message for Jung from Lehder. A third of the cocaine—five kilos—was Jung's to do with as he wished. The rest was Lehder's. Jung was to pay the women and Shea out of his proceeds. Jung quickly sold four of his kilos for $45,000 apiece. He paid Shea $25,000 and gave the women a kilo to split. Starting off with such a huge supply of pure cocaine, Winny Polly soon fell into a habit that ultimately led her to injecting the drug directly into her veins. (She eventually fled in desperation to Medellín to try to get clean at—of all places—Carlos Lehder's house.) Jung held on to Lehder's kilos and waited.

A month after the last Antigua trip, Jung turned over Lehder's kilos to Cesar Toban and Jemel Nacel, Lehder's Cuban-American girlfriend, at the Sheraton Hotel in Boston. By this time Jung's girlfriend, Betsy, had 'fessed up about sleeping with Toban. But Jung was willing to overlook it; there was too much money involved to let emotions get in the way.

DESPITE the initial successes with suitcases, the ultimate goal was still to smuggle cocaine by private airplane. But Frank Shea, their would-be pilot, was upset at his cut of the Antigua deal and had dropped out. Jung had to find someone else. He went looking during the Fourth of July weekend on Cape Cod. He figured that with it being the nation's two hundredth anniversary and parties overfilling the cape, there had to be a pilot among the crowd. A friend set him up with Barry Kane, a practicing attorney and, far more important, a pilot who owned his own plane. Kane, who was something of a playboy on the Cape Cod social scene, handled divorces and real estate transactions. He was already quite rich, with homes in Chatham, Fort

Lauderdale, and Nassau. Jung spent hours feeling Kane out during a boat ride to look at the tall ships gathered at the cape. Jung finally asked if Kane was interested in smuggling cocaine from South America.

Kane immediately said yes.

Jung told Kane that he and Carlos Lehder had planned in Danbury to set up a transportation business for Colombian cocaine producers. If they could involve a pilot like Kane, they could all grow very rich.

Jung and Kane flew in Kane's plane to Toronto to meet Lehder. The three men talked for several hours at a Holiday Inn. Kane figured he could carry up to three hundred kilos in his plane. Lehder said there would be no problem with the pickup in Colombia. They would use an airstrip near Medellín on a ranch owned by Pablo Escobar. The authorities would be paid to leave the plane alone.

Kane provided the rest of the plan: his connections with Bahamian officials through an attorney named Nigel Bowe would allow him to refuel his plane at the airport in Nassau. Once there, he would file a flight plan for the remote outer islands. But instead he would fly to Colombia. Returning to Nassau, he would park the plane at the airport and wait until Sunday. Then he would blend in with the mom-and-pop traffic that flew between the United States and the Bahamas on weekends. Staying only a few hundred feet off the ground, he would follow the coast up to a private strip in the Carolinas.

Lehder was delighted. He and Jung had no concept of the Bahamas, figuring all along that they would do their smuggling through Mexico. But the Bahamas seemed perfect. On the spot Lehder wrote Kane a check for $50,000 to pay for the extra fuel tanks needed to increase the range of Kane's plane. The three men agreed to a fee of $10,000 a kilo, of which Kane would keep $6,000.

When the meeting ended, Kane announced he was flying back to the United States alone. He wasn't going to take Jung because Jung, a parolee, was out of the country illegally. Kane said Jung could take a commercial flight into Portland, Maine, where he wouldn't be bothered by Customs.

WITH Kane in the fold, the cocaine dreams of Danbury took another step toward reality. There was a significant hitch: Lehder and Jung didn't have the money to finance such a large smuggling venture; Jung didn't know it, but Lehder didn't even have enough to cover the $50,000 check he wrote to Kane. To generate cash they planned another suitcase trip. Jung sent a woman with suitcases to Venezuela, but Lehder failed to meet her. On October 19, 1976, Colombian police arrested Lehder for smuggling Chevrolet wagons into Colombia.

This time prison set Lehder back for only a short while. He and five thousand other inmates occupied Bella Vista, a new prison in Medellín. But while most prisoners curled up on dirt floors or stone slabs and ate a thin broth of rotten horsemeat cooked in a gigantic pot called *el bongo,* Lehder enjoyed the best accommodations available. He stayed in a cell block with real beds known as *el patio especial*—"the special terrace." Admittance required a bribe of 1,500 Colombian pesos, about $75.

As he had done in Danbury, Lehder spent his prison time cultivating a gringo who could help him smuggle cocaine. Stephen Yakovac was a onetime auto mechanic and computer repairman in his late twenties, a self-described hippie who wore his hair long and liked to smoke marijuana. Yakovac had come to South America to collect Indian trinkets with his wife. The trip was a rolling nightmare: the couple's car broke down in Central America, and then they were robbed on a bus in Colombia. When they tried to return to the United States for the bicentennial, Yakovac made the mistake of packing a pound of Colombian marijuana; he was now serving three years in Bella Vista, and every day brought its own special agony, dulled only by marijuana. At six four and two hundred pounds of taut, wiry muscle, Yakovac endured the anti-American taunts of the shorter Colombian inmates and considered himself "a cat surrounded by mice."

To Steve Yakovac, Carlos Lehder was a godsend. Instead of calling Yakovac "gringo" as everyone else did, Lehder called him *paisa.* The two prisoners passed their days smoking marijuana and playing Monopoly.

Lehder regaled Yakovac with his dream of smuggling cocaine by air. He said the idea was to form "a conglomerate of small-time cocaine producers and to put all their merchandise together into one shipment so it would pay for the equipment necessary to get into the United States."

The beauty of Lehder's plan was that it didn't require much investment on his part. He would merely charge his clients in kilos—onefourth of their shipments. Lehder envisioned a worldwide network of cocaine smugglers linked by his transportation pipeline. And that was not the end of his daydreaming. He said he hoped to be president of Colombia one day.

Years later, Yakovac would remember Lehder's prison ramblings: "He wanted to pull Colombia up by its bootstraps. He wanted to oust the imperialist Yankees and build a kingdom based on cocaine in

Colombia. . . . He wanted to use cocaine in an almost military way. He wanted to—he was very bitter because of his incarceration in the United States and the fact that he was banned from ever returning to the United States. And he likened himself to Hitler in that he was a small man and could take over the world. . . . He respected, almost idolized Adolf Hitler . . . in his strong-arm tactics, his ruthlessness, making the best out of what resources he had at hand. And to him, that was cocaine."

Lehder spent only two months in Bella Vista, getting out just in time for the Christmas holidays. When he left, he wrote his name, phone number, and a post office box number in Yakovac's diary.

"I want you to come work for me when you get out," Lehder told him.

On Christmas day, Lehder sent in a roast pig for his old pals in the special patio, but Yakovac fell into despair. He figured he would never hear from his friend Carlos again.

OUT of prison, Lehder called George Jung from Toronto—in Danbury they had planned to have their meetings in Canada because of Lehder's problems entering the United States. Lehder told Jung he needed money.

Jung sent a friend with $30,000 taped inside a weight belt. A few days later Jung went to Toronto himself to meet Lehder at the Holiday Inn. They had a problem. While Lehder sat in prison, his $50,000 check to Kane had bounced. Kane had told Jung, "Lehder's credibility on a scale of one to ten just hit minus one."

Lehder said he would take care of the bounced check. Also, Jung should not worry about the mishap in Venezuela: "Let's look to the future," Lehder said.

In the middle of the night, Lehder called Jung and asked if he would come to his room.

"I think I'm going to marry Jemel," Lehder told him. "What do you think about it?"

Wonderful, Jung said. Naive, he thought. But he told Carlos she was a very nice girl. The partners talked for an hour or so, and Lehder suddenly announced he was going to call Jemel on the spot and have her fly to Toronto for the wedding.

Jemel Nacel arrived the next day. She was a dark-haired, petite Cuban beauty. She and Lehder rushed around getting the necessary papers and blood tests. The wedding took place in the cellar of the house of a justice of the peace. Jung was best man. A 45-rpm record provided the music. The marriage certificate was dated February 17, 1977. The wedding party returned to the Holiday Inn and celebrated with Dom Pérignon. Then Lehder instructed Jung to go to Miami, pick up fifty kilos of cocaine, and hold it in Boston.

Jung, who had never been to Miami before, checked into the Fontainebleau Hotel on Miami Beach and called his contact, an impatient Colombian who brought a suitcase to Jung's hotel room. Inside was more cocaine than Jung had ever seen—fifty kilos wrapped in cellophane and covered with duct tape. The packages looked like footballs. Jung spent several hours repacking the cocaine in shelving paper, the kind used in kitchen cabinets; his marijuana days had taught him that dogs could not sniff through it.

Jung returned to Massachusetts with the cocaine and paid a friend to drive to Toronto and bring Lehder across the Canadian border into Boston. Security was lax, and Jung figured Lehder could make it through the cursory customs check.

The crossing was set for St. Patrick's Day, but that night the friend's wife called Jung. She was hysterical. Her husband had been detained at the border. Lehder's whereabouts were unknown. Border patrol officers sweated the friend for four or five hours and finally released him.

Two days later Jung learned from the friend what had gone wrong. Lehder had changed the plan at the last instant, deciding he wanted to sneak across the border on foot. Lehder ordered the friend to turn around right before the border. On a side road, Lehder got out of the car and trekked off in his street shoes into the snow-carpeted Canadian woods. But a border patrol officer had spotted the car backing up and disappearing into the woods, only to return minus a passenger. Opening the trunk, the border guards found a suitcase containing Colombian pesos and Carlos Lehder's Colombian passport. They ran his name in the computer and suddenly wanted to know more about this Carlos Lehder Rivas.

Lehder, meanwhile, was running through the woods pursued by dogs. He crossed the border and after walking several miles found a rooming house run by an elderly lady. She believed his story about being lost in the woods and gave him a bed. The next day, he rode a bus to New York City.

Jung didn't know what happened to Lehder in the woods and was extremely nervous about baby-sitting fifty kilos of cocaine. He decided to run. He flew to Los Angeles and turned the drugs over to his old marijuana contact in Manhattan Beach. The connection was a hairdresser whose hip boutique—there was a pool table in the waiting room—catered to a Hollywood clientele. The hairdresser tested the cocaine, melting it on tinfoil above a butane lighter. It turned out to be nearly pure. The budding California cocaine market, never before exposed to fifty uncut kilos, snapped them up. It was as if the giant city itself had inhaled the drug. Within two weeks the hairdresser sold all fifty kilos and gave Jung $2.2 million. Neither of them had ever seen anything like it. Jung took the money back to Boston in three aluminum camera cases, which he hid in the attic of a friend's house on upper Cape Cod. Then he waited for Carlos Lehder.

About a week later Jung's mother telephoned and said there was a nice young man looking for him. She put Carlos Lehder on the line. Jung told him he had taken care of everything. He joined Lehder in the restaurant of a Hyatt Regency Hotel in Cambridge. Lehder recounted the mishap at the Canadian border, and Jung scolded him and told him to be more careful the next time because he didn't want to go back to prison.

Then Jung related his news: he was holding $1.8 million for Lehder, his end of the fifty-kilo sale. There was a great untapped market for cocaine in Los Angeles, the potential was limitless. Lehder was very pleased at Jung's honesty and enthusiastic about California. The two men decided on the spot to move to Miami and start shipping cocaine to the West Coast.

Several weeks later Jung drove to a hotel in Hyannis Port for a breakfast meeting with Lehder, Jemel, Lehder's mother, and his brother, Guillermo. Jung took the Lehder family sightseeing around Cape Cod. Lehder wanted to buy a car, so Jung took him to a BMW showroom. Lehder saw a car he liked and gave the salesman $10,000 in hundred-dollar bills. He gave his name as "Jose N. Leone," a New York restaurateur, and listed Jung's parents' address. Horrified, Jung shrank from the showroom.

When they were alone, Jung rebuked Lehder. "Even the Kennedys don't pay cash for their automobiles," Jung said. "This is asking for trouble, inviting the police to come down on us."

Lehder shrugged. He said he wanted to go up the street and look at a Datsun 280-Z.

LEHDER made arrangements to drive down to Miami in his new BMW with his new wife. He told Jung that his Colombian contact Pablo Escobar was very impressed with the potential of the California market. The sale of the fifty kilos had turned Carlos Lehder into an important man in Colombia. He went from being a kid who moved a couple of kilos to the man who had suddenly disposed of fifty of them and collected more than $1 million. Above all, he made it look easy.

Carlos, Jemel, and Jung moved into a fourth-rate hotel in Little Havana, the heavily Cuban section of Miami. But Jung spotted drug dealing in the other rooms and wanted a place that was both more secure and less obvious. They went to the Ocean Pavilion Hotel on Collins Avenue in Miami Beach, where they leased a two-bedroom condominium on the eleventh floor. Carlos wanted all three of them to live together.

"Well, you're newlyweds," Jung said. "I don't think I'm needed here. Why don't I just get another place?"

But Lehder insisted. Soon the operation was running smoothly. Lehder brought the cocaine in grocery bags and shopping carts up the service elevator to the eleventh floor. The kilos always came in football-shaped packages, covered with cryptic letters and numbers. Lehder explained that the scrawlings indicated the owners of cocaine in Colombia.

Once or twice a week Jung carried an aluminum camera case bearing fifteen to twenty-five kilos on the 5½-hour United Airlines red-eye flight to his hairdresser contact in Los Angeles. On the return flight, Jung's case brimmed with hundred-dollar bills in $10,000 stacks—the money collected for the previous week's kilos. Jung usually carried more than $1 million a trip. Lehder and Jung each kept $100,000 and sent the rest down to Medellín.

Lehder sent most of his money back to Autos Lehder in Medellín hidden in Chevy Blazers. After the money was removed, the Blazers went out on the auto showroom floor. Sometimes Lehder would give Jemel $20,000 to go shopping at Neiman-Marcus in the nearby Bal Harbour shopping plaza. Jung spent most of his money on Porsches, chartered jets, Dom Pérignon, French Bordeaux, cognac, women, and, increasingly, cocaine for his own personal use. At first Jung had been businesslike about cocaine. But soon, with everybody he knew trying it in California, he plunged in. He found it intensified the thrill he got from smuggling. Jung thought cocaine was harmless, mentally addicting, maybe, but not physically. And nothing could control his mind. After all, he had tried everything—LSD, marijuana, mescaline —and never been strung out. Lehder smoked a lot of marijuana, but he was careful never to use cocaine. Once, when Jung snorted a couple of lines for a quick pick-me-up before catching the red-eye to

California, Lehder remonstrated with him: "How can you do that and get on an airplane? That stuff's poison." Soon Jung was snorting a couple of grams a day.

Jung returned from California one day and noticed aviation brochures scattered throughout the apartment. Jung and Lehder began visiting small airports in south Florida, looking at planes. They were eager to advance beyond suitcases and implement the Danbury plan. The partners spent time in the Bahamas that summer, looking for an island that could serve as a refueling stop for planes coming up from Colombia with cocaine. Lehder had never given up the idea of creating an island sanctuary for drug smugglers. And he had not forsaken his political dreams, either. The strange combination of hippie and Hitlerite persisted. Gradually, Lehder's anti-Semitism emerged. It nauseated the liberal in Jung, but he thought Carlos would grow out of it. Once, at dinner in a Miami restaurant, Jung suggested steak and potatoes, and Lehder replied that "potatoes are for peasants." He quoted Hitler's instructions on the conquered people of Poland: "Teach them only to read road signs and allow them only to eat potatoes."

His anti-Americanism also came forward. Lehder said he hated the United States. He thought it was an imperialist police state. He told Jung that he hoped to flood the country with cocaine and disrupt America's political system and tear down its morality.

By summer 1977, Jung was burning out. He was spending fifteen hours a week in the air, and the time changes and the sheer hammering adrenaline of carrying cocaine through airport security had taken its toll. On one California trip, the cocaine was so high-grade and sold so fast that Jung's contact immediately begged for more. Jung was too tired to fly to Miami, so he called Lehder and asked him to send somebody else with the cocaine.

"I will call you as soon as I have that person in transit," Lehder said.

The next day, as promised, Lehder called.

"I have someone," said Lehder. "They're on the plane now."

"Who is it?" Jung asked.

"It will be a surprise," Lehder said.

The following day, Jung heard a knock at the door of his room at the Holiday Inn in Hawthorne, California. When he opened the door, he saw a bellboy with luggage escorting a short, gray-haired woman. It was Carlos Lehder's mother, Helena. She shook with nerves. Jung ushered her in and opened her suitcase. It contained eight kilos of cocaine.

I've done things in my life, dealt drugs and what have you, but I never sent my mother anyplace with a suitcase full of cocaine, Jung thought.

He ordered a drink for Helena. Then he called Carlos in Miami and asked what the hell he was doing.

"Everybody has to work," Lehder said. "And she wanted a free trip to Disneyland."

4.

THE BAHAMAS PIPELINE

The dream of smuggling cocaine by private aircraft became a reality when Carlos Lehder and George Jung finally met up with Barry Kane in Miami during the first week of August 1977. Kane said he was ready, after a year of waiting and delays, to fly cocaine for them.

Kane took off from Nassau, the fuselage of his small twin-engine aircraft outfitted with collapsible rubber "bladder" fuel tanks to increase its range. He navigated by a nautical Loran, a radio beacon capable of guiding him to within a few miles of his target. Over Colombia, a co-pilot sent along to spot for Kane pointed out a small private landing strip at a farm outside Medellín. It was Pablo Escobar's *finca*.

With 250 kilos of cocaine on board, five times as much as Carlos Lehder had ever handled, Barry Kane returned to Nassau, refueled, and sneaked into U.S. airspace. The cocaine was off-loaded in the Carolinas and transported to a Fort Lauderdale condominium parking lot. Kane divided the load in half and put it in the trunks of two used cars. When the Colombians came, he gave them one car and held the other until they paid his fee. Kane had his money in forty-eight hours. Jung and Lehder split a cool million. Everything had gone like clockwork.

Soon, however, tension built between the partners. Just a month after their triumph Jung began suspecting that Lehder was going behind his back. Before Kane's trip, Jung had finally given in to Lehder's badgering and introduced Lehder to his hairdresser connection in California. This was a tremendous act of trust. The hairdresser was Jung's ace in the hole; if Lehder could deal directly with the hairdresser, he wouldn't need Jung, and he could save millions. Jung knew this, but he had come to love Lehder like a brother.

Now Jung grew worried. He had taken to using cocaine to stay alert during the long flights to California and had become addicted. He was consuming five to eight grams in a single, monstrous binge, and going three and four days without sleep. Jung got so he could do a gram—usually enough to keep a disco queen going all night—in a single snort. The Colombians called him "I-95" because the long white lines he snorted reminded them of the interstate highway in south Florida. Jung's habit fed his suspicions about Lehder.

While Lehder busied himself preparing to move his operations to the Bahamas, Jung felt more and more isolated. He no longer lived with the Lehders at the Ocean Pavilion apartment, having moved out after the couple started arguing and breaking furniture. (Jemel had complained to Jung that Carlos was only interested in Chevy Blazers and airplanes.) A lot of the time Jung didn't know what Lehder was up to anymore.

Jung finally arranged a meeting with Lehder in Nassau. He brought his new wife, who happened to be the sister-in-law of one of Jung's fellow smugglers, a Colombian named Humberto Hoyos. He and Lehder rented a charter boat and spent most of the day looking at the Bahamian island of Norman's Cay two hundred miles southeast of Miami. Lehder said he was considering a ninety-nine-year lease. He was also looking at another island thirty miles south. Both islands had airstrips, but Norman's Cay was better because it was smaller. It would be easier to force fifty people to leave an island than two hundred, Lehder said.

After the boat trip, Jung laid out his suspicions in the lounge of the Holiday Inn in Nassau. "I think you've been going behind my back," he told Lehder over drinks. Lehder looked like he had tears in his eyes. "No, I wouldn't do that," he said. But Jung could see it in his eyes. And he could feel it all around him.

JUNG returned to the United States, and Carlos Lehder turned his attention to Norman's Cay. Situated in shallow water forty miles southeast of Nassau, the cay was one of the most beautiful of the seven hundred islands that make up the Bahamas. Named for a Caribbean pirate and shaped like an upside-down fishhook that had been squeezed between the fingers of a giant, the cay's slender, 4½-mile-long landmass curved to form an ideal harbor for yachts. Along the island's northern end, the hoop of the fishhook, a dozen Cape Cod–style, weathered-wood beach cottages looked out on a rocky coast. The cay's southeastern tip, the point of the fishhook, was undeveloped and vacant. At the cay's southwestern tip, the shank of the fishhook, a concrete airstrip stretched three thousand feet. On the western edge of the airstrip were four miles of sparkling white-sand beach that gently curved along an expanse of water known as Smuggler's Cove. Atop a hill east of the airstrip sat the Norman's Cay Yacht Club, which had a four-stool bar, a restaurant, and the island's lone telephone. The yacht club looked down on a twelve-room hotel, a company store, and a wooden, L-shaped dock with fuel pumps. Conditions were rustic. Water for the island came from cisterns and electricity from fuel-driven generators. Scrub vegetation and sea grape covered the cay, and hills afforded privacy.

In May 1978, Lehder bought the Beckwith House on the northeastern bend of Norman's Cay for $190,000. He paid cash, handing a suitcase full of money to Charles Beckwith in Beckwith's office at Ocean World in Fort Lauderdale. Beckwith demanded the money be counted and to his chagrin found Lehder was about to overpay him by $8,000. Later that year Lehder appeared in the Nassau office of the Guardian Trust Company and opened a large attaché case filled with $1 million in U.S. currency. He made no attempt to hide the money, which caused quite a stir in the office, making everyone a bit giddy. He said he was a wealthy Colombian money exchanger who wanted to develop Norman's Cay into a yacht haven. Lehder struck the Bahamians as intelligent and perfectly charming. He asked everyone to call him "Joe." The attaché case was open on the desk, revealing the blue-green glint of hundred-dollar bills. The money was deposited in the Bank of Nova Scotia on Paradise Island. The bank had never seen such a large cash deposit and introduced a "counting charge" of one percent—$10,000 per million—on subsequent large cash deposits. The deposit was staggering even to Bahamians hardened to the ostentatious displays of the very rich. Soon many influential Bahamians wanted to meet this charismatic twenty-eight-year-old.

Lehder opened seven accounts in corporate names through Guardian Trust. One of these accounts, International Dutch Resources Ltd., purchased lots four and five on Norman's Cay for $875,000 on January 31, 1979. The purchase encompassed 165 acres on the western and eastern tips of the island, including the airstrip, the clubhouse, the hotel, and the dock. Lehder submitted a development plan for a one-thousand-foot airstrip extension and a marina for forty yachts.

For years Norman's Cay had been a favored stop for boaters in the Exuma chain. The cay was perfect for a one-day sail from Nassau, with a channel no more than twenty feet deep stretching the entire forty miles. Now Lehder set about converting the cay into his own private island. The yacht club shut down. The hotel stopped taking reservations. The airstrip closed. The dock refused to sell yachters fuel. CBS News anchorman Walter Cronkite, an avid yachtsman, sailed up in his forty-two-foot yacht during his Christmas vacation in 1978 and was surprised to find the harbor empty. When he dropped anchor to investigate, a man on the pier shouted, "You can't dock here, and you can't anchor out there."

At the next island, Cronkite was told Norman's Cay had been taken over by people who didn't want visitors. Everyone in the Bahamas knew that.

People had counted as many as twenty Doberman pinscher guard dogs housed in pens near the airstrip. Blond men with German accents and black satchels patrolled in Toyota jeeps and Volkswagen vans. When boats got too close to the island, a helicopter sometimes buzzed overhead. A sophisticated communications tower went up on the island, and navigational aids were installed for night aircraft landings.

Soon the island was bustling with activity. Airplanes flew in and out every day, bringing supplies for the new venture. Lehder's employees and associates, an odd collection of Americans, Germans, and Colombians, occupied several houses on the island. A laundromat serviced their needs. Lehder's boats—the sixty-five-foot *Margaret Lee,* the fifty-eight-foot *Chelique IV,* and the thirty-three-foot *Fire Fall*—docked in the protected anchorage. He drove around in a 1932 Ford Replicar, part of his twenty-two-vehicle motor pool. On occasion he was accompanied by one of his baby daughters.

As Lehder moved in, others who had been on the island for years were forced to move out. Philip Kniskern, who owned three vacation villas next to the airstrip near Smuggler's Cove, depended on his guests having access to the airstrip. But he was told by Lehder he could no longer accept bookings. Kniskern was forced to lease his properties to Lehder's employees. Richard Novak, a college professor who leased a diving business from Kniskern, started asking questions about the new crowd on the cay and was suddenly told that there was to be no more diving. When Novak returned a month later for his diving gear, his airplane was surrounded by Lehder's employees. They prevented him from reaching the building housing his equipment. Back at the airstrip, Novak found the fuel drained from his plane. He was forced to take off and make an emergency landing on the beach at South Eleuthera about thirty miles away.

Both Novak and Kniskern complained about Lehder to the police, but nothing seemed to come of it. On Norman's Cay, Joe Lehder had become a law unto himself.

One of those ordered off Norman's Cay was Charles Kehm, who had brokered the sale of the Beckwith house to Lehder. When Kehm refused to go, Lehder had a Bahamian immigration officer deport him, even though Kehm was in the Bahamas legally. Kehm returned, and Lehder threatened his life.

"In case I didn't make myself clear, if you're not off this island today, your wife and children will die," Lehder said.

Kehm left.

AT the time Carlos Lehder took control of Norman's Cay, he was also building his own cocaine distribution network in the United States. He had some money, but he needed a lot more to get a big-time air cocaine operation off the ground. He started with Jung's hairdresser contact and an associate of the hairdresser's, a Miami dealer who had been selling ounces of cocaine since high school. It was a neat arrangement. The hairdresser had the California distribution, the Miami dealer had some start-up money, and Lehder contributed the cocaine. They added a friend of the hairdresser's who owned a recording studio and brought in another friend to help him distribute to the music crowd. But the real problem was pilots. Having made his money, Barry Kane had bowed out. Lehder desperately needed people to fly cocaine.

The hairdresser knew a hulking marijuana pilot who knew a dishwasher from Park City, Utah, and a disc jockey from Los Angeles, all of whom agreed to enroll in flight school. The Miami dealer brought in two high school buddies, one of them another pilot. This was how the early network grew, friends brought in by friends, all of them American.

Lehder rented a house in Beverly Hills to serve as his West Coast headquarters and tooled around Los Angeles in a blue Porsche. He started to compartmentalize his operation, letting his various pilots and distributors have information only on a need-to-know basis. While George Jung had been burning himself out riding the red-eye to Los Angeles, Lehder and his new friends had scouted islands in the Bahamas and rural landing strips in Florida. He bought a smuggling airplane, a Piper Navajo, for $125,000 cash in California. Soon everything was in place.

ON June 11, 1978, Stephen Yakovac, still sitting in a Colombian prison, got an unexpected visitor:

"I couldn't speak," Yakovac wrote in his diary. "My jaws opened and my mind whirled. Carlos. It had been almost a year, a year and a half since we had spoken, and I had just about given up on seeing him again. See him again I did. What a trip. We spoke a little of old times, new times and problems. In one fell swoop, he eliminated our present money dilemma with a gift of 10,000 pesos, and he lifted my spirits incredibly by telling me of his success."

Lehder was returning to Colombia in triumph. He said he had successfully smuggled several loads of cocaine through the Bahamas into the United States and he had a job for Yakovac.

A month later when Yakovac was released, Lehder sent a chauffeur to pick him up. Carlos told him more details about Norman's Cay. He had bought a house there, and he said he was paying the governor of the Exuma island chain $50,000 a month for protection.

"Let's go to work, let's become millionaires," Lehder said.

Lehder asked Yakovac if there was anything he needed. Yes, Yakovac said, a watch. Lehder took the Rolex off his wrist and gave it to him.

Yakovac, his new wife—he had divorced his first wife and married a Colombian prostitute in prison—and their newborn baby flew with Lehder to the Bahamas on a rented Learjet. Also on board were three Colombian prostitutes hired to service Lehder's men on the cay. At first Yakovac stayed in Lehder's house, a spacious affair with a round center and two wings that slanted off at an obtuse angle. The house sat on a narrow bend of the cay flanked by water on both sides and had a conical roof that came to a point, leading Lehder's band to rename it "Volcano."

Yakovac went to work flying shotgun once a month on cocaine loads from Norman's Cay into the United States. He was paid $5,000 per trip. The flights were scheduled for weekends, when Lehder's planes were camouflaged in the small-aircraft traffic from the islands. The smugglers had learned that weekends were also a good time to go through U.S. Customs; in the Customs shack at Fort Lauderdale Executive Airport, Yakovac found the inspectors routinely distracted by TV sports. Yakovac's job was also to inventory the cocaine. In seven flights in 1978, Yakovac helped smuggle 1,358 kilos (nearly 1½ tons) of cocaine into the United States.

On the return trip to Norman's Cay, Yakovac brought back money, once as much as $1.3 million. At first Lehder's men took the cash to the volcano house, put it on Lehder's bed, and spent all night counting it by hand. As they got more sophisticated they added electronic currency counters. The planes carrying the cocaine from Colombia to

Norman's Cay landed at night by the light of portable strobes. Usually a different plane was used for the second leg into the United States. While the crew waited for the second plane, Yakovac supervised the off-loading of the cocaine, sometimes hiding the kilos in sinkholes. The word "cocaine" was never said out loud. Lehder had taken to referring to the kilos as "the children," and the others copied him. Lehder's pipeline soon served a wide variety of clients, from the gringos who worked as Lehder's distributors to Colombians who merely used Lehder's transport service. Among the latter were Griselda Blanco, Pablo Escobar, and Jorge Ochoa.

NORMAN'S Cay was a microcosm of the cocaine business at the time, growing geometrically and becoming increasingly sinister as esculating amounts of cocaine and money poured in. The atmosphere started out fairly informal, just a bunch of guys in cutoff shorts having a good time and getting rich. The entire operation had a 1960s counterculture feel. Lehder's five-bedroom house was open to his men, and the sound system piped the Beatles, the Rolling Stones, and Joan Baez into every room. Wild parties were held to relieve the tension of the smuggling missions.

Cocaine was the product of Norman's Cay, and it was the privilege of everyone to partake of it, even Carlos Lehder, who had finally succumbed to his own endless supply. A little cocaine stimulates the central nervous system, producing exhilaration, euphoria, and a tremendous sense of well-being and power. A lot of cocaine, over time, produces paranoia. The cay was a situation unique in the history of the drug: for the first time a large group of people had access to pure cocaine in unprecedented quantities. It was as if a giant laboratory experiment was under way to see how people would react when confronted with an unlimited supply. The results were quickly apparent.

The island soon became an armed camp of tense, haggard men. Scores of weapons were flown in from south Florida. Yakovac carried a .357 Magnum and sometimes dressed in army fatigues. Lehder favored a chrome-plated .45 automatic. He also paid a German security firm to provide guards for his operation. Seduced by more money than they'd ever seen, the guards left their agency and became Lehder's personal palace guard. Lehder had a boat dragged to the top of a hill on the island to serve as a post for armed guards.

Lehder's own heavy cocaine use—he preferred to smoke cocaine "base," the purest and most addictive form of the drug—boosted his megalomania into the stratosphere. He began to affect a regal, reckless air. His obsession with power increased, as did his fascination with things German, particularly Hitler. Cocaine fed his grandiose dreams. He was studying a book entitled *How to Speak in Public* and planning a political career in Colombia. He had achieved almost everything he had imagined in Danbury: the transportation network, millions of dollars, even the island sanctuary for drug smugglers. The only thing that eluded him was the presidency of Colombia.

Yakovac and others worried that Lehder's flamboyance was getting out of hand. It threatened everyone's security. The story about Walter Cronkite getting kicked off the island was known to everybody.

He has set himself up as a king on this island, Yakovac thought.

Lehder didn't like having his authority questioned. "I'm the boss, like it or leave," he told Yakovac.

One of the things Yakovac didn't like was the way Lehder was clearing the island of people. To discourage vacationers, he had ordered Yakovac and others to "leave a bad taste in their mouth so they wouldn't come back." This was sometimes accomplished by driving around in the Volkswagen van with weapons on open display. A few people were allowed to stay, mainly those who owned property on the cay and had not run afoul of Lehder. Ed Ward, an American pilot from Jacksonville, was one of these. Lehder told Yakovac that Ward was a marijuana smuggler and Yakovac should be cordial to him but not too friendly.

ON August 16, 1978, the biggest cocaine load yet arrived at the cay on a Mitsubishi, a high-performance twin-engine turboprop airplane. Sixteen suitcases full of 314 kilos of cocaine filled the plane from floor to ceiling. The aircraft also carried its owner, twenty-eight-year-old Jorge Ochoa.

Once the kilos were off-loaded, Lehder himself tested the powder, seeking to take his own share from the highest-quality cocaine in the shipment. The cocaine ranged from 88 to 94 percent pure. Some of the kilos were marked with the letters "CIA," which was the Spanish abbreviation for *Compañía,*—"Company," one of the nicknames used by the emerging conglomerate of cocaine producers.

Yakovac was just thrilled to be in the same room with all the kilos. "Never had such a rush in my life," he said later. "We're talking well over $15 million, to use a good round figure, wholesale, in one room, at one time." At the time, the DEA was busying itself making one-ounce busts on the streets of Miami.

Lehder's men loaded the shipment onto a Cessna 206, the traffickers' workhorse smuggling plane, and sent it to the United States. Ochoa stayed overnight on the cay.

Ochoa was not the only young drug lord to visit Lehder. His friend and occasional smuggling partner, Pablo Escobar, also came to the cay, according to Yakovac. One day Yakovac took Escobar and Ochoa and their wives to open bank accounts in the Bahamas. The Colombians spoke no English, so Yakovac did the translating. The Colombians wanted Bahamian banks to serve as a channel for transferring their money to their accounts in Panama. Lehder was simply to deposit the cash for them in the Bahamas, and then it would be sent by wire to Panama. Such trusting rapport was critical to their success. The close relationship between Ochoa, Escobar, and Lehder provided the nucleus of a coalition that would rule the cocaine trade during its period of greatest expansion.

AS Carlos Lehder's business boomed in the Bahamas, George Jung's anger about being eased out of control simmered to a flash point. He traveled in the small circle of Colombian drug smugglers, and every time he went to a party he was introduced as the man who had set up Carlos Lehder. While Lehder had become a legend in the business, Jung was looking like a fool, reduced to moving five to ten kilos at a time. It was driving Jung crazy. In the spring of 1978, Jung returned to the Bahamas for another confrontation with Lehder. Again they met in the cocktail lounge of the Holiday Inn in Nassau. This time Lehder came accompanied by two German bodyguards, who stood behind him while he and Jung sat and talked. Jung could see that the bodyguards made Lehder feel more secure. He sensed that he was no longer dealing with a friend but a fawned-over minidictator. Jung pointed out that he had helped start the business, had risked his life creating cash for the aircraft and the leasing of Norman's Cay, and now he was making $500,000 a year in little kilo coke deals while Lehder was raking in tens of millions. Why had Lehder betrayed him? In his own heart, Jung thought he knew the answer: he had been Lehder's big brother in the business, constantly correcting him and teaching him. Lehder, obsessed with power, didn't want to be reminded of the youth he had been.

"I'm not going to let you get away with this," Jung warned. "There's only one end that can result from this."

Lehder stayed cool. "It's over," he told Jung. Lehder suggested Jung go to work distributing kilos for Humberto Hoyos, Jung's Colombian brother-in-law in New York City. Jung left, unsatisfied. Back in Boston, he approached some gangsters he had met in Danbury with a plan to kill Lehder. Jung was serious enough to make a down payment of $125,000. But Hoyos talked him out of it. If Lehder died, it would cause tremendous problems with the traffickers in Colombia. Lehder had become untouchable. Jung canceled the contract. The down payment wasn't refundable.

Like Jung before him, Stephen Yakovac was eventually forced out of Lehder's organization. Lehder had become increasingly demanding, always finding fault and making crazy accusations.

"I'm the leader of this gang," Lehder said. "This is it. I make the rules. You live by them, or you leave."

Yakovac chose to leave. When he returned to Norman's Cay for some personal belongings, Lehder met him at the airstrip with the ever-present German bodyguards. Lehder held his chrome automatic beside Yakovac's ear, pointed it toward the ocean, and fired. "Get off this island and don't come back," he said.

A few months later a forty-nine-year-old Nassau businessman deliberately swam into the heart of the new cocaine business. Norman Solomon had heard the stories about Norman's Cay for months and finally decided to do something about it. Solomon wrote a newspaper column on the side in Nassau, and he had been a member of the Bahamian Parliament for twelve years. More important, he was the leader of the Bahamian opposition and a man not afraid to challenge the official order of things.

Solomon had a good guess about what was happening on Norman's Cay. So while boating through the Exumas on July 18, 1979, a week after the bloody shootings across the water at the Dadeland Mall in Miami, Solomon purposely drifted close to the cay. Through his binoculars, he noticed pickup trucks paralleling his boat's course on the land. The men in the trucks watched him through their own binoculars.

Returning through the area several days later, Solomon decided to go ashore. He told his captain to stay in radio contact with Nassau while he jumped overboard and swam toward land. Onshore, he walked the beach, careful to stay on sand below the high-water mark, which throughout the Bahamas is by law the property of the queen and therefore public. Soon a large blond man in tight white pants appeared and told him he was on private property. The man had a German accent.

Solomon explained about the high-water mark and kept walking.

The big blond man left and returned with three other men. Two of them had German accents, and the third seemed Spanish. They surrounded the 140-pound Solomon. He could see bulges in their clothes that he imagined hid weapons. He told them all about the high-water mark.

The men were very insistent that Solomon get lost. He was very insistent that they get lost. A standoff ensued.

Then someone who described himself as the "island manager" appeared. He told Solomon he could stay, but his safety could not be guaranteed if he crossed the high-water mark. Having proven his point, Solomon swam back to his boat. When he got home he wrote a letter to the Bahamian police commissioner.

5.

THE KING OF COCAINE TRANSPORTATION

Carlos Lehder was constantly in need of pilots to ferry his cocaine to the United States. So it was only a matter of time before he turned to Ed Ward, the marijuana smuggler whose operation shared Norman's Cay with Lehder's.

Edward Hayes Ward had found the island two years before Lehder. He liked it for the same reasons; it was remote, it had no police force, and it was located between Colombia and the United States. In short, it was the perfect smuggling base.

Though they lived on the same island, no two smugglers had less in common than Lehder and Ward. Ward was an ex-marine who had worked as an aircraft mechanic for the Navy and settled into a routine middle-class life in Jacksonville in the early 1970s. First he sold furniture at Sears, and then he sold insurance, doing pretty well at both but not getting rich. Then he got divorced, and with three children he found the alimony and child support payments more than he could handle. Along with some relatives and Greg Von Eberstein, a co-worker in sales at Sears, Ward entered the marijuana smuggling business. He and his partners were all slightly conservative family men in their thirties, and they went about smuggling as if it were just a mid-career change. Marijuana, they reckoned, wasn't all that harmful, and people did want to smoke it. Ward went to his mother to borrow the $30,000 to buy his smuggling plane, a twenty-year-old twin-engine Beechcraft Bonanza.

The Ward gang set about flying 1,200-pound loads of marijuana from Colombia into Florida and Georgia at $50 a pound. Soon they had more money than they ever imagined. They created front businesses, purchased a marina in Jacksonville, and acquired property in North Carolina and Florida. Ward and Von Eberstein bought fancy houses close to each other on posh Admiral's Walk East in suburban Orange Park, a few miles outside Jacksonville. They wallowed in their newfound wealth. One day a neighbor kid saw a sack of cash emptied out on one of the beds in Ward's house.

The conspicuous consumption of Ward's band of smugglers attracted heavy police surveillance in Jacksonville. The DEA became interested after one of Greg Von Eberstein's brothers paid cash out of a paper bag for a car without even looking at the sticker price. Watching Von Eberstein led the federal agents to Ward, and soon they were going through his trash and staking out his house in Orange Park. By now Ward was remarried to a thirty-one-year-old dental technician. Ward confessed his true business to his new wife, Emilie "Lassie," Ward, but he told her he was less worried about getting arrested for smuggling than he was about having his assets seized by the IRS. He thought he had come up with a foolproof way to smuggle drugs. Soon Lassie was part of the business, counting and banding the money when it came in and playing devil's advocate with Ed to help bolster security.

ED Ward first spotted Carlos Lehder on Norman's Cay while Ward was dividing his time between Jacksonville and the Bahamas in late 1977. Ward knew immediately that Lehder was a drug smuggler. After all, Ward was one, too, and it took one to know one. Ward saw Lehder's Piper Navajo sitting day after day at the landing strip on Norman's Cay and knew it was too expensive a piece of equipment to lie idle for so long. A legitimate owner would have it in use.

Ward was worried that Lehder would think he was a DEA agent. There's two people that look like drug smugglers: drug smugglers and drug agents, Ward thought.

So one day in early 1978 Ward went over to Lehder's house on the northeast end of the cay and asked to speak with him in private. The two men took a walk on the ocean side of the house. Ward was direct. He shook hands, told Lehder he was a drug smuggler and thought Lehder was one, too. He didn't want Lehder to be concerned about Ward's operation affecting his. Lehder said virtually nothing. But for a time the two smuggling groups coexisted peacefully on the island.

A few months later, Lehder asked Ward if he wanted to become a cocaine smuggler.

Ward considered it. He was essentially a square person. He had carried marijuana for over a year before even sampling his own product. Cocaine meant dealing with rougher people and bigger penalties if you got caught. There is a saying in the drug trade: A marijuana deal is done with a handshake and a cocaine deal is done with a gun. But there was more money in cocaine, and it would be easier to fly because it was less bulky than marijuana. Sometimes with marijuana you had to stuff the plane so full the pilot wouldn't be able to get out of the cockpit if the plane went down. Ed Ward was a practical man. He had seen Carlos Lehder start small on Norman's Cay and in a very short time graduate to Learjets. Ward felt he hadn't earned enough for all the effort he had put into marijuana smuggling. He decided to give cocaine a try.

In late August 1978, Greg Von Eberstein brought a "two-gram tooter" home to suburban Orange Park. Ed and Lassie and Greg and his wife, Gail, snorted it together.

"He wanted to show us that it wasn't like heroin, that nobody was going to die from it, and you didn't get addicted to it," Lassie Ward recalled. Greg wanted to go into the cocaine business with Ed, but Gail opposed it. None of the wives wanted their men in cocaine.

Ed Ward needed to put Lehder's proposition to the rest of his band of marijuana smugglers. On September 6, 1978, eight of them had a meeting on Norman's Cay with Ward and Lehder. Lehder had brought a four-inch brown vial filled with a quarter ounce of cocaine. It was white and sparkly, and everybody thought it was really good stuff. Ward invited all his men to go into the cocaine business. Nobody was enthusiastic about the idea. They mulled it over while they drank beer and played cards. They considered themselves a different breed from cocaine smugglers, more easygoing, less prone to violence. They put their concerns directly to Lehder.

"What about violence?" asked one of Ward's men. "Have you ever killed anybody?"

"Every once in a while in this business somebody has to die," Lehder said.

None of Ward's men were immediately willing to switch.

Ward and Lehder entered into a ten-point agreement: Ward would make ten smuggling trips of 250 kilos a trip for $400,000 each. Lehder told Ward he would have to buy a new airplane. He lent Ward $604,000 for a Swearigen Merlin III, a twelve-seat corporate turboprop.

IN January 1979, Ward, Lehder, and Ward's co-pilot, a fifty-five-year-old ex-navy War World II aviator named Lev Francis, made the first trip in the Merlin carrying five hundred kilos of cocaine from Colombia to Norman's Cay. The airstrip was muddy, Ward's plane had been loaded with double the agreed-upon amount, the gas from the refueling was bad, and Ed Ward was furious. Thereafter Ward averaged about one smuggling trip a month for Lehder, but he hated being Lehder's contract employee. Ward, who was so precise in every detail, detested working for the sloppy, free-wheeling Joe Lehder. He said repeatedly he only wanted to work for Lehder long enough to get himself started in the cocaine business.

Sometimes Ward brought the cocaine up to the Bahamas from Colombia in the Merlin and a smaller plane took it into the United States. By this time Lehder's organization had changed. Gone were the early people like Stephen Yakovac. Jack Reed, a dishwasher from Park City, Utah, who had turned cocaine pilot, was now Lehder's right-hand man. Reed was nineteen years older than Lehder.

The operation was growing. Lehder's island staff now numbered between thirty and fifty. He had two or three Colombian pilots and three or four American pilots. None of his pilots knew what the others were doing. More than half a dozen planes now crowded the airstrip at Norman's Cay, including a Sabreliner and a Learjet. The jets were sometimes used to transport money to Armenia, Lehder's birthplace.

Lehder's obsession with security worsened. When the planes came in with the cocaine, the Colombians and Germans went into a frenzy, brandishing weapons and scurrying about the island as if an air raid were in progress. Ward asked Jack Reed to try to reason with Joe Lehder.

"Can't you talk to him?" Ward asked Reed. "You know, there's too much attention being drawn to the island. It's not like it used to be. It's not fun anymore."

Ward, the straight-arrow ex-marine, was getting seriously strung out on cocaine. He had made the mistake of regularly using the product soon after he'd started transporting it for Joe Lehder. He couldn't stop himself: he would go into the bathroom of his house on the cay so his kids wouldn't see him using it and just stay in there, withdrawn and miserable. He got so fond of cocaine that he held an entire kilo out of one of the shipments for his own personal use. He buried the kilo in the backyard, figuring he'd dig it up whenever he wanted some.

"After two or three nights of getting up in the middle of the night to go out and dig it up, Ed said, 'This stuff is going to the States in the morning,' " Lassie recalled. " 'It's going to kill us,' he said." Still, Ward couldn't stop.

"Even when we started seeing that it did have adverse effects, it was still too good because you could feel really lousy and really depressed and you'd do cocaine and the depression and that lousy feeling just completely went away," said Lassie.

Ed and Lassie Ward had much to feel depressed about. Ward had loaded up his family and moved to Norman's Cay for good in the summer of 1979 after learning that the IRS was hot on his trail. As the Wards left Jacksonville, the IRS slapped a lien on the house on Admiral's Walk and accused Ed Ward of failing to report $900,000 in income in 1977 and 1978.

Now the law was moving in on their island sanctuary as well. On the afternoon of September 13, 1979, Ed Ward took off from the cay and flew at low altitude toward Nassau. In the air he saw three Royal Bahamian Defense Force boats coming in a line from Nassau to Norman's Cay. Ward did a 180-degree turn and flew back to the cay. He told everybody a raid was coming.

It had been common knowledge for weeks that the cay was about to be raided. Lehder himself was predicting it; he always seemed to have advance knowledge about police comings and goings. But the longer they went without a raid, the more it began to seem like crying wolf. The attitude about the police had grown lax. After giving his warning, Ward took off again and flew to Nassau for the night.

The next morning, more than ninety officers of the Royal Bahamian Defense and Police forces raided Norman's Cay as part of "Operation Raccoon." Bahamian authorities had known for a long time what Lehder was up to. Nearly a year earlier, the DEA had asked and received Bahamian government approval to conduct undercover operations on Norman's Cay. The DEA, trailing Ed Ward from Jacksonville, had happened onto Carlos Lehder. In March 1979 a senior police official pointed out that Lehder had gained control of almost all the island. Three villas at the airstrip were full of armed Colombians who discouraged visitors. The officer recommended a major raid. Three months later the police received Norman Solomon's outraged letter at having been driven off the beach at Norman's Cay.

The raiding officers were told they were confronting a large, heavily armed drug trafficking operation run by "Latin-looking people who control the entire island." Police intelligence said the ringleader was "a very rich man who has good connections worldwide to enable him to conduct a lucrative business." But it was a crude, poorly coordinated raid. Several senior officers later said they weren't even told they were looking for Lehder.

At seven A.M. on raid day, a Bahamian police corporal landed on Norman's Cay beach in a rubber dinghy and saw a man run to a white Volkswagen bus. The corporal fired warning shots, but the man drove off. The corporal later identified the man as Carlos Lehder. Fifteen minutes later, Lehder ordered the mate of his thirty-three-foot powerboat *Fire Fall* to get under way for Nassau. As the *Fire Fall* headed out of the sound, a defense force boat signaled it to stop. Lehder, at the helm, ignored the signal. Two marines in a rubber dinghy fired at him. He increased his speed. The defense force vessel pursued. Its commander saw a man on the *Fire Fall* dumping a white powdery substance from a plastic bag into the water. The *Fire Fall* entered shallow water on the western side of the cay, and a police sergeant fired at it from shore. Finally Lehder gave up and allowed the *Fire Fall* to be taken in tow.

On shore, Lehder, wearing blue jeans, a thick gold chain, and an expensive watch, got out of his boat and started walking away. A Bahamian inspector shouted, "Joe!" and Lehder turned. He was arrested and handcuffed. Caught in a bedroom at Lehder's house was his German teacher, a young woman named Margit Meie-Linnekogel, who was later alleged to be a German terrorist. A small child was with her. Police searching the bedroom also found a .357 Magnum and small amounts of marijuana and cocaine. Open on the bed was a red Samsonite suitcase with a combination lock. The suitcase held U.S. currency.

Lehder, in handcuffs, complained bitterly as he watched the search of his house. He was overheard saying he was investing $5 million on the cay, and he was going to pack up and leave because of the police harassment.

The prisoners were brought to the airstrip around noon. There, Lehder continued ranting. He denied any knowledge of the items seized inside his house except for the red suitcase, which he said contained the cash payroll for his employees. Assistant Police Commissioner Howard Smith, the commander of the raid, ordered one of his men to give Lehder the suitcase. Lehder opened it and started counting the money in front of the police.

AFTER spending the night in Nassau, Ward and his wife decided to fly back to Norman's Cay despite the raid. They figured they had no reason not to. After Ward landed on the cay, defense force officers with drawn guns told him they had a warrant to search his house. Inside, they found cocaine and marijuana residue and a small amount of ammunition. They also found $10,000 that Lassie Ward had wrapped in a scarf. The money later disappeared.

The Wards were taken to the villas at the airstrip, where they saw

Lehder, also under arrest. But Lehder was taken outside the villas to talk with Assistant Commissioner Smith. Smith had Lehder's handcuffs removed. Lassie Ward saw Lehder leave with a couple of officers and come back with Manfred, one of his German bodyguards. Lehder carried a red suitcase.

Lehder walked over to his girlfriend, a dark-skinned Colombian woman who went by the name Chocolata. She was standing next to Lassie Ward and crying hysterically. He told her not to worry. Everything was going to be fine, he said. He had paid the police off. They would let her go as soon as they finished the paperwork.

"Everything is copacetic," Lehder said.

"Are they taking you to jail?" asked Chocolata.

"No, I don't have to go," he said.

"Why aren't you going?" she asked.

He soothed her in Spanish.

In all, thirty-three people were arrested, nearly everybody in Lehder's organization except Lehder and Manfred. The Bahamian police seized eight handguns, two automatic rifles, one shotgun, thirty-five sticks of dynamite, and 618 rounds of ammunition. The police transported the prisoners to Nassau on a DC-3. Lehder spoke to them before they left and told them not to worry, he'd be there to pick them up tomorrow. Everyone was angry, Lassie Ward recalled, especially the men. "The men were upset that Joe was not being arrested," she said.

As the plane took off, Ed Ward looked out and saw Lehder, standing on the airstrip with Manfred. Lehder waved. Lassie Ward heard later that Joe had refused to stay on the island without a bodyguard.

Several police officers wondered why Lehder wasn't going to Nassau, too.

"Don't worry 'bout him," said Assistant Commissioner Smith. "He'll come later."

But he never did.

Ward spent the weekend in jail, sharing a cell with another of Lehder's German guards, Heinrich, an imposing man with a black beard who liked to tuck two .45-caliber automatics into his belt. One of their Bahamian jailers offered to warn Lassie Ward about future raids on Norman's Cay for $500.

Everybody arrested in the raid was released on $2,000 bail. Only one conviction was ever obtained, and that was against a Bahamian who possessed an unregistered shotgun. When Ward returned to Norman's Cay, he asked Lehder how he'd done it.

"I paid money," Lehder told him.

. . .

THE man who decided not to arrest Joe Lehder was Howard Smith, the assistant commissioner of the Royal Bahamian Police Force. Smith, the second-highest-ranking police officer in the Bahamas, later said the evidence against Lehder was lacking. This conflicted with Smith's own preraid briefing: the two ranking officers under Smith said the assistant commissioner specifically told them Lehder was the "boss" of Norman's Cay and should be arrested.

Newspaper reports later said something very curious had happened during the raid. A police constable searched one of the houses on the cay and found a plastic bag in a garbage bin. The bag held $80,000 in U.S. currency, and the constable spent forty-five minutes counting it. He said he gave the money to Assistant Commissioner Smith. The money promptly disappeared. Smith denied ever receiving it. The constable stuck to his story.

Five years later, Smith's finances became a focal point for a Royal Commission of Inquiry investigating drug corruption in the Bahamas. Within three years after the raid on Norman's Cay, Smith paid $7,500 for a Toyota, $17,500 for an Oldsmobile Cutlass Brougham, and $18,000 in cash for a house under construction. He invested $30,000 in a shipping company and took out a $25,000 loan for yet another car while his bank balance stood at $29,500. The commission looked at Smith's bank accounts and found $57,000 that Smith couldn't account for. Asked about this, Smith said he "played the horses, the numbers, and the dogs."

The commission concluded that "Lehder did bribe the police to ensure his freedom, and we find that there must have been complicity on the part of Assistant Commissioner of Police Smith and other senior police officers."

But four days after the Norman's Cay raid, Lehder was mad enough to try to make good on his threat to leave the Bahamas. "For Immediate Sale: The Norman's Cay Yacht Club, Norman's Cay, Exumas," read the ad in *The Miami Herald*. Lehder offered to sell his entire operation: the airstrip, the clubhouse, the marina, ten vacation villas —all 165 acres. He threw in twenty cars, vans, trucks, and tractors; eight boats, and two of his best smuggling planes. Total price: $2,932,000. "Only serious qualified enquiries considered," the ad warned. Interested persons were to contact International Dutch Resources Ltd., Lehder's corporation.

In the wake of the raid, the ad was strange enough to generate news stories. DRUG FUGITIVE OWNS MYSTERIOUS NORMAN'S CAY, *The*

Miami Herald headlined. The story went on in some detail about Lehder's operation: "Norman's Cay, the Drug Enforcement Administration suspects, has been used for most of this year as a staging area for the smuggling of cocaine and marijuana into the United States."

But even with the police heat and the publicity, business on the cay resumed as usual. Only days after the raid, Ward flew a 250-kilo load from Colombia to Norman's Cay and on to Reidsville, Georgia. The cocaine trip went off without a hitch, but Ward's tax problems in Jacksonville followed him to Georgia. At the airport in Atlanta, the IRS seized Ward's aircraft, the Beechcraft Bonanza. Ward was present when it happened, and at first he thought he was being arrested for smuggling. When the authorities seemed interested only in the plane, he got his luggage and paid an airport mechanic to drive him away. The Bonanza was only a temporary loss; Ward just had his attorney line up a third party to buy it back from the IRS. It cost $40,000—$35,000 for the plane and $5,000 for the third party—and Ward had the plane back within a month. In four months the plane carried another 350 kilos through Norman's Cay and into the United States for Carlos Lehder. In all, Ward transported 3,000 kilos—more than three tons—for Lehder. The cocaine was worth $150 million wholesale in the United States. Lehder funneled more than $22 million through Bahamian banks—the "counting charge" alone came to $205,590. A lot of Lehder's money ended up in the pockets of Bahamian officials.

THE Bahamas in 1979 was a nation for sale, and Carlos Lehder wasn't the only one buying. More than a dozen marijuana and cocaine entrepreneurs independent of Lehder had set up pipelines of their own on seventeen Bahamian islands. The seven hundred islands of the Bahamas were scattered over one hundred thousand square miles of ocean, and it was simply impossible to police them. Raids had little effect, court prosecutions went nowhere. The nation had turned into the prime way station for America's drug habit.

It's not clear when various Bahamian officials decided to start profiting off something they could do very little to stop, but by the beginning of the 1980s the Bahamas had become, in the words of one smuggler, "a payable situation."

The extent of the corruption Carlos Lehder sowed in the Bahamas would take years to surface. The evidence indicates he was merely taking advantage of a system that was already in place. Lehder's lawyer was Nigel Bowe, who had once paved the way for Barry Kane's smuggling flights through the Bahamas. Bowe was a well-known fixer for his wealthy drug clients. Court cases against his clients seldom brought prison sentences. Bowe was also very close to Prime Minister Lynden Pindling. A DEA informant later said Bowe visited Norman's Cay on the twenty-second of each month, allegedly to pick up $88,000 in bribe money destined for Pindling. Another informant eventually charged that Lehder paid a flat $200,000 a month to Pindling. Lehder gave the money to Bowe, who in turn funneled it to Everette Bannister, a notorious bagman who was very close to Pindling, according to the testimony of Bannister's son, Gorman, who much to his father's dismay developed a cocaine freebasing habit.

The Royal Commission of Inquiry considered Pindling's finances and concluded that "the Prime Minister's expenditure over the years from 1977 has far exceeded his income." But the commission could not determine if Pindling took drug money. The prime minister denied every allegation against him. The commission made a harsher determination against Nigel Bowe, finding that "Mr. Bowe's involvement with drug traffickers far exceeded a lawyer/client relationship and that he benefitted materially from his numerous associations with them."

The fact that cocaine smuggling continued on Norman's Cay after the September 1979 raid was well known in the Bahamas. Two months after the raid, Norman Solomon spoke out in the House of Assembly that the island was being used "as one of the biggest drug smuggling operations in this part of the world." Two years later Solomon's house was firebombed.

In December 1979 Carlos Lehder was officially told to leave the Bahamas. At first the pressure didn't budge him, and the smuggling went on.

Mysterious things continued to happen near Norman's Cay. On July 31, 1980, boaters found a drifting yacht, the *Kalia III,* her decks slick with blood. A shotgun blast had perforated the teakwood, and a man's corpse, the scalp nearly peeled from the head, lay facedown in a trailing dinghy. When the Bahamian police arrived a day later, the body was missing.

The *Kalia III* belonged to a retired Fort Myers couple who had set out on a six-month cruise to the Bahamas. The couple disappeared without a trace, and the crime was never solved. Years later one of Carlos Lehder's smugglers would testify that at the time that the *Kalia* disappeared Lehder had sent out his German bodyguards to "take care of" a sailboat hovering too close to Norman's Cay.

There were two more police raids, in 1980 and 1981, but Lehder was tipped off each time. Sometimes he merely got in his Learjet and flew back to Colombia, always returning to keep the business going. Carlos Lehder remained on top of the cocaine world at the beginning of the 1980s. In the fall of that year, he told one of the smugglers on Norman's Cay he had brought in "10,000 children"—kilos—and earned $30 million.

IT was during this period that an old friend went to Colombia for an audience with the man they now called, with utmost respect, Don Carlos. George Jung had never forgotten his onetime smuggling partner. In July 1980 a humbled Jung traveled to Colombia to ask Lehder to take him back. Jung wanted to distribute cocaine again for Lehder in California. Jung was asking to come back not as a partner, but as an employee. He was nervous, but determined. He still felt Lehder owed him. Only now he was willing to settle for much less.

Jung went to the Intercontinental Hotel in Medellín, called Autos Lehder, and left word. In a few hours Lehder showed up at his hotel room with his bodyguards. All of them, Lehder included, were dressed in combat fatigues. Lehder and Jung had some drinks and snorted some cocaine. Jung thought Lehder looked like something off the cover of *Soldier of Fortune* and told him so. It was the first time Jung had ever seen his former partner use the drug. Jung himself was now extremely wary of cocaine and considering giving it up. Two years earlier, he had suffered a mild heart attack during a marathon eighteen-hour cocaine binge while waiting out the birth of his daughter.

Finally Jung made his pitch to return to Lehder's fold.

Lehder said yes. He was in an expansive mood, and the cocaine made him talkative. He said he had control of Norman's Cay and a fleet of aircraft, and he was transporting most of the cocaine out of Colombia into the United States. He bragged of his influence in the Bahamas. He said that Robert Vesco, the financial swindler, had introduced him to Bahamian Prime Minister Lynden Pindling.

Lehder described Vesco, who had embezzled $224 million from American investors in the early 1970s as a financial genius. A fugitive hiding in the Bahamas, Vesco was now telling Lehder what to do with his millions, schooling him in the use of offshore banks to launder money. And, Lehder said, Vesco had introduced him to Fidel Castro. Lehder himself was supporting the M-19, a revolutionary group in Colombia. He seemed very pleased with himself. To Jung his ego seemed as big as the hotel. Lehder had always admired Che Guevara, and now he was starting to emulate Che by wearing fatigues and growing his hair long. Jung reminded Lehder about what happened to his idol, Che. Mixing politics with the drug business was a recipe for disaster.

"This is going to destroy you," Jung said.

Lehder just gave Jung a cryptic smile.

He bragged to Jung that he had made several hundred million dollars. He called himself "the king of cocaine transportation, the king of cocaine." By now Jung had made a few millions in cocaine himself, but the comparison with his former partner was painful, something he would never completely get over. But the meeting had gone well. Jung was full of optimism.

Jung returned home and was promptly arrested on drug charges in Massachusetts. He would not speak with Lehder for five years.

ED Ward left Norman's Cay in the summer of 1980. He was on the Bahamian immigration "stop list"—if detained in the islands, he could be deported. And it looked certain he would be facing criminal charges in the United States soon: Ward found out that Lev Francis, the co-pilot on some of his cocaine flights, had turned informant before a federal grand jury in Jacksonville. With no place to go in the United States, Ward tried everything to straighten out his legal quandary in the Bahamas. He retained the services of Nigel Bowe, the Bahamas' all-purpose fixer. He paid $100,000 to Everette Bannister, Pindling's close friend, and Agricultural Minister George Smith, the Bahamian cabinet official who presided over the Exumas chain of islands that included Norman's Cay. Ward believed the money was going to Pindling himself.

"These people came to us and told us that that was the Bahamian way of life, that's the way they did things, and they could help us," Lassie Ward recalled.

But the bribes didn't fix the Wards' problems. Perhaps most important of all, Carlos Lehder wanted him out. As with Jung and Yakovac, Ward had outlived his usefulness to Lehder. It was clear that the DEA had zeroed in on Ward, and Ward and his smuggling planes had become "hot." In April 1980 Ward had to abort a 150-kilo smuggling trip, and one of his men was arrested on the ground in Georgia. Lehder was angry at Ward for bringing the heat down on the island. So one day Ward picked up his family and went to Haiti, where Nigel Bowe had told him there was no extradition treaty. The Wards moved into a three-story luxury residence on a mountaintop overlooking the bay in Port-au-Prince. The two-acre tract was surrounded by an eight-foot wall. From Haiti, Ward did some cocaine smuggling of his own. But without Lehder's connections, he was only able to put together small loads of a dozen kilos or so, which he sent to Norman's Cay for refueling. Lehder was talking about charging his ex-partner $50,000 for using Norman's Cay. And the law was moving in again.

ON January 8, 1981, the hammer dropped in Jacksonville. Carlos Lehder, Ed Ward, Lassie Ward, and eleven of Ward's fellow Jacksonville smugglers were indicted on thirty-nine counts of smuggling, conspiracy, and income tax evasion by the federal grand jury.

Two weeks later, Ed and Lassie Ward, Greg and Gail Von Eberstein, and two other couples from the Ward group went out to a nightclub in Port-au-Prince. "It was kind of a last hurrah," Lassie Ward recalled. "We had the feeling that the chapters were closing in on us, that this was kind of like, 'This is it.' " At the nightclub their suspicions were confirmed: they saw the DEA agent from Jacksonville who had pursued them for three years.

The next day Ward, Lassie, and ten of Ward's men were arrested in Haiti. The police in Haiti tried to solicit a bribe for the Wards' release. "It's just like the Bahamas all over again," Ed Ward told his wife. "I'm not paying another government to stay in their country. I'd just as soon go back and face trial." They rode to the United States in handcuffs, but their spirits soared. Gail Von Eberstein told her husband she was glad he was under arrest; now he could finally get off cocaine. On the DEA plane they sang "Homeward Bound." On the ground back in Jacksonville, Greg Von Eberstein shook the DEA agents' hands and told them: "It was fun while it lasted, but now it's over, and you won."

Carlos Lehder escaped capture, of course. Before the year was out, Ward reached a plea bargain agreement—he would eventually serve five years; Lassie received probation. Ed Ward gave testimony against his old partner before the federal grand jury. Carlos Lehder had now replaced Griselda Blanco as the DEA's most wanted Colombian drug fugitive.

Lehder left Norman's Cay in September 1981. By now he was also on the Bahamian stop list, and the Bahamians had decided to place a permanent police station on Norman's Cay. It was clearly time to go. Lehder, Jack Reed, and several Colombians loaded Lehder's Rockwell 690 Commander with all their suitcases. Everybody shook hands. Jack Reed, an avid pot smoker, laughed and said he was going to go to Colombia to grow high-quality marijuana.

But Lehder merely moved his residence from Norman's Cay, not his smuggling operation. He returned often and kept a contingent of Colombians on the island to look after things. In June 1982 Nigel Bowe brought an American pilot and drug smuggler to meet Lehder on Norman's Cay. Lehder told the pilot he was running a very successful operation and was paying "a lot of money in the Bahamas," but he needed pilots to transport cocaine. Lehder's hand showed again when the Bahamas celebrated its independence from the British Empire on July 10, 1982. Two Bahamian police officers found a Bahamian pilot and four Colombians loading boxes onto an airplane in one of the hangars on Norman's Cay. The boxes held leaflets demanding "Nixon-Reagan's Drug Enforcement Agency Go Home." The aircraft took off and dropped the leaflets into crowds celebrating in Nassau and on Bimini. Several of the leaflets had U.S. currency taped to them; some had $100 bills.

Lehder's symbolic public shower of money on the Bahamas paralleled his secret largesse toward Bahamian officials. The month the leaflets were dropped, a Bahamian police corporal stationed on Norman's Cay said his inspector told him Joe Lehder was vacationing on the island for six to eight weeks and the police were supposed to protect him. The corporal said he was told the order came from Assistant Police Commissioner Howard Smith, who in turn was receiving the command from "cabinet-level" authority. The corporal saw Lehder twice on the cay. Two other constables were nearby, but none made a move to arrest Lehder.

6.

MIAMI 1982

By 1982, things had gotten far worse in Miami. Since the Dadeland shooting three years earlier, killings had continued and the cocaine trade had mushroomed. South Florida reeled from the effects of the Mariel boatlift of 1980, which added 125,000 Cuban refugees—thousands of them former residents of Cuban prisons—to an already volatile mix of trigger-happy cocaine cowboys. Every year murders set a new record, from 349 in 1979 to 569 in 1980 to 621 in 1981. At one point, 40 percent were drug-related; 25 percent of the victims died with automatic bullets in their bodies. The Dade County Medical Examiner's Office was forced to add a refrigerated trailer to handle the overflow of corpses.

The murders were as bold and bloodthirsty as ever. A killer wearing a motorcycle helmet shot a well-dressed Latin man carrying his luggage through Miami International Airport's baggage claim area and then jumped on a black motorcycle and sped off. Three bodies turned up in the trunk of a car in Kendall. In late 1981 the killings brought action from the DEA, which established a "Centac"—Central Tactical Unit—an elite task force of DEA agents, New York City police, and Metro-Dade detectives funded out of Washington to go after high-level targets in Miami. Centac 26, as it was called, immediately set its sights on the worst of the cocaine cowboys: Griselda Blanco, Paco Sepulveda, and El Loco. Still, the bloodshed continued.

The flow of cocaine also surged to record levels. At the same time —and as a direct consequence—money was flowing out of the country—drug money. Money laundering was epidemic through Miami banks, and the astronomical amounts of cash made some people realize, in a way the murders and cocaine did not, just how encircled they were by the drug trade. In 1979 the Federal Reserve Bank of Miami reported a $5.5 billion cash surplus, which was greater than the combined surpluses of every other Federal Reserve Bank branch in the country.

The next year Operation Greenback, a combined U.S. Customs Service–IRS probe, began to make the first real progress against the Colombian traffickers. Greenback caught a young Colombian woman at Miami International Airport trying to smuggle $1.5 million in cash out of the country in six Monopoly boxes. It was a record seizure, but it was surpassed within three months, when police at the Opa-Locka airport seized $1.6 million from a private plane bound for Colombia.

Soon the Greenback task force was zeroing in on the failure of bank officials to comply with the Bank Secrecy Act. The law required the filing of Currency Transaction Reports (CTRs) with every deposit or withdrawal of more than $10,000 in cash. Before the Greenback crackdown, the traffickers brought millions of dollars into banks stuffed in suitcases, cardboard boxes, and duffel bags. Some bank officers just looked the other way. Customs investigators estimated that $3.2 billion in cash went unreported in south Florida in 1981. Early that year Greenback agents searched the Landmark Bank branch in Plantation, a suburban bedroom community west of Fort Lauderdale. Hernan Botero Moreno, a soccer team owner from Medellín, was charged with laundering $56 million through the bank. Operation Greenback was on a roll. Three weeks later the agents raided two Miami banks, the Bank of Miami and the Great American Bank of Dade County. Isaac Kattan Kassin of Cali, a plump balding man with two teenaged daughters, was charged with laundering $60 million through Great American Bank. Kattan, forty-six, drove a Chevy Citation and looked so much like the prime minister of Israel that the investigators watching him on surveillance code-named him ''Begin.'' The United States attorney for Miami called Kattan the biggest drug financier in South America.

The truth was that the feds were merely catching up with the cocaine trade's subcontractors. Botero and Kattan were just currency dealers—Colombian businessmen whose firms converted foreign currencies, including U.S. dollars, into Colombian pesos and vice versa. The money merchants provided support services to the real drug lords, who stayed well out of harm's way in Medellín.

DEATH, money, and drugs: the gaudy, violent kaleidoscope fed a fear, and the fear created a ground swell. Miami was outgunned and overrun. In December 1981 four powerful men from Miami ventured to the White House with a plea that conjured up visions of a beleaguered cow-town sheriff calling on the U.S. marshal. The delegation was led by Eastern Airlines chairman Frank Borman and Knight-Ridder newspapers chairman Alvah H. Chapman, Jr. (Knight-Ridder owned *The Miami Herald*). They had joined together to form Miami Citizens Against Crime. Miami wanted federal help. Its wish was granted.

On January 28, 1982, President Reagan announced a cabinet-level task force to coordinate a federal offensive against drugs in south Florida. Reagan called Miami "the nation's major terminal for the smuggling of illegal drugs" and named Vice President George Bush to lead what quickly became known as the Vice President's Task Force on South Florida.

"The nearly two million people of south Florida are unfairly burdened financially in addition to being denied their constitutional right to live in peace without fear and intimidation," Reagan said.

A formidable "federal posse" was heading to south Florida—more than 200 federal lawmen, including 130 Customs agents, 60 DEA agents and 43 FBI agents. The Bureau of Alcohol, Tobacco and Firearms added 45 agents to crack down on the proliferation of automatic weapons. IRS agents promised to target money laundering. U.S. Army Cobra helicopter gunships, used for fire support in Vietnam, were brought in to chase drug planes. U.S. Navy Hawkeye E2-C radar surveillance planes were added to help spot smuggling flights. Navy ships were authorized to board boats smuggling drugs. For the first time since the Civil War, the Army and Navy were helping to fight civilian crime. It was an unprecedented response to an unprecedented problem. U.S. CAVALRY IS COMING, AND IT'S ABOUT TIME, headlined *The Miami Herald*.

Yet in the real corridors of federal power in Miami, where one could finally get a good look at the progress of "the drug war," the view was bleak indeed. The U.S. Attorney's Office was such a place, and it faced serious problems in the effort to stem the flow of drugs. The office handled every case made by the DEA, Customs, and all the other federal agencies fighting the drug war. But it was woefully understaffed, with only seven full-time prosecutors assigned to major drug cases. Turnover was high, and sights were set low. Seizure cases came in piecemeal and were tried as such. Nobody followed the trails up the pyramid of the cocaine trade. Nobody had the time. Manpower was one problem, and adequate laws were another. The powerful Racketeer Influenced Corrupt Organizations (RICO) Act, which provided for the seizure of a criminal organization's assets and which had been used to great effect against the Mafia, was seldom invoked. Money laundering alone was not even a crime; agents had to find a drug connection or a currency transfer violation before they could move. Cooperation between agencies was often a joke; Customs and DEA had feuded openly for years. And rivalry within agencies was just as bad.

Nobody tried to put the big picture together. Agents were rewarded by the amount of drugs and money seized, which encouraged a "body count" mentality, an unsophisticated rush to see who could put the most "powder on the table" at the press conference. Agents were also rated on the significance of the traffickers they arrested, but here, too, the sights were low. The highest level of trafficker—"a class-one violator"—was someone capable of moving merely one hundred kilos a month. Nobody seemed to be targeting the people moving tons of the stuff. By the end of 1982, the DEA knew about the big Colombian cocaine organizations, but the significance of Jorge Ochoa and Pablo Escobar was known only to a few agents.

OPPOSING the government's lawyers was an armada of high-priced legal talent, including many former prosecutors gone off to quadruple their salaries as defense attorneys working for the men they once pursued. The "drug lawyers" packed gold Rolexes and roamed the federal courthouse like gunslingers in three-piece suits. They were expert at obtaining lenient sentences. "I don't think I have a single client who got a two-year sentence, or anything near that, for a [drug] conspiracy in the Southern District" of Florida, bragged "Diamond Joel" Hirschhorn, one of the best drug lawyers, in 1981. When the government wasn't losing in court, it found ways to botch things up in the field. The Suarez case was the crowning embarrassment. Roberto Suarez Levy, the twenty-three-year-old son of Bolivian coca king Roberto Suarez Gomez, was caught in a sting operation that yielded a U.S. record 854 pounds of cocaine base. The elder Suarez, then considered the largest known source of cocaine, offered to turn himself in and pay off the Bolivian national debt—estimated at just over $2 billion—if the U.S. government released his son. The offer was turned down. But young Suarez was freed anyway in 1982 because a Miami jury believed his word over that of four DEA agents.

Along with the additional drug agents, the South Florida Task Force promised more resources for the Miami U.S. Attorney's Office. Stanley Marcus, a Harvard Law School graduate who had led the Justice Department's Strike Force in Detroit, was putting together a new team of prosecutors. Marcus called on Dick Gregorie, a career strike force prosecutor like himself, to be his narcotics chief. Resources were always a problem, but Marcus added people rapidly, luring bright young legal talent from the private sector. A vigorous leader who projected a can-do image, Marcus would pump up a prosecutor by telling him he was working on "the most important case in the office." The joke quickly went around that there were twenty "most important" cases in the office.

Five days before the task force agents arrived in Miami, everyone got a glimpse of things to come during a routine cargo inspection by Customs agents at Miami International Airport.

Transportes Aereos Mercantiles Panamericanos—TAMPA, for short—was a two-jet Colombian air cargo company that had operated between Miami and South America since 1979. In the spring of 1982, an informant caught in a seventy-pound coke deal in Miami fingered TAMPA as a smuggling pipeline. The airline was already on notice for an earlier seizure of eight pounds. And about this time, the word came up through DEA channels in Colombia to expect a big load of cocaine in a shipment of blue jeans on a cargo flight from Medellín to Miami.

The three Customs inspectors had no idea what they would find when they showed up on March 9, 1982, to meet the 3:15 P.M. TAMPA flight from Medellín. Based at Miami International Airport, the inspectors were part of a Customs team that regularly checked incoming flights from South America. The team looked for cocaine in cargo and luggage. For cargo, the procedure was known as an "LQV" —landed quantity verification—which simply meant the inspectors verified that the cargo brought in was properly listed on the flight's manifest. The inspectors were always hearing that cocaine was coming up on TAMPA, but they heard that about every airline that flew between Colombia and Miami. There were more flights than they could possibly check.

When the inspectors arrived at TAMPA's warehouse at the airport, hundreds of cardboard cartons of "wearing apparel" were already stacked on pallets not fifty feet from the Boeing 707 that had carried the cargo up from Colombia. Seeing the inspectors, the dockworkers began to drift away from the pile of boxes. The inspectors saw that a number of the brown boxes were haphazardly labeled and unnumbered. Most of them were bound with thin yellow plastic banding, but several had white banding. The inspectors also noticed a sharp, medicinal scent in the air—ether. Inspector Tony Knapik pushed a short screwdriver into one of the cartons with the white banding. It was labeled "JEANS." When he pulled out the screwdriver, white powder poured from the box. Inspector Jerry Dranghon, who was standing nearby and saw Knapik's find, had a flash that a van would appear carrying machine-gun-wielding assassins.

Dranghon radioed his boss, Vann Capps, the chief of the Customs contraband search team.

"Hey, Chief, we got a bingo with TAMPA," Dranghon said. Capps, who was in his car patrolling the airport, immediately began calling for reinforcements to set up a perimeter around the TAMPA warehouse.

Meanwhile, Dranghon and the other inspectors noticed that the warehouse workers were taking off.

"They saw us hit it," Dranghon told Capps. The inspectors field-tested the cocaine and found it was pure. Then they began going through the boxes. "It looks like a good load," Dranghon radioed.

"I'm en route," Capps radioed back.

"It's a big load," Dranghon said. "You better bring a truck, it's so big."

Capps got to the TAMPA warehouse within five minutes. He was the fourth man on the scene. They were badly outnumbered to be sitting on such a big cocaine load. They went through the rest of the boxes; the ones with yellow banding held clothes; every one of the twenty-two boxes with white banding held nothing but cocaine. The symbolism of the white banding was brazenly obvious. The smugglers hadn't even tried to hide the cocaine inside the boxes. Five of them were solidly packed with white powder and weighed 195 pounds each. The seventeen others held the kilo-size "footballs" that were the standard of the Colombian cocaine trade. The kilos were wrapped in yellow plastic and covered with cryptic markings: RC, TOTO, M1, X100.

Soon the place was filled with Customs and DEA agents. The area was quickly cordoned off, and klieg lights were mounted, making the whole place look like a movie set. The agents began to interview the remaining TAMPA employees in the loading area.

Capps called Regional Commissioner Robert Battard, the top Customs official in Florida.

"Oh, shit, you're not going to believe this one," Capps said. "We had three inspectors doing an LQV on TAMPA, and they hit it—it was a cold hit. Mr. Battard, you're not going to believe it. It's nothing but cocaine. Nothing but boxes of cocaine."

At first Capps estimated five hundred pounds, which would have put the seizure among the largest ever found in airport cargo. But Capps quickly radioed back. "It looks like maybe one to two thousand.'' The last time he called, his estimate was three to four thousand pounds. Nobody believed him.

The TAMPA seizure finally added up to 3,906 pounds of pure cocaine. The load was worth more than $100 million, wholesale. Just short of two tons, it was more than four times larger than the previous U.S. record cocaine seizure.

It was even more remarkable for what it suggested about the Colombian cocaine trade. No one single trafficker could have amassed a two-ton load. The TAMPA seizure indicated cooperation among the Colombians on a scale far beyond what U.S. law enforcement thought possible. Every previous assumption about the traffickers was dwarfed by the TAMPA load. No one was arrested that day at the Miami airport, nor was anyone ever charged with bringing in the record load. The DEA determined the cocaine represented the collective efforts of fifteen separate trafficking organizations, including those of Jorge Ochoa and Pablo Escobar. The DEA was getting its first look at the shadow of the beast.

7.

JOHNNY PHELPS

Johnny Phelps arrived in Bogotá in mid-1981 to take over as DEA special agent-in-charge for all of Colombia. He had thirteen men working for him in Bogotá and in branch offices in Cali and Barranquilla on the northern Caribbean coast. He also had a newly opened but as yet unproven bureau in Medellín staffed by one man. Information was pouring in, choking Phelps's single storage vault. Paper threatened constantly to overwhelm him.

Phelps looked like Central Casting's idea of what a narcotics officer should be. He was six feet four inches tall, red-haired and apple-cheeked with a slow Texas drawl and an easy way about him. He was a Dallas Cowboys fan.

Phelps was thirty-seven years old when Washington sent him to Colombia. He had never had a foreign posting and had spent much of his career, first with the Immigration and Naturalization Service, then with the DEA, making heroin and marijuana cases on the Mexican border. He was a prodigy of sorts, moving rapidly upward in the DEA hierarchy without a whole lot of visible credentials. He looked good in a dark suit and the boots he loved to wear, spoke excellent Spanish, and gave a good talk for visiting congressmen and others he needed to impress.

But Phelps was no pretty boy. He had been born poor and grew up in west Texas, a holes-in-the-pants country kid who learned his Spanish from Mexican *bracero* farm workers.

Phelps got married right out of high school and went to work immediately as a lineman for the local power company. He endured it for three years, escaping when he saw a chance to get a job with the Border Patrol. From that moment law enforcement was his life.

In 1973 Phelps joined the DEA in San Diego and spent the next eight years on the Mexican border, making cases either as an undercover agent or in joint operations with Mexican police. He specialized in playing the dumb *gringo* buyer, slightly naive and baby-faced with an "aw, shucks" demeanor. It was an act, to be sure, because the real Phelps was a hardhead and a driver, street smart, stubborn, ambitious, and absolutely single-minded. He didn't party or make small talk, and he didn't joke around with the guys. He came on hard if he thought one of his agents was easing off.

He brought this style with him to Colombia, and at first the hard line didn't go down too well. Phelps didn't care: "You have to volunteer to come to Colombia," he explained. "Why volunteer if you're not prepared to work? When I see people who aren't doing the best they can, my tolerance level is very low."

PRACTICALLY from his first day, Phelps was certain that cocaine was "the coming thing," even though there was little evidence—at least on the surface—to support his theory. The TAMPA Airlines seizure, the event that would permanently alter U.S. law enforcement thinking, was almost a year away. Up to 1981 the biggest seizure in Colombia had been the six hundred kilos found in an airplane in Cali six years earlier. The biggest recent bust was a four-hundred-kilo seizure at a Bogotá lab.

Phelps was puzzled by this. He had helped seize large lots of Colombian cocaine coming across the Mexican border, and in his first few weeks in Colombia he had overflown the Guaviare region in the eastern *llanos* (plains) and spotted huge coca cultivations. Everybody knew that Colombian jungle coca made lousy cocaine, but if the traffickers were planting the bad stuff in such quantities, imagine how much high-potency Bolivian and Peruvian coca must be around.

Law enforcement had dropped the ball by focusing so heavily on marijuana, and Phelps figured politics, more than anything else, was the cause. Shiploads of marijuana were leaving north coast ports every day, and bales of it were washing up on the beaches of south Florida every week. Congress was leaning all over the brand-new Reagan administration to do something about it. Hardly anyone, as yet, was thinking about cocaine.

Except Phelps. Within five months he had instructed his field officers in Medellín, Cali, and Bogotá to devote themselves full-time to cocaine intelligence. He wanted to know everything about cocaine, who was selling it, how much they were moving, how much it cost, where it was going.

Phelps immediately discerned that the tools available to go after drug traffickers were severely limited. The government had given the Colombian army control over the Caribbean coast marijuana traffickers, but the army had botched the job. The minister of defense said he didn't want his soldiers working with drugs anymore and virtually admitted that the traffickers had corrupted them so badly that they were useless as a police force.

The government was creating a special Anti-Narcotics Unit within the National Police that would eventually take over marijuana, cocaine, and everything else. But until the unit was in place, the DEA's counterparts in Colombia would come from a grab bag of agencies: F-2 police intelligence, generally quite good, but overworked; DAS, uneven everywhere, hopeless in some places; the attorney general's police, horribly corrupt in Medellín and in some other substations but possessed of helicopters and other riches obtained in the late 1970s when they were the DEA's pet organization.

Spotty law enforcement was one thing, but what exasperated Phelps most of all was the laissez-faire attitude that many Colombian officials had toward trafficking. Colombians could tolerate a high degree of everyday lawlessness, and anyway, the argument went, marijuana and cocaine were harmless vices. It wasn't the same as, say, rifles, so what was wrong with a little smuggling?

BY the end of the year Phelps had his first list of "top ten" traffickers. From Medellín, there were Pablo Escobar, Jorge Ochoa, Jose Ocampo, and two remaining old-timers—Santiago Ocampo Zuluaga and Manuel Garces Gonzalez. Jose Ocampo was a former cabdriver and was known as Pelusa ("Curly") because of his spectacular pompadour. Ocampo Zuluaga, no relation to Jose, was in his fifties, a classic smuggler/trafficker and a semiretired rancher who served as an occasional counselor and elder statesman for the young Turks. Manuel Garces, about forty-five, had a lot of legitimate business interests —mostly in real estate—and was the only front-rank trafficker Phelps knew who dealt in marijuana as well as cocaine.

From Cali there were Gilberto Rodriguez Orejuela, "the Chess Player," and his sidekick, Jose Santacruz Londoño, "the Student" or Don Chepe, a pair of onetime kidnappers now using cocaine to turn themselves into a business conglomerate. Bogotá had Veronica Rivera, a former street vendor and fence who had killed half of a leading Bogotá crime family to gain control of its trafficking network. Bernardo Londoño was an elderly money launderer known as "the

Diplomat,'' and finally there was Gonzalo Rodriguez Gacha, ''the Mexican,'' the one who was so tight with Escobar and the Medellín crowd. Just after the ''top ten'' was Carlos Lehder, the Armenia loudmouth wanted by the U.S. attorney in Jacksonville.

THE traffickers were career criminals, tough, smart, and in many cases deadly. They had survived and thrived for years in one of the world's most dangerous businesses, and thus far they had managed it largely without disturbing the national consciousness.

This was because Colombia had made violence a national trademark long before drug trafficking came along. Phelps, like every other foreigner who worked in Colombia, began learning about Colombian violence from the moment he arrived in the country. In perpetrating kidnaps, street murders, and massacre, drug traffickers were simply following Colombian tradition.

In fact, the benchmark event in modern Colombian history was known simply as La Violencia, a back country bloodbath between rival militiamen belonging to the country's two traditional political parties, the Liberals and the Conservatives. La Violencia began in 1948 and lasted through most of the 1950s, killing an estimated three hundred thousand people before the army arranged a truce and prevailed upon the two political parties to share power in a ''National Front.''

The National Front stopped La Violencia and achieved a certain degree of social peace for most of two decades, and for that reason alone it could be accurately described as a brilliant idea. But government remained a cooperative affair, and by the time Phelps arrived in 1981, Colombia's ''democracy'' was widely criticized as a glorified old-boy network at the service of the country's Liberal and Conservative mandarins.

With no way to let off steam, political outsiders of the left and right resorted to violence. Colombia in 1981 played host to half a dozen guerrilla groups of various persuasions. The army spent most of its time and resources dueling them in vicious little pitched battles across the country. Right-wing ''death squads'' periodically entered the fray to ''restore order'' in particular cities or towns. Everybody involved was well schooled in the savage skills needed to keep the war going. In this context, the drug traffickers were simply one more violent outfit.

La Violencia had taught Colombia everything it needed to know about violence. The National Front provided a mechanism to manage the strife and contain it, protecting Colombians from themselves. But there were limits to what the Front's creaky institutions could tolerate. The Medellín cartel would cross these limits repeatedly.

Colombia in 1981 was a nation of twenty-six million people—third largest in South America after Brazil and Argentina. Besides its reputation for violence, the rest of Latin America knew Colombians for their beautiful spoken and written Spanish (Gabriel García Márquez, Latin America's best-known novelist, is from Cartagena). Bogotá, the capital and biggest city, was famous for cultural and intellectual erudition; Cali was known for beautiful women; Barranquilla for salsa music and tropical hustle; Cartagena for prizefighters. And then there was Medellín.

PHELPS'S resident agent in Medellín was thirty-two-year-old Errol Chavez. He had opened the office a couple of months before Phelps arrived in Bogotá, and his brief was to find out everything he could about cocaine. Like Phelps in Bogotá, he was immediately swamped. He had no secretary, no files, no typist. He worked up to fourteen hours a day, seven days a week, and couldn't ever seem to get ahead.

Everything was brand new. First, identifying the drug traffickers. Ochoa cropped up all the time. There were Jose Ocampo and Santiago Ocampo, or were they the same? There were Fabio Ochoa Restrepo and Fabio Restrepo Ochoa. And what about the Pablo Correas, Correa Arroyave, and Correa Ramos? Which was which?

Next, sources. He spent his mornings at the National Police headquarters. DAS and police F-2 intelligence were telling Chavez from the day he arrived that there were shipments of anywhere from two to five tons of cocaine moving regularly out of Medellín to the United States. Chavez tried but failed to get independent confirmation, so he didn't report it because he didn't believe it at first and because he didn't want to be laughed at. Someone in Washington will think I'm snorting some of that stuff, he thought.

Chavez divided the Medellín traffickers into two groups, "brokers" and "others." "Brokers"—maybe a dozen crime families led by Ochoa, Escobar, and a couple of others—were those traffickers capable of putting together a big load of cocaine, financing it, and arranging for transportation and insurance. The definition of "big load" in 1981 was "several hundred kilos."

"Others" were invited to piggyback on the brokers' loads, sending one or two kilos, or fifty or one hundred. The broker called a meeting at a Medellín restaurant or hotel and invited anyone who wished to contribute to a load. Brokers brokered for other brokers or for as many "others" as wanted to participate. Each trafficker, big or small, packed his cocaine in kilos and coded them with his personal combination of colors and symbols. These were the ciphers that U.S. Customs would later spot on the TAMPA Airlines cocaine. Some traffickers had more than one set of codes; some changed their code periodically. The main broker and his distributor in Miami, Los Angeles, New York, or elsewhere, had a list of codes so they could handle the accounting for the load.

Chavez stayed in Medellín for two years and developed six informants. Every one of them was murdered. Every time he found somebody, or every time somebody came into his office, he'd say the same things: "We appreciate that you're trying to help the DEA, but don't try to call us directly, don't try to work undercover, and don't try to negotiate any deals." They never listened.

Pablo Escobar's cousin, a down-and-outer who had lost all his money in Peru, approached the DEA and hired on. Chavez gave him some money, told him to be careful. He immediately tried to do a two-hundred-kilo deal with Escobar. He was found naked, hands bound behind his back, shot six times.

Jorge Ochoa's brother-in-law, a pilot, made the mistake of calling Chavez on the telephone and meeting in public with DEA agents. A brace of Ochoa's hired killers met him at the airport when he landed one day, but he managed to run to his Bronco and drive off, the gunmen in hot pursuit. He drove into a shallow riverbed, apparently hoping to shake the tail. Police found the abandoned Bronco that afternoon. They found Jorge Ochoa's brother-in-law a couple of days later, washed up in a culvert. Someone had gouged out his eyes.

Finally there was the time when Chavez's father, a law officer back in the United States, came down for a visit at Christmas. Both men were walking in Chavez's backyard one morning when they spotted something odd lying on the lawn.

"Is that what I think it is?" asked Chavez.

"It sure is," his father replied.

It was a human tongue. The previous week police had found one of Chavez's informants with hands tied behind his back, apparently hacked to death with a machete. Chavez didn't know whether or not this was the tongue from that corpse. He didn't want to know.

Chavez, his wife, Julia, and his three small children were protected twenty-four hours a day by six national policemen. Chavez rode to work in a police-escorted jeep with a machine gun tucked out of sight on the floorboards between his feet. He wore a 9-mm Smith & Wesson pistol on his waist and later added a .38-caliber revolver in an ankle holster. When he went to lunch, he took an escort; when he went out for a drink, he took the escort; when he saw an informant, he took the escort.

He and the public affairs officer who shared the U.S. consulate requested Medellín be made a hardship post so they could get some extra money. The city's homicide rate, they noted, was "64 per 100,000," more than twice that of any city in the United States and five times that of most.

Drug killings, their report said, "were entirely commonplace," and the public affairs officer had twice seen corpses in their bullet-riddled cars "only moments after a 'Mafia hit.' Mob killers use machine guns and often strike in public places, shooting all in sight to ensure the killing of a single victim."

Police told Chavez "everybody knows who you are," and he had no reason to doubt it. One trafficker bragged around town that he had Chavez's phone tapped. Chavez brought in technicians to sweep the building. They found multiple taps on his lines, inside his office, and outdoors. More than once he dialed Bogotá only to get an empty, moaning sound on the line that required him to yell to be heard. Sometimes the information he had was so important that he had to pass it anyway. One of the cables he dictated to Bogotá was found almost verbatim in the handbag of a trafficker's wife arrested in Miami.

Chavez's marriage was in trouble when he got to Medellín, and soon it collapsed altogether. He couldn't blame Julia; Medellín was hard on the nerves. But several things made it worth the trouble. Most important from Chavez's viewpoint, the work was fascinating and important. Practically every scrap of information he produced was new. The traffickers were everywhere, and Chavez saw them constantly. He saw them at restaurants, discos, hotels. He practically sat next to Jose Ocampo at the bullfights, bending over backward to try to take his picture. He saw the Ochoas at a horse show. He trailed after Escobar when he went into the slums to hand out twenty-dollar bills. Every day Chavez listened to traffickers talk over their phone patches to distributors in Miami, telling which color- and number-coded kilos of cocaine went to which client. Deals were going down constantly, and for the first time the DEA was in a position to get a steady supply of usable information from Medellín and act on it.

And with Johnny Phelps in Bogotá, Chavez had the confidence that every report he filed, every phone call he made, and every cable he sent were getting into the right hands. This was because under Phelps,

Bogotá, which for so many years had given almost all of its attention to north coast marijuana, had awakened to cocaine.

What Chavez didn't know until much later, however, was that Phelps lived in mortal fear of what could happen to his branch office field agents, especially Chavez. Phelps believed the Medellín police were either compromised or terrorized and not to be trusted. He wondered constantly whether he should scale back Medellín or shut it down altogether. Phelps tried to get to Medellín fairly often to check on Chavez and show the flag, but it was a delicate exercise. Phelps wanted to show his appreciation for Chavez's enthusiasm, but he didn't want to get him killed, either.

Phelps needed some way to send a signal to the traffickers that the DEA was serious about its business. The opportunity came in February 1982, when a north coast marijuana trafficker kidnapped two DEA agents and tried to kill them on the highway outside Cartagena.

Neither man was badly hurt, and Phelps stayed on the road for the next two months until he and Colombian police hunted down and arrested the trafficker. The incident made Phelps's reputation in Colombian law enforcement and gave him the unequivocal respect of his own agents. Johnny Phelps, one of his subordinates said later, "takes care of business."

Twice during the Cartagena investigation, Phelps contacted and met with one of Colombia's leading cocaine traffickers. He wanted his agents' kidnapper, he told the cocaine boss. The first time the trafficker stalled, but the second time he admitted he knew the kidnapper: "He's crazy, he's causing us a problem. He's bringing a lot of heat down on us."

The heat was Johnny Phelps. Soon Medellín police confirmed to Chavez that Phelps's visit had shaken up the traffickers. The big American with the Mexican accent was trouble, the traffickers felt, and they didn't want anything further to do with him. Phelps had made his point.

8.

THE CARTEL'S GOLDEN AGE

On April 18, 1981, just before Johnny Phelps arrived in Bogotá, Colombia's rising young cocaine lords gathered for a summit meeting at the Ochoa family ranch at Hacienda Veracruz on the Caribbean coast near Barranquilla. The theme was expansion. The Ochoas had so much cocaine backlogged that they needed more and better ways to move it to the United States.

The invited guests arrived by private plane at the ranch's five-thousand-foot paved landing strip—big enough to accommodate commercial jets. Jorge Ochoa also used the occasion to bring some of his stateside distributors to Colombia. Pablo Escobar didn't attend, but Pablo Correa Arroyave, one of Escobar's top lieutenants, represented Los Pablos. Correa Arroyave had the additional advantage of being Jorge Ochoa's brother-in-law.

Jorge and his younger brother, Fabio, met each plane in a white Chevrolet pickup truck. It was raining for much of the day, and Jorge insisted that his guests ride in the cab while he sat in the bed of the truck.

Hacienda Veracruz was big enough to encompass several small towns within its borders. It was entirely self-sustaining, producing everything from cheese to ice. The Ochoas had constructed a bullring and a private lake, and a man-made island in the middle of the lake was being prepared to accommodate several lions and tigers. The ranch already resembled a zoo: elephants, giraffes, and buffalo freely roamed the rolling pastures. Herds of cattle dotted the landscape.

The ranch house was low-slung but magnificent, a big, sprawling, country-style mansion with a red-tile roof. Armed guards hovered discreetly in the distance. Jorge Ochoa, unlike Carlos Lehder, did not flaunt his security.

Carlos Lehder was an honored guest at the summit. Although still well established on Norman's Cay, Lehder, like Ochoa and Escobar, knew that the tiny island could not handle the volume that the U.S. cocaine market now demanded. The traffickers needed more planes, more pilots, and more transportation routes. At Hacienda Veracruz the young traffickers strengthened the links first forged at Norman's Cay. The deepening alliance marked the beginnings of what would come to be known as the Medellín cartel.

AT the summit Ochoa outlined plans for expansion. The previous year his family had imported a U.S. engineer to establish a long-range navigational and communications system at Acandi on Colombia's northwestern edge a few miles from Panama. With this system the Ochoas could route and track all their flights into the United States. The family liked to have four or five groups of pilots operating at any one time, but each had its own distributors and its own routes. All were strictly compartmentalized. If the DEA penetrated one group, the others would remain intact.

Ochoa and Los Pablos were interested in sharing loads, dividing up the jobs and bringing a greater degree of control to the business. Escobar dominated cocaine production and enforcement. He ran labs, bought coca paste, paid necessary bribes, handled security, and, when expedient, killed whoever needed killing.

Lehder's Norman's Cay operation was still an extremely lucrative concern, but it was now one among several. What Lehder still had, however, were contacts with distributors and pilots all over the Caribbean and the United States. No one could match his address book, and his value as a counselor was immeasurable. In future Carlos Lehder would not lack for either power or prestige.

But Jorge Ochoa had now clearly assumed Lehder's old role as "king of cocaine transportation." The Acandi beacon, the runway at Hacienda Veracruz, and the network of pilots and planes that the clan had set up in the United States and Colombia were unique in the cocaine business.

The results were immediately apparent. In Miami during the months after the summit one of Ochoa's distributors alone coordinated cocaine flights totaling nineteen tons—easily dwarfing the 3.3 tons that Ed Ward had moved through Norman's Cay for Carlos Lehder the previous year. And that was only one network. At the same time, other Ochoa smugglers were moving 450-kilo loads into Louisiana, Alabama, Tennessee, and Georgia.

. . .

CARLOS Lehder's departure from the Bahamas and the emergence of Ochoa and Pablo Escobar signaled a fundamental restructuring of the cocaine industry, a reorientation away from Miami and the Bahamas and back to "corporate headquarters" in Colombia.

The process of transforming cocaine into a multinational enterprise took several years, but it was a time of spectacular growth for the Medellín cartel. Escobar and Ochoa brought greater cooperation to the industry. Cooperation was what produced multiton cocaine loads.

The realignment in Colombia, as in Miami, was a bloody, terrifying saga punctuated by kidnappings, torture, and murder. The eye of the storm was Medellín, and police could do nothing to stop the bloodshed. By 1982 the city belonged to the young cocaine traffickers. Police and politicians took bribes and kept their mouths shut. Otherwise they died. Cocaine traffickers did not go to trial.

The old-time smugglers had no place in the new scheme and for the most part gave ground gracefully. They had neither the imagination nor the will to compete with the up-and-comers, and most retired. Others evolved and adapted, content to take a subordinate position in the new order.

The few who wouldn't go along were forced out or killed. Griselda Blanco was an early casualty. She had worn out the goodwill of her peers by failing to pay for cocaine deliveries and creating ugly messes like the Dadeland shooting. She refused to change her style, and by the beginning of 1981 her star was fading rapidly and she had to leave Medellín. It was a new time now, a time for team players, not mavericks.

ESCOBAR and the rest of Los Pablos were progressing rapidly, buying businesses and property all around Medellín, elsewhere in Colombia and in Miami. In March 1980 Escobar bought a Miami Beach mansion for $762,500, making a down payment of more then $400,000. Almost exactly a year later he paid $8.03 million for the King's Harbour Apartments in Plantation, Florida, north of Miami.

Jorge Ochoa's father had left the restaurant business forever, selling Las Margaritas to an old family retainer so he could devote himself totally to breeding walking horses. Young Fabio was learning the cocaine business in Miami, and Jorge's older brother, Juan David, was useful if not particularly inspired.

As time passed, the Medellín underworld began to refer to Escobar respectfully as El Padrino, "the Godfather," and to Jorge Ochoa as El Gordo, "the Fat Man," but at first it was difficult to separate the two biggest bosses from the rest of the nouveau riche young traffickers swaggering around town. Pablo Escobar fancied race cars and sponsored a team in local rallies and formula competitions. Jorge Ochoa, old Fabio, and Juan David loved walking horses and kept large stables. Young Fabio had pretentions as a bullfighter. It was this that brought the lone cloud on the Ochoas' otherwise sunny horizon. On July 21, 1981, Jorge Ochoa was indicted by a Customs court in Cartagena for importing 128 Spanish fighting bulls to Hacienda Veracruz without proper licensing. The bulls were infected with hoof-and-mouth disease and had to be shot. Jorge Ochoa, meanwhile, had his first legal black mark in Colombia. It didn't seem like much to worry about—at least not at first.

THE big traffickers were just a few among Medellín's growing corps of conspicuous consumers. Cocaine was the vice of the eighties, money was pouring into the city, and there seemed to be a race on to see who could spend most lavishly. The golden age had arrived.

Office buildings, apartment houses, hotels, and discotheques sprouted up all over town and spilled into the beautiful hillside suburbs south of the city. The traffickers' chief watering holes were Las Margaritas, the Intercontinental Hotel, and Kevin's. All had spectacular mountainside views of Medellín and parking for as many Mercedes-Benzes and four-wheel-drive Broncos as cared to make the trip.

The Intercontinental, where George Jung had his final confrontation with Carlos Lehder, had Muzak, coffee shops, and ample meeting rooms where traffickers could gather for fun or business. Griselda Blanco and her second husband put on what many remembered as the most spectacular party ever seen there, renting out the grand ballroom and inviting all their *campesino* laboratory staff in for a huge celebration. Half the guests arrived wearing ponchos and sandals, smashed already from drinking shots of licorice-flavored *aguardiente* on the trip in from the countryside. After a couple of hours of Black Label Scotch and champagne, the merrymakers were retching on the ballroom floor, pissing in corners, and trying to chop each other up with machetes.

Kevin's was owned by former cabdriver and current cocaine boss Jose Ocampo, who also owned a huge *finca* outside the city, where he paid a famous international chef $12,000 a month to cook for huge house parties. The food was served outside on long tables and was replenished for as long as guests kept coming, sometimes for days. A kilo of pure cocaine was served as an appetizer. Ocampo's most talked about show occurred the day a drug pilot buzzed the crowd in one of his small planes, then flew straight up into the air until his engine stalled. He crashed and burned. It was sensational.

The traffickers outdid themselves in their rush to buy up or build the most spectacular houses in the city. One homeowner opened his door one morning to confront a twenty-five-year-old kid wearing a fortune in gold jewelry and inquiring politely about the possibility of buying his house. "Oh, I wouldn't take less than one million dollars U.S.," the man said offhandedly, not taking the boy seriously and not wanting to sell anyway. Suddenly he had a suitcase in his hand.

"Count it," the young man said.

The traffickers loved ornate, garish Louis XIV furniture, the more grotesque the better. Every mantelpiece had to have a painting of Jesus with a bleeding heart hanging above it. The idea, in this as in practically everything the traffickers tried to do with their money, was to buy respectability and status, to be accepted as *paisa* aristocracy.

AMONG those living it up in Colombia was Carlos Lehder. By 1980 he was twice divorced, unattached, and thirty-one years old; his millions were intact and burning a hole in his pocket. He decided to invest them in his hometown of Armenia, where he had not lived for fifteen years.

Armenia, some 180 miles south of Medellín, had about 180,000 people. It was the capital of Quindio province in the heart of Colombian coffee country. It was a homespun city, not particularly attractive. It looked like a backwater, and it was.

But what Armenia lacked in sophistication, it more than made up in prosperity. The farmers of Quindio were rich and comfortable, but they kept their money and their pride on their *fincas*. Most of them spent as little time in town as possible. Armenia was where they bought tractors.

In November 1978, the Quindio governor received a letter from one Carlos E. Lehder Rivas, who identified himself as "president" of Air Montes Company Ltd. of Nassau, the Bahamas. Air Montes, said the letter, "is a business dedicated to the international buying and selling of airplanes." Each year, "per our bylaws," the company donated airplanes "to deserving communities who lack air transport of their own.'' Air Montes, the letter continued, had chosen the province of Quindio as the 1978 beneficiary of this largesse. A Piper Navajo 1968, serial number 31-196, was arriving forthwith.

After checking around, the leading citizens of Quindio determined that Carlos E. Lehder Rivas had to be a son of Wilhelm Lehder, the German immigrant engineer they called ''Guillermo'' or ''Bily.'' Guillermo lived quietly in a modest second-floor walk-up apartment in a stucco building in downtown Armenia.

No one could remember seeing anything of Carlos himself since his student days at Carlo Magno High School fifteen years earlier. Townspeople recalled a high-spirited, generous boy who often shared his lunch with his fellow students. He did not take discipline well, however, and once hurled an inkwell at the blackboard, prompting his teacher to expel him. He was smart, aggressive, and resourceful, with a massive ego and a large helping of *paisa* adventurism. His dream, his father would say later, was to go to Hollywood and become a movie star.

The Piper Navajo was flown to Armenia during the Christmas holidays by a tall, blond gringo in his mid-twenties who did not speak a word of Spanish. The pilot waved at the reception committee, handed the technical manuals to the nearest Quindio official, smiled at everyone, and left in a chauffeur-driven car, never to be seen again.

The state of Quindio then began a long and ultimately fruitless effort to resolve the ''airplane affair.'' The Navajo had arrived without documents, and throughout its first year in Armenia officials had to fend off U.S. firms who claimed the plane had been stolen. Quindio finally obtained unrestricted title to the plane but then had to figure out how to use it. Quindio was a tiny province, and Armenia was its only airport. Where was the governor supposed to fly the plane? The plane sat on the tarmac at Armenia's El Eden airport and gathered dust.

LEHDER himself began making forays to Armenia in 1979, breezing in periodically with a batch of glittery friends to raise a little hell, spend some money, open some businesses, make some pronouncements, and generally portray himself as an international mover-and-shaker newly arrived to share with his countrymen the fruits of his business genius.

By 1981 Lehder was spending as much time in Armenia as he was in the Bahamas. With his fast cars, gold jewelry, and fancy friends he was already the most fascinating man Armenia had seen recently, and he had all that money. Lehder was a rich, handsome world traveler.

He spoke excellent English and German and managed easily in Portuguese and Italian. He explained nothing and with effortless aplomb transformed himself into "German-Colombian industrialist Carlos Lehder" virtually overnight.

He bought huge tracts of farmland north of the city and announced he was going to build a gigantic tourist complex with a Bavarian motif. He commissioned Rodrigo Arenas Betancur, Colombia's finest sculptor, to craft him a seven-foot bronze of the Beatles' John Lennon to serve as the project's centerpiece. He tramped his holdings in a hard hat and boots and said important things about Quindio economic development.

In town he bought townhouses, office buildings, and condominiums, prompting local businessmen to engage in a surge of real estate speculation, driving prices to double and triple what they had been.

Headquarters for the Lehder empire was Cebu Quindio, S.A., his all-purpose holding company on the Avenida Bolivar in front of the Parque de los Fundadores. The building had a huge parking lot, which was soon filled with exotic vehicles: armored four-wheel-drive wagons, Mercedes-Benz sedans, Porsche sports cars, and stretch limos of various types. The cars came and went at all hours, seven days a week, sometimes alone, sometimes in convoy, zooming up and down Armenia's normally empty streets.

People wanted to know where Lehder got his money. One boyhood friend asked him the question in 1981:

"I worked in restaurants in New York," Lehder said. "Then I sold cars; and later I sold airplanes in the United States." In the next three years Lehder would be asked the same question many times and would answer it in many ways. Sometimes he would almost tell the truth.

Lehder's presence in Armenia had a profound effect on the city's teenagers. Boys imitated his center-parted, tousled haircut and called him Don Carlos in the street. Teenagers hung out at Cebu Quindio waiting to carry a message, wax a Mercedes, or go out for coffee.

And women thought he had fallen from heaven. Lehder was charming, polite, and always elegantly turned out. Mothers loved him almost as much as daughters. He organized fantastic parties, knew fascinating people, and told wonderful stories about faraway places. A little later, when some of the daughters started having drug problems, mothers would change their thinking. Still later, when four or five of the daughters showed up pregnant with Lehder's children, mothers would warn their daughters away from Lehder.

But in the early days it was all a lark. Lehder had realized the *paisa* dream. He had gone away at a young age, made his fortune, and returned in triumph.

IT was only a question of time before it occurred to someone that there was big money to be made by kidnapping Lehder. Colombia— even sleepy, conservative Armenia—was not the same as the Bahamas or the United States. In Colombia kidnapping was an art. It paid and paid handsomely for those with the necessary skill and audacity.

In November 1981 Lehder left Cebu Quindio in midafternoon in a chauffeur-driven car en route to his favorite *finca,* Hacienda Pisamal, about twenty minutes south of Armenia.

He ordinarily carried a handgun and usually traveled with either an escort car or a pair of *pistoleros.* Still, he had no regular bodyguards, and for some reason on that day traveled without a personal weapon and with only his driver to accompany him.

The car drove south through the city and took the highway toward Cali. About eight miles out of town, near the airport, an automobile was stopped in the middle of the road with its hood up and its driver bent over, peering inside. Lehder ordered his chauffeur to pull over, and both men got out of the car. The chauffeur left his pistol on the front seat.

Suddenly two men appeared brandishing pistols. They gagged Lehder's chauffeur and left him by the roadside. They bound Lehder's hands behind his back and tossed him on the floor of their car in the backseat. Then the hood came down, the ignition turned, and the car sped away with its hostage.

As Lehder told the story to his friends, muscular coordination saved him: "Since I studied karate, I knew several things I could do to free myself." He squirmed out of his bonds, opened the car door, and flung himself onto the highway verge, rolling down a grassy slope into a recreational park.

Then he was up and running, his erstwhile captors spraying bullets in his path. One slug hit Lehder high in the back, knocking him down, but he scrambled to his feet and took off again. His pursuers kept up the chase for a while but soon broke off.

The would-be kidnap caused a sensation in Armenia. Radio commentators interrupted regular programming to talk about the attack against the "German-Colombian investor." Police mobilized for a massive manhunt. Reporters hung around Quindio Central Clinic in downtown Armenia, waiting for news.

Lehder spent about two weeks in the hospital, attended by the best doctors in Armenia, wished well by legions of fans. His entourage hung around the clinic waiting for the latest bulletin on his condition. It was all gratifying to Lehder the "industrialist," but Lehder the drug trafficker had learned a lesson. He would never again be without an armed escort, and he would do his best to take revenge. At the same time that he played the innocent in the Central Clinic, his own *pisto-leros* were out looking for answers.

Soon they had them. The kidnap was the work of the April 19 Movement, or M-19, an urban guerrilla group of about 2,500 cadre whose stock-in-trade was the spectacular guerrilla stunt. M-19 had started out as an ultranationalist, right-wing radical movement but in recent years had drifted into nebulous leftism. It had no coherent program and was known to do occasional contract work for drug traffickers or anyone else who could pay well for organized mayhem. Kidnapping was an M-19 specialty, but so was the double cross, as Lehder now had good reason to know. A year earlier he had bragged to George Jung about his revolutionary alliance with M-19. Now the group had kidnapped him.

Still, there was no real contradiction. M-19 had no enduring loyalty to Colombia's drug lords. Working for them paid well, but working against them could pay better. Kidnapping them would seem to pay best of all. The drug lords had as much money as anyone in Colombia, and there was nobody in the country less likely to call the police. The traffickers were easy prey.

Or at least they seemed to be.

Medellín auto dealer Carlos Lehder, circa 1976. Looking to set up a successful cocaine smuggling operation, he returned home after two years in federal prison at Danbury, Connecticut. (CHARLIE CECIL)

Miguel ''Paco'' Sepulveda. Medellín hitman and Griselda Blanco's chief enforcer. Working out of New York and Miami, he is believed responsible for several of the Cocaine Cowboy murders in the 1970s and early 1980s. (DEA)

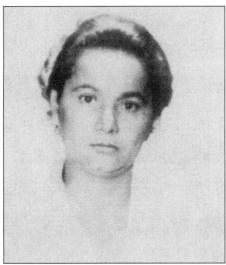

Griselda Blanco, ''La Gaga,'' or ''the Godmother.'' First indicted in New York in 1974, she was a prime mover in Miami's Cocaine Cowboy wars in the late 1970s and early 1980s. (DEA)

Conrado Valencia, "El Loco." Legendary machine-gun–wielding hitman arrested in Miami after the infamous turnpike shooting in 1979. (DEA)

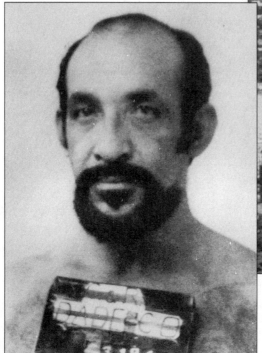

Three photos of the white "war wagon" delivery truck used by the killers at the Dadeland shooting. Sides of the truck show the name written in two different ways. The back of the truck shows bulletproof vests hanging from the ceiling and quarter-inch steel plates lining the inside. (METRO-DADE POLICE DEPARTMENT)

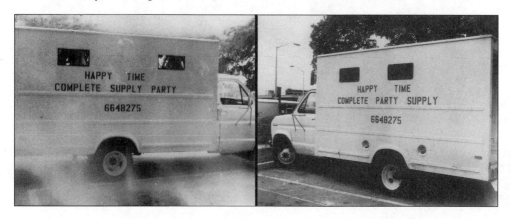

Right: Old Medellín. In 1954 Medellín was a picturesque provincial city with streetcars, palm trees, and lots of open space. *(THE MIAMI HERALD)* *Above:* Modern Medellín. By the mid-1980s Medellín was a city of glass-and-steel skyscrapers. It is Colombia's industrial hub and the center of the Colombian cocaine industry.

Mayo-Junio 1976

El DAS de Antioquia descub
kilos de cocaína entre una ll

Con medio millón pretendieron sobornar a los d

Pablo Emilio Escobar Gaviria

Marco Alonso Hurtado

Hernando de Jesús García

Gustavo de Jesús Gaviria

In 1976 the Colombian Department of Administrative Security in its internal newspaper described the biggest cocaine bust in Medellín for that year. DAS arrested six young Antioqueños in the case, including Pablo Escobar Gaviria (top left) and his cousin Gustavo Gaviria Rivero (center right). *(EL ESPECTA-DOR)*

Carlos Lehder sampling the product, Norman's Cay, 1978. Lehder's onetime prison buddy Stephen Yakovac holds the spoon. (U.S. FEDERAL COURT)

Norman's Cay, around 1981. In the late 1970s Carlos Lehder bought this fishhook-shaped coral island in the Bahamas off the coast of Florida and converted it into a way station for the international cocaine trade. In the foreground is Lehder's airstrip.

In 1980 Pablo Escobar bought this luxury Miami Beach home for $762,000. Escobar made a $420,000 down payment and paid off the $342,000 mortgage in sixty-seven days. *(THE MIAMI HERALD)*

Jorge Luis Ochoa Vasquez,
''El Gordo.''
(COURT PHOTO)

Pablo Escobar Gaviria,
''Godfather.''
(DAS)

Carlos Lehder Rivas,
"Joe Lehder."
(THE MIAMI HERALD)

Jose Gonzalo Rodriguez
Gacha, "the Mexican." (DAS)

Pablo Escobar was thirty-one years old when he bought the King's Harbour Apartments in Plantation, Florida, in 1981 for $8,034,000. (DEA)

Sign in Medellín advertises the first installment of low-income housing built by Pablo Escobar for his development, Barrio Pablo Escobar. The inscription reads: Medellín Without Slums. Under construction in this sector, 1000 homes to be donated without any cost whatsoever to the families who live in the municipal dump. (JEAN-BERNARD DIEDERICH/ CONTACT)

U.S. Customs agents Jerry Dranghon (left), Tony Knapik (center), and Al Tagliaferro (right) examine some of the 1,775 kilos (3,906 pounds) of cocaine seized at Miami International Airport aboard a TAMPA Airlines plane March 9, 1982. The record seizure was an early indication to U.S. law enforcement that the Medellín cartel operated on a scale way beyond anything imagined up to that time. (MARICE COHN/ *THE MIAMI HERALD*)

Johnny Phelps arrived in Bogotá in early 1981 to take over as the Drug Enforcement Administration's Special Agent-in-Charge for Colombia. He would play a key role in some of the biggest and most successful drug busts in the history of U.S. law enforcement, yet when he left in 1984, the Medellín cartel was stronger than ever.

The Ochoa clan: Fabio Ochoa Restrepo, "Don Fabio," the patriarch, aboard his prize walking horse Rescate (Ransom), circa 1982. Reporters speculated that Ransom might have been bought with the money Ochoa did not pay to rescue Marta Nieves, his kidnapped daughter. *(EL TIEMPO)*

Left: Juan David Ochoa Vasquez, oldest of the three Ochoa brothers. (DAS) *Middle:* Fabio Ochoa Vasquez, "Fabito," youngest of the three Ochoa brothers. (DAS) *Right:* Rafael Cardona Salazar, "Rafa," chief cocaine distributor for the Ochoa family in the late 1970s and early 1980s. He murdered a man in front of Max Mermelstein in late 1978, binding Mermelstein to the traffickers. (DEA)

Gateway to Hacienda Napoles, Pablo Escobar's zoo and *finca* on the Magdalena River. The airplane mounted above the gate reputedly flew Escobar's first load of cocaine.

"Paisa Robin Hood." Pablo Escobar kicks off to commemorate the installation of lights for nighttime soccer at a stadium in one of Medellín's northern slum neighborhoods. *(EL TIEMPO)*

Camel in the road at Hacienda Napoles, Pablo Escobar's zoo in the Magdalena River valley. In 1983 the zoo, with animals roaming freely about the grounds, was the most popular in Colombia.

Panamanian Military Commander General Manuel Antonio Noriega met most of the members of the Medellín cartel in 1982 and, according to court records, carried on a profitable association with them for the following three years. (AL DIAZ, *THE MIAMI HERALD*)

9.

MAS

The small airplane described lazy circles in the Sunday afternoon sky above Cali, waiting for the soccer match to get under way far below. It was a big game, between America, the local favorite, and Nacional, the hated rivals from Medellín. As the whistle blew to open the first half, the plane's crewman opened a stern hatch, slid a bale of leaflets to the doorway, snipped the string binding, and pushed them out. Soon a cloud of paper was fluttering toward the midfield stripe.

The leaflet, dated December 3, 1981, was a manifesto. In stark, chilling language it spoke of a recent "general assembly" in which 223 top-level Colombian "businessmen" decided they would no longer tolerate ransom kidnappings by guerrilla groups seeking to finance their revolutions "through the sacrifices of people, who, like ourselves, have brought progress and employment to the country." The "businessmen," it transpired, were Colombia's 223 top drug traffickers. No one who attended the assembly made a secret of having been there.

Each of the conferees, the manifesto said, agreed to contribute two million pesos ($33,000) to a common defense fund and ten men to a common vigilante force. The new organization would be known as Muerte a Secuestradores—"Death to Kidnappers," and that was exactly what it had in mind:

"The basic objective will be the public and immediate execution of all those involved in kidnappings beginning from the date of this communiqué."

The manifesto offered twenty million pesos ($330,000) reward for information leading to the capture of a kidnapper and guaranteed immediate retribution. The guilty "will be hung from the trees in public parks or shot and marked with the sign of our group—MAS." Jailed kidnappers would be murdered, and, if this proved impossible, "our retribution will fall on their comrades in jail and on their closest family members."

The formation of MAS marked the beginning of a new era in the history of Colombia's cocaine lords. Before MAS the bosses cooperated with each other in business; they had partied together; they had even taken the first steps toward building a common cocaine trafficking policy. But until MAS, they had never taken a joint public position on any matter in which they had an interest. MAS marked the consolidation of the Medellín cartel.

Kidnappings among traffickers themselves were commonplace. If a cocaine boss couldn't collect from a colleague, he would kidnap his colleague's daughter and use her for leverage. Traffickers also had been known to provide another trafficker with a wife or a son as a security deposit during a complicated business deal. But recently it had escalated, the M-19's attempted kidnapping of Carlos Lehder being the most notorious instance.

The Lehder kidnapping was not, however, what brought MAS into existence. The pivotal event was the M-19's November 12, 1981, abduction from the University of Antioquia of Marta Nieves Ochoa, youngest sister of Jorge Ochoa. The guerrillas demanded anywhere from $12 to $15 million—accounts differed—probably to make a big weapons purchase. The Ochoas did not intend to pay.

The traffickers' "general assembly" took place in late November. Jorge Ochoa called the meeting and set it for Medellín at Las Margaritas, although some accounts name the Intercontinental Hotel as the site, while still others say it occurred in Cali. Accounts also differ regarding the number of traffickers in attendance. Some suggest there were only 20 bosses—the top names in cocaine—but most agree that the 223 described in the Cali manifesto showed up. These included cocaine traffickers from all over the country, the north coast marijuana smugglers, and the airplane pilots that served both groups.

Lehder, still convalescing from his gunshot wound, played a major role in the assembly, but Ochoa—seconded by Pablo Escobar—ran the meeting. The traffickers drafted the communiqué, agreeing to distribute it in Cali, Colombia's third-largest city, rather than Medellín, in part to give MAS a more national flavor. Also, however, the idea was to catch partisans from two important cities in the same place at the same time. The America soccer club, Cali's pride, was owned by the Gilberto Rodriguez Orejuela crime family, while Nacional of Medellín belonged to money launderer Hernan Botero.

The traffickers elected Santiago Ocampo, Manuel Garces, and Jorge Ochoa as president, vice president, and treasurer of MAS. The first two were well respected and middle-aged, big names from the past. Ochoa was the future.

After the communiqué was written and the meeting broke up, Escobar lieutenant Pablo Correa Arroyave invited everybody to a big picnic at his *finca* outside Medellín. The bosses ate, drank, and chatted, finding they had quite a bit in common.

But before the new feeling of fellowship could take hold, there was the matter of Marta Nieves to resolve. On the night of December 30, 1981, a badly frightened woman named Marta Correa de Bernal was found chained to the barred steel gate of *El Colombiano* newspaper in downtown Medellín. A placard hanging around her neck identified her as the wife of the M-19 chieftain who kidnapped Marta Nieves Ochoa. Bernal's daughter had also been kidnapped but was left with relatives, a MAS communiqué said, because MAS could not "do harm to innocent children."

By mid-January the list of deeds attributed to MAS had reached mythic proportions. The gang was supposedly cutting through M-19 like a hot wind, reputedly killing or turning in more than one hundred guerrilla militants in the six weeks since MAS's formation. Squads of gunmen were reported quartering the countryside, pounding on doors, asking questions, and drubbing to death or shooting anyone they thought could conceivably have had anything to do with the Marta Nieves kidnapping.

It was impossible to determine how much of this was true, but MAS's verifiable acts were impressive. In January MAS captured the Antioquia province chief of M-19, stripped him, tied him up, dumped him in a vacant lot in northern Bogotá, and called the police. In early February MAS smuggled a loaded pistol into a jail outside Medellín, where a convict used it to murder two street punks imprisoned as kidnappers.

It also became clear that a lot of free-lancers were using MAS's smoke screen to settle scores of their own. In January five goons carrying machine guns walked into a real estate office in Medellín's fashionable El Poblado section and opened fire, murdering all six people inside. They were looking for the owner of the office, a second-echelon cocaine trafficker named Joaquín Builes Gomez. Builes was out.

And on January 26 Medellín union leaders denounced MAS to the Attorney General's Office, charging the gang was nothing more than a bunch of management stooges sent out to intimidate labor. Thugs identifying themselves as MAS members had murdered three union bosses in the previous week.

In all, police counted thirty homicides in Medellín in the first two weeks of 1982. On February 6 MAS issued a new communiqué demanding Marta Nieves: "Our patience is wearing thin."

Marta Nieves was released unharmed on February 17, 1982. The next day MAS freed five of its own hostages, all M-19 cadre. Rumor had it that the Ochoas in the end never paid a centavo, that through the force of the MAS example they had demonstrated to M-19 the folly of what they had done. Better to give back the girl and forget it happened. Later in 1982 fat Fabio Ochoa, the family patriarch, appeared in local horse shows riding Rescate ("Ransom"). Was the horse bought with the money Fabio didn't have to spend on his daughter?

In fact, the Ochoas did negotiate with M-19, and they did pay a ransom. One police report said M-19 settled for $535,000. Other sources said the payment was much higher and may have been made with a combination of money and guns. The talks took place in Panama over several weeks, most likely under the auspices of the Panamanian armed forces and with the participation of at least one Panamanian government go-between. The behind-the-scenes supervisor of the negotiations was Panama's chief of miltary intelligence, Colonel Manuel Antonio Noriega.

Sources familiar with the negotiations cited the Marta Nieves affair as Noriega's first opportunity to meet the young Colombian traffickers, and it was the beginning of what became an extremely profitable association. Court papers filed much later in Miami said Noriega in 1982 closed a deal with Escobar and his cousin Gustavo Gaviria allowing the traffickers to transship cocaine through Panama for a fee of $100,000 per load. Escobar's people trained Noriega's pilot to fly Escobar's personal Piper Cheyenne, loaded with cocaine, back and forth between Escobar's ranch and Panama. By the end of 1982, the documents said, Escobar had moved four hundred kilos of cocaine to Panama, and Noriega had upped the price to $150,000 for the next load. Both sides seemed satisfied, and it soon became obvious that the traffickers had picked the right ally. In 1983 Noriega became chief of the Panamanian armed forces and the most powerful man in Panama.

THE MAS affair gave a tremendous boost to the mystique of Medellín's drug lords. Regardless of what had really happened, Colombians began to see them as omnipotent. They had captured M-19's top man in Antioquia, something the Colombian army had tried and failed to do for years. They had wanted M-19 to give up Marta Nieves Ochoa, and M-19 had complied. They had brought Medellín another blood-bath, and authorities had shown themselves totally unable to cope. When the shooting started at night, the police sat in their cars and waited. When the shooting stopped, the cops picked up the corpses.

And regardless of the size of the ransom, it quickly became clear after Marta Nieves's release that M-19 had no further interest in kid-napping drug traffickers' family members. In coming years M-19 and the traffickers would cooperate much more often than they would clash. The Medellín cartel had won its first war. There would be others.

Finally, the Marta Nieves kidnapping had demonstrated once and for all that Medellín sat at the center of the Colombian cocaine indus-try. When the Medellín traffickers called a meeting, every dope dealer in the country showed up. And when law enforcement wanted to spot new trends in cocaine, Medellín was the place to look. The Medellín cartel was open for business.

FOR the DEA's Errol Chavez, 1982 was a pivotal year. After the TAMPA Airlines seizure, his bosses in Washington finally began to think of cocaine traveling by the ton instead of by the hundredweight. But the high volume meant the DEA had to revise its thinking about the criminals it was chasing. Every day the cocaine traffickers were behaving more like the international entrepreneurs they had become and less like the seat-of-the-pants adventurers they had once been. Cocaine had become big business.

As before, smaller traffickers were piggybacking their cocaine on Escobar's and Ochoa's loads, but, unlike before, the big guys were reported ''unhappy'' if smaller traffickers tried to work indepen-dently. Ochoa and Escobar would ship as small a quantity of cocaine as anyone wanted to send; they would even front cocaine for a little trafficker on the understanding that they would be paid later. They insured all the cocaine in their loads, never shipping unless they had an identical amount of backup warehoused and ready to go in the event of a seizure. This service was sometimes described by U.S. drug agents as ''Lloyd's of Medellín.'' The traffickers made the co-caine trade almost risk free for the small investor—an easy way for a person to earn the cost of a new car, a new house, a new mistress.

But the word was that if you bucked the system, ''you suffered.''

Errol Chavez understood that Escobar, the Ochoas, and a handful of other big traffickers were trying to control the market among both sellers and buyers—create a true cartel. They wanted to sell only as much cocaine as would keep the price high, and their profit margin was enormous. In February 1983 Chavez reported that cocaine cost $8,000 to $9,000 per kilo wholesale in Medellín—at a time when it sold for $42,000 per kilo in Miami.

"There is increasing evidence that numerous cocaine trafficking groups are pooling their resources to a greater extent to market their cocaine in the United States," Chavez reported to the Bogotá DEA office. "These groups are using sophisticated techniques to market multihundred and even multithousand kilo loads."

In 1982 the cartel was also doing research on a new product, the results of which were encouraging. By midyear 1983 Chavez reported that 80 percent of Medellín's drug users had switched from cocaine to a crudely refined and highly addictive form of smokeable coca paste called *bazuko,* driving the per-kilo price of *bazuko* up to the point where it was more expensive than cocaine. At approximately the same time—April 1983—cocaine prices were diving below $5,000 per kilo, an indication that production had taken a quantum leap. By dropping the price, the traffickers had opened a vast new market: cocaine for the masses, a new idea from the Medellín cartel. In the United States, mass cocaine use was preceded by the introduction of "crack," a smokeable form of cocaine base (a purer, more refined, and even more addictive product than *bazuko*). Crack was a child of the great cocaine glut produced by the Medellín cartel in the early 1980s. On the streets of Miami, in the summer of 1983, cocaine was more plentiful, purer, and cheaper—$14,000 per kilo—than ever before.

In Colombia, authorities either weren't catching on to what was happening or simply didn't care. After the Marta Nieves affair, Carlos Lehder went home to Armenia and talked pridefully about how he was a member of MAS and how he and the other "kidnappables" had played a vital role in MAS's formation. Later in the year he boasted that he had contributed generously to the Liberal Party and its presidential candidate, Alfonso Lopez Michelsen. With this indiscretion Lehder did himself and his cartel colleagues the disservice of linking them publicly to both vigilante murder (MAS) and the Colombian political establishment. All the traffickers tried to buy influence, but only Lehder bragged about it.

· · ·

PABLO Escobar was known not to be particularly fond of Lehder, because of Lehder's increasingly obvious cocaine habit and his tendency to say stupid things. Escobar was said to refer to Lehder as *bocón*—"big mouth"—in private conversation. But Lehder's 1982 indiscretions were nothing compared with Escobar's. The quiet, humble-appearing *paisa* was no more. In 1982 Escobar won election to the Colombian Congress as an alternate representative from Envigado. When Jairo Ortega, his partner on the ticket, was sick, absent, or otherwise indisposed, Escobar substituted for him. The richest drug trafficker in Colombia was now a congressman.

Escobar and Ortega were allied with Senator Alberto Santofimio Botero, a Liberal Party boss with enormous power and influence. Santofimio sat on the Liberals' board of directors and at one point harbored presidential ambitions. His association with drug traffickers eventually torpedoed this ambition, but otherwise he suffered not at all. Santofimio was the cartel's favorite politician; he came to symbolize the traffickers' corruption of the Colombian political system.

Escobar served Santofimio well. Even before his election Escobar had been a presence in the slum neighborhoods of northern Medellín. Now he was Don Pablo, a soft-spoken, dumpy man with chino pants, polo shirts, downcast eyes, and a gold, diamond-encrusted Rolex watch. Escobar installed lights at soccer fields, built roller-skating rinks, spoke at public events, and handed out money.

Soon he had a radio show, *Civics on the March,* and a social action program called "Medellín Without Slums." He announced that he would build a one-thousand-unit low-income housing project on a piece of north Medellín landfill, to be called, appropriately, Barrio Pablo Escobar.

A corps of publicists and paid journalists handled his public image. For about two years these sycophants had fairly good luck portraying Escobar as a humble, dirty-fingernailed man of the people bent on giving something back to the poor but proud neighborhoods from whence he came. Escobar's newspaper, *Medellín Cívico,* promoted the cause in a cloud of purple prose. Said one *Cívico* columnist: "Yes, I remember him . . . his hands, almost priestlike, drawing parabolas of friendship and generosity in the air. Yes, I know him, his eyes weeping because there is not enough bread for all of the nation's dinner tables. I have watched his tortured feelings when he sees street children—angels without toys, without a present, without a future."

The campaign's culmination came in April 1983 when *Semana,* Colombia's leading news magazine, profiled Escobar as "A *Paisa* Robin Hood." The article slid by the problem of Escobar's occupation, remarking only that the sources of his wealth "never cease to be the object of speculation." In this particular instance, limited speculation, since the word "cocaine" did not appear in the text.

Semana later won a reputation for hard-hitting investigations of the cartel, but in 1982–83 it clearly hadn't caught on yet. It let the *paisa* Robin Hood do the talking: "When I was 16 I owned a bicycle rental business . . . then I started buying and selling automobiles, and finally I got involved in real estate."

His interest in civic good works, Escobar told *Semana,* dated from his high school student days: "I didn't have any money but as a community action member in my *barrio,* I promoted the construction of a school and the creation of a fund for indigent students."

Escobar fooled a lot of people, but the police knew that whatever else he was trying to become, he remained at heart the same cold killer who used to ride shotgun on five-kilo loads. Escobar's popularity in north Medellín was also predictable. North Medellín was as tough an area as existed in the Western Hemisphere, the place where Colombia's vaunted school for pickpockets was rumored to be, the place where the cartel was said to train its motorcycle murderers.

And, apart from rumors, north Medellín was, without doubt, home for an unknown number of murder gangs. Escobar had stopped doing his own hits long ago, but he always had plenty of dirty work available, and north Medellín was the place to hire it out. More than anybody in the Medellín cartel, Escobar was known as an enforcer. He never forgot an insult; he held grudges; he took revenge.

10.

THE COLONEL AND THE AMBASSADOR

Belisario Betancur won election to the presidency of Colombia in March 1982 and took office in August—the same time Pablo Escobar became a congressman. Betancur was a pillar of the Conservative Party and a would-be reformer whose first priority was to seek peace with Colombia's myriad guerrilla groups, an objective that had eluded his predecessors for nearly twenty years. Second, he wanted to launch an ambitious program of economic and social reforms, particularly in housing and education.

Drug trafficking hardly made Betancur's list. It was a back-burner item, of concern largely because it bothered the gringos so much. Betancur was against drug trafficking when he thought about it, but he didn't think about it very often.

For the Medellín cartel, Betancur's election was good news, at least at first. The new president had pronounced himself "philosophically opposed" to the extradition of Colombian nationals to the United States. Carlos Lehder, who a few months before Betancur's inauguration had been an enthusiastic supporter of Betancur's Liberal presidential opponent, Alfonso Lopez Michelsen, suddenly proclaimed himself "fanatically *Belisarista*." As well he should have been. Lehder led the United States' list of extraditable drug fugitives.

By 1982 extradition had quietly become the drug traffickers' central concern—and the only thing they feared. The United States and Colombia had signed a bilateral extradition treaty in 1979. By mid-1981 both nations had ratified it. These procedures caused little comment at the time; extradition was a mundane matter, not front-page news.

Things began to change with Ronald Reagan's arrival in the White House in 1981 and Johnny Phelps's arrival in Bogotá the same year. Reagan made drugs a top priority in the United States' bilateral relations with Colombia, and Phelps became the treaty's first prophet. In conversations with visiting congressmen and U.S. prosecutors, he tried to spark interest in "a new tool that can be useful."

And by 1982 the cocaine bosses had had enough time to figure out that the document seemed to have been drafted with them in mind. The crucial language was hidden away in article 8, paragraph one: extradition of nationals of one country to the other country "will be granted" even "where the offense involves acts taking place in the territory of both states with the intent that the offense be consummated in the requesting state."

This meant that a Colombian drug trafficker could be extradited to the United States even if he had never left Colombia. All he had to do was organize a criminal conspiracy aimed at the United States—in other words, send a load.

Once U.S. prosecutors figured this out, things were never the same. Article 8 meant the prosecutors could ask for any trafficker they could implicate in a case, and they implicated as many of them as they could. Bosses like Carlos Lehder and Cali's Gilberto Rodriguez Orejuela, who had spent years building false fronts of respectability, suddenly found their names and faces smeared all over the papers just like those of any two-bit street punk. For the traffickers, the extradition treaty was like a cross to a vampire. They came to hate and fear it as they feared nothing on earth.

BETANCUR'S "philosophical opposition" to extradition had nothing to do with his views on drug trafficking per se and everything to do with views on national sovereignty. Regardless of his reasons, the effect was the same: he chose not to enforce the provisions of the treaty. This decision early in his administration had tremendous implications both for the drug traffickers and for law enforcement, for by 1982 extradition was rapidly becoming the axis around which Colombian drug policy would revolve. And despite Betancur's soft line against drug trafficking, his administration soon began making a series of small bureaucratic moves whose cumulative effect would be enormous. By the end of 1982, half the attorney general's police had been fired for corruption, and new Attorney General Carlos Jimenez Gomez was doing the best he could to take the agency out of drug enforcement altogether. The U.S. embassy was looking for a new place to put its antinarcotics aid resources. It did not search for long.

In December National Police Colonel Jaime Ramirez Gomez took over leadership of the still relatively new Anti-Narcotics Unit. He had five hundred poorly equipped men, a tiny basement office in south Bogotá, and nothing to do. There was a list of addresses where drug traffickers might be located, but the police rarely bothered because they believed the bosses were too politically well connected to be seriously molested.

For this reason Ramirez wondered why Betancur's police chief had chosen him. He had a reputation as a hard charger who made lots of waves. If the brass thought he was going to sit in a south Bogotá basement and count paper clips, they could forget it.

Ramirez was forty-one, five feet four inches tall, with a homely houndlike face and a tendency to eat too much too often. He had a small potbelly that he worried about constantly. He talked a lot, laughed a lot, told jokes, and kidded people unmercifully. As a boy he had been an outstanding soccer left-winger; now he loved tennis, but his wife wouldn't play with him because he gave too much advice. Ramirez came across as a man who was pleased with himself, pleased with the world, and happy to be doing what he did. This was understandable, for Ramirez was a terrific policeman, and he knew it.

Ramirez's passion was information—gathering it, evaluating it, holding it, and acting on it. It was the secret of his success. As a street cop his first jobs had been in intelligence, and over the years he had made case after case on the strength of what he knew, what he remembered, or what he could find out from the hundreds of sources he cultivated all over Colombia. He "collected" people, and when he met someone who knew something he wanted to know, his eyes lit up, and he smiled hugely and exclaimed: "You know about helicopters? I don't know anything about that! Sit down, I want to know everything."

Ramirez's people thought he was God. His knowledge of crime in Colombia was encyclopedic; he could tell whether an informant was lying by asking five or six questions. His men called him "the human lie detector" or "J. Edgar Hoover." If somebody needed background information on something, he just asked Ramirez. Ramirez was always correcting his subordinates' intelligence reports, fleshing them out with arcane tidbits and otherwise driving everybody crazy.

Ramirez got along famously with the U.S. embassy and the DEA, no "nationalistic chip on his shoulder," as one DEA agent put it. Ramirez wasn't bashful about looking for help, and he pestered people —gringos and Colombians—until he got it. Johnny Phelps was fascinated by Ramirez's ability to lean on his superiors or end run them if necessary. Ramirez, Phelps thought, "doesn't recognize anything that can't be done." Phelps, long, tall, handsome, and standoffish, and

Ramirez, short, thick, homely, and loquacious, were an unmatched set, but they worked well together.

RAMIREZ moved quickly. Before long he had traded his south Bogotá basement for a pillbox-shaped rooftop office on the new National Police headquarters building in Bogotá's El Dorado district, near the airport. Phelps and Caesar Bernal, chief of the U.S. embassy's Narcotics Assistance Unit, began steering aid, money, training, and other resources toward Ramirez's Anti-Narcotics Unit police.

The unit began to expand, ultimately to triple in size to 1,500 men. In early 1983 Ramirez sent five companies of police up to the north coast to take on the marijuana traffickers. Pretty soon Ramirez's office began reporting enormous pot seizures.

Ramirez then began interviewing specialists for his headquarters team. He and a group of subordinates grilled each candidate separately. Ramirez was determined to keep corruption out of the unit. Just to remind him that his fears were not groundless, the cartel tried constantly to bribe, blackmail, or otherwise put him in their pockets. When money didn't work, they sent beautiful women around with sad tales "that can only be told in confidence, to you alone."

Ramirez politely invited the visitors to sit down, then brought an office full of aides in to stand against the wall. "How can I help you?" he asked the women. "You can speak freely. These are all trusted friends of mine."

Next, the cartel tried to flatter him with attention. Cartel lawyers and confidants approached him constantly, letting him know that Pablo Escobar "wants to talk to you."

"I have nothing to talk to him about," Ramirez said.

And then the approaches got even more direct. Ramirez received as many as ten threats a week, so many that they lost meaning. Every time a DEA agent talked to an informant, the informant told him, "Hey, you know these guys are really mad at Ramirez." Ramirez laughed off some of the threats and paid attention to others. He always felt that as long as he ran the Anti-Narcotics Unit, his intelligence machinery would warn him of any serious plot before it could get off the ground.

He was confident—perhaps overconfident. Like a lot of experienced police officers, he had known some of Colombia's most important criminals for years; he had trouble visualizing them as anything more than the neighborhood punks they had once been. He respected the cocaine bosses' ability to do violence: that fit the profile he carried in his mind. But his family and friends didn't think he respected the bosses' ability to plot and organize. Pablo Escobar hadn't gotten to the top of the cocaine business by thinking like a car thief.

IN April 1983 U.S. Ambassador Lewis Tambs arrived in Colombia. He was fifty-five, a heavy smoker with a loud, abrasive personality that seemed designed to grate the nerves of the very formal Colombians. He was a hard-line Reagan conservative who had coauthored the Santa Fe Report, a blueprint for containing communism in Latin America that was adopted by the Republican National Committee as part of the official party platform in 1980. He was not bashful about voicing his opinions—about drugs, guerrillas, politics, and almost anything else—and from the beginning of his tour he established a combative public persona that frequently irritated his Colombian hosts and made his aides cringe.

Yet he got away with it, for despite everything Tambs was *simpático,* which meant everything in Colombia. He was a warm, friendly, personable fellow who mitigated the ferocity of his opinions by not force-feeding them to others. He told jokes on himself and escaped awkward interviews by rattling off humorous sayings that he collected and wrote down in a little book. Betancur, very nationalistic, very Latin American, and very opposed to Reagan policy in Latin America, nonetheless liked Tambs, and Tambs liked him.

Tambs also took his job seriously. He was a professor of Latin American history at Arizona State University. His Spanish was superb, and he worked long hours studying Belisario Betancur before arriving in Bogotá. He understood the origins of Betancur's *hispanidad* ("Spanishness") and accepted that Betancur would naturally oppose the Reagan administration's tough, interventionist policy in Central America.

Tambs would always be emphatically anticommunist in his public utterances, but the Reagan administration regarded communism as a secondary matter in Colombia. When Tambs went to the White House for his final briefing, National Security Adviser William P. Clark had only one thing to tell him: "We want you to go down to Colombia to do anything and everything you can about the drug problem."

And that was it. Tambs had "two songs on my harp" when he arrived in Bogotá: "marijuana and Marxists; cocaine and communism." He held press conferences, gave speeches, went to receptions, and invited small groups of acquaintances to join him in *tertulias,* informal after-work gatherings that are the social lifeblood of Latin America's professional class.

He saw Betancur at the Nariño Presidential Palace once or twice a week. Sometimes these conversations took place around ten P.M., and Tambs found Betancur, who went to sleep very early and got up before daybreak, in his pajamas, ready for bed. Most of the late sessions involved Tambs getting bawled out for some sort of indiscretion. At one point the Foreign Ministry sent a circular around to all the embassies reminding ambassadors they were not to take public positions regarding Colombia's internal affairs, a clear slap at Tambs. Despite everything, Tambs and Betancur understood and respected each other and never held grudges. Tambs knew that Betancur's "job was to take care of Colombia. He knew what I was doing."

What Tambs was doing was looking for a way to get the Colombian government interested in doing something about drugs. The embassy was pushing hard for both extradition and herbicide eradication of marijuana, but it wasn't getting anywhere. Old hands in the embassy were convinced that the government would never do anything about drug trafficking because Betancur's Conservatives, like the Liberals before them, simply did not see drugs as a problem for Colombia. Tambs spent a lot of time visiting local treatment centers to try to turn this attitude around: "Look, if you want to stay an underdeveloped country forever, get into drugs." But Colombia was not convinced.

Also unsuccessful were Tambs's efforts to promote the idea that drug traffickers and guerrillas were allied in a joint venture aimed at tearing down Colombian society. In 1983 this was thought to be an outrageous idea, apparently the product of Tambs's fertile anticommunist imagination. The MAS affair, still fresh in people's minds, demonstrated that the opposite was true.

Still, Tambs had some ammunition. In the first half of 1983 his DEA agents had received information that a north coast marijuana trafficker had bought a pot shipment from guerrillas and had paid for it with guns. Late in the year, the Colombian army told the embassy that guerrillas from the Moscow-line Revolutionary Armed Forces of Colombia, or FARC, had a training camp in the eastern *llanos* near Villavicencio, an area known for several years to be crawling with coca growers and mom-and-pop cocaine labs.

Tambs coined the term "narco-guerrillas" to describe this phenomenon, but the Colombian public scoffed. Worse, Betancur was clearly irritated. FARC cooperation in a negotiated truce was essential to the success of Betancur's "Peace Process," and Tambs's meddling wasn't helping.

The FARC had been in existence since at least 1963. Its leaders were old-line Marxist-Leninist ideologues, and its soldiers were mostly backcountry *campesinos*. There were about five thousand of them in 1982, and they had strongholds in Colombia's eastern *llanos*, a vast wilderness of savannah and tropical forest, and in the central Magdalena River valley. The FARC financed itself through kidnappings and by shaking down rich rural landowners. The FARC was much bigger than M-19 and was taken much more seriously. Many Colombians believed the FARC was the armed wing of the Colombian Communist Party. In 1982 it was almost inconceivable to think of them as allies of drug traffickers.

BY mid-1983 three dedicated people—Tambs, Phelps, and Ramirez—opposed the Medellín cartel and were ready to do battle. What the three still lacked, however, was a spokesman, a political heavyweight capable of putting narcotics at the center of Colombia's national debate. Tambs was amusing, vocal, and forceful, but he was a gringo. Ramirez was a policeman, prohibited from making public policy statements. If Colombia was to mount an aggressive war against the Medellín cartel, it needed a capable Colombian politician to articulate the strategy and drive it home. Betancur wouldn't do it; there had to be somebody else.

The political issue of the day was "hot money," contributions by the drug traffickers to Colombia's politicians. Opposing candidates during the 1982 general elections had accused one another of accepting hot money and had used the issue as a means to smear entire sectors of the major political parties. Two of the biggest targets were Envigado Congressman Jairo Ortega and his cartel alternate, Escobar.

The principal accusers in the hot money debate were the so-called New Liberals—the reformist wing of the Liberal Party. The New Liberals had made hot money a cornerstone of their political campaigns the previous year and had subsequently brought the debate into legislative committee and onto the floor of Congress.

Under terms of Colombia's National Front, presidents were obliged to allocate a certain number of cabinet posts to the opposition. Betancur, a Conservative, assigned the justice ministry to the New Liberals, and in early August 1983 he appointed Senator Rodrigo Lara Bonilla to the post. (The Colombian justice minister is the equivalent of the

U.S. attorney general. The Colombian attorney general is a public administration watchdog, a sort of national ombudsman.)

Lara Bonilla was thirty-five, a handsome, charismatic, aggressive politician, one of the brightest young lights of the Liberal Party. As justice minister the task of investigating the hot money scandals fell to him. He embraced it both as an honest reformer and as a political pragmatist. Hot money was hot press, and Lara Bonilla was aware of the political gains to be made from a successful crusade.

Lara Bonilla's biggest impediment was official inertia. Betancur had known Lara Bonilla's record on hot money and had appointed him justice minister, so presumably the president was ready to back Lara Bonilla to the hilt. The trouble was that Betancur never said so. He was busy with the Peace Process and economic reform. Lara Bonilla was his hot money man; let him handle it.

This was easier said than done. The suspicion among most journalists and other skeptics was that almost everyone—Liberals, Conservatives, New Liberals, Marxists—had taken hot money. Lara Bonilla and the other reformers were trying to look under the rug, and Colombia's political chieftains didn't like it. Thus, in the absence of a clear endorsement from Betancur, Lara Bonilla's status remained somewhat ambiguous. He was not of the president's party; he was a politician himself and not a technocrat; he was attacking a lot of people from his own party. Many of his targets determined that they could stonewall Lara Bonilla and probably escape unscathed. They decided to sit tight and await events.

The second thing Lara Bonilla failed to anticipate was the power of the Medellín cartel. In 1983 it was still possible to think that a man could build a political career by attacking the traffickers. Everyone knew that the cartel for the last few years had been buying its way into the halls of power, but everyone still thought that the trend could be easily reversed, that state power, when brought to bear, was infinitely stronger than cocaine power.

This was a miscalculation. Betancur himself was making it, ignoring the rot that had set into Colombian political institutions and the danger it posed to the integrity of his government. Politicians down the line were also making it. They had played footsie with the traffickers, taken their money, and pretended they didn't know where it came from or that it didn't matter. They didn't understand the extent of cartel influence. The cartel was not trying to buy favors with hot money; the cartel was trying to buy a government. Lara Bonilla, the reformist political zealot, wandered into this jungle like a child. The traffickers were on him like leopards.

Lara Bonilla thus became something of a reluctant crusader. He was not prepared for the cartel's money, its threats, its intimidation, or the pressure it could put on its enemies. For all that, he was a crusader nevertheless, a courageous man who had accepted—and now had to accomplish—the most dangerous job in Colombia: challenge the Medellín cartel and knock it down.

And he had friends. In 1980 he had served as mayor of his hometown of Neiva when Jaime Ramirez was based there as police chief of Huila province. He was also good friends with the family of Ramirez's wife, Helena, a Huila native. Ramirez counted himself a friend of Lara Bonilla's and determined to help him.

So did Tambs and Phelps. Both already knew Lara Bonilla slightly, and both could see that the enormity of his task threatened to overwhelm him. Phelps, in particular, was extremely irritated that Betancur had not been been more out front in the hot money debate. The president was leaving Lara Bonilla to twist in the wind.

PHELPS and Tambs visited Lara Bonilla together soon after his appointment. Lara Bonilla confirmed he did not feel he had the support of the government. On the other hand, he was politician enough to understand that there was no turning away from the cocaine traffickers. He was the point man, like it or not. Could Tambs and Phelps help him?

They could, and would. As the two Americans left the Justice Ministry, Phelps turned to Tambs and said, "This is a man who's looking for allies."

11.

HOT MONEY

Jairo Ortega began his speech slowly. He welcomed the opportunity to talk about hot money, he said, because he was troubled by a "web of hypocrisy" in government. He had "no personal axes to grind," but the truth, he said, should come out. Furthermore, he wanted to respond to accusations plaguing him constantly about his alleged ties to drug traffickers, his liberal use of hot money, and his alleged association with suspicious characters, among them his own Envigado alternate, Pablo Escobar.

His words carried across the floor of Congress, easily heard by Justice Minister Rodrigo Lara Bonilla and other cabinet ministers on hand for the debate.

Did the justice minister know a citizen named Evaristo Porras Ardila? Ortega asked.

No, the minister shook his head, he did not.

Well, Ortega said, Evaristo Porras lives in the Amazon border town of Leticia and has served time in a Peruvian jail for drug trafficking. In April Porras had written a check for one million pesos ($12,821) to Senator Rodrigo Lara Bonilla to help defray campaign expenses. Ortega raised a photocopy of the check in his right hand and showed it to the assembled lawmakers.

In addition, Ortega continued, the justice minister had in fact spoken with Porras by telephone, had acknowledged receipt of the check, and had thanked Porras for his concern. Ortega then played a tape recording reputed to be the phone call in question. It was incomprehensible.

"Let the Congress analyze the minister's conduct with this person who offered him a million pesos; Mr. Porras is a recognized international drug trafficker, according to Peruvian police," Ortega said.

"But far be it from me to try to detain the minister of justice's brilliant political career. I only want him to tell us what kind of morality he is going to require of the rest of us. Relax, Minister. Just let the country know that your morality can't be any different from that of Jairo Ortega and the rest of us."

Lara Bonilla was in trouble. He had never heard the name Evaristo Porras. He knew nothing of a million-peso check or a telephone conversation with its donor. That said nothing, however. He, like any other politician, accepted campaign contributions happily without questioning their origins very closely. Still, this was one of the practices he wanted stopped, and there was a possibility that he was guilty of it.

But he would deal with that later. Now he stood up to reply. There were two ways to go. One, the bureaucrat's, was to admit nothing, investigate, and talk later; the other, the politician's, was to take the adversary's accusation and fling it back in his face. It was August 16, 1983. Lara Bonilla had been justice minister for less than two weeks; he had been a politician for fifteen years.

"My life is an open book," he began. He was blameless and had always been blameless; there was no way his enemies could discredit him. "Any moment that any suspicion whatsoever falls upon me," he would resign his office "knowing that I will not be followed by complacent ministers affected by the blackmail and the extortion being perpetrated against Colombia's political class."

Warming to his task, Lara Bonilla damned the Medellín cartel practice—again demonstrated by Ortega—of casting aspersions on those allegedly receiving the money instead of those who sent it—"those, who, yes, have to explain here or anywhere else in this country where their fortunes have come from.

"Morality is one thing, but there are levels: one thing are the checks . . . that they use to throw mud at politicians," Lara Bonilla said, a shock of hair falling over his forehead as he leveled an accusing forefinger at his enemies. "But it's another thing when somebody runs a campaign exclusively with these funds."

What about Pablo Escobar? he asked. It was strange how "from one day to the next" Escobar had amassed a "gigantic fortune" from the proceeds of a bicycle factory and other "clever deals." With the money he bought "nine airplanes and three hangars in the airport at Medellín," set up a whole flock of nonprofit organizations "that he uses to try to bribe the people," and "created the Death to Kidnappers movement."

Lara Bonilla was winging it, parlaying the little he knew into a blanket accusation. His political instincts were sound. He had to give people something to think about for a while, gain time so he could better prepare himself. What he had told Congress was hardly earth-shaking news. Escobar's résumé was well known to anyone in official Colombia who listened to gossip. What was news was the fact that Lara Bonilla had spoken out. No Colombian politician had dared do this. With one speech he had forever forfeited any chance of peaceful coexistence with the Medellín cartel. He was now their public enemy number one. Live and let live was over.

Escobar, recognizing what was at stake, picked up the gauntlet, notifying Lara Bonilla August 17 "that you have twenty-four hours to present the proofs" of Escobar's participation in MAS, otherwise Escobar would denounce him in Congress and ask for an investigation. He described Lara Bonilla's rebuttal in Congress as "a show of false moralism"; Lara Bonilla had changed from "accused to accuser" only "when he found himself corraled" by Jairo Ortega.

Evaristo Porras also contributed to the cartel cause. An important Escobar underboss and coca leaf shipper, he was contacted by reporters in Leticia, where he confirmed that he had donated the million pesos to Lara Bonilla and that he had indeed been indicted by Peruvian police for drug trafficking, "a youthful indiscretion." His current immense wealth, he said, was a windfall. He claimed to have won the lottery three times the previous year.

And the battle was joined. Lara Bonilla backtracked slightly, briefly, owning up to having received the Porras check but claiming it was payment for a debt contracted to his family. He visited Betancur, who accepted his explanation. Ortega, Lara Bonilla said, had concocted a "political cock-and-bull story" to discredit him.

Escobar asked for an investigation of Lara Bonilla, and a judge actually started probing the Porras affair. In fact, Lara Bonilla never put the matter entirely to rest, but he didn't need to once he got rolling. Fed by Jaime Ramirez on one side and Johnny Phelps on the other, he had all the information he could use, not only about Escobar, but also about the rest of the Medellín cartel and its underbosses. Lara Bonilla was ready to play for keeps, and the traffickers weren't altogether ready for him.

THE drug lords were extremely exposed and vulnerable by mid-1983. Since MAS and its accompanying bloodbath, no one was left to mount a serious armed challenge to the cartel. Vendetta was bad for business, and revenge killings were being discouraged. Escobar and Los

Pablos, Jorge Ochoa and his clan, and Carlos Lehder dominated the business and set the rules, surrounded by their satellites and a dwindling number of independents. Everybody did fine, and everybody got fat together. The cartel members were living like real people, and their money had begun to make them forget that there were a vast number of honest Colombians who hated what they were doing to the country.

It was easy to forget when you were Pablo Escobar, "*paisa* Robin Hood." Throughout 1983 Medellín Without Slums and *Civics on the March* were constantly in the news. The first two hundred units at Barrio Pablo Escobar were scheduled for completion at the end of the year. Escobar was reported to be worth $2–$5 billion, and everywhere in Medellín, Antioquia province, and beyond, he was Don Pablo.

He could get away with anything. He hosted a charity art auction at the Intercontinental Hotel and called it Pincel de Estrellas ("Paintbrush of Stars"). In April he sponsored a "Forum on Extradition" at Kevin's, which, not surprisingly, found that extradition was "a violation of national sovereignty."

But perhaps his greatest accomplishment was to woo part of the hierarchy of the Roman Catholic church to his cause. From the end of 1982 and through most of 1983 he was accompanied on his civic meanderings by two Medellín priests, Reverends Elías Lopera and Hernan Cuartas. They appeared with Escobar and Jairo Ortega on the board of directors of Medellín Without Slums. They co-sponsored Escobar's soccer benefits, helped with the "Forum on Extradition," blessed his auction, and generally gave him the Church's imprimatur as a doer of good works.

Lopera, in particular, was present everywhere. He tramped the slums with Escobar, introduced him at rallies, traveled with him through Antioquia, and gave speeches. In one memorable appearance he instructed Colombia to "wake up!" and proceeded to enumerate all the economic and social ills from which the nation suffered, twenty-three items in all. Drug abuse was not on the list.

Medellín Cívico, Escobar's newspaper, loved Lopera and ran news stories about him with accompanying photographs, usually side by side with Escobar. In February it published a picture of Lopera in animated discussion with Pope John Paul II, with whom he had managed to obtain an audience. *Medellín Cívico* described this as a "historic interview."

Escobar was able to use the priests for months despite repeated attempts—by lay people and many other churchmen—to denounce them. This was because they were protected, either deliberately or unwittingly, by Medellín's archbishop, Cardinal Alfonso Lopez Trujillo, the leading conservative among Latin America's bishops and one of the most powerful Catholic prelates in the world.

Critics tended to confuse their dislike of the narco-priests with their dislike for Lopez Trujillo's politics and ostentatious lifestyle, prompting Lopez Trujillo to view the denunciations as personal attacks. His own propagandists branded one journalist a "viper" and kept up a steady counterbarrage against anyone with the temerity to question the way he ran his archdiocese. This kind of exchange was never funny in Colombia, a nation where the Catholic Church wields immense political power and moral force. Yet largely because of Lopez Trujillo, Escobar's two priests toiled on his behalf for months without even having their knuckles rapped.

Outside of working hours, Escobar played the gracious host at one of his many estates. His favorite spot was Hacienda Los Napoles in Puerto Triunfo, a seven-thousand-acre *finca* some eighty miles east of Medellín on the Magdalena River. The land alone, Escobar told *Semana* magazine, cost him 4.5 billion pesos ($63 million), but that was only the beginning. He landscaped the property with artificial lakes, a network of roads, and an airport. Then he imported more than two hundred exotic animals and turned them loose. In 1983 some sixty thousand visitors made Hacienda Los Napoles Colombia's most popular zoo. Guests drove through the grounds and viewed the animals as they roamed about. There were camels, giraffes, bison, llamas, hippopotamuses, a pair of black cockatoos valued at $14,000 each, a kangaroo that played soccer, and an elephant that would steal the food out of visitors' cars or pluck the billfolds from their hands.

The entrance to Hacienda Los Napoles featured a cement gate with a small airplane mounted on top. This was reputed to be the plane that flew Escobar's first load of cocaine. At the main house, closed to the public, Escobar could sleep one hundred. He had billiard tables, a swimming pool, and a Wurlitzer jukebox stocked with the records of Brazil's Roberto Carlos, Escobar's favorite singer. The swimming pool was flanked by a marble Venus and a mortar emplacement. Under a canopy Escobar had mounted a 1930s vintage automobile peppered with bullet holes. It was variously described as having belonged to John Dillinger, Al Capone, or Bonnie and Clyde.

Escobar constantly entertained his friends and associates at Hacienda Los Napoles, flying them to his private airport, fixing them up with drinks, swimming, and talk about the events of the day. Father Lopera was a regular visitor, as were Jairo Ortega and the redoubtable Senator Santofimio, Escobar's political godfather.

The Ochoas were not nearly as splashy. In Medellín the family stayed at La Loma, a gorgeous hilltop estate south of the city. Guests driving up the winding road were likely to be met and escorted by a herd of old Fabio's tiny pet ponies, which ate out of a person's hand and snuffled and bunted like affectionate puppies. Old Fabio, Juan David, and Jorge also spent a lot of time at Hacienda Veracruz, breeding horses and tending a zoo of their own. Jorge diverted himself by collecting vintage Harley-Davidson motorcycles. Young Fabio was often in Portugal trying to make a career fighting bulls from horseback. The whole family could be seen regularly at horse shows in Medellín and throughout Antioquia.

IN Armenia, Carlos Lehder's influence had reached its apogee. The Posada Alemana, a huge tourist complex/discotheque/convention center, opened to great civic fanfare in the middle of 1983. Lehder's favorite priest, Pereira Bishop Dario Castrillon, gave the blessing. A year later Castrillon would admit having received money from the cartel "and distributing it to the poor."

Posada Alemana, Lehder's answer to Hacienda Los Napoles, was fifteen miles north of Armenia. It had a rustic Bavarian entrance, but the rest of the estate, which twisted and wound for several square miles about the beautiful, green Quindio hills, was Colombian *campesino*—thatched, two-story stucco bungalows, clubhouses, restaurants, and other outbuildings arrayed amid gardens, gazebos, and wire aviaries filled with exotic birds. Maestro Arenas's statue of John Lennon topped a small knoll just inside the *posada* entrance. Lennon was nude, had a bullet hole in his chest and back and a guitar in his right hand. His left hand was extended outward holding the letters *P-A-Z* —"peace." A pedestal inscription read "To the Greatest Musician of the Century." A gently climbing flight of stairs led up to the statue and a walkway surrounded it. Kids went to the *posada*'s discotheque, danced all night, got stoned, then made a pilgrimage to the Lennon shrine to watch the sun come up.

On March 11, 1983, Lehder founded the National Latin Movement, a new political party whose fundamental purpose was to get rid of the U.S.–Colombia extradition treaty. By this time the Jacksonville case against Lehder was in Colombia, waiting to be examined by the Supreme Court. Lehder was number twenty-two chronologically on a list of more than one hundred extraditions contemplated by the United States, but Ambassador Tambs and the U.S. embassy left no doubt that he was number one in the minds of U.S. law enforcement.

The National Latin Movement set up shop in a garagelike building in downtown Armenia. It had a podium, a small office, and a bunch of benches for the faithful to gather for Saturday afternoon rallies. Behind the rostrum the party mounted a twelve-foot photograph of Lehder giving a speech, making the movement's "maximum chief" a constant, larger-than-life presence even when he wasn't on the premises. The party newspaper, *Quindio Libre,* had a full-color capability and a press run of sixty thousand. Lehder's minions distributed it in Medellín by driving down the street and hurling it into the air.

The movement pitched an ultranationalist, vaguely Third World line with an alarming neo-Nazi flavor. Lehder had a corps of youthful, club-carrying "Woodchoppers" to keep order at rallies and claimed that "an incorrect image has been spread of Germany" and of Adolf Hitler, whom he referered to as "Adolfo." He claimed that "international Zionism" was behind "torture and terrorism" in Central America, and that "rabbis collect taxes for Israel." He said his party was a lot like the West German Green Party, "especially on environmental issues." Green and white were the party colors.

FOUR months after the formation of the National Latin Movement two U.S federal prosecutors and a pair of DEA agents from Jacksonville arrived in Colombia on a secret mission to press the case for Lehder's extradition. The team was led by Robert Merkle, the U.S. attorney for the Middle District of Florida. Merkle was a huge man, nicknamed "Mad Dog" and not known for his delicate touch. But he was a brilliant prosecutor, well able to articulate the U.S. case for extradition. He wanted Lehder, and he was led to believe that the Colombians would give him a sympathetic hearing.

Lehder himself was well aware of the problems posed by the Jacksonville indictment. Not only did he risk extradition from Colombia, but he could be arrested and deported to Florida from any third country that had a U.S. bilateral extradition treaty of its own. Lehder had sent feelers to the U.S. State Department in 1982 and had actually met with a DEA agent in Colombia. He offered to sell Norman's Cay to the U.S government for $5 million if the United States would drop the Jacksonville case. Maybe the U.S. Navy could turn the cay into a base, he said. The DEA passed the offer to Jacksonville. It was rejected.

A year later, in July 1983, Merkle was hunting Lehder, not offering deals. He was unfamiliar with Colombia and Bogotá, a city he found tense, packed with security checkpoints and armed guards. The day after he arrived, Merkle took a rickety cable car into the mountains above Bogotá to attend mass at a primitive church overlooking the capital. During the ceremony, a "worshiper" picked his pocket. Outside again, he discovered the cable car was no longer working. He had to walk down a stone staircase to return to the city.

The following week Merkle and his team presented credentials and documentation at the Justice Ministry. Lara Bonilla, who would make Lehder a test case for extradition a few months later, was not yet in office, and Merkle encountered a low-key, matter-of-fact atmosphere. He came away "hopeful but not optimistic."

LEHDER'S shamelessness, like Escobar's, knew no bounds. Since his kidnap he had given up driving his own car and now traveled with an armed escort composed of twenty-five ex-police officers. In an interview with Bogotá's Radio Caracól in late July, he acknowledged membership in MAS because "kidnap victims have to protect their interests."

He also told Caracól he had bought "my islands" in the Bahamas for "more than $1 million" and had put them "at the service of the Colombian bonanza," which was the euphemism he used to describe the billions of drug dollars that Norman's Cay had helped earn. Without mentioning the word "cocaine," he admitted he was a transport specialist for his friends, an "intermediary, you could say, because of the land I had next to the United States."

He had been arrested and put in a U.S. jail because "I was a Latin neighborhood leader" who wanted to "defend my race, my principles, and my Colombianism." He was looking toward a career as a senator, "to represent the kidnappables and the extraditables of Colombia. I want to represent unions, and I want to represent the poorest of the poor.

"They say that I conspired against the United States," he said. "I would say that not only did I conspire, I also will continue to conspire until the day the extradition treaty is canceled."

Lehder traveled to Bogotá to be present for the Ortega-Lara Bonilla confrontation. Denied entrance to the floor of Congress, he migrated upward to the press gallery, where as publisher of *Quindio Libre* he was guaranteed access. He and his bodyguards cheered raucously for Jairo Ortega and grinned maliciously at the regular reporters covering the event.

But bravado wouldn't be enough. While Lehder was in Bogotá, the

Colombian Supreme Court was nearly ready to rule on the constitutionality of Lehder's extradition. Lehder told reporters at Congress that Colombia would extradite him "over my dead body."

Then, on September 2, 1983, the Supreme Court issued a finding favorable to the United States. Colombia put out a warrant for Lehder's arrest, but Lehder had already disappeared, tipped off, he would say later, "because my friends in the Ministry of Justice alerted me regarding Lara Bonilla's intentions." Lara Bonilla approved Lehder's extradition order and forwarded it to Betancur for his signature.

ESCOBAR was next. In forcing Lara Bonilla to the wall on the Porras check, he had left himself wide open to counterattack. Lara Bonilla had nothing to lose, and, it turned out, he had plenty of help. Others were quick to follow his lead.

On August 25 the Bogotá newspaper *El Espectador* published a front-page story detailing Escobar's 1976 Medellín cocaine bust, the one that had dismissed him as a low-echelon mule working for a larger trafficker. *El Espectador*'s reporters had come across an old in-house newspaper published by the Department of Administrative Security (DAS), the Colombian FBI, that gave details of the arrest and published mug shots of Escobar, his cousin Gustavo Gaviria, and four other defendants. There was no mistaking the pictures or what the story implied. Escobar reacted instantly: thugs driving around on motorcycles or in automobiles bought every single copy of *El Espectador* to reach Medellín. *El Espectador* followed up daily, describing how the case had been passed among different courts and judges, how Escobar had been jailed and freed, how the court records had been misplaced, lost, or "disappeared."

In early September Lara Bonilla, working with information supplied by Jaime Ramirez, asked for an investigation of several private air transport and charter firms believed to be controlled by drug traffickers. On September 8 Colombia's Civil Aeronautics Board canceled flying permits for fifty-seven aircraft, a large number of which were believed to belong to the Ochoas and their charter firm, Pilotos Ejecutivos.

That same day, an investigative judge outside Medellín formally reopened the 1976 case against Escobar. On September 10 Senator Alberto Santofimio, finally unable to take the heat, ordered Escobar dropped from his list of supporters, asked him publicly to get out of politics, and suggested he waive his parliamentary immunity, answer the charges being made against him, and get things cleared up. At that point parliamentary immunity, the constitutional right of every sitting Colombian congressman, was the only thing standing between Escobar and a jail cell.

On September 11 Escobar severed his connection with Santofimio, claiming he had gotten into politics eighteen months ago because "only inside the government could a man best serve the community." Now the community was turning its back on him. He would return the favor. He would not, however, give up his congressional seat or his immunity.

Twelve days later the Medellín judge studying the 1976 case ordered Escobar arrested. The charge: that he had conspired to murder the DAS agents who had originally arrested him. Two had been killed in 1977. Antioquia DAS chief Major Carlos Gustavo Monroy Arenas, the officer in charge of the operation against Escobar, was murdered in Medellín by motorcycle assassins on August 25, 1981.

The only thing restraining Lara Bonilla at this point was Betancur and his continued refusal to extradite traffickers. In October the Supreme Court found in favor of extradition in the cases of two north coast marijuana traffickers. Lara Bonilla approved the order and sent it to Betancur, who refused to sign it and instead remanded the case to Colombian courts. The Lehder order was still unsigned and would remain so for months. The message emanating from the presidential palace regarding extradition was clear—find another way.

So Lara Bonilla kept pushing. On September 26 newspapers resurrected Escobar's 1974 car theft indictment. In mid-October Congress carefully consented to engage the possibility of revoking Escobar's immunity to make him liable to prosecution. Tambs, interviewed in *El Tiempo,* Colombia's biggest daily newspaper, denounced the "penetration of narcotics smugglers into politics" and praised Lara Bonilla for taking steps to control it: "How is democracy going to continue in Colombia if it is managed and manipulated by these criminals?"

In late October, again with an assist from Ramirez, Lara Bonilla dropped another bombshell. Six of the nine teams in Colombia's professional soccer league, he said, were either partly owned or controlled by drug traffickers. He named Hernan Botero (Nacional of Medellín), Cali cartel boss Gilberto Rodriguez (America), and Bogotá cocaine lord Gonzalo Rodriguez Gacha (Millionarios) among others. Next month *El Espectador* obtained a full list and added more names.

Finally, on November 17, Colombia's National Institute of Renewable Natural Resources fined Pablo Escobar 450,000 pesos ($5,000) for bringing eighty-five zoo animals into the country illegally in 1981. The list included two camels, two elephants, two elk, six ducks, three Canada geese, a capybara from the Amazon, and assorted others.

For Escobar this was the last straw. On January 20, 1984, in the formal, polite language for which he was rapidly becoming known, Escobar sent a message to Jairo Ortega announcing his withdrawal from public life: "The attitude of politicians is very far from the people's opinions and aspirations." Ramirez and Lara Bonilla had finally put fear into the hearts of the Medellín cartel bigshots.

12.

THE ETHER TRAIL

On February 9, 1984, the Medellín cartel gathered at Kevin's disco to celebrate the baptism of the son of one of Jorge Ochoa's key Miami cocaine distributors. Ochoa stood godfather at the event. Two thousand guests munched quail eggs dipped in honey, drank Dom Pérignon, and strolled Kevin's terrace gazing down the green-clad mountainside to the city of Medellín far below.

The week of the party served as one continuous cartel summit. Jorge Ochoa usually presided, but Pablo Escobar chimed in when he wanted. Escobar was "elegant and eloquent," one guest said, but both he and Ochoa were low-key, unfailingly courteous, and respectful. Part of this was *paisa* formality, but part of it was caution. Both men now had the power to kill anyone in the group who displeased them. Each needed to take great care in how he acted and how he addressed his underlings. An offhand remark or a frown of displeasure could be interpreted as a death sentence.

The traffickers referred to themselves as Nosotros ("Us") or El Grupo ("the Group"). As always, the cartel discussed market expansion. The traffickers wanted to add more smuggling routes, more pilots. They talked about other means of transportation—cargo containers, ships, even submarines. Ochoa complained that the kilos of cocaine his planes were "air-dropping" to speedboats off the Bahamas were getting wet and had to be reprocessed in Miami. New waterproof packaging was needed.

There was a pressing need for more and better transportation, Ochoa explained, because the cartel now had more cocaine than ever. A vast complex of laboratories in the Colombian jungle *llanos* had come on line the previous September and was now producing nearly four thousand kilos a month. Tons of cocaine were quietly accumulating in the jungle, far from law enforcement. Ochoa boasted that he was ready to start moving two thousand kilos a week.

WHAT Ochoa described was unprecedented—a set of integrated factories capable of producing more than half of the seventy tons of cocaine estimated to be entering the United States each year. Making cocaine is complicated, even in a backyard lab, but in the cartel's new facility it was a mammoth logistical task, requiring tons of chemicals, the most important of which was ether.

COCAINE production begins in Peru or Bolivia between 1,500 and 6,000 feet above sea level in the mist-filled valleys on the eastern slope of the Andes. There water vapor from the Amazon rain forest rises upward, providing the proper warmth and wetness for the shrubs that bear the coca leaf.

Like caffeine, nicotine, codeine, morphine, and heroin, cocaine is an alkaloid, a psychoactive compound produced by a plant. Most cocaine comes from one of two varieties of coca leaf. The Bolivian plant has a leaf that is glossy, greenish brown, and elliptical; the Peruvian leaf—also grown in Colombia but with poorer results—is smooth but not shiny, pale green, and oval.

The shrubs bearing these leaves can grow to twelve feet. They are planted in small, terraced plots of usually not more than two acres called *cocales*. The *campesino* coca farmer is called a *cocalero*. The *cocalero* plants about seven thousand shrubs per acre. After four years the shrubs begin producing coca leaves, which are harvested as often as four times a year, mainly by women and children who stuff the leaves into flour sacks tied at the waist. A day's work for an entire family—twenty-five kilos of wet leaves—yields ten kilos of leaves when dried in the sun.

Coca is legal in Bolivia and Peru. For more than two thousand years the leaf has been chewed by Indians and *campesinos* seeking to ward off hunger and the chill temperatures of the Andes. By the end of 1970 coca outstripped tin as the leading source of income in Bolivia and was doing equally well in Peru, where *campesinos* could make four times as much from coca as they could from any other crop.

A certain amount of coca leaf is legally turned into pharmaceutical cocaine, which is used as a local anesthetic in operations conducted near masses of fine blood vessels. In the United States the leaves are sent to the Stepan Chemical Co. of Maywood, New Jersey, which extracts the cocaine and distributes it to pharmaceutical companies. The residue from Stepan's leaves—but none of the cocaine—goes to Atlanta, Georgia, where it still figures in Formula 7x, the secret recipe for Coca-Cola.

Pharmaceutical cocaine, at 99 percent pure, sold for about $3 a gram with a prescription in the early 1980s. It brought sixty times that on the street. Consequently, the vast majority of coca leaf entered the illegal market.

The cocaine pipeline begins when *campesino* harvesters carry the leaves, sometimes by llama, to itinerant paste labs near the coca fields. The dried leaves are treated with an alkaline solution—lime, sodium carbonate, or potash—which begins to break down the leaf's fourteen alkaloids, only one of which contains cocaine. The next day the leaves are soaked in an oil drum or plastic vat filled with kerosene. The leaves are sometimes pressed, like grapes, to help extract the alkaloid-rich kerosene from the soggy plant matter. When the alkaloids in the leaf have fully dissolved into the kerosene, the dead blackened leaf is skimmed off and sulfuric acid is added into the mix. The acid interacts with the alkaloids now contained in the kerosene to form a collection of salts, one of which is cocaine sulfate. The kerosene is siphoned off, and more alkaline is added to neutralize the acid. A gummy, grayish goo collects in the bottom of the vat. This substance is coca paste. A thousand kilos of leaves yields just ten kilos of paste.

The paste producers in Bolivia and Peru usually sell their product to the Colombians. In Colombian towns paste is mixed with tobacco and smoked as *bazuko*.

But the Colombians refine most of the paste they buy. The process continues with another kerosene bath. The alkaloids settle in layers. The mushy crystals at the top are crude cocaine, about 60 percent pure. The crystals are scraped off, washed in alcohol, filtered, dried, and then dissolved in sulfuric acid. The acid once again binds with the alkaloids. Potassium permanganate is added to destroy the noncocaine alkaloids. What remains is filtered to remove manganese oxide and other impurities. Ammonium hydroxide is added, and the resulting precipitate is again filtered and dried. What is left is a very pure cocaine alkaloid known as cocaine base. It takes 2½ kilos of coca paste to produce one kilo of cocaine base.

The base is not soluble in water, and though it can be smoked ("freebased"), it cannot be inhaled through the mucous membranes in the nose. To create a powder good for inhaling, the base must be dissolved in ether. Hydrochloric acid is added along with acetone.

The result, after filtering and drying, is cocaine hydrochloride, the white powder that in 1984 was being used regularly by five million Americans. A kilo of base makes a kilo of cocaine hydrochloride.

Each kilo of cocaine requires seventeen liters of ether. U.S. annual production of ether was only sixty million pounds from five producers. And there were only seven foreign producers of ether in the world. Follow the ether, find the cocaine. Johnny Phelps and his men knew most of this, but Phelps saw something else that made ether even easier to track in Colombia. Not long after he arrived in Bogotá in mid-1981, Phelps found a report in an old file, in which a DEA agent named Lon Sturock had noted that Colombia's cocaine traffickers needed to import many of the "precursor chemicals" used to produce the drug—including ether. This should mean that all the ether in Colombia came through Colombian Customs. To find out where the ether was going, all law enforcement had to do was read the manifests. By cutting off or controlling the ether supply, law enforcement should be able to put the processors out of business.

Phelps decided to test this idea with a survey. His staff would examine Colombia's imports of ether and a second chemical, acetone, and see what the figures showed. Was cocaine the small, urban-lab cottage industry that local seizures seemed to suggest? Or was there something the DEA had missed?

Phelps's study, code-named Operation Steeple, used informants, court-ordered wiretaps, and undercover visits to Colombian chemical firms. The study took about a year. Agents examined records of Colombian imports of ether and acetone from January 1, 1978, to June 30, 1981. No one had any idea that the DEA might be interested in ether and acetone, thus no one had made any effort to conceal how much was coming into the country. The data was put together by a DEA analyst in Bogotá. The study was completed on December 14, 1981. Its findings, couched in dry bureaucratic language, were a revelation:

"A major vulnerability to Colombia's traditional status in the world cocaine trafficking community is its dependence on the importation both of acetone and ether, neither of which is produced in appreciable quantity internally," the report stated. After that dry introduction came a bombshell: "While acetone has fairly wide industrial application in Colombia, ether does not, with perhaps as much as 98 percent of the latter believed to be destined for illicit users."

Ninety-eight percent. Nearly all of the ether in Colombia was going for the manufacture of cocaine. Phelps was astounded. Colombia's cocaine industry, the DEA study found, was supplied by a vast network of illegal ether brokers who imported the chemical into Colombia for resale to the traffickers. The study identified thirty-seven illicit distributors and only twenty-two legitimate ones. The importers brought a total of four thousand metric tons into Colombia, enough ether to produce three hundred tons of cocaine. The DEA's highest estimate for the amount of cocaine consumed in the United States in 1981 was only forty-five tons.

Ninety percent of the ether came from the United States and West Germany. The ether exports of one American firm, J. T. Baker Chemical Supply Co of Phillipsburg, New Jersey, broke down this way: 758.8 tons to illicit and highly suspect users and only 3.3 tons to legitimate users. "J. T. Baker is the largest ether supplier to the Colombian narcotics trafficking community," the study concluded.

The scale of the illegal ether business was awesome. Merck Colombia S.A., the subsidiary of the German pharmaceutical firm and Colombia's largest legitimate ether importer, brought in only thirty metric tons in the entire 3½ years covered by the study. In a single shipment to one of the illegal distributors in June 1981, J. T. Baker exceeded thirty-two metric tons.

Phelps couldn't believe what he was reading. Was it possible, he asked, that some of the ether was being transshipped to, say, Peru? No, his investigators told him, they had checked that. That meant, Phelps realized, that cocaine production in Colombia had reached a magnitude that had never been imagined.

The conclusion of the report was inevitable: "The Drug Enforcement Administration can effect major damage to the Colombian cocaine processing industry through the denial of selected precursors, namely acetone and ether," the Operation Steeple study stated. "Of the two, ether by far is the most vulnerable. . . . If the Drug Enforcement Administration can successfully cut the availability of these precursor substances through timely, coordinated action, the coca processing industry in Colombia could founder."

The study recommended that the DEA pressure companies supplying ether to refuse orders from illegal distributors and tip the DEA off to suspicious buyers. The study suggested limiting orders to highly suspect distributors to half a metric ton. No firm, legitimate or not, should receive more than twelve tons a year. One proposed tactic was stalling: take a suspicious ether order, delay filling it, and then cancel it. This would cause the traffickers to draw down on their stocks, creating shortages.

The study also recommended briefing the "host countries"—Colombia, Ecuador, Peru, and Bolivia. Also to be told were Europe and the State Department's Bureau of International Narcotics Matters.

Finally, the study suggested some tactics for the DEA's men in the field. "Bogotá District Office might also consider establishing a 'dummy' chemical supply corporation to supply ether to the narcotics trafficking community selling 'bugged' barrels along with adulterated chemicals to foul laboratory operations."

Phelps waited until mid-1982, when the Betancur administration took office. Then he gathered his statistics, his graphs, and his flow charts and prepared to present them to two governments. He forwarded the results to DEA headquarters in Washington, but Washington was skeptical at first, not yet prepared to believe in cocaine by the ton.

Colombian Attorney General Carlos Jimenez Gomez was another matter. Phelps scheduled an appointment for his team and presented his numbers. Jimenez Gomez examined them for himself, mulled them over, and made up his mind:

"You're absolutely right," he told Phelps.

Jimenez Gomez immediately restricted ether and acetone imports, but with a glut of ether in Colombia it would take a while for the effects to be felt. There was nothing to do but wait. Still, if Phelps and his staff were right about Colombian cocaine production, inventory would be drawn down eventually. Then something would happen. Phelps would wait for the reaction.

ON November 22, 1983, Frank Torres walked into J. T. Baker in Phillipsburg, New Jersey, with a big order to fill. He wanted to buy 1,300 fifty-five-gallon drums of high-grade ethyl ether. He wanted to pay cash, about $400,000. He wanted the drums unlabeled, and he said he would take delivery anywhere in the United States. He did not hide the fact that he was Colombian, and he said he would take care of the shipping arrangements to Colombia himself.

The amount of ether Torres wanted was ridiculous. It came to nearly two hundred metric tons, roughly equivalent to half the ether imports for all of Colombia in 1980. During the entire 3½ years studied by Phelps's Operation Steeple investigators, the largest single order had been seventy metric tons. The bulk of the illicit orders averaged between ten and twenty metric tons. Legitimate orders were all usually below one metric ton.

By 1983 a lot had happened to the Colombian ether market. Jimenez

Gomez's licensing requirement had been in place for a year. Intelligence reports told Phelps that a drum of ether now cost $4,800 on the Colombian black market. Ether stocks were dwindling in Colombia.

A lot had also happened at J. T. Baker since Operation Steeple. The DEA had approached the chemical company with the survey results, and the company, tagged as the Colombian cocaine trade's biggest ether supplier, changed its ways. There were still no restrictions on the sale of ether in the United States—a fifty-five-gallon drum sold for about $300. But instead of filling Torres's order without question, the J. T. Baker salesman stalled him while he called the DEA in Newark. The salesman then told Torres he would not be able to fill the order immediately.

A week later Torres got a long-distance call out of the blue. Somebody named Mel Schabilion, who said he worked for North Central Industrial Chemicals in Chicago, offered as much ether as Torres needed. Schabilion had heard about the delays at J. T. Baker and wanted to help out. An overjoyed Torres jumped at the offer.

It was a trap. NCIC, which operated out of a Chicago storefront, was a DEA sting run by Schabilion and Harry Fullett, two DEA agents who had been partners for years. They complemented each other perfectly. Schabilion was aggressive, gregarious, big as a pro football lineman, with a sharp street intelligence. Fullett was smaller, quieter, and wore a gold earring in one ear. The duo had a sense of humor about the trade. Schabilion had named the storefront so that its initials matched those of the National Crime Information Center, the FBI's computer-access repository for the criminal records of millions of felons. It was the kind of inside joke dear to DEA agents.

Four days after Schabilion's call, Torres met with the two agents at the Ramada Inn in Miami. Torres said he wanted three hundred drums of ether immediately. He wanted the labels changed on the drums. Instead of "ethyl ether," they should read "ethyl formate" and "ethylene glycol." The following week Torres flew up to Chicago to visit NCIC. Hidden cameras filmed him making a $15,000 down payment. Torres struck the DEA agents as incredibly naive, playing at being cloak-and-dagger and cautious one moment, talking too much the next.

BY now DEA headquarters in Washington was coordinating the burgeoning Torres investigation. The DEA suspected something big but didn't know exactly what it was. Francisco Javier Torres Sierra was a friendly Colombian family man in his forties who ran a small import-export business in Miami, one of many that sprouted up to cash in on the Latin American business boom of the early 1980s. Torres was married and had two daughters and a house in Kendall, a Miami suburb. He went to mass every day and had no criminal record. Yet Torres wanted to buy enough ether to produce almost thirty thousand pounds of cocaine. Who was behind him?

The DEA got a partial answer to that question from Torres's telephone records. Before making his $15,000 down payment to NCIC, Torres twice called a Barranquilla number registered to Armando Bravo Muñoz, a known cocaine trafficker. But this only made things more curious. Bravo Muñoz was not big enough to handle all the ether Torres wanted.

At Torres's instruction, NCIC sent seventy-six drums of ether to the Port of New Orleans. Two of the drums, however, were equipped with radio transponders installed by the DEA's Technical Operations branch.

About the size of cigarette packs, the "beepers" were anchored in Styrofoam and surrounded by a bulky long-life battery pack. The entire package was set in a false bottom welded into the drums. Thin filament antennae ran up the sides of the drums. The antennae were barely noticeable lines, like a slight crack in the paint on the outside of the drums. Once a day the beepers "spoke" to U.S. National Security Agency satellites circling the Earth. The satellite recorded the precise location of Torres's ether shipment.

The DEA lost the signal when the shipment got to New Orleans. Agents in Washington, Chicago, and Miami spent a nervous day, waiting. The next day the signal reappeared in New Orleans. The day after that, the beepers were broadcasting from Colombia.

On March 4, 1984, Herb Williams, the DEA's resident agent in Barranquilla, fielded a three-way conference telephone call linking him with the DEA's cocaine desk in Washington and with the DEA's El Paso Intelligence Center in Texas, nexus for all U.S. drug intelligence. The ether, Williams was told, was now at latitude 10 degrees 34 minutes 20 seconds north by longitude 75 degrees 3 minutes 24 seconds west. The shipment was somewhere outside Barranquilla near Colombia's Caribbean coast.

A Colombian police officer went to check the coordinates. Williams had a pretty good idea what he would find. On March 5 the officer confirmed the suspicion: the ether had passed through Hacienda Veracruz. Williams described this in his report as "a ranch owned by the Medellín, Colombia, cocaine trafficking family Ochoa. The ranch has been identified to be sometimes used as a deembarkation point for cocaine shipments belonging to the Ochoas destined for the United States.''

WHILE events unfolded in Colombia, Torres was having second thoughts in Miami about his Colombian clients. He was nervous, and it made him talkative. He told Schabilion and Fullett he wanted to stop handling ether, but his clients were putting pressure on him to fill the 1,300-drum order, and it was bothering him.

Up to this point, Torres had been careful not to mention cocaine, but now he began to open up. His clients were killers, he said. Only money meant anything to them. Life meant nothing. Torres regaled the agents with details about the cocaine business in Colombia, dropping the names of Jorge Ochoa and Pablo Escobar, saying that five families controlled the business. The agents couldn't decide whether Torres's information was accurate or not.

By March 5 the ether had already left Hacienda Veracruz, traveling south by plane. On March 6 the beeper signals came out of Colombia's eastern *llanos,* a vast area of savannah, tropical forest, and little else.

Johnny Phelps waited a day, but the ether didn't move. On March 7 he decided it was time to act. Apparently the ether had reached its final destination.

Phelps drove over to police headquarters to see Jaime Ramirez, something he usually did at least twice a day. On the days when Phelps didn't visit Ramirez, Ramirez visited him.

Ramirez, as usual, was sitting in his office writing reports and listening to his radios. He didn't have a ham operator's license, but he was crazy about radios and had them installed in his offices, in his car, and at home. He listened to the police, the army, and smugglers talking on their CBs. He knew most of the frequencies that drug pilots used on their way in and out of Colombia, and his scanners found others. This had been very useful to the DEA on several occasions. Now Phelps was telling Ramirez something he had never heard before.

"You're kidding," Ramirez said.

"No," Phelps said. "We think there's a major lab in the jungle."

"Where exactly is it?"

"Here."

Phelps went to the map, put his finger down in the remote southeastern reaches of Caquetá province: latitude 0 degrees 1 minute 4 seconds north; longitude 72 degrees 41 minutes 11 seconds west. Almost exactly on the equator at the confluence of the Yari and Mesay rivers, a jungle wilderness.

Phelps didn't tell Ramirez how big the ether shipment was, because he had doubts the Colombian police could actually put together a big operation and get the people on the ground at the site. Ramirez's men had never before tried to bust a lab in the middle of nowhere. It was going to be a logistical nightmare.

Ramirez looked at Phelps's mark and wondered, not for the first time, how and where the DEA got its information. His people had nothing in the *llanos*. Then he thought about planes, helicopters, and fuel. It would take a couple of days to arrange, but maybe with a stop at San José del Guaviare. . . .

He smiled. "Hell, let's do it."

TRANQUILANDIA

As far as anybody could tell, the place where they were going was
about 160 miles south of San José del Guaviare. At 9:20 A.M. on
March 10, 1984, Lieutenant Colonel Ernesto Gilibert Vargas, second-
in-command of the National Police Anti-Narcotics Unit, ordered his
men aboard two Bell 212 helicopters and a de Havilland Twin Otter
airplane. There were forty-two men, Anti-Narcotics Unit veterans
backed by a fully equipped police Special Operations Group, or
GOES, the Colombian equivalent of a SWAT team. Ron Pettingill,
forty-five, a DEA agent in Colombia for four years, was the expedition's special guest, the only gringo making the trip. The task force
was going to pay a visit to the tiny slice of jungle where the DEA's
shipment of bugged ether was giving off signals.

Jaime Ramirez had moved quickly. After Johnny Phelps told him
about the "major lab" in the eastern *llanos*, he and Phelps had gone
to police headquarters to get permission for the operation. Once that
was accomplished, Ramirez briefed Gilibert, got himself a GOES
team, and arranged the aircraft. The plan was to leave early from
Bogotá, fly two hundred miles southeast to San José del Guaviare,
refuel from the army there, take off again, and hit the target as soon
as possible. The aircraft would be carrying bladder tanks with extra
fuel, but still there was no turning back. Once helicopters were in the
air in rural Colombia, people knew a military maneuver was under
way. Give the traffickers any time at all to warn their friends, and you
could kiss your operation good-bye.

Phelps picked Pettingill to accompany the police because he could
operate the portable videocamera and because he had spent a lot of
time flying the *llanos* looking for coca plantations. Pettingill also knew
the area around San José del Guaviare, the market center of Colom-

bia's not particularly prosperous coca leaf industry. This was as close as anyone ever got on a regular basis to the place where the ether was.

On March 9 the Colombian judicial police issued orders for the assault: "Based on information from the anti-narcotics command, it has been learned that in the jurisdication of the eastern *llanos* there is a laboratory." On March 10, at six A.M., the team gathered at the military airport in Bogotá and took off.

Now it was well past noon, and the helicopters were almost out of fuel. Pettingill was in the Twin Otter, trailing behind at high altitude out of gunfire range. The choppers were down near the treetops.

The airstrip, when they spotted it, was covered with junk—oil drums, tree trunks, and the like. Pettingill could see puffs of smoke coming from the trees. The helicopter pilots confirmed sniper fire, but it dissipated quickly. Still, the raid was a surprise. Ramirez and Phelps, listening to the radio in Ramirez's Bogotá office, remarked on it simultaneously.

The choppers swept around the airstrip in tight circles, found landing zones, swooped low, and touched down. Flak-jacketed GOES men, carrying Israeli Uzi submachine guns, fanned out to secure a perimeter. They waited for the shooting to start, but there was silence. They took a look around.

There was a lot to see. First, there were people, about forty-five of them, mostly men of disparate ages, with a smattering of women. They were all badly dressed and unarmed. Some tried to run into the jungle, but most milled about or stood quietly, waiting to see what would happen. The police gathered them in a bunch, patted them down, and started asking for ID. The people wouldn't talk much, but they didn't have to. Five words out of their mouths branded the majority as Antioqueños, the kind of sullen north Medellín street people the cartel hired by the dozen to do scut work, everything from message carrying to contract murder. These were the *lavaperros,* "dog washers" in Colombian slang.

The GOES members put the prisoners to work clearing the runway, and soon the Twin Otter landed. The choppers fueled up from the bladder tanks and got back into the air to fly reconnaissance. If the snipers were thinking about coming back, the police wanted to know about it.

The airstrip was bulldozed from the jungle on a north-south axis. On the west side there were ten large sheds with raised wooden floors and zinc roofs covered in plastic. Some of the sheds had clapboard sides, and some were open. At least three looked like offices of some sort; a third was a dormitory with berths for one hundred people.

There were sixteen more sheds beyond the north end of the runway, at least one of which, the police could see easily, was a modern, fully equipped cocaine laboratory. On the eastern edge of the strip were four small airplanes. There was a helicopter near the lab.

Pettingill was sweating in the humid afternoon and filming for all he was worth. His arms and neck were bitten constantly by tiny gnats and mosquitoes; he was thankful he had worn a long-sleeved shirt, and he rolled down his sleeves.

As the police picked their way through the encampment, elation began to build. This was no stash area. This was something else, much more than a "major lab." This was a fully integrated cocaine factory that employed one hundred people, fed them and clothed them. There were generators, showers, washing machines and dryers, bulldozers, four-wheel drive vehicles, pumps, and other machinery. Pigs, turkeys, and chickens foraged in a garbage dump behind the sheds.

At the edge of the jungle the police picked up some discarded khaki uniforms and some automatic rifles. In one of the sheds they found more uniforms and bolts of cloth to make others. There were also more weapons: handguns, rifles, and shotguns. Obviously the snipers were security guards of some kind, perhaps even guerrillas.

Back at the landing site, the police began to get an idea of how big the laboratory operation had to be. They counted 305 drums of acetone at the site, 363 drums of ether, 482 jugs of red gasoline, and 133 jugs of aviation fuel. It was an enormous inventory for an enormous enterprise.

The police soon saw why. A discarded logbook showed the airport had received 15.539 metric tons of cocaine paste and base between December 15, 1983, and February 2, 1984. It was unbelievable, Pettingill thought. They had found a grandfather lab.

Finally there was the cocaine. Pettingill filmed it in the sheds at the north end next to the lab. There were about one hundred big plastic garbage cans full of semi-liquid, mushy cocaine hydrochloride with the ether evaporating out of it in a sickly-sweet-smelling cloud.

Gilibert got on the radio to tell Bogotá what his men had found so far. He voiced his fears that the snipers might return and told Ramirez he had helicopters flying the area for security. His men would sleep on the airstrip away from the sheds.

He needed reinforcements, and quickly. He recommended Ramirez pull together a second expedition as soon as possible. He had to get the prisoners out of the camp, and he had to be able to start looking around some more. The helicopter pilots were telling him they had found other airstrips, but he couldn't explore without some backup. He suspected there were other complexes to go with the airstrips, and some of the prisoners had all but confirmed it. By the way, he told Ramirez, the camp they were investigating now was called Tranquilandia—"Quiet Village."

THE next day in Bogotá an automobile stopped outside the cozy row house of Francisco Ramirez, Jaime Ramirez's younger brother and closest friend. It was nine A.M., March 11. Four men emerged from the car, rang the doorbell, and waited. Francisco, himself a former cop, met the four in the street. They were polite, soft-spoken. They had a message for his brother:

"Tell him there's $400,000 for him if he stops what he's doing and forgets about it," one of the men said. "We will put the money in Panama, in the United States, wherever your brother wants it."

"I'll speak to him."

"Tell him the message is from Los Pablos."

Francisco called Jaime immediately and told him what his visitors had said. "What's going on?" he asked.

"Don't mess with this," Jaime said. "Even better, get lost for a while. This is very dangerous. Tell them that I don't know what they're talking about."

The next day the four returned. Francisco followed orders, but the spokesman was quietly insistent: "Of course, we understand. Just tell him again about the $400,000."

But Francisco couldn't reach Jaime. The next day he saw why. His brother, two companies of counterinsurgency soldiers, and what looked like half the Colombian press corps were on national television examining the biggest load of cocaine any of them had ever seen in his life.

RAMIREZ arrived at Tranquilandia with the relief column on March 12 and took command. He sent the prisoners out on what was to become a daily air shuttle service to Bogotá. Then he talked to Gilibert, who told him about another airstrip about sixteen miles to the north. Before dawn the next morning Ramirez scrambled helicopters to the new site.

The workers there had simply dropped their work and fled, leaving behind plastic bags, tape, paper, test tubes, pipettes, thermometers, heaters, presses, and bags of lye. They also left behind a ton of cocaine dumped in fifty huge ceramic jugs.

In all there were twenty sheds at the new site. Like Tranquilandia, the complex had laundry machines, kitchen appliances, generators, cots, mattresses, electric pumps, food, and bedding. There was also earth-moving equipment, boats, chain saws, and a milling machine.

The complex was called Villa Coca 84 or Cocalandia, the police weren't sure which. The task force explored further, found a path, and followed it to yet another lab site. This they immediately dubbed Cocalandia 2. It was well stocked with drums of ether and acetone, but there was no cocaine.

Not believing this, the police retraced their steps to the Villa Coca airstrip and hunted around. There it was, partially hidden in the brush: 140 pails full of cocaine, another five hundred kilograms in all. They took the cocaine and put it in the sheds with the mattresses, the chain saws, and the machinery. Unlike the traffickers, the police didn't have the resources to move anything except themselves. They torched the whole mess and burned it to the ground.

Pettingill reluctantly flew back to Bogotá on the first shuttle to report to Tambs and the DEA but returned to Tranquilandia in time to film the March 14 seizure of Tranquilandia 2 just across the Rio Mesay from the first site. Here the police found four metric tons of cocaine packed in fifty-five-gallon drums, the biggest single cache of the drug ever seized up to that time. The police burned all of it.

Everyone was ecstatic. "Incredible," Pettingill told his office. "We're knocking off a lab every day."

And so they were. On March 15 the police destroyed El Diamante, half a ton of cocaine, six sheds, and a dormitory. On March 16 they found Tranquilandia 3, Palmeras, and an unnamed site without labs but with an airfield, a ramp for launching boats, and a pair of small cocaine testing facilities. This, they determined, was where deals were closed. On March 17 they hit Pascualandia, took one airplane as the spoils of war, and burned another one.

It was also March 17 when the soldiers found the base camp of what they believed to be a detachment of guerrillas belonging to the Revolutionary Armed Forces of Colombia—the FARC. Like the cocaine complexes, the camp had a dormitory, kitchen, and communications center. The soldiers confiscated an assortment of automatic weapons, including several machine pistols (Israeli Uzis and MAC-10s). They also found a base plate for a mortar and a few semiautomatic rifles. There were piles of Leninist tracts and other guerrilla documents and manuals, bolts of blue and green uniform cloth, sew-on triangles of yellow fabric bearing the FARC insignia, and military badges and the rest of the accoutrements of a full-scale tailor shop, including sewing machines.

Like the police a few days earlier, the soldiers concluded that the guerrillas were supposed to be handling base security for the traffickers, a task they had apparently performed without distinction, disappearing into the jungle as soon as the police arrived. It appeared that the army's (and Ambassador Tambs's) long-held suspicions about a "FARC-narc" connection were true.

In all, the police and soldiers in a little more than a fortnight sent 13.8 metric tons of cocaine up in smoke, along with fourteen labs and encampments, seven airplanes, and 11,800 drums of ether, acetone, and other chemicals. In an interview Johnny Phelps called it a "cocaine industrial park" and the "Silicon Valley of cocaine." Tambs flew to Washington to brief the State Department and tell reporters that Ramirez and his men had set "a world record in terms of the money, the product, and the amounts seized." Colombian authorities estimated the jungle labs were likely to have put $12 billion in the coffers of the Medellín cartel in two years. What the police destroyed was conservatively estimated to be worth $1.2 billion.

For Phelps and Ramirez, the mere fact of Tranquilandia had enormous implications. The raid clearly demonstrated that the cartel no longer put together its gigantic cocaine shipments by pooling the output of dozens—or hundreds—of tiny, ill-equipped backyard labs. Phelps had never seen labs like those at Tranquilandia, and nobody in Colombian law enforcement, as far as he knew, had even suspected such labs existed. Tranquilandia explained the 1982 Miami bust of TAMPA Airlines. There, law enforcement found that the traffickers were moving cocaine to the United States in enormous lots. In 1984 at Tranquilandia, law enforcement found out where it was coming from.

For Ramirez Tranquilandia nevertheless remained something of a mystery. The DEA didn't tell him about the transponders in the ether barrels, and he continued to wonder how Phelps had found the dope. Either he had a terrific informant—the thought made Ramirez jealous —or he had access to some sort of satellite "eye in the sky" that could spot cocaine labs through the jungle canopy.

Tranquilandia posed a challenge neither Phelps nor Ramirez could ignore. If there was one "Silicon Valley of cocaine," then there were probably others. It would be Ramirez's job to work out a method of finding the labs and seizing them. It would be Phelps's job to ensure that Ramirez got the equipment he needed.

Resources would be relatively easy to obtain, at least in the short run. Phelps could—and did—use the success of Tranquilandia to pry funds out of the U.S. government. Tranquilandia was the sort of coup that could suddenly make everything easy: "See, sometimes your tax dollars are being put to good use."

As for Ramirez, before Tranquilandia he was one of several rising stars in the upper ranks of the Colombian National Police. Now he was the nation's top cop, responsible for the most spectacular drug bust in world history. His career was made.

Ramirez understood this and took it as his due, for he was not a modest man. He loved the spotlight, and he fully expected to be Colombia's chief of police one day. At the same time, however, Ramirez had no intention of resting on his laurels. He was a hunter before anything else, and one success simply made him hungry for others. His men had kicked the drug traffickers in the face. Now it was time to stomp them.

The army, for its part, did its best to expand on the narco-guerrilla evidence uncovered at Tranquilandia. It circulated excerpts from what purported to be the final document of the FARC's Sixth Conference in May 1982. The document detailed plans for the guerrillas to collect a *gramaje,* or per-gram tax, of 80 pesos (75 cents) from traffickers processing cocaine in guerrilla-held or -influenced areas. Caquetá, the jungle province where Tranquilandia was located, had been a FARC stronghold for years. Where possible, the document said, the guerrillas should concentrate "on the big traffickers, seizing the merchandise [for ourselves] or demanding large sums—but taking care that the movement does not appear to be implicated."

Like the army, Ambassador Tambs sounded the theme of "narco-guerrillas" constantly to the considerable irritation of Belisario Betancur, who still hoped to woo the FARC to his Peace Process. Betancur wasn't convinced of guerrilla involvement with the traffickers. He thought the evidence too thin to put the Peace Process at risk.

Colombia still wasn't ready for narco-guerrillas, and the army's cause was not helped either by Tambs's loud voice or by its own proselytism. The most revealing comment on the matter, oddly, came from FARC second-in-command Jacobo Arenas, who responded to a reporter's question two months after Tranquilandia: "I don't think you can generalize. It could happen that once in a while some of our people may have received money—freely offered—from people we might describe as narcotics trafficking people. We have said that if we find a wallet filled with money lying in the street, we'll pick it up because it's there.''

Phelps and Ramirez had only a passing interest in narco-guerrillas. They were more interested in evaluating the information they had obtained. The presence of so many Antioqueños at Tranquilandia—two of whom turned out to have rap sheets—said something about the involvement of the Medellín cartel. Efforts by Los Pablos to get Ramirez to lay off spoke volumes more about Pablo Escobar's role.

The Ochoas' presence had been established when the plane with the bugged ether refueled at Hacienda Veracruz. And at Tranquilandia, account books listed four Medellín telephone numbers for Fabio Ochoa and recorded his acknowledgment of having purchased seven hundred kilos of cocaine base from Roberto Suarez, Bolivia's cocaine czar.

But the major revelation from Tranquilandia was that Bogotá cocaine boss Jose Gonzalo Rodriguez Gacha had had a huge investment in the jungle. Rodriguez Gacha, now thirty-six, had been regarded as a second-level trafficker. He came from the town of Pacho, north of Bogotá, and had gotten his start as a specialist in the transport of coca leaf from Peru and Bolivia. He was short, squat—five feet five, 175 pounds—and somewhat eccentric. He loved Mexico and things Mexican, especially mariachi music, and named his *fincas* after Mexican cities. For this he was generally known as El Mejicano. Others called him "Big Hat" because he always seemed to be wearing a straw fedora. He was also believed to be deeply interested in the possibility that Colombia, despite an adverse climate, might in the future grow its own coca leaf. He was believed to be experimenting with large coca nurseries in Guaviare.

Although Johnny Phelps had had Rodriguez Gacha on his "ten biggest" list in 1981, neither the DEA nor the Anti-Narcotics Unit had ever regarded Rodriguez Gacha as anything more than Pablo Escobar's man in Bogotá—perhaps a member of Los Pablos, but certainly a subordinate.

Tranquilandia suggested something different. The first hint that "the Mexican" was active in the *llanos* came from a wrecked plane found on one of the jungle airstrips. Civil aviation authorities listed the owner of record as Justo Pastor Rodriguez Gacha, Gonzalo's brother. The plane had lost its license because of an accident in September 1983.

Next came a letter to the Anti-Narcotics Unit from the police chief in Leticia, the Amazon river town where the cartel brokered Peruvian coca leaf. The word there, the chief said, was that Rodriguez Gacha got murdered financially at Tranquilandia. His sources had told him that Rodriguez Gacha had been flying paste and base to the Yari River area from Peru since the middle of December 1983, and had had a huge sum of money tied up in his *llano* labs. Besides his brother's wreck, the chief added, the narcotics police at Yari had seized at least one other of Rodriguez Gacha's planes. Finally, although "the Mexican"—or Don Andres, as he was known along the Amazon—had once lived in Leticia and was still well-known there, he had not been seen in town since last October.

This meant that Rodriguez Gacha was probably a much bigger player than law enforcement had at first believed, the big loser in the biggest cocaine operation law enforcement had ever seen. From that moment law enforcement stopped thinking of Rodriguez Gacha as a member of Los Pablos and began to think of him as a partner in the Medellín cartel.

BEFORE the Tranquilandia raid, the per-kilogram wholesale price of cocaine in Miami was $14,000. Immediately after the raid it started to rise, an indication of scarcity for the first time in three years. Law enforcement took heart. The *llanos* raid, the biggest cocaine bust in history, had damaged the cartel. But how serious was it? And what was the cartel going to do about it?

14.

THE WHITE MERCEDES

Justice Minister Lara Bonilla's nerves were wearing thin. Phelps could tell whenever he went for a visit. The cartel had terrified the family of Rodrigo Lara Bonilla long ago; now the strain was beginning to prey on the minister himself.

Lara Bonilla had begun his tenure as a reluctant crusader, prodded into action after Pablo Escobar tried to smear him in the 1983 hot money controversy. The strategy had backfired, mostly because of Lara Bonilla's uncommon courage. Since the hot money affair, the cartel—its immense wealth, its ostentation, its violent history, its bribes, and its corruption—had become a daily scandal served up by the justice minister and presented in grotesque detail by the nation's newspapers and broadcasters.

The results of this had been truly extraordinary. Carlos Lehder had gone into hiding, an order for his extradition signed by Lara Bonilla and lying in the in basket on President Belisario Betancur's desk. More than three hundred small airplanes had had their licenses revoked by Lara Bonilla, including most of the Ochoa family's Pilotos Ejecutivos fleet. Now the Justice Department was investigating the Ochoas' ownership of Hacienda Veracruz, where a plane loaded with ether had stopped to refuel on its way to the cartel's jungle lab complex at Tranquilandia.

And Lara Bonilla didn't stop there. In early 1984, working with information supplied by Colonel Jaime Ramirez and the Anti-Narcotics Unit police, he had denounced thirty politicians for taking hot money in municipal elections. He had continued to seize airplanes and denounce cartel involvement in Colombia's professional soccer league. On April 6, 1984, shortly after the Tranquilandia raid, he an-

nounced that Colombia would begin trial spraying of north coast marijuana fields with the herbicide glyphosate, raising the possibility that
eight years of furious U.S. diplomacy might finally bear fruit.

It was Pablo Escobar who had suffered most at Lara Bonilla's
hands. Driven out of Congress by Lara Bonilla's denunciations and
forced to endure a string of humiliating revelations about his notorious
past and criminal present, Escobar by the end of 1983 had lost whatever pretentions he may have had for a career as a public servant.

But he did not go quietly. Nor did he really go at all. As long as
police were chasing him and Congress was debating whether to re-
voke his parliamentary immunity, Escobar kept a fairly low profile.
But whenever the heat moderated, he was back on the offensive. On
February 13, 1984, the courts withdrew an arrest warrant against him,
and he immediately announced that unless the government abrogated
the extradition treaty with the United States, he and Lehder would
close down 1,500 businesses and put more than twenty thousand people out of work. On March 2 he held his first political rally in more
than six months, denouncing Lara Bonilla as a shill of U.S. imperialism and criticizing the Medellín municipal government for turning off
the lights in his soccer stadiums.

And on March 26, with the cartel reeling from the Tranquilandia
raid, he wrote an "open letter" to U.S. Ambassador Lewis Tambs,
denying any involvement in the jungle labs: "I can only characterize
your statements as tendentious, irresponsible and malintentioned
without any basis in reality; they denigrate the good faith of public
opinion. My conscience is clear."

The letter denounced extradition and labeled "pernicious" Tambs's
contention that Escobar and the rest of the cartel had hired FARC
guerrillas to guard the Tranquilandia installations. Finally, he described Lara Bonilla as "the representative of your government in the
Colombian cabinet."

It was this last remark and others like it that weighed heaviest with
Johnny Phelps. He had the utmost respect and admiration for Lara
Bonilla, but his resentment and contempt for the Colombian government was growing almost daily. During the hot money controversy
and in all the months following it, President Betancur had made few
public statements regarding drug trafficking and had done little to
indicate that Lara Bonilla's policies were his own. He had taken no
action on extradition and seemed to plan none. Now he was sitting by
while the biggest cocaine trafficker in the world—a known killer and
career criminal—was insulting his justice minister.

Phelps was a cop. He accepted risks; it was part of the job. But Phelps was worried about Lara Bonilla. The justice minister was in way over his head, and his boss was ignoring him.

Meanwhile, in Medellín, it was obvious that no matter what was happening to Escobar, the Ochoas, or any other individual trafficker, the cartel still reigned supreme. Errol Chavez had left the city in August 1983, posted to Houston. Before he left he had told his replacement, Mike Vigil, that things were bad in Medellín and getting worse. Vigil had no reason to doubt it. Gunshots echoed through the city so often that no one remarked on it anymore. Perhaps once a week on his way to work Vigil would spot a corpse lying on the edge of the road. No one stopped to stare.

The Medellín police were terrified of trafficker vengeance and would hardly leave their headquarters buildings, let alone make an arrest. After *El Espectador* printed the details of Pablo Escobar's 1976 cocaine arrest, Vigil went down to DAS headquarters to get the police photo file so he could make some mug-shot copies for his own records. The negatives had been stolen and substituted. Vigil's secretary, hired by Chavez after immense bureaucratic wire-pulling, was so scared that she sat in the DEA office with her shoes off "so I can feel the people walking in the corridor." She quit shortly.

Security—guarding people and guarding property—was a huge industry in Medellín, but it was difficult at times to tell whose side the guards were on. Vigil, unwinding at an open-air Envigado cafe one afternoon, got interested in a good-looking woman who said she worked as a secretary for a local security agency—"You know, bodyguards, chauffeurs, armed guards, and that stuff."

A couple of drinks later she confided that her bosses would also murder people for a fee, "you know, hits for hire." Anything complicated—a policeman, a public official, a judge, a politician—had to be negotiated. The low end of the line—a quicky job on a nonentity—was simplicity itself: "We start at $250, you know—cash."

IT was in August 1983 that Colombian F-2 police intelligence agents discovered the first plot against Lara Bonilla. It was a simple assassination organized from Medellín. In those days Lara Bonilla was giving daily bravura performances in Congress and had little real appreciation of who was after him or the resources they could bring to bear: "I am a dangerous minister for those who act outside the law," he said in an August news release. "I only hope they don't catch me by surprise."

Tambs and Phelps, under no illusions, went to visit Lara Bonilla after the plot was discovered. Tambs in particular was emphatic: "You should be more concerned, you should take more precautions." He offered to give Lara Bonilla his own bulletproof vest. Lara Bonilla thanked both men but minimized the problem.

In the corridor with Phelps, Tambs was more insistent: "Here, take the vest and see that he gets it." Phelps gave Lara Bonilla the vest, but he couldn't make him wear it.

The next time Phelps went to the ministry with Tambs, it was to tell Lara Bonilla that the DEA had found that people in Lara Bonilla's own office were passing information to the drug traffickers. Again Lara Bonilla either dismissed the threat or didn't understand it. Phelps told Tambs, "He's not ready to believe what we say."

Tambs tried more often. As time passed he and Lara Bonilla grew very close, partly because they always had business together, but mostly because they both loved to talk. Lara Bonilla was a politician and a left-winger, with little use for the United States' "big stick" policy in Central America. Tambs was an academic and a sharp-tongued Reagan conservative who helped design Central American policy. They were natural foes, but each had an excellent sense of humor and a natural inclination to spend hours discussing what Tambs described as "life's eternal verities."

It was during one of these sessions in February 1984 that one of Lara Bonilla's aides interrupted him to tell him about the whistling sound in his telephone receiver and the difficulty he had making himself heard. The telephones were tapped. And not just here in the office, said the aide, but also at his home. Lara Bonilla was appalled: "How could they!"

Finally, Tambs thought, he's gotten the message.

SOMETIME soon after the Tranquilandia raid—even years later it would not be clear exactly when—a "group of drug traffickers" gathered in a "bunker" in Medellín, according to a secret DAS memo, to pool resources and plan the assassination of Rodrigo Lara Bonilla. One police informant reported that representatives of the cartel had met at a Medellín soda fountain called Cositas Ricas ("Tasty Little Things") to work out the details. The whole job, front money and fees for everyone, would be done for fifty million pesos ($521,000). A DEA informant would tell agents years later that he had heard Pablo Escobar personally order the killing.

The contract was picked up by Los Quesitos, one of several Medellín murder gangs closely identified with and possibly sponsored by the cartel. Los Quesitos sent three field commanders to handle the Bogotá end: John Jairo Arias Tascón, an ex-con with a full rap sheet; Rubén Dario Londoño, alias "Juan Pérez," a young hoodlum standing for election as a Pablo Escobar–sponsored Medellín city councilman; and Luis A. Cataño, who purchased a green Renault, filled it with guns, grenades, bulletproof vests, and the like, and drove it from Medellín to Bogotá.

These three set up in the four-star Nueva Granada and Bacatá hotels in downtown Bogotá. They met several times for meals in La Fonda Antioqueña, where they could sample home cooking and put the final touches on the plan. With them at this time was German Alfonso Diaz Quintana, known as El Ronco ("the Croaker"), a first-rank Medellín hitman assigned as the backup killer in case the initial plot failed.

The chosen killer was Iván Dario Guizado, thirty-one, "Carlos Mario," a strung-out drifter with fifteen prior arrests for murder, robbery, and assault dating back to 1969. The driver would be a kid, Byron Velasquez Arenas, one of Pablo Escobar's gofers.

The team sat in Bogotá and waited, speaking Antioqueño dialect, eating in Antioqueño restaurants, and making toll calls to Medellín from their hotels. Londoño called his mother half a dozen times. Others called Cataño's house in La Estrella, a Medellín suburb. Cataño had left his car in Bogotá and gone home. Other numbers were linked to offices and political allies of Escobar's sisters, Alba Marina Escobar and Maria Victoria Escobar de Henao. DAS would say later that the plotters several times called another Escobar sister, Ludmila, directly.

AT ten A.M., April 30, 1984, Tambs received a telephone call from an excited Rodrigo Lara Bonilla. He had now been complaining for some weeks about the threats against him and had been getting progressively more nervous and worried about his family. Finally he had terrific news. The Foreign Ministry was going to get him out of the country, send him to Prague as Colombia's ambassador to Czechoslovakia—deep inside the Communist bloc.

"You'll be safe there." Tambs laughed. "All the terrorists are in the government."

Unfortunately, Lara Bonilla said, clearance from Czechoslovakia was going to take thirty days, and he and his family needed a place in which to hole up for that time. Could Tambs help him?

Tambs could. He called the White House and asked staffers to fix something up. Soon he had confirmation: a hideout in Texas had been found.

With this piece of news in hand, Tambs left his office for a lunchtime reception at the Dutch embassy. He left word with an assistant to tell Lara Bonilla about the Texas arrangement, then he drove to the airport to say good-bye to a departing U.S. Congressional delegation.

AT seven P.M. on April 30, Byron Velasquez and "Carlos Mario" headed into traffic to look for a white Mercedes-Benz limousine. Lara Bonilla always sat in the backseat on the right side. They drove to a residence in the fashionable neighborhood of north Bogotá, to an address they had learned that afternoon when they'd met Cataño's green Renault to pick up the grenades and the MAC-10. Their contact, who called himself John Jairo Franco, had told them people "were talking" about them in Medellín. Translation: Find the target and get it done.

It was just dusk when they spotted the Mercedes. Traffic was fairly heavy, but Velasquez and Carlos Mario were riding a new Yamaha motorcycle and had no difficulty weaving in and out of traffic. Velasquez kicked the throttle and swooped down on the limousine, tucking in easily just behind of the right rear fender. He eased off until the bike held position so that the two vehicles seemed frozen in space while the rest of the world *whoosh*ed by.

They had a nice angle and all the time they needed. Carlos Mario removed the MAC-10 from his jacket, pointed it at the shadow in the backseat of the Mercedes, and pulled the trigger. He emptied the magazine in about two seconds.

Rodrigo Lara Bonilla was pronounced dead at Shaio Clinic at 7:40 P.M., April 30, 1984. He'd taken three .45-caliber slugs in the head, two in the chest, one in the neck, and one in the arm. Lewis Tambs's bulletproof vest was loose in the backseat, tossed there haphazardly. It wouldn't have helped.

After the attack, Lara Bonilla's escort limousine chased down the Yamaha. A bodyguard's lucky shot hit the gas tank, setting the bike on fire and spinning out of control until it crashed into a curb. Byron Arenas Velasquez, shot in the arm and stunned, was arrested. Iván Dario Guizado, "Carlos Mario," was dead in the street, his head practically blown off by bullets from a body guard's machine gun.

· · ·

BELISARIO Betancur and the Colombian cabinet visited the clinic shortly after the shooting, then retired to the Nariño Presidential Palace. The ministers were appalled and disgusted. Betancur was serious, very careful in what he said, very severe. Shortly after midnight he issued a statement proclaiming a state of siege in Colombia and promising to "rescue the national dignity." Then he returned to the conference room, where he remained with the cabinet until three A.M. At one point he polled the ministers on their opinions regarding what else might be done, then announced peremptorily: "We will extradite Colombians."

Lara Bonilla's body, in a closed coffin, lay in state in the Rotunda of the Capitol Building while thousands of Colombians paid their last respects. In the morning, under a bright sky, a military honor guard escorted the coffin across the Plaza Bolivar to the National Cathedral. The plaza was mobbed with people—rich, poor, middle class—crying and chanting in a collective bellow of rage and anguish: "We love you, Rodrigo!" "¡Venganza, justicia!"

Tambs stood inside the cathedral in a roped-off section reserved for diplomats. Betancur arrived along with his cabinet. Most of the Congress was on hand, as were the leading officers of Colombia's armed forces. The memorial service was short but emotional. Outside, the crowd continued restive and outraged. Inside, Betancur stood stone-faced, but the tension had drawn sharp vertical lines in his features.

After the service Tambs walked outside to his limousine. People in the street recognized him, waved at him to get his attention: "¡Viva los Estados Unidos!"—"Long live the United States!" It was not often that he heard that.

Lara Bonilla's body was flown to his home city of Neiva for funeral and burial. It fell to Betancur to deliver the eulogy. He spoke shortly after four P.M. It was not a conciliatory moment, and Betancur was not in a conciliatory mood:

"We have reached a point where we must reflect on what is our nation, what does the word 'citizen' mean?" he said. "Stop, enemies of humanity! Colombia will hand over criminals wanted in other countries so they may be punished as an example." The crowd rose and began to applaud.

Six days later, on May 8, 1984, Betancur signed the extradition order for Carlos Lehder.

Al Líder Máximo del Movimiento Cívico Latino Nacional

CARLOS LEDHER RIVAS

--- Ofrece la Juventud y el Pueblo Bogotano —
INVITADOS: Luis Fernando Mejía - Jairo Herrán Vargas,
Orlando Herrán Vargas.
ORGANIZACION OMAR SIERRA - JULIO CALERO

CON MONUMENTAL PROGRAMA, CONCURSO DE CABALLOS
DE PASO - RIÑAS DE GALLOS - MURGAS - CONJUNTOS
BANDAS PAPAYERAS - MODELOS - MANOLAS - DANZAS Y
ATRACCIONES ESPECIALES - CASETAS DE BAILE

6 Toros serán lidiados 6

POR LOS NOVILLEROS

FERMIN RODRIGUEZ
(Triunfador de Varias Tardes)

GABRIEL ORTEGA
(DEL TOLIMA)

RODRIGO ANDRADE
(EL PILI DEL HUILA)

HENRY GARCIA
(NUEVO EN ESTA PLAZA)

ORLANDO CASTAÑEDA
(ARTE Y CLASE)

EDGAR MENDOZA
(EL BUNDE)

RISAS CON ALEGRE CUADRILLA COMICA

DIRECTOR DE LIDIA - EL FAMOSO NOVILLERO

FERNANDO MOJICA

SALIDA de la GRAN CARABANA de BUSES
9 A. M. AV. CARACAS - CALLE 26 - INVITADO DE HONOR UD.

In September 1983, Carlos Lehder made a pilgrimage to Bogotá to give his National Latin Movement a countrywide send-off. Highlight of the excursion was a Lehder-sponsored bullfight and fair in the town of Guatavita, twenty-five miles outside of Bogotá.

Left: Colombian President Belisario Betancur in 1983. He came to office "philosophi-cally opposed" to the extradition of drug traffickers to the United States. He left office as extradition's staunchest advocate, a bitter enemy of the Medellín cartel. *Right:* Lewis Tambs. This Arizona State University professor of Latin American history arrived in Bogotá in 1983 as U.S. ambassador to Colombia. His instructions: "Do something about drug trafficking." *(THE MIAMI HERALD)*

Colonel Jaime Ramirez Gomez, chief of the Colombian National Police Anti-Narcotics Unit, briefs reporters on the discovery of Tranquilandia, a gigantic cocaine laboratory complex in Colombia's eastern jungle. *(EL TIEMPO)*

Two photos of a Colombian cocaine lab bust.

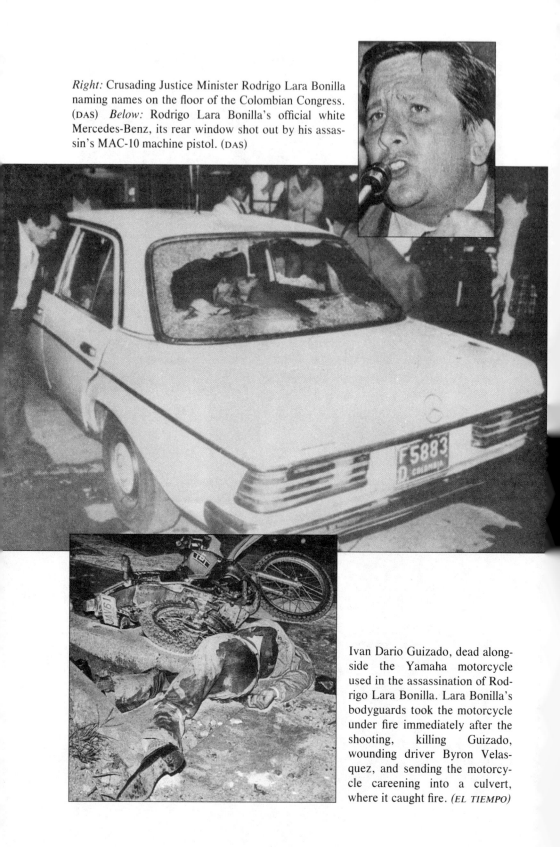

Right: Crusading Justice Minister Rodrigo Lara Bonilla naming names on the floor of the Colombian Congress. (DAS) *Below:* Rodrigo Lara Bonilla's official white Mercedes-Benz, its rear window shot out by his assassin's MAC-10 machine pistol. (DAS)

Ivan Dario Guizado, dead alongside the Yamaha motorcycle used in the assassination of Rodrigo Lara Bonilla. Lara Bonilla's bodyguards took the motorcycle under fire immediately after the shooting, killing Guizado, wounding driver Byron Velasquez, and sending the motorcycle careening into a culvert, where it caught fire. *(EL TIEMPO)*

Agents of the Colombian Department of Administrative Security bring Ochoa family patriarch "Don Fabio" Ochoa Restrepo in for questioning during the crackdown following the murder of Rodrigo Lara Bonilla. *(EL ESPECTADOR)*

Barry Seal (right) and Carlos "Lito" Bustamante plotting a 1,500-kilo cocaine shipment in Miami. Worried about wiretaps, Seal carries a bag of quarters for easy telephone use to discuss business. (DEA)

Barry Seal and co-pilot Emil Camp crashed their Lockheed Lodestar in the Colombian jungle during their first try at flying 1,500 kilos of cocaine for the Ochoas. (DEA)

U.S. government photo taken by hidden CIA camera shows Barry Seal (right) and Pablo Escobar (striped shirt) supervising the loading of cocaine at Los Brasiles airstrip outside Managua, Nicaragua.

Barry Seal gives an interview about his life as a DEA informant to WBRZ-TV in Baton Rouge, Louisiana, in 1984. The documentary, *Uncle Sam Wants You,* outraged both federal officials and the leaders of Medellín cartel. (JOHN CAMP, WBRZ)

On the morning of November 6, 1985, armed guerrillas belonging to Colombia's M-19 guerrilla movement stormed Bogotá's Palace of Justice and took several hundred hostages, among them most of the members of the Colombian Supreme Court. Within hours the Colombian army and national police had the palace under siege with tanks and special attack troops. When the takeover ended a bit over a day later, nearly one hundred people were dead and the building was gutted by fire. *(EL TIEMPO)*

Supreme Court Justice Hernando Baquero Borda, ambushed and murdered by Medellín cartel killers as he drove to work, July 31, 1986. (DEA)

Jorge Ochoa aboard a Colombian C-130 on his way to Bogotá after his capture at a tollbooth outside Cali, Colombia, November 1987. *(EL TIEMPO)*

15.

BARRY SEAL

A month after the fall of Tranquilandia, a pilot known as Ellis Mac-
Kenzie approached the coast of Colombia in a twin-engine Cessna
Titan 404 that had been purchased in Miami for Jorge Ochoa. Mac-
Kenzie rode as co-pilot; a Honduran friend of the Ochoa family pi-
loted the plane. Both men were very tired. They'd left at two A.M.
from South Caicos, an island south of the Bahamas, hoping the early
hour would help them avoid the Colombian air force. Now, near
dawn, they found that the radio beacons along the Colombian coast
had been turned to low power, and they were having a tough time
navigating in heavy fog. Finally they spotted the skyline of Cartagena,
and the plane banked left, crossing the coast several miles east of the
city.

"We'll be going right over Jorge Ochoa's ranch and farm," said the
Honduran, a Vietnam veteran and former commercial airline pilot
named Felix Dixon Bates. "Would you like to see it?"

"Certainly," MacKenzie said.

The Titan circled Hacienda Veracruz, and the two pilots waved to
somebody on the ground. MacKenzie admired the ranch's paved
5,400-foot airstrip as only a good drug pilot could. But the plane didn't
land, continuing instead south along the Rio Magdalena toward Medellín. The Titan finally set down on a five-thousand-foot grassy jungle
airstrip north of the city. As soon as the plane cut its engines, workers
on ladders painted over its U.S. registration number. The new number
would be Colombian, the number of another Titan owned by the
Ochoas that had just been confiscated with cocaine in the Bahamas.
That way, if the Colombian government asked about the seized plane,
the Ochoas could show them the new Titan and claim the other one
must be an imposter.

MacKenzie studied the airstrip cut into the moist, dense vegetation. Rain would make it muddy and dangerous. Large pools of standing water from a recent downpour still spotted the runway. A small plane sat refueling nearby while a tractor towed duffel bags of cocaine out of the jungle. The pilot of the refueling plane told MacKenzie that he was headed to Andros Island in the Bahamas with three hundred kilos.

MacKenzie and Bates transferred to another small plane and flew to a complex of hangars on the outskirts of Medellín. This was Jorge Ochoa's aircraft base, Bates explained, where he kept his private helicopter and jet. A driver picked them up and took them south into the mountains about a mile past the Hotel Intercontinental to a large estate with a winding driveway. This was La Loma, home of the Ochoas.

They were ushered into a sitting room and welcomed by Jorge Ochoa, Fabio Ochoa, Juan David Ochoa, Pablo Correa Arroyave, and Pablo Escobar. Jorge Ochoa presided. MacKenzie did not speak Spanish, so Bates translated for him. Ochoa politely exchanged pleasantries with MacKenzie and acknowledged that they had spoken previously by telephone.

"Yes," MacKenzie said. "I am very glad to meet you after all this time."

MacKenzie was a man on a mission. Actually he had two missions, but the Colombians would have killed him on the spot if they had known about the second one. Ellis MacKenzie was not the pilot's real name. He was Adler Berriman Seal, and he was an informant for the U.S. Drug Enforcement Administration. Born and raised in Baton Rouge, Louisiana, Barry Seal was quite larger than life. He weighed about three hundred pounds, sported big muttonchop sideburns, and had the attitude that Barry Seal was smarter than just about anyone around. Despite his girth, he was something of a ladies' man. He did not smoke or drink. Women and flying were his passions. Most people who knew him and knew anything about flying said he was the best pilot they had ever seen. He didn't fly an airplane, he wore it like a suit of clothes. When he was just twenty-six, he became one of the youngest pilots in the history of Trans-World Airlines.

But Seal got bored with commercial airline flying. He had done a stint in the U.S. Army Special Forces in the pre-Vietnam 1960s, and he'd been flying since he was fifteen. "Full of fun, full of folly," his high school yearbook had said. A born leader who could charm paint off a barn, Seal needed excitement, something more than just putting in his time during the week so he could drift off to the suburbs and follow the LSU Tiger football games. He found the thrill he needed in smuggling. In 1972, when he was thirty-two, Seal got arrested for the first time by Customs in New Orleans in a conspiracy to fly seven tons of plastic explosives to anti-Castro Cubans in Mexico. The arms buyer turned out to be an undercover agent. Although the judge threw out the case, the publicity cost Seal his job with TWA.

Seal then became an "airline broker," a handy euphemism for which the words "all-purpose smuggler" could easily have been substituted. He started flying marijuana in 1976. He had his own group of aviation mechanics and co-pilots, and his business often took him to Central and South America, where his skills as a pilot were much appreciated.

In 1979 Honduran police caught him with an illegal handgun in his cockpit and sent him to jail for eight months. On the flight home he met William Roger Reeves, another smuggler who told him that he worked for the Ochoa family of Medellín. Seal began to fly cocaine for the Ochoas in 1981 and soon found himself dealing with the Colombians directly. One contact was a woman who sometimes dressed in a nun's habit. She was replaced by an Ochoa distributor in Miami who called himself "Lito." Lito's real name, like Seal's, was a closely guarded secret. Seal got in touch with Lito by calling one of three numbers on Lito's pocket telephone pager.

By this time Seal had become something of a smuggling genius. He studied mistakes traffickers made by reading the testimony in big federal drug conspiracy cases. He even attended the trials when he could, soaking up information like a student attending seminars. Ultimately he created a system that was nearly fail-safe. His planes always departed from and returned to his Louisiana bases at night. Like all smugglers, they flew without lights. Seal and his pilots wore third-generation night-vision goggles, which at $5,000 a pair electronically magnified the available light from the stars and moon fifty thousand times. Over Colombia, his planes flew through "windows" in Colombian airspace—precise periods when the military would look the other way—paid for with $25,000 bribes. Reentering U.S. airspace, Seal's smugglers dropped to 500 feet and slowed to 120 knots. On radar screens, they looked like helicopters coming ashore from oil rigs in the Gulf of Mexico.

Entering the United States, Seal's planes would pass over a radio checkpoint. If the man on the ground with the radio determined that the plane was being followed, the mission was aborted. If there was no trailing aircraft, Seal's planes followed radar beacons to drop sites in remote parts of the Louisiana bayou. Duffel bags full of cocaine were parachuted into the swamp. Helicopters swooped down, retrieved the bags, and ferried them to off-loading sites. The cocaine went to Ochoa distributors in Miami by automobile. In 1982 and 1983 Seal brought in more than five thousand kilos and grossed $25 million, even though every drug agent in Louisiana considered him the biggest smuggler in the state.

On stakeouts, agents watched Seal use two pay phones at a time, working from a little green canvas tote bag full of hundreds of quarters. He talked in code to Colombia and sometimes transmitted messages over the line by Hewlett-Packard computer so the agents couldn't listen in. He loved the challenge presented by law enforcement. Seal once bumped into a Louisiana State Police agent on the street in Baton Rouge and told him, "You dumb sonofabitch. You'll never catch me."

When Seal finally got caught, it was in south Florida, not Louisiana. It didn't take any sophisticated hardware, just an informant. The informant worked for Randy Beasley, DEA case agent for Operation Screamer, a mammoth sting aimed at penetrating the network of mercenary drug pilots. The informant led Beasley to a smuggler who knew a hot-shot pilot from Louisiana willing to fly Quaaludes out of South America. Beasley called the DEA in Baton Rouge.

"Hey, I got a guy, he's a pilot, he's from Baton Rouge, and they call him El Gordo," Beasley said, " 'the Fat One.' "

"We know who you've got, and if you've got him, we're going to come down and kiss you," said the agent in Baton Rouge. "We've been working him ten years, and we've never been able to get him."

Based on the informant's testimony and numerous wire-tapped telephone conversations, a federal grand jury in Fort Lauderdale indicted Seal in March 1983 for smuggling two hundred thousand Quaaludes. His name and several of his aliases made the papers in small print with seventy-five others. In fact, for some reason Seal was listed twice, as "Adler (Barry Seal, Bill Elders, Gordo) Seal" and "Adler (Bill) Seal." Either way, his cover was intact. To the Ochoas, he was Ellis MacKenzie; the names Barry or Adler Seal meant nothing to them.

Seal surrendered voluntarily and was freed on $250,000 bond, but he faced sixty-one years in prison in two separate court cases stemming from the Screamer indictment. Immediately he tried to make a deal with the government. Seal approached Beasley and offered to "flip," to turn informant and go undercover. He promised big things, more cocaine than the agents had ever seen, but he wasn't specific. He wanted to travel outside the country with very little control by

DEA. What an ego, Beasley thought. He thinks he's untouchable. Seal even had his own conditions for the government. He wanted the charges dropped against two of his men who were also caught in Screamer. He also wanted to cut the deal without telling his attorney, Richard Ben-Veniste, a former Watergate prosecutor. That made Beasley uneasy. Beasley and the Screamer prosecutor decided to turn Seal down.

Seal then tried to make a deal with the U.S. attorney in Baton Rouge, Stanford Bardwell, a high school classmate. Bardwell knew that Seal was still under investigation by a state and federal task force in Baton Rouge and New Orleans. He refused even to see Seal, explaining later that Seal's request was "too cryptic."

All during this time, Seal had managed to stay in touch with Lito and even moved three cocaine loads for the Ochoas while he was out on bond in the summer of 1983. But as his court date neared, he quit smuggling to prepare his defense, trying at the same time to keep his problems a secret from the Colombians.

This was somewhat difficult. Lito, for one, was perturbed because MacKenzie wasn't bringing in enough cocaine. He pressed MacKenzie to make another trip. Lito's brother had just smuggled three thousand kilos for the Ochoas. Why couldn't MacKenzie do that?

Seal was stunned to hear the Ochoas were bringing in so much at a time. He asked for details. Lito asked if he wanted to make such a trip himself: "Yes," Seal replied. "I'll just have to find an airplane."

Seal went to trial on the Quaalude charges in Fort Lauderdale in February 1984. Things did not go well. On February 17 he was convicted of conspiracy and possession with intent to distribute Quaaludes. He could get ten years in prison. U.S. District Judge Norman C. Roettger was known as the toughest sentencing judge in the Southern District of Florida. And Seal faced a second trial on related Screamer charges that could add forty-seven years to his prison term.

Even so, Seal continued his preparations for a three-thousand-kilo load for Lito and the Ochoas. On March 9 he bought a twin-engine Lockheed Lodestar, a World War II submarine chaser rebuilt into an executive aircraft that could carry a payload of more than three thousand kilos. But the next day Tranquilandia was raided, and Seal's trip was delayed.

By now Seal was getting desperate to cut a deal with the government. He again tried Stanford Bardwell, without success. But when the going got tough, Barry Seal got brash. Finally, he just got in one of his planes, flew to Washington, and contacted the offices of the Vice President's South Florida Task Force. The task force's DEA liaison sent Seal to the DEA's Washington headquarters. Agents there were impressed enough to call Bob Joura, a veteran group superviser newly posted to the DEA's Miami Field Division. Joura asked his men if anybody wanted to handle a guy named Barry Seal. Ernst "Jake" Jacobsen, a hulking Mississippian with a walrus mustache, had heard of Seal when he'd worked with Customs in Gulfport. Jacobsen knew that Seal was big time. "I'll take it," he said.

Jacobsen and Joura met Seal for the first time at a small shopping mall in Miami. Seal, wearing a ridiculous disguise of dark glasses and a hat, jumped into the backseat of the agents' car, very afraid. He didn't want to be seen in the DEA office. The two agents took him driving through Miami and nearby Hialeah to calm his nerves and listen to his story.

It was hard to believe. Neither Joura nor Jacobsen, both of whom were new to Miami, were familiar with the name Jorge Ochoa, but the amounts of cocaine Seal talked about were ridiculous. Jacobsen thought he was blowing smoke.

Seal said he had worked for the Ochoas since 1981, flying or arranging more than one hundred smuggling trips of more than three hundred kilos each. The Ochoas paid an average of $3,500 a kilo. The math was astounding: if Seal was telling the truth, he had moved more than thirty thousand kilos of cocaine into the United States and received $75 million.

Jacobsen was still skeptical; informants always promised a lot. That was how they got attention. But then came the kicker: Barry Seal said he could do a 3,500-kilo cocaine deal with the Ochoas and deliver it in two shipments to the DEA. Seal was offering to nearly double the two-ton TAMPA bust, the largest cocaine seizure in the history of the United States.

Seal continued. The Ochoas wanted a big score now because they were hurting. In addition to Tranquilandia, their Bahamian pipeline was giving them trouble. They had lost several loads in the islands to corrupt police who were turning around and reselling the cocaine— about two thousand kilos—in Miami.

The Ochoas had just bought a new plane in Miami, a Titan 404, to replace one they had lost. They wanted Seal and another Ochoa pilot to deliver the aircraft to Hacienda Veracruz. Seal was to meet with Jorge Ochoa to discuss the 3,500-kilo deal.

The briefing lasted two hours. Jacobsen weighed the pros and cons. The DEA agent and federal prosecutor in Screamer hadn't liked Seal. The DEA and state police in Louisiana were still investigating Seal. But as Seal talked, Jacobsen became more and more convinced.

Things he said checked out. By this time Jacobsen had found out from other agents in the office about the Ochoas. This could be a rare opportunity. Jacobsen and Joura decided to pursue it.

On March 28 Seal signed an agreement to cooperate with the government without his own attorney present; he was so concerned with security that he didn't want a private lawyer knowing the details. He agreed to plead guilty to the remaining charges against him, and sentencing would be withheld to see what he could do for the government. No promises were made, but all parties knew if Seal could deliver, it would significantly reduce his prison time. The next day Jacobsen formally debriefed Seal. Seal was given the informant number SG1-84-0028. That number or the initials CI—cooperating individual—would be substituted for Seal's name on all reports in his case file, which was given the number G1-84-0121. The information Seal gave, Jacobsen wrote, was "relating to the smuggling of cocaine by the Jorge Ochoa family."

On April 3 Jacobsen called the prosecutor supervising Seal's cooperation and told him the investigation was on. The target was Jorge Ochoa.

Four days later, as Ellis MacKenzie, Seal greeted Jorge Ochoa at La Loma, becoming the first DEA informant to penetrate the inner sanctum of the Medellín cartel. The meeting lasted an hour.

Ochoa asked Seal how his friend William Roger Reeves was. Seal said he was glad Ochoa had asked, because Reeves had told Seal that Ochoa owed him $5 million. It was Seal's trademark to take the bold approach, even with the world's largest cocaine trafficker.

"Oh, don't worry about that money for Roger," said Ochoa. "I gave it to a friend of Roger's, and it's all taken care of."

Ochoa didn't speak English, but with translation everyone entered the conversation to some degree except Juan David, the eldest Ochoa brother. Jorge Ochoa told Seal he had an inexhaustible supply of cocaine to fly into the United States. He also had problems. Half the three hundred kilos he sent into the Bahamas each day was getting seized. But that was nothing compared to the catastrophe at Tranquilandia.

Pablo Correa Arroyave, Jorge Ochoa's brother-in-law, said the *llanos* raid had turned up records with several of their names on them. "Things are real tight for us now," Correa told Seal. "People are investigating this large laboratory down in the *llanos* valley that Mr. Lehder was running for us."

"Mr. Joe Lehder?" Seal asked. Seal, like any mercenary drug pilot, knew the name well.

"Yes," Correa said.

Correa said Lehder had hidden the rest of the cartel's cocaine in small underground bunkers throughout Colombia. The Tranquilandia raid and subsequent investigation had forced the cartel to move its laboratories. At this point, Seal said later, the traffickers motioned him forward. They were whispering now. The cartel had struck a deal with some ministers in Nicaragua's Sandinista government. The arrangement, Seal said later, "was at this point in its infancy, and I was not at any time—Felix [Bates] and I were sworn to blood secrecy that we are, you know, not ever to mention the name Nicaragua again. Even in the meetings from then on, it was going to be referred to as Costa Rica."

The Sandinistas were helping the Ochoas develop an airstrip for refueling their planes in Nicaragua. That meant a plane out of Colombia heading to the United States could carry less fuel and more cocaine.

Seal expressed surprise that the Ochoas were dealing with what he considered "communists."

"No, no, no. We are not communist," one of the traffickers told him. "We don't particularly enjoy the same philosophy politically that they do, but they serve our means and we serve theirs."

"Well, I'm not real sure that an American would be welcome in Nicaragua smuggling cocaine," Seal said.

"You have nothing to worry about," he was told.

Ochoa outlined the mission: Seal was to fly to the jungle airstrip north of Medellín, where Seal had dropped off the Titan 404, to pick up the first 1,500 kilos. He would fly it directly into the United States, where half the cocaine would go to Miami, the other half to Los Angeles. The Ochoas planned to stockpile cocaine for the spectators attending the 1984 Summer Olympic Games in Los Angeles.

Immediately after delivering the 1,500 kilos, Seal and Bates were to fly south to the Sandinista airstrip in Nicaragua and wait for the Ochoas to gather another 2,000 kilos. Seal was to make the first flight within ten days.

BACK in Miami a week later, Seal met Lito at Auto World, a luxury car dealership Lito said he owned with Pablo Escobar. Lito said Escobar moved five hundred kilos a week through Auto World.

Lito told Seal that Jorge Ochoa had lost six planes in two days in the Bahamas and was overhauling his Miami distribution network.

The man picked for the job was Lizardo Marquez Perez, a former Venezuelan naval officer. Marquez was wanted in his own country for smuggling 667 kilos of cocaine and joining in an attempted coup d'état. The Ochoas considered Marquez an intellectual and called him El Professor; he had graduated with an electrical engineering degree from Georgia Tech in 1967. He shared the Ochoas' passion for walking horses. When Seal met Marquez in mid-April, Marquez described himself as like a godfather to the three Ochoa brothers.

He also told Seal that the Ochoas were unhappy with Lito's slackness. He and his people had gotten complacent and started talking freely on their home phones instead of using pay phones. "I have to improve security," said Marquez.

Marquez was very orderly. He was buying beepers with security codes for the distributors in south Florida and making notes for a security manual. He showed Seal a draft copy, laid out neatly on a table. Entitled "Notes to Meditate on (Ponder)," the ten-page, single-spaced typed document discussed the advantages and disadvantages of renting safe houses under fictitious names: "The opportunity to obtain credit is lost . . . which makes it difficult in the future to obtain a new residence." But fictitious names allowed "the one who lives in the house" to "appear as the butler of the house. To any question [he can answer] 'the owners are traveling.' " The manual never mentioned the word "cocaine," describing it instead as "the foods" in the house. "If something happens and the butlers are able to escape, no traces have been left on the foods, and so there wouldn't be any connection between: butler and food, between butler and the company and consequently, company and food. For this reason it is always necessary to use gloves."

Minimum standards for the houses included "residential location, preferably in a low traffic street; lots of green space; garage for two cars; garage hopefully not within the neighbor's sight." The persons living in the house should be "preferably a couple with children." The manual also described "Obligations of the Occupants: to live a normal life. . . . Try to imitate an American in all his habits, like mow the lawn, wash the car, etc. He must not have extravagant social events in the house, but may have an occasional barbecue, inviting trusted relatives."

Marquez was pleased that Seal shared his views on the importance of security. That night, though, the DEA had Marquez's beeper number, thanks to Barry Seal.

When Seal and Bates flew to Panama for a business meeting with

Ochoa, Pablo Escobar, and other traffickers, Seal carried a batch of daily reports from Marquez for Ochoa. The cartel leaders were anxious for Seal to fly the 1,500-kilo load as soon as possible. But Seal insisted on inspecting the Nicaraguan airstrip first.

BACK in Miami, Seal and Bates bought a Winnebago to carry the cocaine once it got into the United States. Bates had to put down a $500 deposit and griped that Lito still owed him $100,000 for a load he had flown into the Bahamas.

"If he owns half of Auto World, why don't you tell him that you will take a brand-new automobile as part payment on your bill?" Seal said. "Or two cars. One for you and one for your wife. And give me one while you're at it."

"Well, I never thought about it that way," Bates said.

So Bates and Seal went to Auto World and picked out cars. Seal fancied a big four-door Mercedes 500 SEL priced at $63,585.

"If you want that one, you can have it," Lito said.

Seal took it as an advance on his fee.

The mission was scheduled to go in two days, but Seal blew an engine in the Lodestar during a test flight. It took a week and $30,000 to replace. Then another snag came up in Colombia. The cartel had arranged the murder of Lara Bonilla, and its members were forced to flee Colombia for Panama.

Seal finally met the cartel leaders again in Panama City. It was May 1984, a few days after the Lara Bonilla killing, and everything in Colombia was in chaos. All three Ochoa brothers were staying with their wives, children, and several of their employees in a rented house about ten blocks east of Panama City's Caesar Park Marriott Hotel. Juan David, the eldest and softest of the Ochoa brothers, was teary-eyed, and the rest of the household was in dismay. Old Fabio had been arrested in Colombia and was now in prison.

Pablo Escobar was also in town. He told Seal that Carlos Lehder was hiding in Brazil. Neither he nor Lehder, he emphasized, had had any part in Lara Bonilla's assassination. He speculated it was a DEA or CIA plot to encourage the Colombian government to use the extradition treaty. All the cocaine laboratories in Colombia, Escobar said, had been dismantled and were going to be moved to Nicaragua. Lara Bonilla's assassination had resulted in cocaine supplies being moved into the mountains for safekeeping. In the meantime, Panama would be the home away from home.

Despite current misfortunes, the Ochoas were more determined than ever to move the 1,500 kilos quickly. From now on, the family told Seal, he was to call them at the Panama house for instructions.

On May 20 Seal met the cartel leaders in the basement office of a nondescript, two-story, white stucco house in downtown Panama City. Ochoa and Escobar were there, along with Gonzalo Rodriguez Gacha, Felix Bates, and a man Seal did not recognize. Escobar introduced him as Federico Vaughan and identified him as a government official from Nicaragua. Seal immediately began mispronouncing Vaughan's name as "Frederico."

Escobar said Vaughan would escort Seal and Bates to the Nicaraguan airfield so Seal could inspect it. If they followed Vaughan's instructions, no harm would come to them. Vaughan told Seal he was an assistant to Tomás Borge, the Sandinista interior minister. Vaughan said his government stood ready to process all the cocaine base the Colombians could deliver. The ether was coming from East Germany.

Later that day Seal and Bates took a Copa Airlines flight to Augusto Cesar Sandino International Airport in Managua, Nicaragua. Vaughan was also on the flight but purposely did not sit with them. At the airport, however, he went ahead and smoothed things with Immigration so Seal and Bates could get into the country without having their passports stamped. Vaughan's wife, Marquesa, picked them up. That night they stayed at Vaughan's house on the south side of Managua. The next day Vaughan drove them to the airfield. He told them not to be alarmed by the guards or the checkpoints. It was, he said, a mere formality.

As they drove northwest, the urban landscape of Managua turned rural. About five miles outside the city they came to a large oil refinery, and Vaughan stopped. This was the country's only refinery, he said. Never fly near or over it. He pointed out antiaircraft batteries on the perimeter. Any aircraft that flew over the refinery, friend or foe, would be shot down immediately. That got Seal's attention. They walked a few hundred feet and came to a huge sunken lake, an inactive volcano crater that had filled with clear blue water, about a quarter of a mile across. Vaughan said it was the purest water in the country and the only unpolluted drinking water for Managua. In its own way, it was as vital as the refinery. If they flew near it, they would be shot down.

They continued northwest, around a mountain behind the volcano crater and across a railroad track. Here they turned left into Los

Brasiles, a military airfield with a single paved runway. They passed through several roadblocks and security checkpoints staffed by guards armed with Kalashnikov AK-47 assault rifles, the Soviet bloc's weapon of choice. Vaughan showed them a hangar that was going to be used in the smuggling operation. Inside, he pointed out Pablo Escobar's personal Piper Cheyenne. Seal inquired about the runway length, foundation, and texture, his standard procedure for every smuggling flight. As they talked, Seal, Bates, and Vaughan walked the entire three-thousand-foot-length of the runway. When Seal and Bates ventured into the grass to inspect a drainage ditch on the western side of the runway, Vaughan yelled for them to stop.

"It is mined with land mines," Vaughan cautioned. "If you have any problem landing your aircraft, don't veer to the western side, or you will be killed."

After the tour Vaughan took them to a steak house. On a map of Nicaragua he drew arrows showing the entry and exit routes for their smuggling flights. He also gave a code for entering Nicaraguan airspace. They were to call the Sandino tower on a certain VHF frequency and identify themselves as Yankee November Whiskey X-ray Yankee—YNWXY. The tower would reroute them to Los Brasiles. Seal scrawled the code on Vaughan's map. He wrote Vaughan's home and office telephone numbers and codes for reaching him by high-frequency radio on the map's left-hand corner. Vaughan warned that all the approaches to the city of Managua were covered by antiaircraft guns to protect against night attacks by the contra rebels. On the Managua portion of the map, Seal circled the gun emplacements, the refinery, Vaughan's home, and the headquarters for the Sandinista Peoples' Army.

Seal and Bates then flew back to Panama City to report to Escobar and the Ochoas. The runway was perfect, but the hangar was too small for the airplane Seal intended to use. Escobar asked if his own airplane, the Piper Cheyenne, was still in the hangar. Yes, Seal said. Escobar then added another change to Seal's mission: no longer was Seal to return to Nicaragua for a second shipment of 2,000 kilos after delivering the first 1,500 kilos to the United States. Instead, Seal was to fly to Bolivia to pick up 6,000 kilos of cocaine base for the new cartel laboratories in Nicaragua.

Seal and Bates returned to south Florida via private plane. Upon landing, Seal immediately dashed to the Fort Lauderdale Federal Court House for his sentencing before Judge Roettger. No one had bothered to tell Roettger that Seal had become a valued government informant. Roettger called him "an evil man" and sentenced him to the maximum, ten years in prison. He ordered Seal taken directly to the Broward County Jail. A frantic Seal was now behind bars without an attorney to help him.

The DEA's undercover operation came to a standstill while Seal languished for two days in jail. Finally, Jacobsen and Joura, in a closed hearing before Roettger, convinced him to let Seal out on bond.

16.

THE NICARAGUA DEAL

As soon as Barry Seal got out of jail, he called Felix Bates. They had to get moving. The 1,500-kilo load was set for the next day. Bates asked Seal where he had been. Busy, Seal said.

Then Bates told Seal he thought his wife might be a government informant. She had been arrested in Miami for cocaine possession while Bates and Seal were in Panama, but when Bates got home he found that she had been released. She had accompanied Bates on earlier money-laundering trips to Panama; now he feared she had traded information about those trips for her freedom.

Bates, who freebased cocaine heavily and was getting very paranoid, refused to go with Seal unless he could bring his wife along to keep an eye on her. Seal finally relented, then flew to Louisiana and waited for two days. Bates, always promising to be on the next flight, never showed. Finally Seal prevailed on his best friend, Emil Camp, to fly as his co-pilot. At 2:30 A.M. on May 28, they took off in Seal's Lockheed Lodestar from a small general aviation base in northwestern Arkansas. They landed several hours later at the Ochoas' grassy airstrip north of Medellín.

As Seal feared, recent rains had turned the ground to mush. When Seal questioned the ground crew, they told him to wait for Don Carlos. Soon a long-haired man appeared on a horse, waving a machine gun and shouting orders. Don Carlos, it turned out, was Carlos Lehder, and he was showing more than the ordinary strain of someone who had sat on a cocaine load for a week. The Lehder that Seal had heard about was a legend in the cocaine business. But the Lehder that Seal saw outside Medellín was just a harried, frantic man, spouting anger at the delays. Lehder worried out loud that someone might see

Seal's plane from the air. He wanted it fueled and off the strip right away.

That, Seal said, was impossible. The overloaded airplane would never lift off the muddy strip.

"I don't care what you say," Lehder told him, gesturing with the machine gun. "We are going to load this airplane, and you are going to get out of here. You start loading fuel."

Seal did as he was told. Meanwhile, in fifteen minutes the ground crew loaded 1,500 kilos of cocaine stuffed in duffel bags and burlap sacks, and Seal rolled the Lodestar up the wet runway. It bobbed but could not build speed. At takeoff, Seal lost control and crashed. He and Camp were all right, but everybody had to work feverishly to recover the cocaine just before the plane blew up, severely burning two workers.

THE cocaine went by tractor back for inventorying at its stash sites, and a small plane carried Seal and Camp into Medellín. They took hot showers and freshened up at the home of Pablo Correa Arroyave, who guided them around his huge mansion, showing off his tropical garden, his waterfall, his swimming pool, and his Olympic-sized velodrome. Correa had returned to Colombia while the other cartel leaders remained abroad. Afterward, Correa said he had arranged with Jorge Ochoa and Pablo Escobar to keep the smuggling trip alive by replacing Seal's burned Lodestar with the smaller Titan 404 aircraft that Seal had delivered to Colombia back in April. "Certainly you are not going to be able to carry the full 1,500 kilos that you tried to carry with the larger airplane," Correa said. "Can you carry half of it?"

"No, sir," Seal said. "Because then I wouldn't be able to add any fuel." Seal was afraid of running dry and crashing in the Gulf of Mexico. Until now the plan had been for Seal to fly the cocaine directly from Colombia to the United States without a refueling stop.

"And with a stop in Nicaragua?" Correa asked. "How much can you take?"

"Well, with the stop in Nicaragua, we can probably take 700, 750 kilos," Seal said.

If the Lodestar hadn't crashed, Seal would have flown the cocaine directly into the United States without a refueling stop. Now he was going into Nicaragua sooner than expected. That night from the Hotel Intercontinental in Medellín he called Bob Joura in Gulfport to tell him about the change in plans. Joura and Jacobsen, Seal's two DEA handlers, had driven the Winnebago to Gulfport to await the 1,500 kilos.

The next morning Seal and Camp flew back to the jungle airstrip and amused themselves by taking pictures of each other on top of the burned Lodestar wreckage. They spent the next three days with Lehder in the jungle. The onetime "king of cocaine transportation" was now clearly an underling to Ochoa and Escobar, relegated to guarding their cocaine. Lehder showed Seal a stash of three thousand kilos and said six thousand kilos of base was in northern Bolivia ready to be flown to Nicaragua.

ON June 2 Seal called the DEA. He was flying to Nicaragua the next day. At 10:30 P.M. the following night, Jacobsen got a call in Miami from one of Seal's people in Louisiana who had received a cryptic radio transmission: Seal "was returning to Nicaragua after experiencing some engine trouble." Three hours later Jacobsen learned Seal "was on the ground in Nicaragua, and he might have some legal problems." There was no further contact.

The DEA didn't get a full explanation until Seal returned to the United States with no cocaine three days later. Seal gave the following account at his DEA debriefing:

He and Camp left Colombia in the Titan 404 on June 3 with a reduced load of seven hundred kilos of cocaine. They landed at Los Brasiles as planned, but the refueling ran several hours over schedule. Seal took off in darkness and flew without lights through the Nicaraguan mountains. Just north of Managua, antiaircraft tracers lit the sky around his plane. A round pierced his left engine, and the plane rapidly lost altitude. It was going to crash. Seal elected to go back to Los Brasiles, but the airfield was dark, and landing without lights was suicide. Seal tried desperately to reach Vaughan on the radio, but Vaughan had gone home.

Quickly running out of options, Seal called a Mayday into Sandino International along with the code Vaughan gave him. When he landed soldiers approached, and Seal told them he had to talk to Vaughan. Seal was allowed a phone call, but Vaughan wasn't at home. A Sandinista army sergeant who worked for Vaughan appeared and unloaded the cocaine from Seal's plane. The sergeant told Seal and Camp to keep their mouths shut and go along with what was happening. Everything was going to be fine, he said.

Seal and Camp were jailed overnight at a military compound in downtown Managua that had once served as former dictator Anastasio Somoza's headquarters. The Sandinistas still called it "the bunker." The next day Vaughan obtained Seal's and Camp's release and took them to a hacienda in southeastern Managua, where Seal was reunited with Pablo Escobar, who had moved from Panama to Nicaragua to supervise the cocaine-processing operations there. From the house, Seal could see the mountain bearing the letters *FSLN*, the Spanish acronym for the Sandinista National Liberation Front.

A couple of days later, Vaughan visited, bringing a Nicaraguan newspaper, *El Nuevo Diario*. "This is the reason we wanted you to keep your mouth shut at the airport, because we had to keep this entire incident very quiet in the newspapers. We don't control all the newspapers here," Vaughan said.

The newspaper had printed a two-paragraph Sandinista Peoples' Army communiqué saying that antiaircraft gunners at Sandino Airport shot at an Agrarian Reform Air Transport Co. plane because the plane was unable to signal its location.

"The DAA [Anti-Aircraft Defense] had to signal and fire warning shots to induce it to land at the airport—which happened without untoward consequences," the communiqué said.

Vaughan said the mishap really occurred because he hadn't planned for a smuggling flight in darkness. The gunners didn't see Seal, but they heard him, and they fired at the sound. Obviously the operation needed better communication—Seal was astounded that he hadn't been able to reach Vaughan once he got in the air; he suggested they buy walkie-talkies.

Pablo Escobar told Seal the new Nicaraguan cocaine lab complex was located at a *finca* south of Managua and was now about two weeks from going into full production. Escobar referred to the Bolivian cocaine base that Lehder was now gathering in Colombia: there was ten to fifteen tons, roughly equal to one-fifth of the cocaine consumed in the United States for the entire year.

"Well, that's going to take a real large airplane," Seal said.

Seal suggested they buy a military cargo plane he had seen advertised in an aviation trade magazine. Escobar loved the idea. He said Seal should get the plane and return for the first seven hundred kilos.

"Is that cocaine safe?" Seal asked.

"Every gram of it," Vaughan said. "We haven't lost one single gram."

SEAL and Camp flew home in Pablo Escobar's Piper Cheyenne III, which Escobar was sending for maintenance in the United States. Seal immediately called Lito to present Escobar's shopping list. With $200,000 in cash, Seal bought night-vision goggles and a dozen ITT McKay high-frequency radios, top-of-the-line equipment at $12,000 apiece. Next Seal acquired a Fairchild C-123K Provider, a twin-engined military transport shaped like a whale that had been used extensively during the Vietnam War. Seal called it "The Fat Lady." Seal obtained the C-123K, one of the few in civilian use, by swapping another plane with an airplane broker with known CIA connections in New Smyrna Beach, Florida.

By now the CIA had signed on to the Seal mission. Two weeks earlier, while Seal was in Colombia with Lehder, the CIA had checked Seal's description of Los Brasiles. "The CIA has provided us photographs of this airfield, and it matched to perfection the description given by the informant," noted a DEA agent in the Cocaine Investigations Section in Washington.

The CIA's contribution to the Seal case was mainly technological: on June 18 Seal flew the C-123K to Rickenbacker Air Force Base in Ohio. Technicians there rigged a 35-mm camera provided by the CIA in the airplane's nose and another inside the plane in a fake electronics box atop a bulkhead facing the rear cargo doors. The box had a pin-hole lens to allow the camera to film anybody loading onto the rear of the plane.

Back in Miami three days later, Seal called Vaughan in Managua. He secretly tape-recorded the call for the DEA.

"I was going to see my grandmother at noon on Saturday," Seal told Vaughan.

That was the code for the cocaine pickup.

Seal told Vaughan about the C-123K. "It's a big Cadillac . . . very big, big car. . . . I just wanted to make sure that my grandmother, uh, was going to tell the landlord that the . . . that the car was very big so that the landlord wouldn't be uh, uh, excited when, when, when they saw it."

The "landlord" was the Sandinistas. Seal was worried about getting shot down again.

"No, no, no," Vaughan said. "Everything is okay about that."

Seal called Vaughan again on June 24, the day before the flight, and again talked about "the party tomorrow" at his grandmother's.

"Uh—I mean, everybody is coming to the party, and you've notified those, uh, boys in green?" Seal asked. He was still worried about getting shot down.

"Right," Vaughan said.

"They're all—everybody is notified?" Seal asked.

"Yes," Vaughan said.

"Excellent," Seal said. "Okay. I just want to make sure, I don't want any problem."

"Yes, everybody is going to be there," Vaughan said.

"Okay, good," Seal said. "And is Pedro coming? Because I have that liquor for him."

Pedro was Pablo Escobar. The liquor was the list of things Escobar wanted in Miami.

"Uh, yes, yes, he's coming," Vaughan said.

Seal said he was leaving for the party at midnight. He asked if it had been raining on "the yard where we park the cars at the party." In other words, was the airstrip muddy? Vaughan assured him it was dry and hard and only a little bit muddy in one small area.

"I can't stay at the party long," Seal said. "I have to try to leave as soon as possible." He wanted to refuel as fast as possible.

"Yeah, we're going to be ready for that," Vaughan said.

"Okay," Seal said. "Now remember this, this uh—motor home is very big, and it's a funny, funny color, so don't let anybody get excited."

The C-123K was painted camouflage green according to U.S. military specifications. Seal was still scared the Sandinistas would shoot it down on sight.

But Vaughan only laughed. "No, that's perfect, that's perfect," he said.

SEAL took off from Key West and landed the C-123K at Los Brasiles at one P.M. June 25, 1984. When the loading began, Seal noticed that the radio-controlled trigger for the hidden cameras was malfunctioning. Seal or his co-pilot had to operate the rear camera by hand. Seal could clearly hear the shutter clicking inside its box. But the camera worked. It caught Seal loading twenty-five-kilo duffel bags of cocaine with Pablo Escobar, Gonzalo Rodriguez Gacha, and Federico Vaughan.

At 4:50 A.M. the next day, Seal landed the C-123K at Homestead Air Force Base south of Miami with seven hundred kilos of cocaine aboard. That night he called Lito and set up a meeting at Dadeland Mall. The two men talked in Lito's car in the parking lot.

"Where is the load?" Lito asked.

"It's sitting right there in the Winnebago," Seal said.

Lito didn't like that. It was nearly ten P.M., and the parking lot was emptying rapidly. The Winnebago would stick out like a sore thumb.

Seal left Lito at the Winnebago. A team of DEA agents watched a
white Chevy truck drive up. A man in a white T-shirt got out, un-
locked the Winnebago's door, climbed inside, and drove off. Agents
in several cars and a helicopter followed the Winnebago onto U.S. 1.
The Chevy truck and a gray Mercedes-Benz also followed. At the
chosen moment, a DEA agent in an old white Buick junker picked for
the task smashed into the camper. On cue, a Florida Highway Patrol
car drove up.

The DEA had hit on a daring plan to keep the Seal investigation
alive as long as possible. By law, U.S. agents are not allowed to let
drugs pass through their hands and onto the streets, even if it means
ending an undercover investigation prematurely. The seven hundred
kilos had to be seized, but to keep the investigation going, the DEA
wanted the smugglers to think that it was just an accident. The DEA
staged its own traffic accident: ram the Winnebago and have a trooper
just happen by. The trooper was instructed to allow the driver of the
camper to escape.

The plan almost worked. The young Colombian inside the Winnebago produced his license but could not find the vehicle's registration.
He asked the trooper if he could go across the street and make a
telephone call. The trooper said yes. The man got across the street to
a Wendy's restaurant. One of the surveillance agents did a play-by-
play on his car radio as the man walked behind the restaurant and
bolted: "He's crossed the street, now he's rounding the corner. And
. . . there . . . he goes."

But the DEA hadn't counted on the instincts of a civilian crime
stopper blowing its most sensitive investigation. A bystander who had
seen the accident chased the young Colombian when he started running and tackled him. They fought until a Coral Gables police car
pulled up. Now the police had no choice but to make an arrest.

At 2 A.M. that night Seal got a call from Paul Etzel, a Colombian
who sold cars in Miami and worked for Lito.

"Have you heard the news?" Etzel said. "The load got busted."

The next day Seal got a message that Lito wanted to see him immediately. Seal thought his life might be in danger and asked Jacobsen
to arrange surveillance. Seal and Lito met at a Tony Roma's restaurant near Dadeland. Lito said that the highest-ranking member of
Ochoa's organization in Miami, a man he described only by the name
"Jota," Spanish for the letter *J*, wanted to see everybody immediately.

"One of our people was following the Winnebago, and he said he saw a car ram into the side purposely," Lito said with Etzel translating. "He is trying to say it was a setup."

Seal got in a station wagon with Lito, Lito's wife, Luz, and Etzel and rode to a condominium off Brickell Avenue, an exclusive address just south of Miami's midtown skyline. The four of them took an elevator up to an apartment where Jota and a group of Colombians waited. Jota said he had been asked to investigate the seizure. He ordered the young man who had followed the Winnebago to speak. Etzel interpreted for Seal. The young man said he saw a driver deliberately ram the Winnebago.

"He doesn't know what he's talking about," said Lito, who as architect of the deal felt a vested interest in showing the seizure was nothing but an accident.

Jota asked Seal for his opinion. Seal said that if Jota thought there was something wrong, they should immediately shut down. There was brief conversation that wasn't translated for Seal's benefit. Then Jota asked Seal to show him his driver's license. Jota told Seal he would get back to him. Then everybody was forced to wait until Jota left the apartment. He did not want to be followed.

Lito called a day later with the good news that everything had been settled. He asked Seal if he would be willing now to return to Nicaragua and pick up more cocaine. Seal said yes, then called Vaughan in Managua. He mentioned the accident.

"My friend told me that everything was okay," Vaughan said.

"Yeah, only one person in the hospital, and he seems to be okay," Seal said. He meant only one person was under arrest. Seal complained to Vaughan about the bust and said someone with authority needed to make changes. Vaughan said everyone would listen to Seal.

"They have a very, very good and special, uh, consideration for you," Vaughan said. He told Seal that "our common friend"—Pablo Escobar—wanted a favor. Vaughan struggled with the name of what Escobar wanted.

"Sometimes my English is not so good," Vaughan said. "Small water vehicle for, uh, to have fun. . . . It's some kind of boat. Water boat."

Seal figured out that Escobar wanted a rubber raft with an outboard motor. Escobar had given Seal another shopping list on his last trip into Nicaragua. Part of it was practical, airplane parts and so on, but it also contained capitalist consumer goodies hard to get in Nicaragua: video recorders, ten-speed bicycles, Johnny Walker Black Label Scotch, Marlboro cigarettes.

Escobar also wanted Seal to bring him $1.5 million in cash. The money was needed to pay the Sandinistas for landing rights in Nicaragua. Lito took his time getting the money together, and soon Seal was pressing the deadline for his next flight. So from his suite at the Omni International Hotel in Miami, Seal called Escobar directly. Etzel, on hand to translate, got on the line in the suite's sitting room, and Seal picked up the receiver in the bedroom. When the call went through, Seal attached a small suction cup from a Sony Walkman recorder to the receiver. Etzel could not see Seal and was unaware that he was taping the call.

"It's MacKenzie, calling Pedro," Etzel said in Spanish to the male voice that answered in Managua. "What will I tell him?" Etzel asked Seal.

"Tell him that they're jacking me around," Seal said. "That you and MacKenzie are preparing to leave tomorrow night, and we have all of the airplane parts and everything, that the bill is about $150,000, and they won't give us that money."

When Escobar came on the line, Etzel translated Seal's message for him.

"The gentleman with whom he works didn't deliver anything to him?" Escobar asked. Told no, Escobar said he didn't have anything to do with that—Lito worked for Jorge Ochoa, after all. But Escobar said he would call Los Amigos—"the Friends."

Then Etzel gave Escobar the rest of Seal's message: "And about the material for you, the big one, they say they don't have any."

The big one was the $1.5 million Escobar wanted.

"Oh, I see," Escobar said. "I'm going to get in contact with them, then, to see what the problem is."

A little later, Seal got an angry call from Lito.

"I am down in the Keys vacationing, and I just got notified you need this million and a half dollars," Lito said. "And I got it from Pablo Escobar and his people, and I don't work for Pablo Escobar and his people. I work for Jorge, and I don't appreciate getting called out at this time of night to bring you this million dollars."

The next day, though, Lito brought the money to the Omni in three suitcases and a cardboard box. When he had left, Seal called Joura, who sent a DEA agent over to his room to photograph the cash, $1,553,500.

SEAL left in the C-123K for Nicaragua a day later on July 7. When the plane landed at Los Brasiles, Seal told Vaughan he had received a radio message in the air from one of his men in Mississippi that the off-loading site was under police surveillance. Seal wanted to leave the load on the ground in Nicaragua. Vaughan took Seal to see Escobar, who listened to Seal's arguments and thanked him for being cautious. In the future, Escobar suggested, Seal might consider digging underground hiding places near his landing strips, as he, Escobar, had done in Colombia. The second Nicaraguan load, nine hundred kilos, stayed on the ground at Los Brasiles.

Seal's apparent concern was an act. If Seal brought in the load, the DEA would have to seize it, just as it had with the first load. The agents wanted to pursue the case much further, and after the Winnebago bust they felt they could not explain away a second seizure. Joura wanted Seal to fly the Bolivian cocaine base up from Colombia so the DEA could identify the cartel cocaine labs in Nicaragua. Most of all, he wanted Seal to lure Ochoa and Escobar into a country where they could be arrested and extradited to stand trial in the United States.

Now, with Seal preparing to return to the United States from Los Brasiles empty-handed, Escobar talked again about the Bolivian cocaine base destined for the cartel's labs in Nicaragua. Seal would fly the finished cocaine in the C-123K from Nicaragua to a landing strip in northern Mexico. Rodriguez Gacha, head of the cartel's West Coast distribution, had acquired this Mexican airstrip. Pilots in small planes would take the cocaine from Mexico to the United States. One of the small planes would head to a strip in Georgia controlled by a friend of Carlos Lehder. Escobar wanted Seal to inspect the strips in Mexico and Georgia, and Seal agreed. The DEA hoped to seize the cartel leaders in Mexico.

THE DEA was poised for what might have been a sensational coup, but the case suddenly unraveled. The Sandinista involvement was so politically hot that it burned a hole through the investigation. On June 26, the day Seal arrived at Homestead Air Force Base south of Miami with the seven hundred kilos, details of his secret mission were already known to Lieutenant Colonel Oliver North, the National Security Council adviser who ran the Reagan administration's secret aid pipeline to the contra rebels fighting the Sandinistas.

That day North jotted the name "Freddy Vaughan" into his desktop notebook. Underneath that he wrote "Works for Tomás Borge" and "Photos show Vaughan and Nic Int Troops." Finally, he added, "750 pounds of cocaine."

Ron Caffrey, chief of the DEA's cocaine desk in Washington, had personally briefed North and CIA official Dewey Clarridge about Seal's flights into Nicaragua. In late June or early July, Caffrey said North and Clarridge already had the Seal photographs when Caffrey arrived to brief them at the Old Executive Office Building on the White House grounds. Caffrey was furious at the security breach.

North asked if the story could be leaked to the press, Caffrey recalled four years later during hearings in Congress. A key vote on contra aid loomed and evidence of Sandinista complicity in drug trafficking could only boost the contra cause.

But Caffrey told North a leak would end Seal's usefulness to the DEA and ruin the mission. The briefing ended with the general understanding that Seal was going to continue with his undercover activities and return to Nicaragua with the $1.5 million bribe for the Sandinistas. If Seal could fly money into Nicaragua, North asked Caffrey, why couldn't he land the plane somewhere outside the airport in Managua and turn the money over to the contras?

The suggestion was ignored by DEA.

A day later, Army Lieutenant General Paul Gorman, commander of the Panama-based U.S. Southern Command, told a U.S. Chamber of Commerce audience in San Salvador that the United States "now had firm proof that the Sandinistas were actively and recently involved in drug trafficking, and the world would soon be given proof." On July 6 North wrote concerning a call from Clarridge that "DEA thinks CIA leaked info to Gorman."

When Seal returned from Nicaragua on July 8 after leaving the nine hundred kilos behind, Joura got even more troubling news. He learned that the right-leaning *Washington Times* newspaper, a Reagan administration favorite, was about to leak details of Seal's mission. The source of the leak was obvious to DEA.

Joura knew he had to wrap up the case quickly. He told Seal to set up a meeting with Lito and Etzel. At the Skyways Motel in Miami on July 17, the DEA arrested both men. Lito produced a driver's license that said he was Jorge Negrete, but by now the DEA knew his real name: Carlos Bustamante. He had no passport. He told the agents he made his living washing cars on a football field. The agents caught Felix Bates at the Miami Airport Hilton with $20,000 in cash. Safely outside the United States, Vaughan, Escobar, Ochoa, Lehder, and Rodriguez Gacha all escaped.

The *Washington Times* story appeared the day of the arrests. The article and the follow-up stories it generated in newspapers throughout the country focused on the Sandinistas' role in the case. Nicaragua denied the charges: "It would be a lack of seriousness on my part if I responded to that accusation," said Interior Minister Tomás Borge, Federico Vaughan's alleged boss.

The Sandinista connection eclipsed the fact that the leaders of the Medellín cartel had been indicted together for the first time. Politics grabbed the headlines, while the cartel leaders largely escaped notice. They were variously described as "often accused Colombian cocaine barons" and "top-level traffickers in Colombian cocaine." The head-line in *The New York Times* read U.S. ACCUSES MANAGUA OF ROLE IN COCAINE TRAFFIC. The *Times* story didn't mention Ochoa or Escobar until the ninth paragraph, and then it misidentified Escobar as Nicar-aguan. The significance of the Medellín cartel was lost beneath the politics.

17.

CRACKDOWN

The assassination of Rodrigo Lara Bonilla had put the Medellín cartel on the run for the first time in its existence. The problems in Nicaragua were only a symptom of a much graver malaise. For three months after the Lara Bonilla murder, everything the traffickers touched turned sour.

Worst of all, the cartel had disgraced the nation and insulted its president beyond endurance. Before Lara Bonilla no sitting cabinet minister had ever been killed in Colombia. It was an appalling act of consummate arrogance, and Belisario Betancur could not afford to ignore it.

In addition, drug trafficking was destroying Colombia's international image. Betancur wanted to raise Colombia's profile in Latin America, but all anyone ever wanted to talk about at inter-American gatherings was drug trafficking. Now Betancur was branded as the president of a country where drug bosses killed cabinet ministers.

Lara Bonilla's murder marked the moment when Colombia first identified the Medellín cartel as the enemy: savage, ruthless killers willing to challenge the integrity of the Colombian state. There was no more talk of drug trafficking being a "U.S. problem and not our problem." There was no more discussion of the drug traffickers' capitalistic enterprise and creativity. The days when Pablo Escobar and Carlos Lehder could strut their stuff across Colombia's political landscape were over.

Under Betancur's May 1 state of siege, drug defendants were to be tried in military courts and would not be offered bail. Conviction brought heavy prison sentences with no possibility of parole. On the street, police acquired broad powers of search and seizure and arrest and could hold somebody for questioning without probable cause.

They were also allowed to pull the gun permit of anyone suspected of drug trafficking. It was this measure that had prompted the detention of old Fabio Ochoa.

Within days, hundreds of suspected traffickers were rounded up and thrown in jail. Police searched more than one hundred buildings believed to be owned by the cartel. Planes, cars, trucks, and other property were seized all over the country.

In Medellín police raided one of Pablo Escobar's apartments and found Escobar's address book open on a settee beside the telephone. Someone apparently had warned Escobar that the police were coming, and he had escaped just in time.

Police also invaded Escobar's Hacienda Los Napoles and traipsed all over his fancy mansion. Within a couple of weeks Colombia's humane societies were complaining that Escobar's zoo animals were starving. The government took over the zoo and reopened it as a tourist attraction. Masons resumed pouring cement for the brontosaurus that Escobar had wanted to use as the centerpiece for a new theme park.

Carlos Lehder, too, had lost his favorite plaything. His staff at Posada Alemana hadn't been paid since he'd left for the jungle after Lara Bonilla signed his extradition order the previous September. Now his people quit en masse—perhaps two hundred families—leaving his prized pair of tigers to starve. The tigers required a regular diet of freshly killed horses at $70 apiece. The Humane Society put the tigers on the dole. The rest of the estate languished, the bungalows and outbuildings scarred by rain damage and fire. John Lennon endured, the lone reminder of the *posada*'s past glories.

MOST of the cartel, as Barry Seal had discovered, decided to sit out the crackdown in neighboring Panama. It was a good choice for a number of reasons. The traffickers had been familiar with Panama for several years, ever since they began setting up dummy holding companies there and laundering drug money through Panamanian banks in the 1970s. They had also often used Panama as a meeting place or a vacation playground. Panama City was less than an hour from Medellín by plane.

More important, however, the cartel had a Panamanian patron. General Manuel Antonio Noriega was chief of the Panama Defense Forces and the most powerful man in the country, able to make and unmake presidents at will. Noriega was the only friend an outsider needed in Panama.

The traffickers had known Noriega personally at least since early 1982, when, as chief of military intelligence, he had helped the Ochoas during the Marta Nieves kidnap negotiations. By the end of that year Escobar had set up a deal with Noriega to use Panama as a transshipment point for cocaine loads headed from Colombia to the United States, with Noriega collecting fees for all services rendered.

Sometime around the end of 1983 the cartel-Noriega association moved into a new, more ambitious phase. The traffickers built a large cocaine lab on the Rio Quindio in the Darién jungle of southern Panama, some fifty miles from the Colombian border. Cartel members—Ochoa, Escobar, and probably others—paid $5 million to high-ranking Panamanian military officers to ensure they would not be bothered. It was not clear whether Noriega received the money directly, but it would have been impossible for a lab of that size to be built without the general's knowledge and approval.

This was a dangerous game for Noriega, but if anyone could play it, he seemed to be the man. He was a small, gnomish career officer with an acne-pitted face that caused him unending embarrassment and earned him the nickname Cara de Piña—"Pineapple Face." He had no public presence, projected no human warmth, and had no visible political skills. But he was, in fact, politically brilliant, a manipulator and tightrope walker capable of posing as a Third World leader and friend of Cuban Communist leader Fidel Castro while at the same time remaining in the good graces of the United States and serving as a CIA asset. Rumors of corruption, drug trafficking, gun running, and worse swirled about him for years, but he was able to weather every storm because the gringos felt he was the key to Panamanian political stability and the unhindered operation of the Panama Canal. He was untouchable and as well connected as any man in Latin America.

After the Lara Bonilla murder, Noriega took the cartel exiles under his wing. He provided them with bodyguards, listened to their complaints, and gave them counsel. Ochoa, in addition to his rental house near the Marriott, often stayed at the Continental Hotel in Panama City's banking district. Escobar stayed at the El Valle and Bambito hotels or at the Holiday Inn in Paitilla, near the municipal airport. The cost for sanctuary, for Escobar alone, was $1 million, payable to the general.

THE cartel wanted a truce with the Colombian government, and an opportunity presented itself almost immediately. Panama was holding presidential elections May 6, and a flock of prominent Latin American politicans was streaming into town to serve as observers.

The chief Colombian delegate was former President Alfonso Lopez Michelsen, who had lost his bid for a second presidential term to Betancur in 1982. Lopez Michelsen was a tall, distinguished, vigorous man in his mid-seventies, an elder statesman in the Liberal Party and the current patriarch of one of Colombia's most influential families. He was also a political maverick with a sardonic wit and the instincts of an alley fighter. His campaign, like Betancur's, was widely reported to have been tainted by "hot money" from Escobar, Ochoa, and other cocaine traffickers. A Metro-Dade police document said his campaign manager "had a relationship" with Jorge Ochoa and Pablo Escobar.

Still, Lopez Michelsen was no dirtier than anyone else and had, in fact, been vigorously defended by Lara Bonilla during the minister's days on the floor of Congress. For a variety of reasons, Lopez Michelsen was the traffickers' perfect vehicle: he was widely respected, politically astute, and accustomed to hearing all sorts of strange propositions. He even advertised his availability as a go-between, often describing himself as "a mailbox" for anyone who wanted to send a message.

Lopez Michelsen's advisers received word that the cartel wanted to talk to him once he got to Panama City. Lopez Michelsen had no idea how the contact would be made, but he telephoned Betancur to inform him what was planned. Betancur took the information under advisement.

Lopez Michelsen arrived in Panama City May 4 and checked into the Marriott. He was still unpacking his bags when one of his advisers called. Escobar and Jorge Ochoa were in another suite in the hotel. They wanted to meet now. Was that all right?

Lopez Michelsen went to the indicated room, knocked on the door, and was greeted by two nondescript-looking men in sport clothes, one short, one tall, both slightly heavy. The short one was Escobar; the tall one was Ochoa. They introduced themselves politely and invited Lopez Michelsen, who had never before met either man, to sit down.

They began by explaining how disturbed they were about the Lara Bonilla killing and the "persecution" they and their families had suffered as a result. Escobar insisted that neither he nor anyone closely connected with him had had anything to do with the murder. He had been trying to discredit Lara Bonilla with the Porras check, he said, so "it made no sense for me to kill him."

Lopez Michelsen nodded, signifying that he had heard what Escobar had said. Otherwise he was noncommittal. He had listened to plenty of nonsense in his life and could listen to more, if that was what this was.

Two things, though. First, Escobar and Ochoa seemed very disturbed, anxious, maybe even scared. Sitting in Panama did not seem to agree with them. Second, they spoke convincingly and well. Lopez Michelsen had been led to believe that they were low-lifes; instead he found them soft-spoken and polite. It was true they didn't look like much, but they were extremely astute politically, something Lopez Michelsen could appreciate. Also, Lopez Michelsen was looking for hierarchy here but couldn't find it. The two took turns speaking, neither man dominating the conversation.

The two traffickers said they represented a "large group" of people involved in the drug trade, everyone but Carlos Lehder. They had broken with Lehder, they said, because of his distressing habit of talking too much. Lehder had also tried to compete with them as a cocaine producer. They didn't like that. They were disposed to return to civilian life and to get involved in legitimate business. They also said they planned to bring their money home. The pair kept the discussion away from specifics. They asked for no commitments from Lopez Michelsen, and he gave none, simply nodding his head that he understood. After an hour or so they were finished.

Lopez Michelsen observed the Panamanian elections, a fraud-tainted fiasco resolved after a fashion when voting officials proclaimed Noriega's candidate the winner. Then Lopez Michelsen flew to Miami for a few days of sun and shopping. He called Betancur and told him what had transpired with the cartel bosses. Then he forgot the entire matter.

THE Lopez Michelsen meeting marked the begining of an ambitious "two-track" recovery policy by the Medellín cartel. On one hand the traffickers were trying to reach an agreement with Colombia in hopes that the slate might eventually be wiped clean, all sins forgiven. At the same time they were running a big lab in Panama's Darién jungle, talking about setting up others in Nicaragua and fixing up the details of a 1,500-kilo cocaine shipment with Barry Seal. Thus, if Colombia wouldn't accommodate them, Nicaragua would. Or Panama. Or somewhere else. Cocaine was a movable feast.

The success of this strategy depended on secrecy and the cartel's ability to maintain a low profile while they remained in hiding. But suddenly everything seemed to fall apart in Panama. Almost immediately following the election debacle, the Defense Forces discovered the Darién lab and arrested twenty-three people—all Colombians. What the hell was going on? The cartel was supposed to have a $5 million fix in. Enraged, the traffickers approached the government for an explanation. General Noriega was in Europe, Panamanian officials said. We don't know what happened. Well, find out, the cartel demanded.

Discussions took place in Havana under the sponsorship of Cuban President Castro, who had served in the past as an intermediary for the traffickers in some dealings with Colombian guerrillas—specifically M-19. Castro also had a long-running and cordial relationship with Noriega. The cartel and a Panamanian government official held a preliminary conference before Noriega flew in from Europe. The general then talked privately with Castro and returned to Panama. The twenty-three Colombians were immediately released, some of the lab equipment was returned to the traffickers, and $3 million in cash was returned to the cartel.

After the Darién affair, both Noriega and the cartel leaders sought a meeting to clear the air. Noriega also wanted to discuss how long the cartel planned to stay in Panama; he gave permission for the traffickers to host a second meeting with Colombian government officials, this time with Attorney General Carlos Jimenez Gomez. The meeting, like the Lopez Michelsen encounter, would be a "secret" affair managed exclusively by the cartel.

JIMENEZ Gomez left Bogotá with a somewhat sizable delegation on the afternoon of May 26. His ostensible mission was to find out about $13.5 million in Colombian government monies that had apparently disappeared from the Chase Manhattan Bank. The traffickers called Jimenez Gomez at the Hotel Soloy in downtown Panama City. A spokesman said he represented "various Colombian citizens who wanted to discuss their situation." Jimenez Gomez agreed.

They met that night. This time there were about seven traffickers, chief among them Escobar, Jorge Ochoa, and Rodriguez Gacha. Jimenez Gomez listened to them, agreed to carry the traffickers' message to Betancur, and suggested they put it in writing.

The next day the traffickers returned with a six-page letter addressed to Belisario Betancur. Jimenez Gomez took it and flew home to Bogotá.

The traffickers described this extraordinary document as a "unilateral declaration" outlining our "frank and honest position on the subject of narcotics trafficking." After discussions among themselves, the traffickers said, they had decided to "simply and openly ask you, Mr. President, to consider the possibility of our reincorporation into Colombian society in the near future."

The first part of the memorandum was a brief history of drug trafficking in Colombia. It contained the assertion that "our organizations . . . today control between 70 and 80 percent of the total volume of Colombia's drug traffic" representing "for us an annual income of around $2 billion."

The memorandum then repeated the assurance made earlier to Lopez Michelsen that "the organizations that we represent" had no responsibility "either directly or indirectly" for the murder of Lara Bonilla. Furthermore, the traffickers denied any connection with Colombia's guerrillas or any desire to change "the democratic and republican system currently in place in Colombia." The traffickers had gotten involved in politics, they said, "exclusively" to lobby for the abrogation of the U.S.–Colombia extradition treaty.

The second part of the memorandum outlined the deal the traffickers were offering. They would turn over all clandestine airstrips and laboratories, dismantle their infrastructure, stay out of politics, bring their money home, help develop crop substitution projects to replace coca and marijuana, and "collaborate with the government . . . in campaigns for the eradication of domestic consumption of drugs and the rehabilitation of addicts."

In return, the traffickers wanted Betancur to lift the state of siege, restructure extradition procedures, and agree not to apply the extradition treaty for offenses committed before the date of the letter.

In other words, amnesty. If the traffickers earned $2 billion per year and kept a lot of it outside the country, the amount of money that could come back to Colombia was hard to imagine. It was a colossal bribe.

THE cartel members heard nothing about the proposal from Betancur or anyone else and continued to mark time in Panama while their fortunes collapsed around them. Relations with Noriega, sensitive since the Darién affair, were further exacerbated on June 15, when U.S. Customs at Miami International Airport seized 1.2 metric tons of cocaine sealed in freezers and packed in cartons labeled "perfume" aboard a cargo jet belonging to a Panamanian charter company. A week later Panamanian drug agents confiscated 6,159 drums of ether in the Colón Free Trade Zone, at the Atlantic terminus of the Panama Canal. And a week after that the fourth man in Panama's military chain of command was arrested, publicly disgraced, and forced to retire from the Panama Defense Forces for conspiracy to traffic in ether. The same officer had served as Noriega's bagman in the cartel's $5 million Darién payoff. Relations with Noriega were supposed to have been smoothed over, so what was going on?

The cartel members were defenseless and trapped in a foreign country while disasters occurred all around them. There was simply too much public scandal. By the end of June the first reports were surfacing in Colombia about the cartel's Panama meetings with Lopez Michelsen and Jimenez Gomez. The next month in Washington the Nicaragua case broke on the front page of the *Washington Times*.

It was obvious that the cartel was going to have to get out of Panama. Neither Escobar nor Ochoa felt comfortable outside of Colombia, and the Panamanian experience had confirmed their worst fears about how fast things could go to hell if nobody was watching the business. The traffickers began looking for new foreign sanctuaries. They also began to look wistfully at Colombia. Ultimately, they knew, they would be safest at home, where their money could buy them the protection they needed and where their hired killers could keep their enemies at bay.

But Betancur showed no sign of easing off. To succeed Lara Bonilla as justice minister, Betancur named another drug hard-liner, Enrique Parejo Gonzalez. Parejo was a New Liberal also, and just as tough as Lara Bonilla. Unlike Lara Bonilla, he could count on Betancur's support. By the end of the summer, the United States had initiated extradition proceedings on more than sixty Colombian defendants. By the beginning of November, Colombian authorities had thirteen of the fugitives in jail. At midmonth Parejo approved five extraditions, and on November 16 Betancur signed two of them.

It was also Parejo, working closely with Jaime Ramirez and the U.S. embassy, who helped obtain final approval for herbicide spraying of marijuana. After full-scale spraying started in the fall, the north coast marijuana business, the United States' primary drug target in Colombia for more than a decade, started to collapse almost immediately.

FOR Lewis Tambs and Johnny Phelps, the twin victories on extradition and marijuana spraying meant that they had fulfilled their two most important missions. Tambs called 1984 a "breakthrough" year. Phelps, skeptical and more cautious, was nonetheless finally pleased with Betancur. The president hadn't moved until Lara Bonilla was murdered, but now that he had finally made up his mind, "he stuck with it."

And on August 14, Bogotá Superior Court Judge Tulio Manuel Castro Gil issued a summons and preliminary finding against fourteen suspects in the Lara Bonilla killing, including most of the Quesitos hit team and the alleged "intellectual authors" of the crime: Pablo Escobar, the three Ochoa brothers, Gonzalo Rodriguez Gacha. On that day Escobar had five arrest warrants pending against him: two for homicide in the murders of Medellín DAS agents, one for questioning in the Lara Bonilla killing, one for smuggling animals for his zoo, and one for extradition to the United States as a drug trafficker. On October 19 Castro Gil indicted Escobar for the murder of Rodrigo Lara Bonilla and named the Ochoas and Rodriguez Gacha as material witnesses.

The case against Escobar rested primarily on the testimony of Jaime Ramirez, who appeared twice before Judge Castro Gil prior to the Lara Bonilla indictment. The cartel knew Ramirez was denouncing them and apparently received a blow-by-blow report. In 1986 police searching an Escobar *finca* would find a copy of Ramirez's deposition lying open on a coffee table. Possession of the document was a felony.

Ramirez didn't care what the cartel knew about him. He felt somewhat responsible for Lara Bonilla's death, felt he should have warned the minister of the risks attendant in making public the dirty cartel secrets Ramirez had in his files. When Lara Bonilla was killed, he promised that "I will fight even harder."

And he did. By mid-1984 Ramirez had 1,200 men in the police Anti-Narcotics Unit. He was making gigantic marijuana seizures in the north almost every week. He was hitting cocaine labs constantly and developing new sources of intelligence to such a degree that he and most of his men were in the field almost all the time.

And after Tranquilandia, Ramirez and Phelps found that success bred success. New informants began coming unsolicited to the police and the DEA with news about labs "like that one you found in Caquetá." As the two lawmen had suspected, rural labs were the rule in Colombia rather than the exception.

Whenever police or DEA agents received a tip, they attempted to verify it with aircraft overflights and aerial photographs. The hunters always looked for the rural lab signature: a water source, lake, or river; and an airstrip. Without these two things, no cocaine processor could do business.

In the first seven months of 1984, police seized 1,500 metric tons of marijuana, 26 metric tons of cocaine and cocaine base, and 37 metric tons of *bazuko*. The 63-ton haul represented an elevenfold increase over all cocaine seizures in the previous four years. The police also counted 84 labs destroyed and 144 drug-trafficking airplanes seized.

While it was relatively easy to seize property, labs, or even cocaine on a rural raid, Ramirez was frustrated that it was almost impossible to catch a big trafficker. It was just too hard to get to a jungle lab, and the traffickers always knew when the police were coming. On May 4 Ramirez's men missed Carlos Lehder at Airapua, in the *llanos* one hundred miles southeast of Bogotá, by about four days. Ramirez felt there was no way his men could have come any closer.

For Ramirez, Lehder became a special project. Unlike Escobar, Ochoa, and Rodriguez Gacha, hiding out in Panama, Lehder was available in Colombia. And unlike the expatriates—and much more important—Lehder's case was closed. Ramirez was a realist, and he knew that even if he arrested Escobar or Ochoa, it would be a miracle if a Colombian jail could hold either man. History had shown that the Medellín cartel bribed or murdered anyone who opposed it, and there wasn't a judge or a prison warden anywhere in Colombia likely to escape one of these two fates. Even though the United States had asked for extradition, there would be a long legal road to travel before anyone in the Medellín cartel was sent north.

Except Carlos Lehder was different. Betancur had signed Lehder's extradition order; his appeals were exhausted. The Justice Ministry soon confirmed what Ramirez suspected: if he arrested Lehder, he could quite likely simply put him on an airplane and send him to the United States without any bureaucratic hassle whatsoever.

Ramirez began to stalk his quarry. He set his men to work collecting intelligence and developing informants. The Airapua incident had not scared Lehder off. In fact, within two months he was calling up radio stations and sending "open letters" denouncing "U.S. imperialism" and predicting his return to public life. He told *Semana* magazine that he was "not hiding, simply extremely busy. Soon I'll be in Bogotá without any problems at all, because they're going to fix my case."

In early 1984 Lehder had tried unsuccessfully to sell Norman's Cay. In June 1984 the DEA reported sighting Lehder in Miami, possibly visiting a nephew. In November Ramirez's men tracked him to Finca Chipre near Magangue, about one hundred miles southeast of Cartagena in the Magdalena River valley. There he was supposed to be setting up a new smuggling operation. Police busted it November 18, seizing 230 kilograms of cocaine, but Lehder wasn't there.

At the end of the year Ramirez's informants traced Lehder to Colón, where he was reportedly living in a three-story, red-roofed house about three blocks from the Panama Canal. A little over a week before that, the informants said, he had been in Medellín. Clearly he was back in touch with his colleagues. Lehder now had twenty-five aliases and passports from Colombia, Uruguay, and West Germany. He was corresponding with Bogotá lawyer Pablo Salah Villamizar, a favorite of the drug dealers, which was probably the way his news releases were getting out.

Finally, in February 1985 he gave an interview to Spanish television from one of his *llanos* hideouts. It was the usual neo-Nazi claptrap but this time overlain with a touch of paranoia. Too much cocaine? Lehder was bearded and shaggy, dressed in fatigue pants and a sleeveless black vest and sitting on a chair with his back to a river. He told the television reporters he was planning to form a "five-hundred-thousand-man" army to "defend the national sovereignty." Lara Bonilla, he said, was "shot by the masses" in self-defense.

"The extradition problem has grown to become a problem of national liberation," he said. "It was the people who shot Lara Bonilla before he could—with imperialism's help—send more than three hundred Colombians en masse to be processed in the United States."

Lehder deftly skirted, as always, the question of what he did for a living. Then his interviewer asked him how he could get good ideas from Adolf Hitler, who, "among other things, killed six million Jews."

"That is misinformation," Lehder said. "We know that there were never more than one million Jews in Germany. Half of the blood running through my body is German, right? In other words—if there is someone who can talk about Germany, it is not the Jew, it is the German! If one can talk about Colombia, it is the Colombian! It shall not be a Brazilian or a Czechoslovakian. Am I right?

"I say with all honesty that—Adolf, along with six million soldiers, eliminated twenty-one million communists, right? And he eliminated ten million Allied enemies. In other words he, Adolf, is and shall be . . . right? . . . until someone surpasses him, he shall be the greatest warrior the world has ever seen."

Lehder meandered rhetorically, with little regard for ideology. Along with "Adolf's" anticommunist Nazism, he blithely embraced modern revolutionary socialism. He denounced the United States as a society "guided by *Playboy* magazine . . . drunk on pornography" and "guided by a military industry that forces the United States to open fronts of war and fronts for the sale of arms, and one of the newest and most novel excuses [to do this] is the struggle against drug trafficking. . . ."

18.

DRAWDOWN

Apart from the tragedy of the Lara Bonilla killing, 1984 was looking like the year of successful moves against the Medellín cartel. The Tranquilandia bust, the beginning of marijuana spraying, and the enforcement of the extradition treaty had given both the Colombian and U.S. governments cause for optimism.

But almost immediately after Belisario Betancur proclaimed a state of siege, law enforcement began to notice that crackdown had its limits. Arrests in the aftermath of the Lara Bonilla assassination reached the impressive total of 398, but few of the suspects could be held beyond questioning. For example, the weapons charge against old Fabio Ochoa collapsed, and he was soon released.

Furthermore, police only picked up two "extraditables" in the post–Lara Bonilla dragnet. Johnny Phelps, still not particularly trusting of the Betancur administration, immediately called a news conference at the U.S. embassy in which he described the prisoners as a "test case" of the Colombian government's new resolve to extradite drug traffickers. By the end of the year the United States would have more than one hundred extradition requests filed in Colombia. Phelps wanted to hold Betancur's feet to the fire.

Phelps was one of the first to realize that the Lara Bonilla killing had dramatically raised the stakes in the drug war. If Colombia wanted to arrest traffickers, it better have the laws to prosecute them and the security to keep them in jail. And if Colombia wanted to extradite traffickers, it better have the institutional strength to endure the cartel's threats. The Colombian justice system was going to be tested as never before.

The traffickers, hunkered down in Panama or hidden away in jungle *fincas* in Colombia, had no intention of backing off: "I am a symbol of those men who battle imperialism,'' said Carlos Lehder from his *llanos* hideout. ''In this struggle the end justifies the means.''

Suddenly Colombia was a much more dangerous place. In July Betancur told an audience of Roman Catholic priests that traffickers had threatened him on his private telephone line at the Nariño Presidential Palace. Only his closest advisers were supposed to know the number. Betancur, who used to seek out the multitude to bask in its adulation, now traveled in an armored car and showed up for appointments at odd times. In the days when he was ''philosophically opposed'' to extradition, the cartel had left him alone. Now that he had declared ''all-out war'' on drug trafficking, he was their enemy.

LEWIS Tambs had begun to notice his deteriorating security almost from the moment he arrived in Colombia. At first he had ridden in a U.S. Army armored Cadillac limousine and had a ''follow car'' loaded with security agents to back him up. He carried a .357 Magnum revolver at all times. But early on he had discovered that he could outshoot every one of his Colombian bodyguards. Since Tambs knew he was no Wild Bill Hickok, this was, as he put it, ''unnerving.''

So he took his bodyguards to a firing range and practiced with them regularly, both with pistols and with Israeli Uzi submachine guns. It was good for morale; everybody liked to shoot, Tambs included. He got to where he could hit 242 out of 250 with the pistol, and his bodyguards, thank God, did better than that.

As time passed, Tambs's security advisers kept adding cars to his convoy. By the time of the Lara Bonilla killing he had five: a ''scout'' car, a ''lead'' car, his limo, and two follow cars. He had two personal bodyguards besides his regular escort and could draw reinforcements from a corps of five hundred Colombians assigned to guard the U.S. embassy and its personnel.

The rest of the embassy staff rode to work in heavy, armored black four-wheel-drive vehicles. Embassy kids rode to school in buses escorted by army jeeps with machine guns mounted on the back. Tambs had forced everybody to move out of houses and into apartments and had provided everyone with armed guards.

Three times Washington re-called Tambs to question him about the drug traffickers' threats and to talk about security. In late May 1984, shortly after the Lara Bonilla killing, the White House sent Tambs a team of specialists to advise his security people. This was after an empty automobile rolled downhill toward the U.S. embassy residence, collided with a curb, and exploded, sending flames shooting three hundred feet into the air. With a slightly better angle, whoever was responsible could have put the car at the gate of the residence. Tambs took a look at the wreckage and found only a front axle. The rest of the car had disappeared.

The White House team stayed a few months, then went home. Nevertheless the threats still came regularly, by phone and in the mail. Now, in October 1984, Tambs felt the embassy was under siege, and Washington agreed. The State Department cabled him to "draw down" the official U.S. delegation to a bare minimum. Tambs first asked for volunteers to leave Colombia, then made up an additional cut list. In all, he reduced the staff by 30 percent.

JOHNNY Phelps spent the final months before his midyear departure riding to work in an armored van, carrying a Swedish machine gun along with his usual pistol, living in an apartment with security guards and listening to running gun battles in the neighborhood practically every night. His daughters had watched a shooting from their school-bus, and his eight-year-old son had seen a dead man lying in the street beside a police van. In the United States for a visit after a particularly long stay in Colombia, he had stared through a friend's picture window, feeling slightly bemused because there were no bars on it.

And if this was "success" in Colombia, it had failed to make any lasting impression in the United States. After Tranquilandia, the wholesale per-kilo price of cocaine had risen above $25,000 in Miami. Five months later it was back at $14,000 and dropping lower than at any time in history. The Colombian foreign minister, frustrated at the lack of progress and disturbed at the damage that was being done to Betancur's presidency, complained repeatedly to Tambs: "We have been able to capture more drugs than any country in the world, why can't you stop consumption?" Tambs had no answer.

IN the immediate aftermath of the Lara Bonilla assassination, all but the biggest chieftains were back in Medellín. And in September, resident DEA agent Mike Vigil spotted Pablo Escobar, his wife, and a retinue of bodyguards at the bullfights. Crackdown, it seemed, was over.

A secret police memo dated in August reported that Escobar and Gonzalo Rodriguez Gacha were living in a house in a fashionable residential district of Medellín. They were in town for the christening of Escobar's newborn daughter and getting ready to visit a *finca*.

Young Fabio Ochoa, the memo said, was driving a yellow-and-black municipal cab for fun and wearing a beret. Two police captains periodically briefed the cartel members so they could avoid arrest.

And even if the cartel chieftains were seldom seen, their presence was everywhere felt. Besides their informers in the police department, the traffickers had so many bodyguards and hired gunmen that it made no sense to try to arrest them. Anybody who wanted to question Pablo Escobar had better show up with a platoon of soldiers.

As if to drive this point home, the rumor spread in October that ambitious underworld types had sensed weakness in the traffickers and had kidnapped Escobar's seventy-three-year-old father, Abel de Jesús Escobar Echeverri, hoping for a quick payoff from the absent "Godfather." Within hours, the rumors said, Escobar put as many as five thousand gunmen in the street, scrambled helicopters, and started turning Medellín and the surrounding countryside inside out. Escobar's father was released unharmed after sixteen days. Not a centavo was paid. No one was ever able to figure out if the story was anything but a publicity stunt, but true or false, the message conveyed was clear enough: Escobar was back; Escobar was in control.

Escobar's money was everywhere. On October 23 Judge Tulio Manuel Castro Gil, who had indicted the cartel in the Lara Bonilla case a few months earlier, was met outside a Medellín courthouse by an Escobar bagman with a proposition. He sought the "temporary dismissal" of the indictment:

"Ask for whatever you want, and they'll put it wherever you want it, in Colombia or outside the country," the bagman said. Once he made up his mind, he should get in contact with one of Escobar's sisters.

"Then you can relax," the bagman concluded. "Neither your life nor the lives of your family members will be in danger."

THE Lara Bonilla assassination had caused Phelps to revise his thinking about his Medellín office. On the one hand, he regarded the murder as an incredibly stupid stunt for which the traffickers had paid dearly. On the other hand, it was a warning. First with Errol Chavez and now with Mike Vigil, he had perhaps blithely assumed that the cartel wouldn't dare touch the DEA in Medellín. The Lara Bonilla murder had changed that. If they would hit a sitting cabinet minister, they would hit anyone. This was true everywhere in Colombia, but it would happen first in Medellín.

Vigil's security was negligible. He drove everywhere with the window down so he could hear the motorcycles when they came up behind him. He was deathly afraid of the motorcycles, especially in the traffic circles where the killers could sneak between lanes of cars, murder their victims, and scurry down a side street leaving everyone else mired in a traffic jam. Once, driving home at night, Vigil heard a motorcycle behind him but couldn't see any lights. He sped up, dodged back and forth in the roadway so the bike couldn't come up alongside, then screeched into his driveway and ran for cover. He spotted the motorcyle as it drove by. There was a passenger who held his hands between his legs, looking at Vigil. Sorry he missed his mark? Or wondering about the crazy driver? Vigil ran up to his apartment and had a double shot of Jack Daniel's.

Like Chavez before him, Vigil lost all six of the informants he developed, many of them in grotesque ways. One man was beaten and tortured with pins jammed beneath his fingernails, then shot in the head and tossed in the street with a sign around his neck: "Killed for Being a DEA Informant."

AS the year wore on, it became obvious that the crackdown had failed. The flow of cocaine to the United States had not been interrupted and the drug traffickers had not been scared away, extradited, or even arrested in meaningful numbers.

After several months Colombians began to get weary of the tension. Public opinion alternated between outrage and resignation, crackdown and appeasement. These wild mood swings would occur again and again in Colombia, with increasing frequency and intensity—a collective manic depression.

The first spasm happened less than three months after Lara Bonilla's death. *El Tiempo* in Bogotá leaked the news of the cartel's May meeting in Panama with Alfonso Lopez Michelsen; soon the Jimenez Gomez encounter was public knowledge, along with the cartel's famous proposition. The revelations caused a sensation.

At first they brought widespread condemnation from most influential Colombians. One senator said talking to drug traffickers was "like inviting bank robbers to a symposium on bank security."

But Lopez Michelsen refused to be chastised about it. He again said that he was willing to act as a "mailbox" and then said nothing further. Congress summoned Attorney General Jimenez Gomez and demanded that he defend himself, but it got little satisfaction:

"I told them I would deliver their note, but that obviously it should be understood that it was a unilateral declaration, that it could not be interpreted as a promise of an agreement or as a bilateral treaty," Jimenez Gomez said. "I did not expect, nor do I expect, any answer because it was a unilateral declaration."

Betancur, prodded to make some sort of a statement, waited a week after *El Tiempo*'s revelations before condemning the cartel's proposal: "Under no circumstances will there be a dialogue. . . . There haven't been and there won't be negotiations between the government and the authors of the memo."

Yet Betancur did not convince. *El Tiempo* noted that letters in favor of talks with the drug bosses were running slightly ahead of letters opposing them. A television poll found that 48 percent of respondents favored talks. And even Justice Minister Parejo Gonzalez, hardest of the hard-liners, defended Jimenez Gomez: "What the attorney general did was try to find a solution to the problem."

Finally, there was no denying that the cartel still wielded considerable political influence. Even with its "maximum chief" hiding in the jungle, Carlos Lehder's National Latin Movement in the 1984 off-year elections managed to win two seats in the Quindio provincial legislature and four city council seats.

In addition, on July 9 Pablo Escobar gave a telephone interview to Bogotá's Radio Caracól from "somewhere" outside Colombia. It was a classic Escobar political pitch, carefully worded and tedious as an address to a Communist Party congress: "People who know me understand very well that I am involved in industry, construction, and ranching," he said. He described his role in narco-dialogue as that of an "intermediary," claiming that "the fact that I attack extradition does not make me extraditable." The Lara Bonilla indictment was a "gratuitous and capricious accusation." He had left Colombia because he "had no guarantees of any kind."

What gave credence to this debate was the public's knowledge that the hard line didn't seem to work. Escobar was unrepentant, alive, and well. The cartel's proposal outlined what could be a peaceful solution to an impossible problem. The government may have scoffed, but a lot of Colombians thought maybe the government should take the proposal seriously.

SHORTLY after midyear Ramirez's antinarcotics police could see that the cartel was building new labs and growing new coca fields in several *llanos* provinces. Escobar was heavily involved, but the leading figure was Gonzalo Rodriguez Gacha, now Escobar's frequent partner and constant companion. It was Rodriguez Gacha who put the *campesino* growers on the payroll and negotiated the per-gram coca tax with the FARC guerrillas who provided security. The FARC-narc relationship was ambiguous and changeable as always but seemed to survive as long as both sides profited from it. On August 9 soldiers had a firefight with FARC guerrillas and recovered documents suggesting the rebels were financing weapons purchases with cocaine profits. On October 12 the FARC attacked police raiding a jungle lab. Later in the year army intelligence reported the FARC had taken sixteen people hostage near Tranquilandia and released them five at a time in return for 150 barrels of ether and acetone, 592 kilos of cocaine, and 25 million pesos ($250,000). At the end of the year an informant told police that Escobar had five hundred acres of jungle coca with accompanying labs and that a one-hundred-man FARC column was not only providing security but also operating both the farm and the factory. On Christmas Eve Escobar visited the site to pay Christmas bonuses.

IT was the guerrillas who finally decided things for the DEA in Medellín. In November Vigil got tipped off that the traffickers had put out a kidnapping contract on him and a guerrilla hit team had picked it up. Shortly after the warning, Medellín DAS agents told Vigil they had discovered people watching him and tracing his movements. Vigil called Bogotá and talked to George Frangullie, Phelps's successor. Frangullie told Tambs, and Vigil was gone before Christmas. The DEA closed its Medellín office.

At the same time, Tambs in Bogotá was taking even more precautions. After the embassy drawdown, he ruled that only single people or couples without children could stay. Next he put the embassy on "flex time" so people would show up for work at different hours. Then he fed the work schedule into a computer so that it would become even more random. On November 26, a small white Fiat sedan exploded outside the U.S. embassy, breaking windows up and down Eighth Avenue and covering the streets with debris for two square blocks. Six people were seriously injured, and one woman passerby was decapitated by a sheet of flying glass.

In early December Tambs's security staff told him they believed one of his Colombian bodyguards had been bribed to kill him. The State Department wanted him out of Colombia on Christmas Eve. Tambs stalled, then took a "vacation" and flew home with his family December 26. After he left, his security officers gave everyone on the staff a lie detector test. One man, the one who had aroused suspicion, refused to take it, resigned, went down to his bank, and withdrew a lot of money.

In the United States, Tambs was told that his wife and children were not going back to Colombia. A few days later Tambs was informed by the State Department that his Colombian tour was over.

FROM mid-1981 to the beginning of 1985, four men had hounded the Medellín cartel without mercy. Their achievements were impressive, but their failure was also evident. The cartel had suffered badly at their hands but had fought them to a draw. It had murdered Rodrigo Lara Bonilla; it had outlasted Johnny Phelps; and now it had chased away Lewis Tambs.

That left only Jaime Ramirez.

19.

THE AUDIENCIA

By the fall of 1984, the Medellín cartel had begun to recover its power and influence. Pablo Escobar and Gonzalo Rodriguez Gacha were back in Colombia, quietly reestablishing their processing and trafficking networks after five months of neglect. Carlos Lehder remained in internal exile in the *llanos,* but Escobar and Rodriguez Gacha had enlisted his help as an overseer for the cartel's burgeoning jungle operations and as a diplomatic go-between in guerrilla relations. Old Fabio Ochoa was living quietly and breeding horses at La Loma and Hacienda Veracruz. Sons Juan David and Fabio were keeping a lower profile but were hardly invisible. They were back in Medellín and back in business.

But nobody had seen or heard anything from Jorge Ochoa since Carlos Jimenez Gomez's visit to Panama in May. When the Nicaragua deal blew up in a cloud of publicity, Jorge Ochoa had seemed to vanish.

In fact, sometime in July or early August Ochoa had emigrated to Spain with Cali cocaine boss Gilberto Rodriguez Orejuela. Ochoa showed up in Madrid as "Moisés Moreno Miranda," while Rodriguez Orejuela held a Venezuelan passport in the name of "Gilberto Gonzalez Linares." Both men were traveling with their wives, and both appeared outwardly respectable.

Shortly after their arrival, the wives began to deposit large amounts of U.S. dollars in local banks—$370,000 in all. Ochoa bought an eight-thousand-square-foot mansion on a huge tract of land in one of Madrid's most fashionable suburban neighborhoods. He had a swimming pool, tennis courts, a storehouse, and a discotheque to go with the four Mercedes-Benzes parked in his garage. He registered his five-year-old son in the bilingual American School.

Rodriguez Orejuela stayed in a fancy downtown hotel, but he bought two huge apartments, one of them still under construction, and picked up his own pair of Mercedes sedans. Both men had made their purchases through holding companies set up in their wives' names.

At the end of August a tipster approached Spain's Special Prosecutor for the Prevention and Repression of Drug Trafficking and suggested that "Moreno Miranda" was not who he pretended to be. The prosecutor went to the Group IX judicial police, who put "Moreno Miranda" under surveillance.

What the police investigators saw at first was a married couple having a grand time eating in fancy restaurants, going to concerts, and driving around in beautiful new automobiles. They discovered that the "Moreno Mirandas" socialized with a Venezuelan couple named "Gonzalez Linares." Soon after that they found where the two men lived, watched their wives prowling around banks during the day, and came to the conclusion suggested by their informant: "Moreno Miranda" and his friend were probably drug traffickers seeking to resettle in Spain. Their wives were laundering drug money. The police also noticed that the two men met frequently at an empty downtown apartment, where they apparently did business.

The Spaniards ran the two men through their mug books and identified Rodriguez Orejuela almost immediately. Soon they had Ochoa identified as well. By September 25 the police had five wiretaps in place. Ochoa had been calling Colombia, London, Panama, and Belgium.

The judicial police told the DEA in Madrid, and the DEA cabled home: "Intelligence . . . has indicated that suspected Colombian trafficking group intends to create investment company with unlimited funding and is in the process of purchasing several extremely expensive residences, indicating intent to remain in Spain."

Rodriguez Orejuela had been sought since 1978 on Los Angeles and New York drug trafficking warrants; Ochoa was sought in the Nicaragua case. The Justice Department prepared extradition requests on the two fugitives and gave them to the State Department, which passed them to the U.S. embassy in Madrid. On October 17 the ambassador passed a "verbal note" to the Spanish Foreign Ministry requesting the arrests of both men.

Altogether, Spanish police watched Ochoa and Rodriguez Orejuela for 2½ months, growing increasingly nervous as time passed. The stakes loomed much larger in November when investigators found out that Ochoa was planning to buy ten thousand acres of ranchland in southern Spain. Police feared what this might be used for. One of their internal reports said, "In Colombia right now, the cocaine traffickers have a serious problem finding ether and hydrochloric acid." Spain, the report said, "could be converted into a world cocaine distribution center."

On November 15, 1984, the Spanish judicial police arrested Ochoa, Rodriguez Orejuela, and their wives, froze all their bank accounts, and seized $90,000 in cash lying loose in their residences. In Rodriguez Orejuela's hotel room they found an account book describing 1983 sales of more than four metric tons of cocaine. The DEA saw to it that Ochoa's son was taken out of the American School.

FOR the Reagan administration, the capture of Jorge Ochoa seemed like a gift from God. Not even four months had elapsed since the U.S. government had named Ochoa and the rest of the Medellín cartel as criminal partners of Nicaragua's Sandinista government. Now the Spaniards had caught Ochoa, and he stood an excellent chance of being extradited to the United States. The political advantages to be obtained from such a circumstance were enormous.

The Spaniards seemed cooperative. DEA agent William Mockler had arrived in Madrid a couple of days before Ochoa's capture to assist the Spanish police and the DEA's resident agent in Madrid, Jimmy Kibble. Mockler had been stationed in Miami and was familiar with the Nicaragua case and with events in Colombia since Tranquilandia. More important, he was the DEA's expert on Rodriguez Orejuela.

Spanish police telephoned Mockler and Kibble a couple of hours after Ochoa and Rodriguez Orejuela had been picked up. The two DEA agents arrived at the station about 10:30 P.M. and took a look at the defendants through a one-way mirror. The two Colombians were casually dressed and grim-looking.

Mockler identified Rodriguez Orejuela and chatted with the Spanish police about Colombian cocaine dealers in general and the Medellín cartel in particular. He made a formal deposition, describing what he knew about both defendants, what he called "information from investigations," as well as "general facts" about Colombian cocaine trafficking.

It took about thirty minutes, and the Spanish were impressed. Mockler taught them how to read Rodriguez Orejuela's account book, showing them in the process that they were holding a man accustomed to dealing enormous quantities of cocaine. The Spaniards noted that they had seen such books before, but until then had never known what they were. In Spain in 1984, three kilos of cocaine was a big bust.

The Spanish police's frame of reference for cases like Ochoa's was political. The Spaniards didn't know a great deal about international drug trafficking, but they were accustomed to terrorism and ideological extremism of all types. In Spain political tolerance had been almost unheard of until the last ten years or so.

The Spanish police knew that Ochoa was wanted for running cocaine through Nicaragua with the help of the Marxist government there. This gave them a political peg that they could understand. Mockler took it further. He was able to connect Ochoa to Tranquilandia, which, he said, had been guarded by "M-19 guerrillas." The Nicaragua operation had been handled at a military airstrip with Nicaraguan soldiers loading the cocaine. For the Spaniards, all of this tied together: Rodriguez-Ochoa, M-19, Nicaragua. In other words, cocaine, terrorism, the Soviet bloc—the triple nightmare of the free world.

The Spaniards announced that Ochoa would be held on special antiterrorist laws pending a review of the charges. Throughout the case the Spanish would treat Ochoa the way they treated imprisoned Basque separatists—as an extremely dangerous man with extremely dangerous friends. This was probably wise. Ochoa was dangerous enough, and although he didn't have dangerous friends immediately available to him in Spain, he certainly had the money to hire some.

It was clear from the beginning that the terrorism-communism-drugs link—accurate or not—offered a comfortable framework within which U.S. and Spanish law officers could discuss the Ochoa case. The Spaniards knew a lot about terrorism but almost nothing about cocaine traffickers who dealt in tons. The Americans knew a lot about big drug lords but almost nothing about terrorism (Mockler in his deposition confused M-19 with the FARC at Tranquilandia). In lumping everything together, however, both sides could appear knowledgeable about the case, even when they weren't.

Unfortunately, this strategy backfired in Spain as it did in the United States. Many Spaniards regarded the Spanish police and the DEA, like the Reagan administration, as so virulently anticommunist that they would go to any lengths to discredit the Sandinista government—even to the extent of accusing it of dealing drugs. For its part, the Nicaraguan government was quick to denounce what it described as U.S. deceit. Nicaragua, in a statement issued by Interior Minister Borge's office, rejected "in absolute terms the false accusations made by the American government, whose objective . . . is to discredit our country and justify the illegal war of aggression promoted and directed by the United States.''

Such sentiments had a certain resonance in Spanish America's mother country, and Ochoa's lawyers quickly recognized the advantage and exploited it. As Kibble and Mockler left the police station, Mockler told the inspectors that they could expect large numbers of attorneys to show up momentarily. The inspectors chuckled. Three lawyers were at the station within an hour; withing two days each defendant had around ten, including some of the most eminent jurists in the country.

And on November 27, 1984, only twelve days after Ochoa's arrest, the lawyers filed a complaint charging that DEA agents had participated in the initial police interrogation of Ochoa and Rodriguez Orejuela. At the agents' behest, the complaint charged, Spanish police tried to induce both defendants to denounce the Sandinistas as drug traffickers. In return, the complaint said, the U.S. government had offered to ensure that documents required to complete the extradition package would "arrive too late." Ochoa and Rodriguez Orejuela declined the offer, the complaint said.

Kibble later described the allegations as "100 percent, unequivocal nonsense" concocted by the Spanish press, probably with the help of Ochoa's people. Neither he nor Mockler, he said, ever spoke a single word to either defendant.

Still, there was reason for the Spaniards at least to consider the story. The Reagan administration, in its haste to smear the Sandinistas, had already blown the DEA's Nicaragua investigation. What was to stop it from trying to do something else in Spain?

The United States formally requested Ochoa's extradition on the Nicaraguan indictment shortly after his arrest in Madrid. Extradition for Rodriguez Orejuela was also quickly filed, based on two older trafficking cases, from Los Angeles and New York. The Spanish government examined the documents and on January 10, 1985, submitted them to the Audiencia Nacional for review. Five days after that, Colombia asked for Ochoa's extradition on charges of "falsifying a public document"—namely the license to import 128 Spanish bulls into Cartagena in 1981, or smuggling. On February 23 the Spanish Justice Ministry sent the Colombian request to the Audiencia Nacional as well. The battle was on.

AT the outset of the Ochoa case, the United States appeared to be in a stronger position. Drug trafficking is more serious than bull smuggling; the U.S. claim had been filed first; the Spanish government was known to favor the U.S. request over the Colombian.

The defense team had to whittle away these advantages or circumvent them. Within six months Colombia had submitted a second request for Ochoa's extradition, this one sent from Medellín and based on the Nicaraguan indictment on file in Miami. Clearly what had happened was that an Ochoa crony had gone into Miami public records, photocopied the Nicaragua indictment, taken it home, and sent it to a district court in Medellín. As a result Colombia now had two requests to the United States' one, including one that was just as serious as the U.S. accusation. In fact, it was the same one. Rodriguez Orejuela worked the same scam with his indictments. Both his cases were refiled in Cali.

The legal battle in Spain bore little resemblance to the courtroom cases of the United States. The Spanish justice system, like the Colombian, was "Napoleonic" rather than "adversarial." Verdicts were made on the basis of interpretation of written laws rather than legal precedent and juries' decisions. The judge was in charge of the criminal investigation of a case, and judge, prosecutor, and defender met together to present arguments, hear evidence, and file motions. This took place not in a public courtroom, but in the privacy of the judges' chambers. Everything was written down, studied, and discussed, and a conclusion was arrived at. The case was summarized and the verdict announced after a single hearing, the only time the public had a chance to see the defendant.

In Colombia the traffickers took tremendous advantage of these procedures. Since so much of the case took place in closed rooms, it was an easy matter to intimidate or otherwise manipulate judges. On the other hand, defendants seldom saw their accusers or the witnesses arrayed against them. Judges taking depositions in chambers or a closed courtroom were extremely kind to hearsay evidence, as Mockler had found. In Colombia Jaime Ramirez had become the chief prosecution witness in the Lara Bonilla killing largely by recounting what he knew of Pablo Escobar's life history and the reason Escobar would be likely to want to murder the justice minister.

In Spain the integrity of the courts was more rigorous than in Colombia, but there was plenty the defendant could do to play on public opinion. The first news accounts of the arrest and interrogation of Ochoa and Rodriguez Orejuela invariably referred to the two men as "Colombian *mafiosi*." As the months passed, however, the pair frequently appeared in print as "Colombian rancher Jorge Luis Ochoa, 36," and "Colombian banker Gilberto Rodriguez Orejuela, 46."

Headline writers never altogether lost their affinity for "Colombian *mafiosi*," but the cartel publicity machine was getting its message across.

Also pure cartel was an April 2, 1985, story in the Madrid newspaper *El País* citing unnamed Spanish and Colombian "diplomatic sources" as saying the CIA was responsible for shooting at the Spanish embassy in Bogotá on two occasions "to justify and accelerate the extradition of the drug traffickers and to discredit them before the public." In June *El País* printed a story about the DEA's attempt to induce Ochoa to denounce the Nicaraguan government. It was accompanied by Mockler's testimony. The U.S. embassy told Mockler he would be well advised not to return to Madrid.

One Ochoa lawyer denounced the Reagan administration's "dirty war against Nicaragua" and portrayed his client as a pawn in a dishonorable political chess game. Ochoa's attorneys also took advantage of hearsay, citing statements by conservative U.S. Senator Paula Hawkins and other U.S. dignitaries who spoke out about Sandinistas and drugs. At one point the lawyers even quoted a midwestern farmer willing to do "anything we can do to support President Reagan in Nicaragua." The plan was to portray "Colombian rancher" Jorge Ochoa not as a drug trafficker, but as a victim of U.S. politics.

The prosecution could not match the defense in publicity, but it did have a few tricks of its own. At one point the story spread that friends of Ochoa had tried to break him out of jail with a daring helicopter rescue attempt. And a couple of days after the Mockler story was leaked, "police sources" told the Spanish news agency EFE that Ochoa and Rodriguez Orejuela had attempted to bribe the police in charge of the case. The sources also denied they had tried to get Ochoa to denounce the Sandinistas. The sources did not say whom, specifically, Ochoa had tried to bribe and for how much. The EFE story described Ochoa as the "viceroy of world cocaine traffic" behind Escobar.

THE cases against Ochoa and Rodriguez Orejuela were handled in the penal chamber of Spain's Audiencia Nacional—roughly translated as "National Court." Spain had no state or provincial justice system or specialized courts, so the "National Court" absorbed huge numbers of cases that in the United States would be parceled out among several jurisdictions.

The Audiencia Nacional examined the evidence for nearly nine months. Ochoa pronounced himself willing to stand trial for bull smuggling in Colombia but professed innocence in the drug charges and refused to accede to a trafficking trial either in Colombia or the United States. Ochoa's lawyers continued to push the political nature of the accusations and tried mightily to discredit the U.S. case by ridiculing Barry Seal, denouncing him as a criminal and a liar.

The prosecution handled these objections capably, assisted on several occasions by lawyers sent to Spain from the U.S. Department of Justice's Office of International Affairs. The visitors explained grand juries and plea bargaining and "flipping" drug offenders to turn them into informants, the latter two practices virtually unknown and viewed with extreme distaste in countries that use a Napoleonic justice system.

And in the matter of Seal, hearsay again came to the rescue. Newspapers described Seal as the only witness against Ochoa and questioned his reliability, pointing out that he was a crook cooperating with the DEA only to stay out of jail himself. Seal was, in fact, the only witness, but the defense was forced to acknowledge depositions submitted by Seal's two case agents. These were nothing more than the Seal story retold by the people who debriefed him—that is, hearsay—but under Spanish law they were admissible. So the prosecution now had three witnesses, only one of whom was a flipped felon.

THE Audiencia Nacional's public extradition hearing was held September 17, 1985. The case rated a special courtroom built for dangerous defendants. It was copied from the 1975 film *The Man in the Glass Booth*, about the trial of Adolf Eichmann. Pews for the public—enough seating for perhaps eighty people altogether—occupied the back half of the room. The public was set off from judges, defendants, and prosecutor by a three-foot-high wooden panel and a floor-to-ceiling sheet of bulletproof glass. The audience could see and hear the proceedings but could not breach the glass wall. This discouraged political activists from interrupting trials with a grenade.

A panel of three judges sat behind a wood podium at the front of the room, gazing out over the courtroom. Defense and prosecution were installed on either side of the judges, facing one another. The accused sat before the judges on a low wooden bench backed up against the glass dividing wall. In addition, there was a specially constructed bulletproof "bullpen" for extra defendants.

On trial day the gallery was almost completely filled with Colombians—members of the Ochoa family and others whose purpose was not immediately apparent. A handful of nervous lawyers from the

U.S. Justice Department were also on hand, curiosity overcoming caution. The atmosphere was noisy and vaguely unpleasant at first, but the crowd quieted immediately when the hearing began. Ochoa, in a dark suit, sat quietly with his back against the glass wall, flanked by two policemen wearing berets. He looked good; he'd lost a lot of weight. He was well groomed, hair neatly trimmed, no mustache, no fat cheeks, no hair tonic. He was quite the prosperous young Colombian businessman. Except for the eyes, noted DEA agent Kibble. The eyes were those of a man much older than Ochoa. Anybody who saw the eyes could tell Ochoa was no fool.

The hearing lasted about three hours, which was longer than usual. The three-judge penal court panel opened the proceedings and invited the prosecution to summarize its case. Then the defense made its response, the prosecution delivered a rebuttal, and the defense closed with a rejoinder. The judges interjected a few questions, but this was largely a formality. The case had already been presented and compiled in lengthy legal-sized tomes stored in chambers. The judges would consult these later. The hearing served two largely ceremonial but nevertheless important purposes: an oral, public confrontation between prosecution and defense and a public affirmation that the court had done its duty.

The judges closed the hearing, dismissed everyone, and retired to confer. On September 24 they spoke: by a vote of 3–0 they denied the U.S. petition for extradition because of its "political context." Ochoa would be sent to Colombia to stand trial for bull smuggling.

"To accede to the petition formulated by the United States," the finding said, "the defendant could run the risk of seeing his situation aggravated because of political considerations." The judges noted that Seal "has a direct interest" in denouncing Ochoa because "of a pact he had with American authorities to obtain a pardon for a sentence of ten years." The court did not find convincing the U.S. argument "implicating the government of Nicaragua" given "the notorious animosity between the current U.S. government and that Central American Republic."

Ochoa's lawyers had won the game by playing the anti-imperialist card, denouncing Seal, and expressing willingness to allow their client to be extradited to Colombia. "The finding has been juridically correct," said Enrique Gimbernat, one of Ochoa's lawyers.

But it was not the last word. The prosecution filed an appeal, also within the Audiencia Nacional, also within the penal chamber. This time all seven of the chamber's judges would examine the evidence. The prosecution argued—and forcefully enough to convince the court to reexamine the case—that "the fact of bad relations between governments" had nothing to do with the merits of a legal case in any nation "ruled by law." The United States was such a nation.

And, incredibly, on January 21, 1986, the Audiencia Nacional by a vote of 4–3 reversed itself and agreed to send Ochoa to the United States. The court noted that besides Seal, the United States had presented evidence from two "American agents" (Seal's DEA case officers). Finally, the judges said, "the notorious and undoubtable fact" that the United States and Nicaragua had unfriendly relations "does not constitute a legal impediment to extradition." Ochoa was accused of drug trafficking, which could not be "reconstituted as a crime of a political character."

The defense immediately appealed.

UNCLE SAM WANTS YOU

When Jorge Ochoa was arrested in Spain, Barry Seal's value to the U.S. government skyrocketed. If Ochoa was extradited to the United States for trial in Miami, Seal would be the only eyewitness to his crimes. Yet despite the fact that Seal had made the most important case in the history of the U.S. Drug Enforcement Administration, federal officials in Baton Rouge and New Orleans had not given up trying to indict him for drug smuggling in Louisiana.

Federal law enforcement is broken up throughout the United States into fiefdoms known as federal districts. Seal's problems centered on crimes he allegedly committed in the Middle District of Louisiana before he became an informant in the Southern District of Florida. Seal had been targeted by a joint federal and state task force run out of Baton Rouge and New Orleans by veteran federal Organized Crime Strike Force prosecutor Al Winters, a big, bearish man with a rumbling basso voice. As a strike force prosecutor, Winters worked directly for the Justice Department out of Washington, but the man who ultimately called the shots on the Seal investigation was Stanford Bardwell, the U.S. attorney for the Middle District of Louisiana. Bardwell was a political appointee of the Reagan administration, a civil lawyer who had never tried a criminal case. But like the rest of the law enforcement community in Baton Rouge, Bardwell badly wanted to indict Barry Seal.

Soon Al Winters found himself caught between two federal districts with wildly conflicting visions of Barry Seal. Louisiana knew Seal as a cunning, arrogant manipulator who had made fools out of law enforcement in Baton Rouge while bringing tons of cocaine into the state. But in the Southern District of Florida, Seal was the contrite informant who had had a change of heart and become the DEA's most productive undercover operative. Both visions were accurate. "Miami thinks the guy is the greatest thing since sliced bread, which is usual because he's helping them," Winters said. "And Baton Rouge thinks he's the worst drug dealer in the history of Louisiana, which he was."

Federal drug conspiracy investigations are usually made with informants. Federal prosecutors find some of them by inducing convicted drug dealers to "flip." Others are intimidated by the threat of a federal grand jury, where witnesses can be summoned to testify under oath without an attorney present and can be thrown in prison if caught in a single lie.

When Seal found out in August 1984 that a federal grand jury in Baton Rouge was hauling his friends in, he held true to form and took the offensive. First he tried to get his federal friends in Miami to intervene. It seemed logical. The federal investigation of Seal in Louisiana made the south Florida feds uneasy. An indictment of Seal in Louisiana could damage Seal as a witness in Florida. The Miami feds understandably wanted things resolved in Louisiana before Seal testified for them. But the Louisiana feds thought they had a case against Seal, and they intended to make it. The U.S. Attorney's Office in Miami and the Justice Department in Washington both took the position that if Louisiana had a case, they should pursue it. Nobody wanted to stand in the way of a legitimate investigation. The situation was extremely tricky, calling for a delicate balance between three parties with different goals—the Louisiana feds, the Miami feds, and Seal.

The solution was a plea bargain. Everybody hoped to make a deal that would satisfy Seal and the feds in Louisiana yet preserve Seal's credibility as a government witness in Miami. The man whose job it was to work this out was Thomas D. Sclafani, Seal's attorney. Sclafani, a graduate of Notre Dame and Brooklyn Law School, was savvy about the workings of federal law enforcement, having served as chief of narcotics in the U.S. Attorney's Office in Miami. Sclafani figured the Louisiana feds had a very weak case or they would have indicted Seal long ago. His suspicions were confirmed early in the plea negotiations, when he learned they were trying to tie Seal to a mere two-hundred-kilo load that had been seized in Louisiana in the early 1980s. Louisiana offered Seal a ten-year sentence in return for his guilty plea. Sclafani scoffed and told them no thanks: "Take your best shot."

As the negotiations foundered, the friction increased between Louisiana and south Florida. In Miami, DEA agents Bob Joura and Jake Jacobsen stood as Seal's biggest supporters. They had gotten very close to Seal, who had made the biggest cocaine case in the history of DEA for them.

In Louisiana, on the other hand, drug agents and prosecutors looked with suspicion on Seal's relationship with Miami DEA. The Louisiana State Police believed Seal still smuggled drugs into Louisiana while using the Miami DEA as his shield against investigation. The state police continued to stake out Seal's aviation office in Baton Rouge long after he became an informant for Miami DEA. Things got so bad that Jacobsen and Joura were told to stay out of Baton Rouge.

When Seal learned that the state police were trying to corner him, outrage was added to his normal competitiveness with law enforcement. Ken Webb, a troubled drifter whom Seal helped out from time to time, had been approached to turn informant against his benefactor. Webb claimed the state police told him they would do whatever they had to do to get Seal, even if it meant putting cocaine in the wheel well of a tire.

Feeling desperate, cut off from Miami DEA, and pursued by the Louisiana feds, Seal devised his own plan. In September 1984 he called John Camp, a veteran, prize-winning investigative reporter at WBRZ-TV channel 2, and told him about his undercover exploits for Miami drug agents and the CIA. Seal showed Camp videotapes of network news broadcasts corroborating portions of his story. Seal gave Camp an earful of allegations about how the U.S. Attorney's Office in Baton Rouge had tried to set him up. Camp was skeptical at first. He didn't see a lot to be gained by taking up the cause of an admitted drug smuggler against law enforcement officials, some of whom were news sources and personal friends.

But a lot of what Seal said checked out. Seal even allowed Camp's camera crew to secretly film a meeting in Miami between Seal and one of his DEA handlers. John Camp began to believe Barry Seal.

As word got around that Camp was making a documentary with Seal, things thawed a bit. In Miami, Assistant U.S. Attorney Richard D. Gregorie, who now held Sclafani's old job as chief of the narcotics section, had monitored the Seal negotiations with great concern. Gregorie knew Seal's tremendous potential as a government witness and was anxious for a solution. Gregorie was also a friend of Al Winters; both had backgrounds as longtime Organized Crime Strike Force prosecutors. So Gregorie called Winters and got the talks started again.

In November 1984 Winters and Bardwell traveled to the U.S. Attorney's Office in Miami to meet with Seal and his two lawyers, Sclafani and Lewis Unglesby of Baton Rouge. Up to now, Unglesby had handled Seal's problems solely with the Baton Rouge grand jury and was unaware of Seal's cooperation with Miami DEA. He was a sharp Baton Rouge lawyer, but he'd never heard of the Medellín cartel. He learned that his client was a witness against the most powerful drug smuggling organization in the world over breakfast with Seal and Sclafani at the Hyatt Regency Hotel in Miami.

"We really shouldn't be sitting next to Barry at this public restaurant," Sclafani said.

"Why?" asked Unglesby.

"What do you mean, why?" Sclafani said. "Don't you know there's a contract out on him?"

"You're kidding," Unglesby said.

"Don't worry," said Sclafani. "He's sitting closer to me than he is to you."

After breakfast the three men made the short walk to the U.S. Attorney's Office overlooking the Miami River. After several hours of negotiations, the parties reached agreement that Seal would plead guilty to charges in Baton Rouge and in return would be sentenced to whatever time he ended up getting from Judge Roettger in Fort Lauderdale on the Quaalude smuggling charges; Roettger was considering a motion to reduce Seal's ten-year sentence based on his cooperation with Miami DEA. The Baton Rouge sentence would run concurrently with the final sentence from Roettger. Bardwell and Winters left happy, expecting Seal to serve at least three years in prison. Getting Seal to do time was the moral victory they sought.

Seal was also happy. Once again he had resolved his problems with the legal system. And he expected to be rewarded by Judge Roettger. After the meeting, Seal, Sclafani, and Unglesby left the U.S. Attorney's Office and walked a block south to a public parking lot under an overpass. It was Veteran's Day, and downtown Miami was nearly deserted as twilight approached. Just to needle Unglesby, Sclafani said, "Gee, Lewis, this is a great place for a hit."

Bardwell, Winters, Seal, and Sclafani signed the deal roughed out in Miami on November 19, 1984, in the offices of the Organized Crime Strike Force in New Orleans. Seal agreed to plead guilty to two counts: conspiring to possess with intent to distribute 462 pounds of cocaine and failing to file currency transaction reports for $51,006.04 deposited in four Baton Rouge banks. The sentence on count one, the drug charge, would match the sentence Seal ultimately received from Roettger. On count two, the money laundering charge, Seal would receive no prison time. U.S. District Judge Frank Polozola would merely be allowed to set conditions of probation for Seal: "As to count two of the instant indictment, the defendant will receive a period of probation to be determined by the Court."

On November 20, Camp's documentary, entitled *Uncle Sam Wants You*, aired on channel 2 in Baton Rouge. Camp opened his piece by showing footage of the meeting between Seal and Jake Jacobsen in Miami.

"Barry Seal is an enigma," Camp said. "On one hand he has been working closely with federal drug agents in Miami and with the Central Intelligence Agency. He is a key witness in one of the most significant drug investigations ever conducted in south Florida. But at the same time here in his hometown of Baton Rouge, the veteran pilot has been a target of an intensive, and what he describes as unfair, investigation."

Seal appeared on camera wearing sunglasses and a combat flight suit. He was arrogant and baiting.

"I'm not a drug smuggler," he said. "I say prove it. Where is the proof?"

"A gun smuggler?" Camp asked.

"No," Seal answered. "Where's the proof? Why am I not on the front page of the paper at Ryan Airport or any other airport with a load of dope, with a load of guns? If they're such good agents and I'm so big, the biggest in the world, you know, the biggest in the world don't get away from the law and from justice, you know that."

Seal accused Baton Rouge drug agents of asking him to set up a drug bust and then trying to set him up when he refused.

"The bottom line was, 'How about helping us make a bust? How about setting somebody up? Give us a load. We'll let you get away . . . if you don't help us, we're going to get you anyway.' I said, 'Well, it's real hard for you to knock on the door of my airplane at night, when I'm doing two hundred miles an hour and say, "You're under arrest." You're not going to involve me with anything.' "

Camp said Baton Rouge investigators had gone to "extreme lengths" to prove Seal was a major air smuggler. He went on to present an account of the Louisiana investigation. It must have seemed like Stanford Bardwell's worst nightmare.

"I think that the investigation being headed up now by Mr. Bardwell has floundered," Seal said. "I don't think that they—in fact, I'm positive they have no evidence of wrongdoing, because they have threatened grand jury witnesses, they have threatened attorneys, local attorneys. These are things that just aren't done. I'm not caught up in a feud between two government agencies. I think what we're caught up in here, as I mentioned before, is now Mr. Bardwell has found himself in the middle of a cover-up.''

Seal accused the local federal prosecutors of forcing witnesses to lie to the grand jury and on camera offered the testimony of Ken Webb, who said the federal government had pressured him to do ''whatever it takes'' to get Seal. Webb said he had lied to the grand jury about Seal.

Seal continued, laying it on thicker as he went:

''The federal authorities are, I think, for the most part good people. I think that there are bad eggs in every nest, but I think there's no real mystique about me. Most of what I do is out in the open. I don't hide anything I'm doing. When I'm employed by government agencies and they ask me to keep discreet what they tell me, I do. I try to move in the method and the ways that they ask me to move, and maybe to some of the local authorities it may seem that sometimes it's on the border of criminalism, sometimes—sometimes not. But I think that the overzealousness of the local federal authorities in the Middle District of Louisiana has caused them to cross their fine line that they walk also between right and wrong.''

Seal described himself as ''an aviation consultant'' and expounded on his life of adventure:

''The cost of living an exciting life is high. You can't sit in Baton Rouge and go to work from nine to five on Monday through Friday and go to the LSU football games on Saturday night and church on Sunday and have an exciting life. That may be exciting to ninety-nine percent of the population, but to me it's not. And the exciting thing in life to me is to get into a life-threatening situation. Now, that's excitement. . . . Whether you call it soldier of fortune or what, it's a way of life to me. I enjoy it, and I'm going to keep doing it.''

Camp asked about rumors that the Ochoa family had put out a $350,000 murder contract on him.

''John, there's a risk in all covert operation work,'' Seal said. ''There's risk in everything you do in this line of work. That's why the pay is so good. . . . If you can't stand the heat, don't work in the kitchen. I can take the pressure. I'm not worried about the contract. If it comes, it comes.''

Camp asked Seal, ''Do you see yourself getting indicted?''

''No,'' Seal said. ''If they indict me, it means that I go to court. It means that then I get to tell my side of the story. All of this and much, much more that you're now hearing from me will be put out in the public eye. The Justice Department is not going to tolerate this. There's no way they can indict me.''

Camp summed up:

"It is not the purpose of this report to suggest Barry Seal is innocent, or for that matter guilty of anything other than those crimes for which he has already been convicted. Certainly Seal had chosen a lifestyle that lends itself to suspicion. His association with Colombian cocaine suppliers and his involvement in exotic plots hatched by the CIA and DEA have given him a certain mystique. He claims it is this mystique that has made him a target of overzealous investigators.

"We have repeatedly sought comment from U.S. Attorney Bardwell and other officials about the allegations of investigative and prosecutorial misconduct. They have refused to be interviewed and expressed considerable resentment that Seal was even given a forum to express his complaints. But Barry Seal and others have made allegations that go beyond their own personal problems with prosecutors. The targeting of individuals, the pressuring of witnesses, and the abuse of the grand jury process raised questions about the integrity of our system of justice. And when such questions are raised, regardless who asks them, they deserve to be answered.

"I'm John Camp, channel 2, *Eyewitness News*."

The show badly embarrassed the Baton Rouge feds. Bardwell's refusal to be interviewed meant the documentary could not help but be one-sided. Lewis Unglesby, Seal's Baton Rouge attorney, thought it amounted to "a declaration of war on the federal government here. You don't spit in the eye of a hurricane and then not plan to evacuate."

MAX

The Federal officials in Louisiana weren't the only ones watching *Uncle Sam Wants You*. Shortly after the program aired, a private investigator in Baton Rouge slipped a Betamax videotape of the documentary into a mail pouch destined for Fabio Ochoa in Medellín.

A few days later Max Mermelstein, a stocky Jewish engineer, drove by on his daily visit to Rafael Cardona's office in a house north of Miami. Mermelstein worked for Cardona in the cocaine trade.

Inside the house, Max greeted his boss and several other Colombians, among them Carlos Arango, better known as Cumbamba, one of the most feared hitmen of Miami's cocaine wars, and a man named Cano, whom Max knew to be an employee of Fabio Ochoa. With Jorge Ochoa in jail in Spain, Fabio now ran things. Cano's brother had been the administrator of Tranquilandia. Mermelstein learned that Cano had traveled from Colombia with a videotape from Fabio Ochoa. Cano had come to the United States to see if he could straighten out the Ellis MacKenzie situation. Max learned that MacKenzie had flipped and was going to testify against Jorge Ochoa and Pablo Escobar.

Rafa Cardona put the tape in a video machine, and he, Cano, and Max sat down to watch. As the tape rolled, Max learned for the first time that MacKenzie's real name was Adler Berriman Seal.

Afterward they talked about the need to locate MacKenzie. Cano had flown with MacKenzie several times as guide pilot on smuggling trips to Colombia. He discussed MacKenzie's habits while Rafa made a list. Cano gave Max Seal's home address in an exclusive section of Baton Rouge, the models of the cars his wife and secretary drove, descriptions of several of his aircraft and their registry numbers, and the names of several restaurants he frequented. Cano said they would prefer a kidnapping of MacKenzie. For a kidnapping they would pay $1 million. But if that couldn't be accomplished, they must do whatever had to be done to quiet him. For MacKenzie's murder they would pay $500,000. The contract came from Fabio Ochoa and Pablo Escobar.

It dawned on Max that he was being asked to kill MacKenzie. Max had been chosen because he was an American. Rafa told Max that he would be going out to Baton Rouge because Colombians would be too conspicuous there. Rafa told Max to make whatever arrangements he needed to silence MacKenzie. If it was to be a murder, the cartel wanted it to look like a traditional organized crime hit.

Max accepted the contract. Turning it down, he felt, would amount to forfeiting his own life.

Then Rafa called Colombia and handed the phone to Max, who found himself talking to Fabio Ochoa. Fabio thanked him for accepting the contract and wished him luck. He told Max it was necessary but he seemed reluctant about killing MacKenzie. He preferred a kidnapping. Then Fabio said there was somebody else who wanted to speak with him. Pablo Escobar got on the line and also thanked Max. Fabio got back on the line and asked him if he needed any expense money. Yes, Max said. They asked him how much, and he told them to use their discretion.

After the phone call, Cano mentioned that Seal was married and had some small children. Max said he wanted absolutely nothing to do with killing women and children. If it had to be done, it had to be done, Rafa said.

Before the meeting ended, Rafa asked Max if he could handle another chore. He said Lito Bustamante had been arrested as a result of MacKenzie turning informant in the Nicaraguan deal. Bustamante was in the federal Metropolitan Correctional Center in South Dade, the holding facility for federal prisoners awaiting trial. His trial was set for the summer. Could Max arrange to get a helicopter and pilot to fly into the prison and break Lito out?

MAX Mermelstein had become sort of an all-purpose gringo handyman for the Medellín cartel. He had come a long, circuitous route from his childhood in Brooklyn. Mermelstein's father had put Max to work at thirteen "to learn what money was all about." He earned his own tuition to a New York community college, where he graduated in 1963 with an associate's degree in applied sciences. He worked for consulting engineers by day and studied mechanical engineering at the

New York Institute of Technology by night. But he got bored sitting behind a desk and drawing board all day, so he went into sales. He sold air-conditioning and heating equipment to contractors, but that also bored him. He went through a divorce and moved to Puerto Rico to make a clean break of things in the early 1970s. There he became the chief engineer for a chain of shopping centers and department stores, then rose to the same job at the Sheraton Hotel in San Juan. After six years he moved to the chief engineer's job at the Princess Hotel in Freeport, the Bahamas.

By then he had a Colombian wife whom he had met in Puerto Rico. To help out her family, he set up a pipeline to smuggle illegal aliens through the Bahamas into the United States, a kind of underground railroad for Colombians seeking a better life in America.

In 1978 Max had moved to Miami and gotten a job as chief engineer at the Aventura Country Club. Even with Mermelstein gone, Colombians still passed through the pipeline he had set up in the Bahamas. One of those who used it was Rafael "Rafa" Cardona Salazar, a Colombian in his mid-twenties from Medellín. Rafa came to see Max when he got into the United States. He'd drop by the house, and he and Mermelstein would go out together. Slowly, trust was building.

Cardona eventually told Max that he smuggled cocaine, up to fifty kilos a week. Gradually he drew Mermelstein, up to this point nothing more than a mere alien smuggler, into the cocaine business.

One day a long-haired kid named Fabio showed up at Max's house with a kilo for Cardona. To Max he looked like a high school kid, carrying schoolbooks under one arm and a plastic bag containing the kilo under the other. Just out of his teens, the boy smuggler dressed punk, wore his hair long, and drove a Datsun 280Z car. But he was extremely mature, with fine manners and elegant Spanish.

A few weeks later Max accompanied Cardona to a stash house at a garden apartment complex in Kendall. Cardona was picking up another kilo. Rafa left Max in the car when he went inside the apartment. While Max waited, Fabio appeared with another man and put a package in the backseat of the car. Fabio then asked Max to come inside the apartment, where Rafa and several other people lounged about. Rafa took Max into a room and showed him two steamer trunks containing hundreds of kilos of cocaine. In 1978 that was an unheard-of amount of cocaine.

Max had no idea how important the long-haired kid was until Rafa told him when they left the stash house. Fabio Ochoa Vasquez was one of the Ochoa brothers from Medellín. The Ochoas, Max learned, were about as big as anybody ever got in cocaine. Fabio Ochoa had been sent to the United States by his family to handle the distribution in Miami after Jorge was nearly arrested the year before outside the Dadeland Theatre. Cardona himself distributed for the Ochoas in the southeastern United States.

For a few months Max dabbled in the cocaine business, distributing a kilo here and there. Then, on Christmas Eve, 1978, everything changed. That night Max threw a party at his home west of Miami. Rafa was one of those in attendance. After all the guests had gone, Rafa returned with a friend, Antonio "Chino" Arles Vargas. They roused Max from sleep at 2 A.M. They had been drinking and using cocaine, and Rafa asked Max to drive them home.

Max took the wheel of Rafa's white van, and the three men set out on the empty streets of suburban Dade County. Rafa sat in the passenger seat and Chino, who worked for Rafa, sat in back. Rafa and Chino were arguing. It turned out that Rafa had shot a man in the face that night at another party. The man had said something Rafa didn't like, and Rafa just shot him. Chino told Rafa the shooting was stupid.

Rafa still had his gun with him in the van. Suddenly he twisted and emptied five or six bullets from the .38-caliber revolver into Chino.

"All I saw were the flashes," Mermelstein said later. "My foot just froze to the gas pedal, and I couldn't move, I just kept driving straight ahead." Max was too stunned to speak.

After they dumped the body in a field off a suburban side street—10800 SW 84th Street—Rafa explained. One of his cocaine shipments were short three kilos. He suspected Chino and another man. So the killing was for the theft—and to impress upon Max that Rafa was not afraid to do what was necessary.

"Basically, from that point on he controlled my life," Mermelstein would say much later. "I saw him commit murder, and he allowed me to live. I think it was a well-thought-out plan."

Max and Rafa then left Miami for a while, Rafa back to Medellín, Max to New York, to work for Colombians there. Rafa called Max about once a week or had one of his men stop in and see him. Max knew he was being watched.

Two years passed, and Rafa finally summoned Max to Miami on February 28, 1981. He wanted Max to go to work for him. Max, Fabio Ochoa, and Rafa met at the King's Inn near the Miami International Airport to discuss a two-hundred-kilo seizure that had occurred in Okeechobee County the day before. Such losses were taken very seriously. Detailed ledgers were maintained, and record-keeping procedures were very strict. Every kilo had to be accounted for. If a cocaine seizure resulted from a legitimate bust or an unavoidable accident, it was written off as a business expense. If someone's incompetence caused it, that person was responsible for paying for the lost load. In many instances the payment was that person's life as Rafa had demonstrated with Chino.

From their lofty perch in Medellín, the Ochoas rarely demanded blood. They didn't have to. Often their lieutenants, feeling the subtle pressure from the boss's accountants in Medellín, took it upon themselves to exact the brutal balance.

In April 1981 Max Mermelstein attended the summit meeting of the rising young Colombian cocaine lords at Ochoa's Hacienda Veracruz ranch. Jorge Ochoa struck Mermelstein as well mannered and down-to-earth. He used his great wealth to collect vintage Harley-Davidson motorcycles. Ochoa was extremely solicitous toward his guest, asking Mermelstein several times if he was "pleased" with being at the ranch. Ochoa did not seem the least bit violent. Max felt Ochoa had "an aura." He was so considerate of Mermelstein's feelings that Max found himself responding in kind. Jorge Ochoa was a hard man to say no to.

Back in Miami, Mermelstein coordinated thirty-eight cocaine flights for the Ochoas, bringing in nineteen tons in the last seven months of 1981. At least once a week Mermelstein was on the phone to Jorge Ochoa, scheduling flights, counting inventory, or discussing distribution and collection. In January 1982, Mermelstein and Rafa attended a planning meeting in Cali for the Tranquilandia labs.

Mermelstein returned to Colombia when the cocaine bosses gathered in Medellín for the baptismal party of Rafa Cardona's son in February 1984. As Rafa's right-hand man, Max had a position of honor at the party. After all, Rafa had stood godfather to Max's youngest daughter back in Miami. Rafa had requested Max make him the child's godfather; Colombians took such family rituals seriously. As in all his dealings with the Colombians, Max felt it was a request he could not refuse.

All the big traffickers were at Rafa's party. Max thought of it as "Apalachin Colombiana," recalling the 1957 summit meeting of Mafia chieftains at Apalachin in upstate New York. Max's ability to speak Spanish, along with his closeness to Rafa and the Ochoas, allowed him to mingle easily among the trafficking elite, even though he was a stocky forty-year-old gringo with a Brooklyn accent. It was at one of the meetings during the week of the party that Max first heard mention of a gringo pilot named MacKenzie who was about to fly a huge load for the cartel. The traffickers referred to MacKenzie as El Pajarito—"the little bird."

Max's transportation group competed with MacKenzie's. Acting on Rafa's authority, Max had subcontracted with a group of American pilots and powerboaters to bring in tons of cocaine for the cartel. Beginning in September 1982, the smuggling group's aircraft, a Piper Navajo, flew from Colombia and air-dropped cocaine into the waters off Long Cay in the Bahamas. The plane then continued on to Nassau, where it picked up "cover girls," women paid $2,000 to pose as tourists for the flight into south Florida. Meanwhile, the floating cocaine was retrieved by crews in speedboats who made the seventy-five-mile run into Miami at speeds of up to ninety miles per hour—each run required a new $100,000 engine. A "spotter plane" circled the drop site looking out for Customs planes. Under cover of darkness, the boat slipped into Biscayne Bay while a lookout with binoculars scanned the water from the eleventh floor of a nearby condominium. A communications center in Miami monitored law enforcement frequencies and provided the radio link-up for the planes and boats. Except for the cocaine getting wet, the system was foolproof. Load after load got through undetected.

When the cocaine came into Miami, Max took care of the accounting and distribution. He earned about $500,000 a year as Rafa's employee, a mere fraction of the money he handled. In three years he had arranged for the importation of more than seventy thousand pounds of cocaine for his bosses and had sent more than $200 million back to Colombia. He lived well but not phenomenally so: he had a $350,000 house in Miami Lakes, an $80,000 yacht, a $30,000 car, $30,000 in jewelry, several small businesses, and $275,000 in stash money. Even so, Max felt sometimes that he was nothing more than a well-paid slave. He had tried to ease his way out of the business four or five times.

Rafa told him: "There's only two real ways to get out—going to jail or getting killed."

Max lived in constant fear of Rafa, who kept two hand grenades under the front seat of his car and $1 million in a nearby suitcase. Rafa was always well armed and usually coked up. He could be the nicest person in the world, or he could be the most vicious stone killer depending on whether he was drinking and using his own product. Unlike the Ochoas and Escobar, Rafa lived the life of a cocaine cowboy. He was very concerned about clothes—his tastes were Italian and expensive—and he spent lavishly. When he gave a birthday party for his four-year-old daughter at the Sheraton in upscale Bal Habour north of Miami Beach, he flew down a twenty-piece orchestra from New York. Rafa's gift to his son on his first birthday had been a kilo of cocaine or, more accurately, the proceeds from the sale of the kilo, about $30,000, which were placed in a bank account in the child's name. Rafa often said he expected his son to take over the business when he retired.

RAFA was plagued by his own craving for cocaine. He was addicted to freebasing "Colombian style"—rolling the cocaine base up in a Marlboro cigarette and smoking it. When he smoked cocaine he became so paranoid that he forced his family to sit at the dinner table with him so he could watch them. He even followed them into the bathrooms of their house in Miami Lakes. Rafa's wife, Odila, blamed their daughter's rare eye disease—she suffered from muscle deterioration behind the eyeball—on the long sessions spent watching Rafa freebase. But cocaine trafficking was a family business for Colombians; Odila kept her husband's books.

Unlike the Ochoas, who stayed far away from the south Florida cocaine wars, Rafa and Max were forced to deal with the many violent and unpredictable Colombians distributing in Miami. Most of the murders in Miami could be traced back to Griselda Blanco, who was still a vicious wildcard in a cocaine world rapidly heading toward an almost corporate order. By late 1981 Blanco had pretty much left Medellín, but Rafa and Max continued to work with her in Miami. Blanco loved killing. She bragged about shooting her second husband, Alberto Bravo, in the mouth. She and her third husband, Dario Sepulveda, argued in Max's living room over who was the better killer. But killing had unpleasant side effects: Blanco said she could not sleep alone. She needed to lie next to a man, whose hand she held in an iron grip while she slept. In her dreams she was haunted by the ghosts of those she had murdered.

Early in 1982 Rafa brought Blanco to Max's house in Miami Lakes and told him that she had tipped him off about an assassination plot and saved his life. He was going to reward her by becoming her cocaine supplier. Thereafter Rafa and Max sent about twenty to fifty kilos a month to Blanco and her organization, which included her son, Dixon, a motorcycle killer, and his two brothers.

Then in late 1983 another cocaine war erupted. Blanco had become estranged from Dario Sepulveda. When he was killed by police in Colombia, Blanco was blamed for his death. She and Sepulveda were in a custody fight for the son, Miguel Corleone Sepulveda, who was so important to Blanco that it was rumored she had a man killed for being twenty minutes late picking him up at Miami International Airport. The death of Dario Sepulveda brought Blanco into direct conflict with her onetime chief enforcer, Dario's brother, Paco. Rafa sided with the Sepulveda faction against Blanco, and Mermelstein immediately moved from the house Blanco had visited to a house at 500 N. Island Drive in Golden Beach. He rented it for $3,500 a month under an assumed name.

With Rafa no longer a source, Blanco found another supplier in Marta Saldarriaga Ochoa, a cousin of Jorge Ochoa. Soon Blanco had amassed a $1.8 million debt to Saldarriaga. Instead of paying it, Blanco simply had the young woman killed, or so police suspected. Marta Ochoa's body, wrapped in a sheet of plastic and perforated with bullets, was fished out of a canal in Kendall. The Miami cocaine community braced for slaughter. But Marta Ochoa's father came to Miami for the funeral and made an impassioned plea to stop the killing. Vengeance was his, he said, and he had decided not to take it. Griselda Blanco moved to California, and the Ochoas did not pursue her.

While Max was lying low in his Golden Beach house, he received a visit from Rafa and Carlos Arango, the jut-jawed onetime Blanco hitman known as Cumbamba who now worked for the Ochoas. Cumbamba carried a black attaché case. He opened the case, and inside was a silenced MAC-10 machine pistol set on blocks and rigged with a trigger mechanism that allowed it to be fired without opening the case. There was a hole in the side of the case for the gun's muzzle. A business card covered the hole. The weapon's serial number had been bored out so it couldn't be traced. Rafa wanted to test-fire it by Max's pool, an idea that Mermelstein nixed. Instead Mermelstein went into the garage and returned with a plastic beer cooler and five telephone books. He filled the cooler halfway with water and soaked the phone books in it. Then he moved the cooler into a small apartment behind the garage and told Rafa to fire away. Rafa took the gun out of the case. The homemade silencer muffled the noise; the only sound was the slapping of the pistol's bolt, like someone clapping his hands. The MAC-10 had too much velocity for Mermelstein's makeshift backstop. Several of the bullets went through the plastic foam and phone books and lodged in a wall. When Max moved out of the house several months later, he had the bullet holes plastered over.

FLIPPING

Max Mermelstein had never killed anybody, and the Barry Seal contract put him in a quandary. But he thought he knew where to turn. He called his friend and fellow trafficker Jon Pernell Roberts, who had once told Max he could arrange it if Max ever needed someone eliminated. Max told Roberts about the contract and gave him a viewing of *Uncle Sam Wants You*. Roberts said he would take care of it.

Then Max picked up a cardboard box full of cash from a young Colombian sent by Fabio Ochoa. Inside the box was $100,000 in twenties. Max was to use this to finance the hit.

The urgency of the mission to kill Barry Seal was underscored on January 5, 1985, when the first four Colombians ever extradited to the United States landed at Homestead Air Force Base. The prisoners arrived aboard a Colombian C-130 cargo plane and were taken into custody by U.S. marshals. None of the four was a kingpin, but a quick look at them revealed that the United States was striking close to the heart of the Colombian trade. Hernan Botero Moreno was a soccer team owner wanted for laundering $55 million through the Landmark Bank in Plantation in 1981. Two others were defendants sought in the Operation Swordfish money laundering case of 1982. The fourth man was Marcos Cadavid, a midlevel trafficker linked to Jorge Ochoa. Extradition for Jorge Ochoa suddenly seemed much more possible— and the damage Barry Seal could do was incalculable.

In late January 1985 Mermelstein and an associate of Roberts's flew from Miami to New Orleans to try to find Barry Seal. While Mermelstein stayed in New Orleans, Roberts's associate drove to Baton Rouge to try to locate Seal. Mermelstein wanted to stay as far from Baton Rouge as possible. He paid the man $28,000 to look for Seal.

The man found many of the restaurants and places Seal frequented, but he returned without spotting Seal. Mermelstein was then forced to accompany the man back to Baton Rouge to help search. They made no progress and returned to Miami.

They had found everything Cano had put on his list except Seal's helicopter business. And they weren't sure the restaurants were the right ones. Max asked if Cano could be sent back from Colombia to help them. Cano returned, and he and Max set off for Louisiana, driving from south Florida in Max's pewter-gray 1985 Jaguar. On the way, Max asked Cano if Jorge Ochoa "was aware of the situation and what was being done about it in Baton Rouge." Cano told Max that Fabio Ochoa had been in touch with Jorge in Spain a number of times, and Jorge had given his approval.

Max and Cano stopped in New Orleans and rented a car; Max didn't want to drive around Baton Rouge with a Latin in a Jaguar with Florida license plates. Once in Baton Rouge Cano pointed out Barry Seal's house, his airplane brokerage offices, and several restaurants Barry favored. They found Seal's white Cadillac. It took almost a full day, but they also found the helicopter business. But they didn't find Seal. From the Holiday Inn on Airline Highway in Baton Rouge, they called Fabio Ochoa in Colombia and Rafa in Miami. By now Max was beginning to wonder if the Colombians had picked up on the fact that he was stalling.

CANO returned to Miami, and Max stayed in Baton Rouge, looking. But he didn't find Seal, and eventually he returned to Miami. One day he was sitting in Papucci Shoes, his import shoe store at the Four Ambassadors Hotel, when Rafa and Cumbamba dropped by. Rafa wanted to know what was going on in Louisiana. Why were they having so much trouble locating Seal? What was taking so long? He said he was getting pushed very hard by the Ochoas and Pablo Escobar. They wanted it taken care of fast.

Max said it took time and Rafa had to be patient. When Rafa left, Cumbamba stayed behind. Max had known Cumbamba for nearly three years. For Griselda Blanco, Cumbamba had been one of the most feared killers in the Colombian drug underground. He didn't look the part. He wore black-rimmed glasses that were nearly as thick as the bottom of Coca-Cola bottles. He had the pale Antioqueño skin and tightly curled black hair. These features combined with his massive chin to make him look slightly retarded.

Cumbamba was angry. He felt left out of the Seal hit. How come a contract was given out and he wasn't involved? He asked Max how much it was worth, and when he heard he got more upset. Why was Max having so much trouble filling it?

Seal lived in a secluded area, Max said. There was one way in and one way out. The road came to a dead end. There was no way the hit could be done unless everybody in the house was taken out, and Max wasn't about to do that.

Cumbamba said that didn't bother him at all.

Max told Cumbamba he had no authority to hand over the contract. Cumbamba had to talk to Rafa, Fabio Ochoa, and Pablo Escobar. Cumbamba said he would do that.

Max made one more trip to Baton Rouge. He drove past Seal's house and saw a blue Chevy pulling out of the driveway. On Cano's list, the blue Chevy was Seal's secretary's car. Max followed the car but got stuck at a light when the woman turned into an industrial park. When he caught up to her, she was somehow behind him. He gave up and went home.

A TASK force of federal and local drug agents arrested Max Mermelstein on June 5, 1985, as he drove his Jaguar through a sparsely populated suburban area about twenty miles west of Fort Lauderdale. The agents moved in on him, and he gave up quietly. The agents later said it seemed that he wasn't surprised, as though he had known all along that he was under surveillance. It almost appeared to them that Max sighed with relief. The agents found a loaded .22-caliber Walther in the glove compartment of the Jaguar. Max lived nearby in a secluded suburban ranch house with his wife and two children, next to neighbors who thought he worked as an engineer. In Max's house the agents found twenty-five more weapons, $73,000 in cash in a wall safe, and $200,000 in a tote bag under his bed.

A few days earlier Rafa had told Max they were about to be arrested. But while Rafa took off for Colombia, Max decided to stay behind. For three months he had known he was being followed. But he felt it was time to get out of the business, and getting arrested was the only way he knew to do that and stay alive.

Mermelstein and Rafael Cardona had been indicted in Los Angeles early in 1985 and charged with smuggling 750 kilos of cocaine into California. Automaker John Z. DeLorean's alleged attempt to use cocaine to finance his failing auto company led the L.A. feds to Mermelstein. The cocaine in the DeLorean case was marked RCX—Rafa Cardona's code. DeLorean was acquitted in 1984 in a controversial trial that courtroom observers saw as a stinging critique of the kind of government "reverse sting" operations later perfected by Barry Seal. But the government's informant against DeLorean also knew Mermelstein. After DeLorean was acquitted, the informant gave the DEA Mermelstein.

The Los Angeles indictment accused Mermelstein of operating a continuing criminal enterprise—the potent "CCE" charge that all drug traffickers feared because it could land them in prison for life without parole. For Mermelstein there was no way out: cooperate or spend decades behind bars. "In the language of *The Godfather*, we made him an offer he couldn't refuse," said James P. Walsh, chief of the major narcotics section for the U.S. Attorney's Office in Los Angeles.

Mermelstein didn't spill his guts at the first opportunity. He didn't tell the feds about the contract on Seal's life until three or four weeks after his arrest. Four months later he sat down for a full debriefing with a single DEA agent in Los Angeles as informant number SR1-86-0015. Mermelstein told about how he'd met Rafael Cardona, how he worked as the Colombians' go-between with American drug smugglers. He told about the baptismal party for Rafa's son in Medellín. He said Cardona told him two days before his arrest that they were going to be arrested. But all that was just the beginning.

When Mermelstein started talking, he proved to be an even better informant than Barry Seal. Seal was a pilot, a transporter of cocaine; Mermelstein was a trusted intimate, a member of the inner circle. Max's position with the Medellín cartel was akin to Joe Valachi's with the Mafia. Like Valachi, whose dramatic testimony before the U.S. Senate in 1963 served as the first public unveiling of the Cosa Nostra, Mermelstein took the feds deeper than ever before into an uncharted area of organized crime. During the debriefing, Mermelstein described how the "Medellín combine" dominated the cocaine trade. He named its members: the Ochoas, Pablo Escobar, and a name little known to law enforcement, Jairo Mejia. He estimated the amounts of cocaine they moved a month: Rafa—800 to 1,000 kilos; Fabio Ochoa—1,200 to 1,500; Escobar—1,200 to 2,000; and Mejia, the largest of them all, at 2,000 to 3,000. Mermelstein described the "Cali group," another powerful Colombian cocaine combine that worked in concert with the Medellín group. He talked about the Marta Ochoa kidnapping and the forming of MAS. Rafa had ordered Max to buy weapons in Miami to arm MAS: 200 Colt AR-15 rifles and 30,000 rounds of ammunition. Mermelstein revealed a smuggling technique of the Cali group—hiding the cocaine in the nose cones of Eastern Airlines jets.

Max claimed that Rafa had met with DeLorean in the Bahamas and later provided the cocaine DeLorean was arrested with. Mermelstein said that he had smuggled accused Miami cocaine queen Marta Libia Cardona and Operation Swordfish money launderer Jose Javier Alvarez Moreno out of the United States after they'd posted bond; the cartel got its fake IDs through a passport office in Puerto Rico at a cost of $5,000 apiece.

Max talked and talked and talked. He recalled Rafa's shooting of Chino in the van on Christmas Day nearly seven years before. He had a phenomenal memory for names, places, and dates.

Max's second debriefing a month later drew a crowd. DEA agents came from Fort Lauderdale, Miami, and Cleveland. The FBI sent a man, and so did Customs. Al Singleton of Metro-Dade Homicide and Centac 26 showed up. Mermelstein addressed the many individual interests of these agents, tying loose strands together. For Singleton's benefit, Mermelstein talked about the Dadeland shooting, identifying one of the Colombian killers in the war wagon. For Bob Palumbo, the DEA agent from Cleveland, he told what he knew about Griselda Blanco; Palumbo had been part of Operation Banshee, the original case against Blanco. Mermelstein told the agents that each kilo contained an identifying paper that could be found only if the kilo was carefully unwrapped. He said that "Mono," Lito Bustamante's brother, now handled the cocaine distribution for the Ochoas in the southeastern United States, moving 1,200 to 1,500 kilos a month.

It was an astonishing performance.

WHILE Mermelstein revealed the cartel's secrets, Barry Seal honed his legend as a DEA informant, working undercover despite the contract on his head. On January 24, 1985, Seal engineered the seizure of ninety kilos of cocaine and the arrests of nine Colombians in Las Vegas. It was the biggest cocaine bust in the history of Nevada.

Less than a month later, Seal scored another amazing coup at a meeting in Miami. He paid a $20,000 bribe to the chief minister of the Turks and Caicos Islands, a British colony south of the Bahamas. The money was for protecting drug shipments. "I don't want you to feel as if I'm trying to push you into anything," Seal told Chief Minister Norman Saunders. "You do exactly what you feel in your heart."

The whole scene was taped by a hidden DEA video camera. Saunders and two other government officials were arrested immediately after a second meeting with Seal in Miami. It marked the first time a foreign head of government had been arrested on drug charges in the United States.

On June 28, 1985, Seal surrendered to U.S. marshals to start serving the ten-year sentence Judge Norman Roettger had given him in the Operation Screamer case in Fort Lauderdale. Seal had to serve the sentence in the federal Witness Protection Program, because by this time his life clearly was in danger.

For the first fifty days he was kept in a windowless, underground cubicle with a bed, a television, and a bathroom, shut off from all the noises of the outside world. He received no visitors and ate all his meals in his room. Then he was transferred to his "permanent protection facility," where he was allowed one hour of exercise a day, according to his attorney, Thomas Sclafani. Seal's wife, Debbie, flew 1,500 miles and tried to visit him with their two small children, but she was turned away because the family's names were not on the visitor's list. Seal, a free spirit who hated confinement, was gradually reaching his limit.

Seal's life turned into a series of courtroom appearances. In the summer of 1985 he was the chief witness in the Nicaragua and Turks and Caicos cases in Miami and in the record cocaine seizure in Las Vegas. Assistant U.S. Attorney Dick Gregorie supervised Seal's testimony for the government at the two trials in Miami. Gregorie had been a successful career Mafia Strike Force prosecutor in Connecticut when he was picked to lead the narcotics division in Miami during the dark cocaine cowboy days of 1982.

An intense, dark-eyed man in his late thirties, Gregorie had a boyish innocence, a single-mindedness that manifested itself in the capacity to become morally outraged at cocaine traffickers. The Medellín cartel incensed him. He had been educated by Jesuits, and his beard and balding head gave him a slightly monkish quality, but he had an easy laugh, and his eyes gleamed when he spoke about his cases. His one extravagance was a Datsun 280Z, which he'd bought cheaply through an FBI contact.

The son of a doctor in Boston, Gregorie couldn't stand the sight of blood and found himself in law school at Georgetown. Not knowing what he really wanted to do with his life, he took an internship at the U.S. Attorney's Office in Boston. The Secret Service was making a big counterfeiting case. For the first time, Gregorie saw informants and federal agents up close; the whole cloak-and-dagger world of federal law enforcement opened up to him like a Technicolor adventure. A young prosecutor in the office named George Higgins was working on a novel that would become *The Friends of Eddie Coyle*. Gregorie was hooked.

Now, nearly fifteen years later, Gregorie warned Seal that he must tell him everything in his background, leaving out nothing that might hurt the government's case.

"Barry, if you've held anything back, the slightest single thing, those defense attorneys will bring it out and crucify you," Gregorie said. "I want to know about everything. If you slept with some pygmy hippopotamus out in some bayou in Louisiana, I want to know about it. There better not be any pygmy hippopotamus out there."

"There's no pygmy hippopotamus, Dick," Barry said.

Seal proved to be an unflappable witness with an encyclopedic recall of drug smuggling minutiae. His first appearance came at the Turks and Caicos trial in Miami, where prosecutors played the videotapes of Seal's meetings with Norman Saunders. It was vintage Seal: "If you're sitting here conspiring, brother, it's called conspiracy," Seal said in his typical bold way on one of the tapes. "You gotta be careful. You gotta know who you're dealing with."

Seal's performance drew grudging praise from several top-flight criminal lawyers who jammed the courtroom to watch the tapes. "This guy is really good," said Jay Hogan, one of the best defense attorneys in Miami.

Seal wowed the jury, too, winning four convictions. Norman Saunders became the first foreign head of government ever convicted on drug charges in the United States.

Then Seal testified in the Nicaragua case, the trial of Lito Bustamante, Lizardo Marquez Perez, Felix Dixon Bates, and Paul Etzel in Miami. In his opening argument, Gregorie called the defendants part of "one of the largest cocaine organizations in the world." Seal called it "the Jorge Ochoa cartel." The case attracted little attention. Cocaine-ravaged Miami had become jaded about big drug trials. The story of the trial's opening ran on page 2B inside *The Miami Herald*'s local news section under the headline: SANDINISTAS LINKED TO COKE CARTEL. Seal spent two days on the stand, and his testimony was devastating. After the first day, Bustamante, Marquez, and Bates all changed their pleas to guilty. Only Etzel saw the trial to the end, and the jury convicted him. Next Seal went on to testify in Las Vegas, where the results were seven convictions. In three cases, Seal's testimony brought seventeen convictions.

Despite their guilty pleas and their looming heavy sentences, Bustamante, Marquez, and Bates apparently didn't plan on spending a lot of time in prison. One of the things Max Mermelstein told the DEA about was a bold plan to break Lito Bustamante and Lizardo Marquez out of the federal Metropolitan Correctional Center in South Dade.

The plot could have been lifted from a bad thriller: land a sleek, jet-powered helicopter inside the prison, blow away the guards with machine guns and hand grenades, and whisk away Bustamante, Marquez and Bates. With Mermelstein's help, DEA agents were able to identify the helicopter, a turbo-powered, black-and-gray Hughes 500 Ranger purchased with $500,000 in small bills. The Ochoas were offering $300,000 to attract a pilot willing to set down inside MCC.

In late October 1985 the agents began round-the-clock surveillance of the teardrop-shaped helicopter at Tamiami Airport. Timing was critical: the three cartel members were going to be sentenced on November 1; afterward they would be moved to more secure federal prisons. The plotters had to strike before the sentencing.

The escape plan threw the DEA into a frenzy of activity. There were only a few days to go until the sentencing, and the agents did not know the exact date of the breakout attempt. The DEA alerted officials at the prison, a forty-two-acre complex that housed about seven hundred inmates under security ranging from minimum to maximum. Bustamante, Bates, and Marquez were held in separate medium-security cell blocks. The three men were allowed to mix with the prison population and had jobs that gave them freedom of movement. Bates worked in the prison laundry, and Marquez was an orderly.

As the November 1 date neared, details of the escape plan became clearer. From the prison, the helicopter would fly low and fast at speeds of up to 160 miles per hour to a nearby farmhouse. There the helicopter would be blown up, and the escapees would be driven to a small airstrip in the Everglades and flown to the Bahamas. From there they would board a jet for Colombia. The DEA agents who watched the plan take shape were struck by the unfathomable arrogance of the Colombians to attempt such an escape. "The motivation was probably ego—to show up the United States," said Billy Yout, one of the agents involved. The agents did not know the day of the planned escape, but they did know the time: seven A.M., when all the prisoners would be in the open yard getting ready for their work assignments. It was the best possible time for a jailbreak.

On October 30 the agents watched the helicopter practicing quick "touch and go" landings and takeoffs. The agents were torn. They wanted to let the plot proceed and then nab the helicopter inside the prison, but that was deemed too dangerous. The DEA impounded the helicopter without waiting to make any arrests.

"Our fear was that there might have been a second helicopter that we didn't know about," Yout said. "We could have pursued the investigation, let it go on longer, but we were running out of time."

Two days later, Bustamante, Bates, and Marquez were taken before a federal judge to be sentenced. Bustamante and Marquez each got forty years, and Bates got twenty. Immediately after the sentencing, the prisoners were taken to serve their time at the maximum-security federal prison in Atlanta. The Medellín cartel had been foiled again. But how long would luck stay on the side of the good guys?

23.

"THIS IS DOUBLE-CROSS"

Barry Seal, the consummate manipulator, ended up out-manipulating himself. At first it looked as though he had pulled it off again, resolving his legal difficulties with another plea bargain and once again having the last laugh on his enemies in Louisiana law enforcement. In December 1984, a month after the *Uncle Sam Wants You* documentary aired, Baton Rouge U.S. Attorney Stanford Bardwell held a press conference to announce Seal's indictment.

In fact, it was merely the formal execution of Seal's plea agreement, consisting of the two counts to which Seal had agreed to plead guilty: a two-hundred-kilo cocaine conspiracy charge and a $51,000 money-laundering charge. But Bardwell staged the announcement as a victory for his office, an attempt to recoup some of the face lost in the *Uncle Sam* debacle. He didn't mention Seal's plea agreement, choosing instead to emphasize the "fifteen-month investigation" that brought Seal down. The top law enforcement officials in Louisiana paraded out for the press conference, but almost immediately the occasion turned into another opportunity for Barry Seal to one-up the government. Once again it was John Camp, the WBRZ-TV investigative reporter, who asked the embarrassing questions.

"Is there a plea bargain arrangement that has been made that will guarantee Mr. Seal not receive any time excessive to what he's been sentenced to in Florida?" Camp asked Bardwell.

"I'm not prepared to comment on that at this time," Bardwell answered.

It didn't help that Bardwell's flustering "no comments" immediately got contrasted with Seal's cocksure grins.

"I've reached exactly the type of settlement that I wanted to reach,'' Seal told Camp on camera. ''Whether they're happy or not, you'll have to ask them.''

While Seal openly predicted he would serve no time in prison on the charges, Bardwell said Seal would have to serve at least a portion of the ten-year sentence Judge Roettger had given him on the Quaalude smuggling conviction in the Operation Screamer case.

''It is my view that the sentence will not be reduced,'' Bardwell told Camp on camera.

But under questioning by Camp, Bardwell seemed uncertain about what the judge would do.

''How could you possibly make that judgment if you haven't talked with the judge?'' Camp asked.

''Well, just based on prior experience, I just have a feeling that he's not in a position—he's—he's got no reason to change it,'' Bardwell said.

Camp concluded that Bardwell was being kept in the dark about the promises being made to Seal in south Florida. Seal had told Camp privately that he had been assured in Miami that he would not serve any jail time. He hadn't been specifically told, but the message had been conveyed through ''nods and winks,'' Camp said.

The next month, when Seal appeared in federal court in Baton Rouge to plead guilty to the charges in Bardwell's indictment, U.S. District Judge Frank Polozola asked him about the statements on *Uncle Sam Wants You*.

The judge, who happened to be a close friend of Bardwell, pointedly asked Seal if he knew of any wrongdoing by federal officials in the Middle District. This time Seal kept his mouth shut.

ON October 24, 1985, Barry Seal appeared before Judge Roettger in a ''Rule 35 hearing,'' a proceeding in which a judge considers the work an informant has done for the government and makes a ruling on whether to reduce that informant's sentence. For informants, it's the payoff at the end of the rainbow, the quid pro quo for risking their lives.

By now Barry Seal was the most famous informant in the history of the DEA. He had single-handedly pulled off three of the best investigations the agency ever had. In the Nicaragua case, he had tied the Sandinista government to cocaine trafficking and brought about the first indictment of the Medellín cartel. In the Turks and Caicos case, he had garnered the first drug indictment of a foreign head of government. In the Las Vegas case, he had set a record for cocaine seizures in the state of Nevada. And it hadn't stopped there. Seal had gone on to testify brilliantly at the subsequent trials. He had shown an enormous amount of courage under fire and put himself at great personal risk. When Barry Seal decided to become a government informant, he set out to be the best.

So it came as no surprise that Seal's Rule 35 hearing collected an impressive array of law enforcement testimonials. Bob Joura appeared for the Miami DEA, along with Dick Gregorie from the U.S. Attorney's Office in Miami, a federal prosecutor from Las Vegas, and a British police official who had worked on the Turks and Caicos case. Seal's attorney, Thomas Sclafani, questioned the witnesses before Roettger.

"DEA considers the Ochoa investigation or the Nicaraguan investigation the most significant investigation that DEA has been involved in since its inception," Joura told the judge. "I have worked with a lot of informants over my career. I have never met someone who had as much potential and produced as much as Mr. Seal did. I have known him for over a year and a half now, and we have had almost daily contact during that time. He has been debriefed extensively. I have never caught him in a lie. I think once he decided to cooperate, he decided to cooperate wholly and completely. I think he has come to realize the effect that cocaine has on the fabric of society in the United States, and I don't think it's something that he totally realized before his arrest when he flew drugs into the country. I think as a person who provided transportation, I don't think he ever considered the impact of what he was doing. I think now, through working with DEA, he has come to have some realization of this, and wants to correct some of the things he has done in the past."

Sclafani asked Joura, "If Mr. Seal had done the things that he has done, and if instead of being a cooperating defendant he was a DEA agent, can you tell us what kind of reward he would have gotten?"

"I suppose he would have been proposed for the Attorney General's Award, which as far as I know is the highest award available to somebody in DEA," Joura said.

Roettger listened to the testimony and then ruled. He referred back to when he'd originally sentenced Seal to ten years in prison the year before. "At the time of trial, I thought the evidence portrayed a defendant who was bright, cunning, and frankly amoral," Roettger began. "I would clearly have given Mr. Seal more than the ten-year maximum at the time of sentencing because, from the evidence I saw, he struck me as being a man who, if I may describe in a word that most

Americans shy away from these days because our language has become very bland . . . I thought he was evil.

"I think well known to all people in this district, promises of cooperation don't cut any ice with me at all, and the only time I let anybody out of jail entirely, rather than just a reduction of sentence, is when their cooperation rises to the level that they have put their life in a position of peril. And when they do that, then I think they deserve to be suitably rewarded.

"Consequently, I am going to reduce his sentence to time served."

Barry Seal walked out of the courtroom a free man.

THE reaction in Baton Rouge was fury. One of the angriest was U.S. District Judge Frank Polozola, a strict law-and-order judge whose hands were now tied by Roettger's sentence. Polozola was bound by the plea agreement not to sentence Seal to any more time than what Roettger had given him.

When Seal appeared December 20, 1985, for sentencing before Judge Polozola, he was accompanied by only one attorney, Lewis Unglesby. Bardwell appeared for the government. Tom Sclafani didn't attend because he considered the matter a foregone conclusion. The plea agreement was very clear: Polozola could not sentence Seal to any more prison time than what had been handed out by Roettger. That meant no time at all.

Polozola vented his anger at Roettger's sentence: "If I had the remotest idea, the slightest idea Mr. Seal would not receive a jail sentence in Florida, under no circumstances, absolutely no circumstances, would I have accepted this plea agreement," said Polozola. "As far as I'm concerned, drug dealers like Mr. Seal are the lowest, most despicable type of people I can think of, because they have no concern for the public. . . . In my own opinion, people like you, Mr. Seal, ought to be in a federal penitentiary. You all ought to be there working at hard labor. Working in the hottest sun or the coldest day wouldn't be good enough for drug dealers like you."

Then Polozola laid out the conditions of probation. If Seal broke any one of them, he could be sentenced to five years in prison. First, Seal would need the judge's permission to travel outside the state of Louisiana; usually convicts on probation needed only to report to a probation officer. The condition applied for any travel, even for work as a government informant.

"I don't care if it is the Drug Enforcement Administration, I don't care if it is the CIA, I don't care if it is the State Department, I don't care if it is the U.S. attorney, I don't care who it is, you don't go any place, any place, without getting my personal written approval in advance," Polozola said.

This was getting to be too much for Unglesby. He couldn't resist a little sarcasm.

"Do you want me to refer all those agencies, since he talks to all of them, to you?" Unglesby asked.

"I don't care," said Polozola. "I don't care who they are. The probation department is going to see it. The U.S. attorney is here. He is the government's lawyer. We only have one government."

"I have found that, in this case, not to be entirely true," Unglesby observed.

Then Polozola stripped Seal of the bodyguards he had hired to protect him in Baton Rouge.

"It's come to my attention that there are certain people around you that carry guns," Polozola said. "If the guns are in your houses, you are going to have a serious problem with revocation [of the probation]."

"I don't possess a gun, and I don't intend to," Seal said. "But I do intend to have bodyguards."

"Well, your bodyguards are going to have to be without guns," Polozola said.

"Well, why is that? If they have legal permits to carry them?" Seal asked.

"You take your chance, Mr. Seal," Polozola threatened.

Polozola then fined Seal $35,000 and ticked off other, routine conditions. Then came the clincher, the one he'd saved for last:

"And as a further condition of probation, the defendant shall reside at the Salvation Army Community Treatment Center, 7361 Airline Highway, Baton Rouge, Louisiana, for a period of six months."

Seal and his lawyer were entirely unprepared for this turn of events. They immediately started whispering to each other. The details of a plea agreement are usually worked out so well in advance of the court date that the sentencing itself is merely a scripted performance. Judges usually ratify what the two sides bring before them. No one had said anything about a halfway house. The judge might as well have ordered a target hung on Barry Seal's back.

"Well, we want to talk about that, Judge," Unglesby said, recovering his composure.

"There is nothing to talk about," said Polozola.

"That's double-cross by the government," Unglesby said.

"That is not double-cross by the government," Polozola said.

"Yes, sir, it is," said Unglesby.

"Read the plea agreement on count two," Polozola said.

"I've read it," Unglesby said. "I'm very familiar with it. I hammered it out, okay? It says no incarceration."

"This is not incarceration," said Polozola.

Seal had walked into a government booby trap. When they drew up the plea agreement, the feds in Louisiana had not intended to hand over all control of the fate of Barry Seal to Judge Roettger in Fort Lauderdale. The indictment worked out in the plea agreement had two charges. On the first and far more significant charge, the two-hundred-kilo cocaine conspiracy, the Louisiana feds had agreed to abide by whatever sentence Roettger finally gave Seal.

On the second charge, the relatively insignificant $51,000 money-laundering count, there was to be no prison sentence. But Louisiana reserved the right to set the conditions of probation. It had seemed innocent at the time, but Louisiana feds had entered into the plea agreement anticipating just such a contingency as Roettger's sentence freeing Seal. The trap was ready to spring when Seal appeared for his sentencing before Polozola. "Looking back, I think I got run over by a truck and should have seen it coming," Unglesby said later.

After Polozola ruled, Unglesby threatened to appeal.

"Let me tell you what," Polozola said. "I'd love for this plea agreement to be broken. I'd love for this plea agreement to be broken right now."

Polozola offered to let Seal withdraw his plea on the spot.

The judge had Seal over a barrel. If Seal took back his plea, he would lose his immunity for all the crimes he had already admitted. Bardwell left the courtroom smiling. He had finally beaten Barry Seal. A private investigator paid by the Ochoas also exited the courtroom.

After the hearing, Lewis Unglesby ran into one of Bardwell's assistants in the hall. Unglesby asked if the judge knew the full extent of Seal's cooperation with Miami DEA.

"You know what he said?" Unglesby said later. "He said, 'That's Florida and Las Vegas. Barry hasn't done anything for us in Baton Rouge, and until he does something for us we're not that concerned about it.' Of course, there wasn't anything for Barry to do in Baton Rouge. Barry *was* Baton Rouge."

All his smuggling life, Barry Seal had bet on his ability to outsmart the government. Up until the Polozola hearing, he had won nearly every round. He'd brought tons of cocaine into Louisiana even though the Louisiana State Police had had him under surveillance, and every fed in Louisiana wanted to indict him. He had worked his way out of a tough jam in Operation Screamer. When the DEA and U.S. Attorney's Offices in two districts had turned down his offer of cooperation, he'd still managed to fly to Washington and go to work for the government on his own terms. In the Nicaragua case he had duped Jorge Ochoa and Pablo Escobar, the world's biggest cocaine smugglers, men who made empires through the sheer force of their ruthless will. He had fooled Carlos Lehder and Federico Vaughan, Lito Bustamante and the cartel security chief, Lizardo Marquez Perez. He had survived a plane crash in Colombia and antiaircraft guns in Nicaragua. He had overcome them all, even the relentless men in Louisiana who wanted more than anything else to see him behind bars. Now, just as freedom was staring him in the face, it began to slip away.

BARRY Seal did not go into the Salvation Army halfway house right away; there were no immediate vacancies. Polozola refused to stay the sentence, but Seal's attorneys asked for and got another hearing set for January 24, 1986. This time they would introduce testimony from the Rule 35 hearing before Judge Roettger in hopes of getting Polozola to change his mind.

On January 21, two days before the hearing, something happened that cast everything into a far more urgent light. A Spanish appeals court granted a U.S. request to extradite Jorge Ochoa to stand trial in Miami. All of a sudden Seal, the only eyewitness against Ochoa, became far more valuable to the federal government—and far more dangerous to the Medellín cartel.

"The case against Ochoa was going to be all testimonial, and it was going to be Seal with very little corroboration," Sclafani said. "Without Seal the case is finished."

Sclafani filed a motion to "correct" the probation set by Polozola. He called Seal "the single most important government witness in the United States today." The motion said Polozola's sentence "will place Seal in a life-threatening position, especially given the anticipated extradition of Jorge Ochoa to Florida."

Sclafani took pains to point out that Seal "has been the subject of an open $350,000 contract on his life." The motion said the contract now stood at $500,000 dead and $1,000,000 if brought back alive to Colombia.

A motion from the Louisiana prosecutors argued against changing the probation: "The government does not see how residing at the Salvation Army imposes any more of a threat than Mr. Seal residing at his home in Baton Rouge, La.'' The motion was signed by Stanford Bardwell and Al Winters.

On January 23, the day before the hearing, Sclafani flew to Baton Rouge, checked into his hotel around noon, and found a note from Lewis Unglesby telling him there was going to be a ''status hearing'' in Judge Polozola's chambers at four P.M. Such status hearings are usually held to see if preliminary differences can be worked out and resolutions reached before the court hearing. At the meeting were Sclafani, Unglesby, Polozola, Winters, the U.S. marshal for Baton Rouge, and the chief federal probation officer for the Middle District. Seal awaited the meeting's outcome in Unglesby's law office nearby.

Polozola made it clear from the outset that Seal would have to surrender at one P.M. the following day. The exchange then got ''relatively free,'' Sclafani said. Sclafani reminded the judge about Ochoa's extradition.

''Judge, my client wants to get out of town,'' Sclafani said.

The judge said that Seal should go into the federal Witness Protection Program. Now it became clear what the halfway house gambit was meant to achieve: the Louisiana feds wanted to scare Seal into the Witness Protection Program—anything to prevent him from driving around Baton Rouge in his big white Cadillac and rubbing his freedom in their faces. Sclafani said Seal wouldn't go for the Witness Protection Program; he hadn't seen his family for three months the last time he was in the program while he was testifying in Miami and Las Vegas.

Sclafani instead suggested transferring Seal to protective custody in another federal district. It wouldn't be the same as the Witness Protection Program; Seal would have more freedom, and his wife could visit more easily. The judge agreed to consider it provided that Sclafani could find another district willing to take Seal. According to Sclafani, the judge chuckled sarcastically and said, ''Good luck.''

That got under Sclafani's skin. He accused the judge of not being concerned that Seal might get killed. Then it was the judge's turn to take offense. Sclafani said the judge launched into an angry tirade, and that his face reddened and his voice thickened as he spoke.

''Let me tell you something about your client,'' Sclafani remembered Polozola saying. ''Your client likes to tell radio stations and television reporters that Judge Polozola does not have the last word. He's right. The court of appeals has the last word. But I'm not going to give him anything to appeal.

''So, in effect, Judge Polozola has the last word. You tell your client the next time he shoots off his mouth to the television cameras about Judge Polozola, he better watch what he says.''

Then the judge paused and said, ''Your client needs to be taught a lesson.'' Sclafani said the lesson could result in Seal ending up with a bullet in his head.

After the hearing in Polozola's chambers, Seal, his wife, Debbie, Sclafani, Jacobsen, and Joura all went to dinner at Ruth's Chris Steakhouse, Seal's favorite restaurant. The mood was one of cautious optimism. Everybody hoped the halfway house sentence would be averted. During dessert, Sclafani telephoned Dick Gregorie in Miami; Gregorie went to work trying to find another federal district that would put Seal in protective custody.

The next morning Gregorie called Winters and told him that the U.S. attorney in the Northern District of Florida had agreed to take Seal as a favor to the U.S. attorney in the Southern District of Florida. Winters said he had no problem with that.

Soon after, Sclafani spoke with Gregorie and learned of the arrangement. But at 9:20 A.M., when Sclafani arrived at the courthouse, Winters and the rest of the Louisiana feds told him they vigorously opposed sending Seal to Pensacola, Florida.

''We can't let him go to Florida, Florida is a drug state,'' Winters said. Sclafani was furious.

All parties met in chambers with the judge. The judge was suspicious of the proposal to send Seal to Pensacola. Why, if cocaine kingpins were threatening Seal's life, would Seal want to go to Florida, the cocaine capital of the United States? The judge agreed to call the chief federal probation officer in the Northern District of Florida. He went to another room to make the call. While the judge was on the phone, Sclafani went down the hall to a witness room and called Gregorie. The arrangement was unraveling before his eyes. Sclafani felt Winters had betrayed him and Gregorie by not supporting the proposal. ''You had one federal prosecutor in Louisiana specifically back-dooring a brother prosecutor in Florida,'' Sclafani said.

''Do you realize Winters didn't go along with it?'' Sclafani told Gregorie. ''What's going on here?''

Then Winters came into the room and got on the phone. He told Gregorie the judge was not likely to accept the proposal. Several witnesses in the room overheard Winters say into the phone that he was sorry, but he just couldn't go along with it. The people from Baton Rouge wouldn't budge, and there was nothing he could do. Twenty-five minutes later the judge emerged from his phone call with the chief probation officer in Pensacola. The judge said they knew nothing in Pensacola about Seal's case or the conditions of his probation. Since everything was so confused, the judge was turning down the transfer.

Time had run out: it was nearly noon. All the parties went into the courtroom to go through the motions. Polozola insisted that Seal enter the halfway house at one P.M. Before the judge ruled, Seal's attorneys desperately sought to have the courtroom proceedings sealed.

"It is our position that this should not be publicly said, any more than necessary, that he is to go to the halfway house today at one o'clock," Unglesby said.

The Louisiana prosecutors opposed closing the hearing; they needed to get approval from Washington for that. Then Polozola refused to grant a gag order preventing all parties from talking to the press.

"Your man is the one who really talks to the press," he said.

Seal was taken directly from court to the halfway house. He was not given time to pack or see his family. Characteristically, he gave a telephone interview from the halfway house.

"I'm trying desperately to understand the logic behind Judge Polozola's ruling," Seal told the Baton Rouge newspapers. "At the sentencing, he said he wanted to make sure I didn't bring any more drugs into the Middle District. I brought twenty thousand pounds of cocaine into the Middle District of Louisiana, nowhere else, and I never left my house. I did it all by phone."

THE HALFWAY HOUSE

No one expected Barry Seal to remain for long in the Salvation Army halfway house. It was absurd. It was too dangerous, and Seal was too valuable a witness. Al Winters thought Seal would give in and finally enter the federal Witness Protection Program. Even Seal didn't have the brass to run around Baton Rouge stripped of bodyguards with a $500,000 contract on his head.

"If this doesn't force him to leave Baton Rouge, nothing will," Winters told Dick Gregorie.

When the weekend came and went and Seal stayed in the halfway house, Winters started to grow concerned. After two weeks he called Gregorie again. They discussed going to Judge Polozola jointly to ask to have Seal moved out of Baton Rouge. But Gregorie said it was no use: Barry was determined to stay in Baton Rouge to serve out his six months at the halfway house and become a free man again.

Seal told Jake Jacobsen that he didn't think the Colombians would try to kill him. "It's just business," he said. He felt relatively safe in Baton Rouge. If any Colombians showed up in that part of Louisiana, they would be obvious.

Cumbamba had taken over Max Mermelstein's contract to kill Barry Seal in May 1985. But Seal entered the Witness Protection Program the next month, and the contract was put on hold. The plot remained dormant until January 21, 1986, when Jorge Ochoa was suddenly ordered extradited from Madrid to Miami. Three days later Seal began reporting to the Salvation Army halfway house at six P.M. every day. He checked out at seven A.M., and his days were his own as long as he returned to the halfway house at night.

· · ·

AFTER Seal had been in the halfway house for fifteen days, three men from Medellín flew to Mexico via Panama and crossed the border illegally into the United States. Four days later Bernardo Vasquez, a Colombian who lived just north of Miami in Hialeah, checked in under his own name in room 270 at the Kenner Airport Hilton outside New Orleans. Cumbamba showed up four days after that, February 16, and rented room 312 under the name Miguel Velez. The next day the three Colombians from Medellín arrived, and Vasquez bought a 1982 gray Buick for $6,500 in hundred-dollar bills. He registered the car in the name of Mary L. Cook. That night Vasquez and one of the Colombians from Medellín went to Baton Rouge and rented room 228 at the Jay Motel Lounge Restaurant, a $15.91-a-day dive next to a used-car lot on Airline Highway. The motel no longer had a lounge or a restaurant, and the second-floor room had no telephone. But it did have a clear view of the Salvation Army parking lot just a few hundred yards away.

The following day Vasquez picked up the Buick and rented a red Cadillac Sedan DeVille from Avis on his American Express card.

The next day, February 19, Vasquez went to Anthony's, a men's clothing store in Kenner, and purchased three baseball caps and two plaid raincoats. That afternoon Cumbamba drove one of the three Colombians from Medellín, Luis Carlos Quintero Cruz, to the halfway house parking lot in the Buick. The new car sticker was still on the Buick's window. Cumbamba backed the Buick into a parking space three spots away from the three large white Salvation Army drop boxes for donated clothing. The boxes sat in the center of the parking lot. Witnesses said later that Cumbamba and Quintero Cruz got out of the car and dropped something into the boxes. Then Cumbamba got inside the Buick and smoked Marlboro cigarettes while he waited for Barry Seal.

In his weeks at the halfway house, Barry Seal had seemed friendly and unafraid. He showed up on time every evening at six. He usually had a friend drive him or follow while he drove into the lot in his father's white 1972 Fleetwood Cadillac. On the morning of February 19, Seal rose and left the halfway house at 7 A.M. as usual. He had no business office to go to. In the first week of his halfway house stay, the IRS slapped a $29,487,718 "jeopardy assessment" lien on all his property. A jeopardy assessment was designed to keep suspected drug dealers from liquidating their assets. Seal's own testimony for the government had done him in: the IRS arrived at the $29 million figure by using Seal's statement in the Turks and Caicos trial that he had grossed $75 million smuggling drugs. While Seal had immunity for any crimes he'd admitted to in his testimony, he had no immunity for civil tax liabilities. The IRS took the white Mercedes convertible that Barry had gotten from Lito, a helicopter, two boats, three planes, Seal's business office, and nearly all the furniture in his house. The house itself was under a seizure warrant.

Seal spent much of his time trying to come up with a strategy to solve his tax problems. "This IRS thing has me very, very time-limited," Seal told John Semien of the *Baton Rouge Morning Advocate* on February 19. "I've been with attorneys twenty-four hours a day. The whole time I'm over at the Salvation Army I'm on the phone with them, and it's gotten to be a very involved thing."

Even so, Seal usually made time for lunch at home with Debbie and the kids. The morning mail brought more bad news. The Federal Aviation Administration was revoking his pilot's license because he was a convicted felon.

Just before six that evening, Seal was speaking on the car phone in his Cadillac with Bill Lambeth, an aviation consultant in Phoenix. Seal wanted to buy an airplane propeller. Seal told Lambeth he would call him back at 6:15 P.M. from the Salvation Army. "He sounded very harried and troubled," Lambeth later recalled.

Maybe he was preoccupied when he arrived at the Salvation Army lot. He drove right past the parked gray Buick and backed the Cadillac into a space flush against the drop boxes. The boxes stood between him and the Buick. They would shield him on the driver's side as he got out of the Cadillac. The car itself would provide cover from the passenger side. He was thirty feet from the Salvation Army's door.

The witnesses who saw Quintero Cruz carry something to the drop boxes were right: minutes before six Quintero Cruz had put something wrapped in a raincoat inside one of the boxes. Then he hid behind the boxes, empty-handed and loitering, as Seal arrived in his father's Cadillac.

When Seal opened his car door, Quintero Cruz reached into the drop box and unwrapped the raincoat from a silenced MAC-10. He leaped toward Seal. With the muzzle less than two feet from Seal's head, Quintero Cruz fired twelve times in two seconds. Even through the silencer the shooting sounded loud, like firecrackers going off. Three bullets hit Seal in the left side of the head. Two of them entered behind his left earlobe, making oval holes in the skin with burned rims one centimeter in diameter. All three projectiles passed completely through Seal's head, severing the cerebrum from the brain stem. A fourth bullet put a red furrow in his scalp. A fifth bullet passed through his upper arm and rib cage. A sixth tore through his chest. All the wounds were "through and through"—none of the bullets were stopped by Seal's body tissue.

After the firing, Seal slumped over, bleeding profusely onto the Cadillac's seat, his hands cupped over his ears as if to shut out all sound.

Inside the Salvation Army building, Major Bennie Lewis heard the popping noise. He ran outside to the Cadillac. He leaned over Seal and saw a hole all the way through his head.

"Barry, can you hear me?" Lewis asked.

There was no response.

At 6:04 P.M., John Camp was in the WBRZ newsroom when the word came over the police scanner:

"There's been a shooting in the Salvation Army parking lot," someone said.

About fifty people were in the room for a staff meeting. The room went dead silent. Camp felt as though he had been kicked in the stomach.

"Jesus Christ, they got him," Camp said.

When Lambeth in Phoenix got tired of waiting for Seal to call back, he telephoned the Salvation Army himself.

"He's lying in the parking lot," someone told him. "He's just been shot."

Lambeth immediately telephoned Debbie Seal at home. Either someone was playing a bad joke, he told her, or she had better get down to the Salvation Army right away.

Debbie Seal called over there. "Miss Seal," someone said, "I don't think you should come out here."

"Then which hospital should I go to?" she asked.

"He won't be going to a hospital."

THE next day U.S. Attorney Stanford Bardwell called a press conference. "He deserved to be prosecuted," Bardwell said. "He deserved to be sentenced."

"Were you trying to teach him a lesson?" asked an angry John Camp. Seal's lawyers had told Camp what the judge had said in chambers.

A pained look crossed Bardwell's face, but he leaped at the question anyway. "Sure," he said. Then he paused, seeming less sure, and added a little too quickly, "Not to get killed."

. . .

BARRY Seal, forty-six on the day he died, had been right about one thing: the Colombians in Baton Rouge were conspicuous. Seal just didn't see them coming. In the pandemonium after the killing, the FBI took only forty-eight hours to trace, identify, capture, and charge six suspects.

Immediately after the shooting, Quintero Cruz, the man with the MAC-10, ran back to the Buick. A witness saw him hand the MAC-10 to Cumbamba in the driver's seat. The Buick peeled out of the parking lot, almost running over another witness. A third witness got a good look at Cumbamba loitering outside the Buick a few minutes before the shooting.

The witness said the driver of the Buick had been wearing green surgical pants.

A quarter mile away in a children's activity center parking lot, the Buick screeched to a stop, and the two men abandoned it, engine idling, the MAC-10 inside on the floorboards. The men ran to a second getaway car, a red Cadillac, parked nearby. They were laughing.

Across the street, two off-duty sheriff's deputies, hired as security for a bingo game, noticed the commotion and got a description.

The FBI immediately flooded the airport with agents. Others began checking hotel registries for guests with Latin-sounding names. The hit team had been extraordinarily sloppy. Vasquez and several others had used their true identities. Vasquez had even used his American Express card to rent the getaway car. And the price tag from the clothing store was still on the raincoat that Quintero Cruz had wrapped around the MAC-10.

At 7:30 P.M. Vasquez and another member of the hit team checked out of their rooms at the Hilton in New Orleans. The Cadillac was abandoned at the New Orleans International Airport. The car entered the lot at 8:36 P.M.

At 8:45 P.M. two FBI agents watched a Latin man approach the Eastern Airlines ticket counter at the airport. The man was sweating and appeared nervous. He had been unable to obtain a direct flight to Miami. The agents questioned him. He played the naive, lost traveler. Although he gave hesitant, uncertain answers, he possessed a proper passport in the name of Miguel Velez. The agents did not yet have the description from the witness who saw the green surgical pants. They had no probable cause to make an arrest; they had to let Velez go. He told the agents he was going to go back to his hotel to call a cab to take him to another airport. About fifteen minutes later, when a description of the killers came over the radio, the FBI agents realized they had had one of them. They checked at the hotels and found that

Velez had rented a cab. The cab was heading to Jackson, Mississippi. An all-points bulletin went out for the taxi.

At 2:20 A.M., in Meridian, Mississippi, a police officer spotted a disabled taxi on the highway. The cab had hit a deer. The officer questioned the passenger, who was wearing green pants. The cabbie couldn't understand why the police were making such a big deal about a dead deer. In the passenger's pocket was $3,270 in twenties and the keys to the rented red Cadillac getaway car. The officer arrested "Miguel Velez" immediately. It turned out that Velez's pants, though green, were not the type worn by surgeons. Later, investigators found the green surgical pants inside Velez's luggage. He had changed clothes after the shooting, but he had made the cardinal mistake of taking off his green surgical pants and putting on pants that were also green.

Bernardo Vasquez spent the night at a safe house, a friend's home in Algiers, a suburb of New Orleans. What he didn't know was that his friend was a confidential informant for the FBI. The FBI arrested Vasquez the next day with $860 in twenties and $9,800 in cashier's checks. Cruz was caught in Marrero, in another suburban safe house, carrying $3,127 in twenties.

BARRY Seal's funeral took place the day after the arrests. The family put a telephone pager and a ten-dollar roll of quarters in the coffin. What was Barry Seal without his quarters and his pay telephones? The Reverend Joe Hurston recited an epitaph that Seal had chosen long ago and written down in his personal Bible: "A rebel adventurer the likes of whom, in previous days, made America great."

No drug agents attended the funeral of the greatest drug informant in DEA history. The bosses in Washington let Jacobsen and Joura know that it wouldn't be a good idea.

Nearly a month after the murder, President Reagan went on national television to pitch for congressional aid to the contras. He displayed the grainy black-and-white pictures Seal had taken on his undercover mission to Nicaragua.

"Every American parent will be outraged to learn that top Nicaraguan government officials are deeply involved in drug trafficking," Reagan said. "There is no crime to which the Sandinistas will not stoop. This is an outlaw regime."

There was no mention of Barry Seal.

. . .

FOUR months after Barry Seal's death, Dick Gregorie and Al Winters went to a secret location outside Miami known as "the submarine." The submarine was a small, windowless living quarters so named because its occupant could not know if he was underground or underwater. It had a bedroom, bathroom, and television set, but there was no door that the occupant could see. Entering the submarine required navigating secret passages. It was the most secure spot in south Florida for a witness, the natural place to put Max Mermelstein.

Seal's death profoundly affected Max, who was now the leading living witness against Jorge Ochoa and Pablo Escobar and thus Barry Seal's successor as the most important drug informant in the United States. The two federal prosecutors had come to debrief Max for different reasons. With Seal dead, Gregorie needed a witness to refashion a case against Jorge Ochoa, whose extradition status in Spain had been thrown into doubt again by Ochoa's lawyers' legal maneuvering. And with Seal's murder, Winters had gone from being Seal's prosecutor to his avenger. It fell to Winters to build the case against Seal's killers in Baton Rouge. Max chain-smoked in the submarine while he heard the details of the hit. Winters told Max that the murder weapon had been a MAC-10.

Suddenly Max started peppering Winters with questions. Did the weapon have a drilled-out serial number? Yes, Winters said.

"Not only can I identify it, the weapon was test-fired at my house in Florida," Max said.

Agents were immediately dispatched to the house Max had rented in Golden Beach. They dug into the wall and, sure enough, found five .45-caliber bullets. The bullets matched the ones that had killed Barry Seal. Max had just directly tied the Medellín cartel to Seal's murder. Based on Mermelstein's information, Fabio Ochoa, Pablo Escobar, and Rafael Cardona were indicted the next month by a federal grand jury in Baton Rouge. The charge: conspiring to violate Barry Seal's civil rights by plotting to kill him.

Carlos Arango, "Cumbamba," the cartel hitman whose signature was to drain corpses of blood and tape their eyes and mouths. He helped plan Barry Seal's murder. (NEW YORK CITY POLICE DEPARTMENT)

Two photos taken by a CIA camera hidden in Seal's plane of the elusive Federico Vaughan, the cartel's contact inside the Sandinista government. Vaughan told Seal his government was willing to process all the cocaine the cartel could supply. Vaughan disappeared after the Seal mission was exposed.

Colonel Jaime Ramirez, commander of the Colombian Police Anti-Narcotics Unit, the year before his death, in a Santa Marta marijuana field, watching herbicide spraying, with members of the U.S. House Narcotics Committee, chairman Charles Rangel on the right. (TIMOTHY ROSS)

A statue of John Lennon on the grounds of Posada Alemana, Carlos Lehder's ranch. Large bullet holes are visible in Lennon's chest and back. In his left hand, Lennon holds the word "PAZ"—peace. *(EL TIEMPO)*

U.S. Attorney Bob Merkle prosecuted Carlos Lehder for the Middle District of Florida in 1987–88. After the trial he announced his intention to run for the U.S. Senate. (C. W. GRIFFIN/ *THE MIAMI HERALD*)

Guillermo Cano Isaza, the crusading antidrug editor of *El Espectador* who was murdered by hitmen following a series in his newspaper on the Medellín cartel. (*EL ESPECTADOR*)

Carlos Lehder Rivas sits aboard a military plane after his arrest, awaiting extradition to the United States. (AP)

25.

PALACE OF JUSTICE

One day in August 1985, Supreme Court Justice Alfonso Patiño was in his chambers in the Palace of Justice in Bogotá when he received a telephone call: "We want you to declare the extradition treaty to be illegal," a voice said.

"What?" asked Patiño, incredulous. "Who is this?"

"We want you to declare the extradition treaty illegal."

And that was all. Patiño thought it strange. Who were these people, and how did they get his private number? He puzzled over it, decided not to tell his wife, María Cristina, then reconsidered. "Be careful," he told her.

"Of what?" she asked. Patiño said it was probably nothing. The court, he said, was examining a challenge to the constitutionality of Colombia's bilateral extradition treaty with the United States. He understood vaguely—he read the papers—that some criminals, drug traffickers, he thought, were especially affected by the treaty. This wasn't any of his business, though. His business was to worry about questions of law. He had nothing to do with drug traffickers. What could they want with him?

In early September Patiño received three letters in the mail. Each one had the same warning as the earlier telephone call, and each one was signed "the Extraditables." Patiño didn't mention it to his comrades in the Supreme Court's constitutional chamber. He didn't want them to know that this was happening; he didn't want to know if it was happening to them.

"I'm having a little trouble," he told María Cristina. "You should change your travel routes during the day, don't talk to me over the phone about your plans, and, really, be very, very careful."

Patiño admitted then, without telling her any specifics, that Colombia's cocaine traffickers were trying to influence his position on extradition. The Colombian Supreme Court had twenty-four justices in four chambers: civil, labor, penal, and constitutional. Extradition was a constitutional question and, as such, would be discussed and ruled upon by Patiño and the other members of the constitutional chamber. Whatever they decided was virtually guaranteed to be accepted by the court meeting in plenum.

At first Alfonso and María Cristina Patiño were more scandalized than frightened by the letters and telephone calls. The Patiños were from one of Colombia's august Conservative families, with a record of public service that stretched for generations. Alfonso was a noted jurist and a member of one of the finest Supreme Courts in Colombia's history. María Cristina was a ranking bureaucrat in the Foreign Ministry, in charge of administering Colombia's diplomatic missions and other real property all over the world. Criminals simply didn't bother people like the Patiños. Until now.

On September 14 the second letter arrived. Alfonso got two copies, and María Cristina got three at home. This one opened, *Hola, Perro* ("Hello, Dog"), and noted that "we know everything about your life." It came with an accompanying tape cassette that contained excerpts from several private conversations by Alfonso and by María Cristina from their respective offices at the court and at the Foreign Ministry. The most useful bit of news in the conversations was about María Cristina's upcoming inspection tour of Colombia's European embassies: "María Cristina will not be alive to make the trip," warned a voice on the tape.

At this juncture the Patiños paid a visit to the Ministries of Justice and Interior, seeking to shake things up. Alfonso came away with a four-man DAS escort, and María Cristina got a bodyguard.

The Patiños also braced the rest of the justices and demanded to know what sort of attention "the Extraditables" were paying to them. Quite a lot, it turned out. All had received the letters. One justice had taken his daughter to the hospital and left her there for a minor but urgent operation. Nurses paged him in the receiving room before he left, notifying him he had a telephone call: "We know where she is."

Another justice had received so many telephone threats on his private line that he'd changed the number. Two days later he received a call on the new line: "Hey, c'mon, don't be an asshole. . . ." A few days later the same justice received a tiny, elegantly made coffin in the mail with a brass nameplate bearing his name. He had a heart condition, he was in a constant state of panic, and he hadn't told his family.

The third set of letters to the Patiños arrived October 15, all of them addressed personally to María Cristina and delivered at home. There was neither wheedling nor insults in this one:

"You must convince your husband to abrogate the treaty," it said. "Remember, we are the same people who dealt with Rodrigo Lara Bonilla. Your bodyguards won't save you, no matter how many you have." There was another casette with more tapes of María Cristina's office phone calls. She changed the number.

Now María Cristina had four bodyguards of her own. Alfonso stopped taking walks. Both Patiños ceased going out at night and invented several number codes to use with one another and with relatives to let them know their whereabouts and plans. Alfonso suggested María Cristina start driving her own car to work instead of riding with him: "That way you'll save yourself."

Then one Tuesday early in November, Alfonso came home from work and confided that the next day the court planned to discuss the constitutionality of extradition. Neither Patiño slept that night. In the morning they dressed, had breakfast, and chatted. Then Alfonso kissed his wife and climbed into his car: "Take great care today." It was November 6.

IN the early days of Colombia's cocaine wars, disputes between the drug barons and the criminal justice system were personal matters to be settled on a personal basis. A drug boss bought the policemen he needed, and, if he got arrested anyway, he bought the judge who had his case. It was easy. In the early days a dismissal cost the peso equivalent of $30,000. More recently the tab had risen to $50,000, but it worked just as well. The judges were still largely the same career-oriented thirty-year-olds as before. They lived in one-room walk-ups, ate red beans and *arepas* (corn cakes) most days and *ajiaco* chicken stew on Sunday, if they were lucky. They made $230 a month prosecuting vomit-covered *bazuko* freaks and hired killers whose future no one cared about. The judiciary was a separate branch of government with no political influence. The judges hated the executive and hated Congress. Congress paid the judges the bare minimum to attract candidates. Judges, after all, had no constituency. No votes, no money.

If bribes were refused, traffickers tried a few threats or maybe paid clerks to steal the briefs. Sometimes the traffickers put a loose tail on the judges for a couple of days, get them to wondering. Or gave them a beating. The possibilities were legion. At some point the judges usually came around. Then they either took the money or quit their jobs so the cases could conveniently get lost.

When none of this worked—and this happened surprisingly often, at least two dozen times, by last count—the traffickers killed the judge. There simply was no other way to deal with an honest judge. And what was the harm? Nobody cared; nobody investigated; nobody was ever arrested.

With the coming of the Medellín cartel, however, patterns of judicial intimidation, like patterns of everything else to do with cocaine trafficking, became institutionalized. By 1985 the cartel's bagmen were hanging around arraignment courts with briefcases full of cash. Everybody knew them. By 1985 the cartel had so many cops on the pad that judges could never tell if their court-ordered bodyguard was protecting them or following them. By 1985 intimidation had become such a science that one of the cartel's heavy breathers could threaten a judge without even naming the case. He was calling on behalf of *all* of the defendants.

In short, by 1985 the cartel had correctly identified the criminal justice system as the weakest link in Colombian drug enforcement. The judges were badly overworked, badly paid, badly protected, and horribly maligned in the newspapers and by public officials. They were resentful of the treatment they received, and they were defenseless—easy targets for intimidation and murder. Why mess with an armed cop when the judge who gives him his orders doesn't even know how to cock a pistol?

And by 1985 the judges had learned the basic lesson well: "You can take the $50,000, or you can die," as one young prosecutor put it. To make sure the judges remembered the maxim, the cartel periodically demonstrated its validity. The Lara Bonilla assassination had done a lot in this regard, but memories faded and needed jogging.

Pablo Escobar, as in the past, was the expert in the field. He was already believed to have murdered almost everyone concerned with his 1976 dope bust, and he had followed that up by getting indicted for killing Lara Bonilla.

On July 23, 1985, five gunmen in a Mazda waylaid Bogotá Superior Court Judge Tulio Manuel Castro Gil outside the University of Santo Tomás and shot him to pieces as he climbed into a taxi. Castro Gil had written the Lara Bonilla indictment and had turned down unlimited money offered by an Escobar bagman the previous year. Escobar was apparently still willing to murder his tormentors. "You can take the money, or you can die."

Extradition had complicated matters, for it took traffickers out of the familiar, malleable Colombian ambience and put them in a place where judges spoke English, didn't investigate cases, and were treated like gods. The whole legal system in the United States was different and, most Colombians thought, merciless. Put a Colombian in a gringo court on drug charges, and he would be sent away forever. In Colombia nobody wanted to try drug cases; in the United States it seemed as though courts were competing for the opportunity.

The cartel had never been able to deal with any of this—it was too foreign—and from the moment the bilateral extradition treaty took hold in 1982, the cartel had lobbied furiously to have it either ignored, declared unconstitutional, or abrogated, preferably all three.

This was an old story, but what made 1985 different was that the traffickers were seeing their worst fears realized. Hernan Botero, the "respectable" Medellín banker extradited in January as a money launderer, couldn't get bail in Miami and was taken back and forth from court in Miami *in chains*. In August a federal jury convicted him; he would be sentenced to thirty years in jail and fined $25,000.

For Marcos Cadavid, extradited at the same time as Botero, it was even worse. He was sentenced to fifteen years for cocaine trafficking after *only three months in the United States*. Colombian traffickers were accustomed to the Napoleonic system with its myriad briefs and endless procedural delays. Marathons like the Ochoa affair in Spain offered all kinds of opportunities for sophisticated legal maneuvers. In the United States, it seemed, defendants were denied bail, went to jail, went to court, were convicted, and went to prison. That was it.

So the cartel did what it could in Colombia. It had the highest officials of the government under constant threat, and it killed when necessary or desirable. First came Castro Gil, then on September 11 motorcycle gunmen murdered La Picota prison warden Alcides Arizmendi. A week earlier Arizmendi had foiled a plot to break out extraditable prisoner and cartel associate Juan Ramón Mata Ballesteros. Minutes after Arizmendi's death, Mata Ballesteros's fellow prisoners began to chant and jeer in their cell blocks. Pablo Escobar called a Medellín radio station to accuse Arizmendi of "mistreating prisoners."

Besides intimidation, the cartel made excellent use of propaganda, focusing its campaign on cultural differences and racism. It was, they said, impossible for a Colombian to get a fair trial or decent treatment in a U.S. courtroom. The press and the DEA had given the gringos the idea that all Colombians were wiry, beady-eyed little brown men and savage killers. Look at the way they shackled people. The chaining of Botero, videotaped and shown on Colombian television, caused such a public uproar that the Foreign Ministry made a protest to the U.S. embasssy. U.S. diplomats explained that U.S. marshals transported all federal prisoners in chains, regardless of nationality.

Still, the nationalist appeal struck a sympathetic chord among a populace grown weary of the endless killing, corruption, and institutional damage. The United States was doing nothing to curtail cocaine consumption, the argument went, and Colombia was paying the price. If there were no extradition, the traffickers would leave us alone.

But the Betancur administration held firm. By September 1985 six defendants had been extradited, nine more were in custody, and 105 U.S. "Requests for Provisional Arrests" were active in Colombia. Justice Minister Parejo Gonzalez, unremitting in his support for extradition, said the United States and Colombia were "cooperating beautifully."

The Medellín cartel had apparently reached the same conclusion a month or so earlier. Extradition, now embraced by both the United States and Colombia, could not be shaken by either public opinion or threats to political officials. The only thing left was to get rid of the extradition treaty itself. That's when the traffickers decided to go after the Supreme Court.

THREE ambassadors were presenting their credentials to President Betancur in the Protocol Salon of the National Palace. Ordinarily the procedure should have taken about forty minutes. It was just after 11:30 A.M., November 6, 1985, on a beautiful Bogotá morning. Betancur had greeted the new Indonesian ambassador and was now receiving the Mexican envoy. There was a playing of national anthems and a presenting of arms by grenadiers in the courtyard. Everything had a certain martial air, so it took a moment for Colombian Foreign Minister Augusto Ramirez Ocampo to register alarm when he heard gunshots in the street outside. Wait a minute, he thought, that's not part of the ceremony.

A courier interrupted briefly, confirmed there was gunfire coming from the Plaza Bolivar about two blocks away. Betancur heard this news and began the ceremonial again, moving quickly this time. The shots continued briefly, then were replaced by the sound of a large number of marching feet. Police, thought Ramirez. What in hell is going on?

. . .

AT 11:40 A.M. about thirty-five M-19 guerrillas, loaded down with machine guns, automatic rifles, and grenades, leaped from the back of a covered truck and flooded into the Colombian Palace of Justice, an unsightly, blocklike, four-story stone building on Bogotá's central Plaza Bolivar. Within minutes they had seized the entire building and more than 250 hostages, including Alfonso Reyes Echandia, chief justice of Colombia's Supreme Court, and the majority of the court's twenty-four associate justices. Alfonso Patiño and the other members of the constitutional chamber were discussing extradition in a third-floor conference room.

Around noon eleven police plainclothesmen tried to break into the palace basement. Guerrillas greeted them with gunfire.

For the next twenty-six hours hundreds of soldiers, police, and commandos attacked the building and tried to subdue its defenders. On the face of it, it was an unequal struggle. The soldiers had tanks, rockets, and helicopters and used them with abandon, blowing great holes in the palace's masonry and bashing in the main door to establish a salient on the ground floor.

But the guerrillas had planned well. Extra combatants had infiltrated the building in civilian clothes before the guerrilla shock troops arrived, and there were more than enough riflemen to cover key entrances and windows. Police helicopters landed GOES units on the palace roof, but guerrilla snipers kept them at bay by shooting through skylights.

Most important, the guerrillas had mounted their heavy machine guns in makeshift pillboxes of furniture, cushions, cabinets, and junk jammed into stairwells throughout the palace. From these strongpoints, guerrilla gun captains had superb fields of fire and could pin down entire police or army units virtually without risk. After the initial probes and fireworks, the struggle quickly reached stalemate.

YESID Reyes Alvarado, a young lawyer working in north Bogotá, heard about the seizure over the radio. He tried to telephone his father, the chief justice, Alfonso Reyes, about 1:30 P.M. Unable to get past a busy signal, he called the secretaries next door. They were scared but reasonably coherent. His father was all right; his bodyguards were with him, and there were no guerrillas on the fourth floor where Reyes and most of the other justices had chambers. His father's line was busy because he was talking to government officials.

Yesid called back a half hour later, got more or less the same report, and began to wonder what he might do to help. Just before he hung up he heard a commotion, and one of the secretaries screamed, "They're coming through the wall!"

Yesid dialed and dialed, getting no answer for more than an hour. Finally, a little after three P.M., he got through on his father's private line. An excited, angry voice yelled at him: "Tell the police and soldiers to stop shooting!"

"Who is this?" Yesid wanted to know. "Let me talk to my father."

His father came on the line then. He was with M-19 Comandante Luis Otero, he said. Otero was in charge of the assault. Reyes was calm; he spoke slowly and carefully: "I'm all right, but see if the DAS and the police will stop shooting. . . ."

Otero's voice cut in: "If they don't stop shooting in fifteen minutes, we're all going to die!"

Yesid called the police to press for negotiations, then reached Otero and his father again. Otero was frantic, almost inarticulate. The government wouldn't talk—wouldn't even begin to talk; the guerrillas were stuck in the palace with nobody to listen to their demands. Nothing. The entire event was rapidly turning into a nightmare.

Yesid's father, by contrast, was still calm, still insistent: "The shooting must stop."

Yesid hung up and dialed Radio Caracól. He spoke to the editors' desk, gave them his father's private number, and suggested they open a line. They did so immediately, and Yesid, along with most of Colombia, tuned it. Again he heard his father urging a cease-fire.

Yesid waited for an hour, then called the palace again to talk to his father, who was finally beginning to sound a bit haggard. "The guerrillas want to negotiate," he said. Then the line went dead. It was just after five P.M.

DOWN the hall from Alfonso Reyes and Comandante Otero, Justice Humberto Murcia Ballen was huddled on the floor of his office, somewhat scared and getting more scared by the minute. He was in the court's civil chamber, had never been threatened, and had scoffed at Patiño and the others when they told him about their problems. His first thought after the guerrillas arrived was that they would "shoot up the place, paint the walls, break some windows, and leave." Then the army came, and he expected negotiations to begin. But instead of peace talks there were bullets whizzing all over the place. Murcia had lost a leg to illness several years earlier, and a bullet shattered his artificial limb during the first hours of the siege. Since then he had been immobilized, which didn't present an immediate problem. He wasn't going to remind anyone where he was or what he did for a living.

The fires started about seven P.M. After the siege ended, some Colombian government and U.S. embassy officials would maintain that the guerrillas lit them so they could purposely burn extradition cases on file in the court archives. Opponents of the government would maintain that the police started the fires in order to burn cases having to do with death squad activity and other sins of the security forces.

Although the fires did indeed destroy extradition cases, death squad activity cases, and much, much more, accusations of arson on either side did not, ultimately, seem credible. The palace was a virtually impregnable fortress for somebody outside trying to get in, but inside it was largely composed of salons broken up by wooden dividers. Anybody who worked there knew the place was a firetrap. Put several hundred men with hand grenades and tracer bullets in there for a nine-hour pitched battle, and fire was inevitable.

It was the smoke that finally made Justice Murcia give himself up. Choking and terrified, he crawled to the top of the fourth-floor stairs and surrendered to the guerrillas below. They hauled him to a bathroom and threw him on top of some sixty other hostages heaped inside. Murcia was sure now that he would die. He thought about his family; then he thought about his life; then he thought about nothing at all.

Early the next afternoon the final assault began. At that point the bathroom was filled with hostages and guerrillas, living and dead. The guerrillas, increasingly desperate, ordered the living hostages to get to their feet, then shoved them out the door. Murcia, supported by another hostage, lurched into a grenade explosion. Stunned and bleeding from the face, he fell to the floor. Most of those who were with him were dead. The remaining guerrillas pitched the corpses down the stairwell—Murcia among them. Then they went away. Murcia waited, then crawled to the cellar. He knew there was a tank on the first floor, so he dragged himself up one flight and peeked over the edge into the lobby. Taking heart, he pulled himself erect and put his hands in the air:

"Don't shoot!"

AT least ninety-five people died in the Palace of Justice, including Supreme Court Chief Justice Alfonso Reyes Echandia, his two bodyguards, and Comandante Luis Otero. Alfonso Patiño and the rest of the associate justices of the court's constitutional chamber all died, probably among the first people killed. In all, eleven of the twenty-four justices died, all by bullet wounds. Early reports said the guerrillas executed the justices, but this was never confirmed.

Apparently all the guerrillas were killed. Twenty-two were identified, and at least nineteen unidentified corpses were believed to have been part of the attacking force. Eleven police and soldiers were killed, as were thirty-two other people: auxiliary justices, secretaries, lawyers, and bystanders of one kind or another.

Belisario Betancur's presidency never recovered from this horror. Early kudos for being "tough" with the guerrillas gave way to bitter recriminations. Why had there never been any meaningful attempt to negotiate? Surviving justices, among them Humberto Murcia, denounced the government in a paroxysm of despair. Relations between Betancur and the Colombian justice system hit bottom.

Justice Minister Parejo expressed the opinion that the seizure was probably a cartel job, but he was the only top-level government official to say so publicly. At first Colombians thought the cartel conspiracy theory was just propaganda to deflect attention from the draconian performance of the government and security forces. But as time passed the conviction would grow that the cartel had indeed been involved. A year later every Colombian in a responsible public position would accept without question that the traffickers ordered and paid for the Palace of Justice assault in a joint venture with M-19: good guerrilla theater, good intimidation for the traffickers.

But this postmortem did Belisario Betancur no good. When he spoke at a memorial mass for the dead justices on November 10, the survivors boycotted the service in disgust. Finally, Betancur believed in narco-guerrillas, just as he had believed, finally, in extradition after the cartel killed Lara Bonilla. Death, it seemed, was a convincing argument. Now the Medellín cartel was killing Colombia.

26.

BETANCUR AT TWILIGHT

In February 1986 President Belisario Betancur was halfway through his last year in office. His presidency had begun with more fanfare and enthusiasm than any in recent memory, but there was little left at twilight.

Betancur had suffered a massive loss of public confidence in the past several months. Eight days after the Palace of Justice bloodbath, a devastating volcano eruption and mud slide buried the Magdalena River town of Armero and killed some 22,000 people. Relief efforts were slow and inefficient, the magnitude of the tragedy not fully appreciated. Scathing criticism rained down on the government, adding salt to Betancur's already festering political wounds.

Betancur was double-damned for the Palace of Justice debacle. He could never adequately explain why he'd failed to negotiate with the M-19 guerrillas in the early stages of the takeover. At the same time, he could never adequately explain why his administration would ever have wanted to negotiate with guerrillas in the first place. Betancur's vaunted "Peace Process" lost prestige. Until a few months before the seizure, the Colombian government had had a cease-fire with the M-19. Did it now make any sense to try to achieve peace with such savages?

Apparently Betancur still thought it did, and as his presidency limped into 1986, he could point to what looked like a solid achievement. While the M-19 peace initiative had collapsed, a truce with the much larger and more prestigious FARC had held. The FARC, the Colombian Communist party, and several Marxist labor groups had united to form the Patriotic Union party and had stated their intention to participate in March parliamentary elections. Betancur could not run for a second term in the presidential balloting two months later, but if he could bring FARC into participation in legitimate governmental activity, his Peace Process still had a chance to go forward. What Betancur chose to ignore was that the Peace Process, like virtually every other political initiative in Colombia, was already compromised by the Medellín cartel. Since Ambassador Tambs had coined the term "narco-guerrillas" 2½ years previously, the conviction had grown in Colombia that the FARC and the cartel were indeed permanently involved with one another in a series of joint ventures and business deals in the eastern *llanos*.

By the beginning of 1986, security forces accepted the connection. Operations against *llanos* cocaine labs were always planned with the knowledge that police would likely be challenged by highly trained jungle guerrilla cadre.

But evidence was also growing that the FARC-narc relationship had started to deteriorate. Virtually from the moment the Patriotic Union put its new electoral organization on display, its above-ground leaders and cadre began to be attacked and assassinated in alarming numbers. Many Colombians, particularly those who lived in the *llanos*, knew that the FARC and the cartel were competing for control of *campesino* coca growers, and that both sides were becoming increasingly impatient with the high-handed way in which the other insisted on doing business. The *llanos* were basically FARC turf, and the cartel knew that it couldn't compete with the guerrillas there. What the cartel could do, however, and do better than anyone, was murder the FARC's urban cadre, that is, prey on the Patriotic Union. It began to do so.

BY 1986 the cartel had moved into direct confrontation with the Colombian government and had begun systematically to attack and destroy any Colombian institution that it could not shape to suit its purposes.

The criminal justice system was a joke. The cartel murdered people at will, and the killers were almost never pursued, let alone caught. The judges were just as poorly paid and poorly protected as ever, working in primitive conditions that made their jobs almost impossible. The atmosphere in the courts was so contentious and embittered by mid-1986 that the conflicts became ridiculous. When the United States tried to give the court system $290,000 for administrative reform, the employees' union rejected it "categorically" as "one further step in [the United States'] abusive policy of intervention in the internal affairs of other states."

The cartel had murdered one of Betancur's justice ministers and had his successor under constant threat of death. Betancur's attorney general, supposedly the watchdog of the courts, had gone to Panama to listen to the cartel's peace proposal. The Supreme Court was devastated. Justice Fernando Uribe Restrepo, successor to Alfonso Reyes Echandia as chief justice, resigned in March after four months in office because of cartel death threats. *His* successor, Nemesio Camacho Rodriguez, would resign in January 1987 for the same reason. On July 31, 1986, motorcycle killers ambushed and murdered Justice Hernando Baquero Borda, last of the court's old-guard, proextradition hard-liners. Baquero was riding in a chauffeur-driven limousine with a motorcycle escort. Besides Baquero, the gunmen also killed a bodyguard and a bystander. Baquero's wife, driver, motorcycle escort policeman, and another bystander were wounded. Betancur blamed "organized crime's hired assassins."

One former justice summed up the sad state of Colombia's Supreme Court at midyear: "A year ago, to be a justice was every lawyer's aspiration; now everybody hides, so they won't be asked to serve."

Many Colombians continued to lobby for some sort of deal with the cartel, arguing as always that cocaine was a gringo problem, not a Colombian problem. But in 1986 even this was no longer true. Cocaine cost $15 per gram in Bogotá, well within the means of any middle- to upper-middle-class Colombian. For the less well-to-do there was always *bazuko,* now widely used in big city slums. While no statistics existed, drug rehabilitation workers estimated users at anywhere from three hundred thousand to three million. Most of the time *bazuko* had traces of leaded gasoline, kerosene, ether, sulphuric acid, and other chemicals used in the cocaine refining process. It could cause permanent brain damage.

Still, Colombians were to a certain extent correct when they said that Colombia "doesn't have a major drug problem." What Colombia had was a major problem with institutional collapse. The courts, the political parties, Congress, the police, most of the professional soccer league, and even the bullfights were compromised by the cartel. Even the guerrilla groups—a Colombian institution for thirty-five years—had been forever tainted by the traffickers.

Despite all this, extraditions continued, and Justice Minister Parejo Gonzalez, with Betancur backing him to the hilt, remained implacable in his pursuit of the traffickers. By the end of 1986 Colombia had extradited thirteen people in all. All but one for drug-related crimes.

But still the cartel leaders eluded capture. Escobar and Gonzalo

Rodriguez Gacha were seen regularly in Medellín, in Cundinamarca province near Bogotá, and in Guaviare where "the Mexican" had his coca plantations. Carlos Lehder was reported in and out of the cities but still for the most part stuck in the jungle. Jorge Ochoa was in jail in Spain, but his organization was intact and functioning well with his brothers at the helm.

And if the cartel members were invisible, their presence was nevertheless felt constantly and as never before. The cartel wanted the extradition treaty done away with, but the government still refused to get the message. In 1986 Colombia would experience a year of violence such as it had not seen in decades. Extradition was the theme; the Palace of Justice was the overture; now came the opera.

THE year opened with a vendetta in Medellín. Rumor had it that the Ochoas had lost a big load in the United States but for some reason refused to pay insurance to its piggybackers. The piggybackers, furious at this behavior, tried to collect from the clan in time-honored cartel style: they kidnapped people and held them against the day their creditors paid their debts. In this fashion around twenty people were murdered at the end of January and in February.

Key casualties included Rodrigo Pardo Murillo, Jorge Ochoa's brother-in-law, who was kidnapped and killed in reprisal for an earlier killing; Pablo Correa Arroyave, another Ochoa brother-in-law and a key figure in Los Pablos, who was ambushed and killed in the street; Pablo Correa Ramos, cartel underboss and softball fanatic, who was hitting fungoes at a Medellín ballpark when two spectators stopped watching him, pulled out machine pistols, and riddled him with bullets.

On March 19, several weeks after these paroxysms, Medellín police found the corpses of two Panamanians: Rubén Dario Paredes Jimenez, son of General Noriega's predecessor as chief of the Panamanian armed forces, and Cesar Rodriguez Contreras, a former military pilot and Noriega confidant. The pair had checked into Medellín's downtown Hotel Nutibara on March 11 and disappeared two days later. In 1988 a U.S. federal indictment would charge that the two Panamanians came to Medellín to meet members of the cartel and negotiate a 322-kilo cocaine deal. The indictment said both men were in Medellín with Noriega's knowledge and support.

This sort of ugly intrigue had long been a staple of the Medellín scene, but the "Orchid City" in the last couple of years had surpassed itself. In 1985 Medellín homicides numbered 1,698, highest incidence per capita in a country that had had 11,000 total murders, a rate higher than any in the world for a country not actually embroiled in civil war. The United States, a nation with almost ten times as many people as Colombia, had 16,000 murders in 1986.

In 1986 Medellín eclipsed these figures. Murder countrywide became the leading cause of death for males between the ages of fifteen and forty, and the University of Antioquia documented 1,155 homicides in the city in the year's first six months, 80.4 percent of them the result of gunshot wounds. For all of 1986, murders in Medellín would reach 3,500—about 10 a day.

Law enforcement in the city was totally paralyzed. Gossip in Bogotá held that there were "20,000 unsolved murders in Medellín and only 20 defendants." DAS in Medellín no longer investigated cases. Instead they were passed to Bogotá, which sent agents from headquarters. If the agents stayed too long, with their cultured Bogotá accents and smooth manner, the north Medellín murder gangs got to know their faces and began following them around.

IN Spain, the Ochoa trial continued to creep through a legal labyrinth that most Colombians had long ago ceased to understand. As expected, the January 21, 1986, Audiencia Nacional appeal ruling in favor of extraditing Ochoa to the United States was far from the last word. The defense filed its own appeal January 24, charging that the prosecution was acting unconstitutionally.

On January 31 the court agreed to consider the new defense motion, and on February 12 it decided in favor of Colombia. In Baton Rouge Barry Seal had a week to live, but it was probably too late to call off the hit, even if the Ochoas had wished to do so.

After the February 12 finding the Ochoa case moved into a new, extremely Byzantine phase that had nothing to do with the political content of the indictments. The case had called into question virtually every aspect of Spanish law relating to extradition, forcing the courts to review their statutes and finally prompting legislators to enact a completely new set of guidelines. For the next round of hearings the courts would rule strictly on the basis of a series of weighted factors: the date of the extradition request, the nature and number of the crimes alleged, and the nationality of the accused and related matters.

The U.S. request looked sadly deficient at this point, and American officials despaired of their chances of gaining custody of Ochoa. Colombian authorities were reaching the same conclusion. It seemed increasingly likely that El Gordo would defeat the gringos and come home. The Seal murder strengthened Ochoa's position still further, removing the U.S. government's chief witness from the scene.

If Ochoa reached Colombia, Colombia was going to have to hold him. The Betancur government got a practical demonstration of what this might entail on March 19, when Honduran prisoner Juan Ramón Mata Ballesteros, wanted for extradition to the United States in the murder of a DEA agent in Mexico, spread about $2 million among eighteen trustees and guards and walked out of Bogotá's Cárcel Modelo. The warden immediately resigned. The previous year motorcycle assassins had killed another prison warden after he'd discovered an earlier plot to spring Mata.

ON May 25 voters elected Liberal Party candidate Virgilio Barco Vargas as Colombia's new president. He won with 58 percent of the vote, crushing his Conservative party opponent by an unprecedented margin. Barco, a colorless engineer educated at the Massachusetts Institute of Technology, was known as an honest man, a capable bureaucrat, and a friend of the United States. He was supposed to be strongly antidrug and strongly proextradition, but drugs had not warranted even a paragraph in his election platform.

Furthermore Barco, like Betancur before him, gave drug enforcement no priority whatsoever. He was interested in abolishing "absolute poverty" among Colombia's twenty-eight million citizens and in dismantling the National Front, the cooperative political venture through which Liberals and Conservatives had jointly ruled Colombia since 1958. Barco wanted a Liberal Party government and had the mandate to impose it. It was an ambitious and worthy plan, a direct attack on the cronyism that had turned Colombian politics into the private domain of the nation's aristocracy.

But again, like Betancur with his Peace Process, Barco was ignoring the Medellín cartel, failing to recognize that the justice system was in desperate straits, failing to recognize that his own party was desperately compromised, failing to recognize that the traffickers were destroying Colombian institutions. Like Betancur, he would not be minding the store when it most counted—at the beginning.

It was not as if clues were lacking. After Barco's election the traffickers embarked on a chillingly efficient assassinations policy, aimed as always at further intimidating law enforcement and at inducing the Supreme Court and other legal authorities to abrogate the extradition treaty.

On July 3 motorcycle killers murdered Avianca Airlines chief of tickets Luis Francisco Briceño Murillo in morning traffic. On September 1 motorcycle killers murdered Avianca security chief Carlos Arturo Luna Rojas a few days after he seized two hundred kilos of cocaine in an airplane tire.

On July 16 Luis Roberto Camacho, *El Espectador* correspondent in Leticia, was killed after a protracted struggle with Evaristo Porras and other drug traffickers over control of the local Chamber of Commerce. On July 18 Rubén Dario Londoño Vasquez, the "Juan Perez" who had helped lead the plot against Rodrigo Lara Bonilla in 1984, was murdered in Medellín as he stepped down from his van. Two weeks later Justice Baquero was killed, and a week after that Parejo Gonzalez, Lara Bonilla's successor, was spirited out of Colombia under guard and sent to Budapest as ambassador to Hungary. Betancur had tried to get Lara Bonilla to Prague two years earlier, but the cartel had moved too quickly. Parejo Gonzales had apparently been luckier.

On August 30 motorcycle killers in the Rio Magdalena town of Barrancabermeja shot alternate congressman León Posada Pedraza of the Communist Party; he bled to death three hours later. On September 1 another set of motorcycle killers shot Patriotic Union Senator Pedro Nel Jimenez just as he was about to get on an airplane to attend Posada's funeral. The Patriotic Union denounced Magdalena landowners and paramilitary death squads; by early 1987 they were also damning Gonzalo Rodriguez Gacha and his gunmen in Guaviare. By that time more than three hundred Patriotic Union militants had been killed.

In Cali the widespread lawlessness inspired a particularly vicious spate of vigilantism. In August and the first three weeks of September, thirty-three people were killed by gangs of murderers, twenty-one of them during a single five-hour period the night of September 4–5. For the most part the victims were whores, pimps, drunks, homosexuals, *bazuko* addicts, and pickpockets and other petty crooks. These targets, police said, were killed by "death squads" or someone with "a personal problem." The victims also included Raul Echavarria Barrientos, managing editor of Cali's *El Occidente* newspaper, staunch supporter of extradition and advocate of the death penalty for drug traffickers. He was shot down by a pair of gunmen who waylaid him outside his house when he came home from work.

ON July 13, 1986, after twenty months, six separate court findings, a final ruling by a special panel, and a succession of motions and appeals so Byzantine that only his lawyers seemed to understand them in the end, Jorge Ochoa came home from Spain. He looked dough-faced and unhealthy, heavyset but not fat. He landed at El Dorado Airport in Bogotá and was taken to DAS headquarters for fingerprinting and mugshots. His father was crying with joy: "I'm very happy that my son has been returned. I think justice has been done."

The Spanish Audiencia Nacional, in its penultimate (fifth) finding, said it had based its decision on the fact that the Colombian petitions ultimately had greater weight than those of the United States. The United States had made its request first but had only made one request; Colombia had two. The charges were equally serious in both countries. The deciding factor, then, said the court, was nationality: "From the standpoint of fundamental rights, it is obvious that [in Colombia] his case would be tried in a country that is his own, where he knows the language, where the environment, the customs, and the Napoleonic legal system itself would permit him greater possibilities of full judicial protection."

Indeed. The way it was supposed to work, Ochoa would first travel to Cartagena to stand trial for "falsification of a public document"— in other words, smuggling 128 Spanish fighting bulls into Colombia in 1981. After that he would have to go to Medellín to deal with the drug indictment lifted from the south Florida Nicaragua case. Then, in theory, he would have to face extradition to the United States.

In fact, however, filing the Nicaragua case in Medellín set up potential double jeopardy, making it extremely unlikely that he would ever be extradited. How could somebody be tried twice on the same charges? Gilberto Rodriguez Orejuela, extradited to Colombia a couple of weeks before Ochoa, had made precisely this calculation and was sitting quietly in a Cali jail waiting for his case to come to trial. Rodriguez Orejuela, a first-rank trafficker for perhaps fifteen years, was a subtle man and probably the financial genius behind the cartel. Not for nothing was he known as "the Chess Player."

Ochoa was taken to Cartagena and on August 1 appeared in a Colombian court—as far as anyone could tell—for the first time in his life. He described himself as a "rancher" and said he didn't have an ID card anymore. Customs Judge Fabio Pastrana Hoyos indicted him for bull smuggling and remanded him to jail to await trial.

Parejo Gonzalez, still in Bogotá but about to depart for Budapest, was mindful of what was at stake and had taken great pains to cover all of Ochoa's obvious paths to legal escape. Chief among his measures was a message he sent to Pastrana instructing the judge not to release his famous prisoner under any circumstances. Regardless of his finding in the bull-smuggling case, Parejo Gonzalez said, Pastrana should hold Ochoa and make ready to transfer him to Medellín.

Days after the message, however, Parejo Gonzalez was gone to Hungary, the Betancur administration had packed its bags, and on August 7 Virgilio Barco was inaugurated as the new Colombian president, bringing in a whole government full of rookie bureaucrats.

Parejo Gonzalez had reason to worry, for the Ochoa family had already sent envoys to Cartagena. Much later, documents seized by the Colombian army would show that the envoys had spread 199 million pesos ($995,000) around the city. The bagman was described as "Misael" in the documents, and the major beneficiary was "the Professor," who collected 132 million pesos ($660,000) for "lowering bail and fines," among other services.

On August 15, Judge Pastrana issued his finding. Ochoa was guilty as charged and was sentenced to twenty months in jail. There was, however, something else. Unknown to virtually everyone in the country, Ochoa had already been released. Two days earlier Pastrana had paroled Ochoa on 2.3 million pesos ($11,500) bond. Ochoa had spent precisely thirty days in jail in Colombia.

Pastrana, who was thirty years old, had told Ochoa to check in faithfully every two weeks. Pastrana was fired August 21, six days before Ochoa's first reporting date.

Ochoa never bothered to report to anyone.

27.

THE RAMIREZ CONTRACT

On January 25, 1986, a middle-aged man appeared at the Bogotá headquarters of Colombian National Police intelligence (F-2). The police knew the man as a sometime informant who had close ties with M-19 guerrillas in Medellín. On the rare occasions when he helped police, his information had always been good. He worked for money and always demanded the going rate—and then some. Police suspected he was a closet gambler or a womanizer who liked to buy expensive presents.

His story that Saturday morning concerned Pablo Escobar. A bit over two months earlier, he said, Escobar had put out a murder contract on an unnamed "police colonel." It was a big job: (twenty-five million pesos ($152,000) plus expenses. Someone had held the contract for two months, then dropped it. A fortnight ago it had been picked up again, this time by the Medellín chapter of the Ricardo Franco Brigade, a particularly savage FARC splinter group that had made recent headlines by torturing and murdering as many as two hundred of its members, charging they were police infiltrators. The Brigade had named "Chief of Executions" Carlos Espinosa Osorio, alias Cuco ("Foxy") to handle the police hit. The informant took care to point out that Cuco had had nothing to do with the Ricardo Franco massacres. He was a killer, yes, but he wasn't crazy.

Escobar, the informant continued, had advanced Cuco two million pesos ($12,000), which the hit team had used for black market purchases in Medellín: four 9-mm Smith & Wesson pistols, one .357 Ruger revolver, and one .45-caliber MAC-10 machine pistol. All of this had been dumped in the back of a rental van and driven to Bogotá with a motorcycle escort. Now everything was lying in the trunk of a red Renault 18 parked in front of an Escobar-owned safe house in the town of Chía, a bedroom community on Bogotá's northern edge. One hit team member was watching it.

The informant didn't know who the target was, but he—and Escobar and Cuco—had a lot of information about him. Much of it was coming from a police lieutenant "who had the colonel's confidence" and was betraying it for five million pesos ($30,000). Cuco and his gunmen knew, for example, that the colonel was going to start a course at generals school on the twenty-fifth "of some unspecified month"; that the antinarcotics police had given him a going-away party at a Bogotá club; that the DEA had lent him an armored Mercedes-Benz; that his mother lived at Diagonal 63, no. 27–43 in Bogotá; that he had a country house in Cajica, north of the capital; that he drove a Toyota camper, license plate AL-26-18.

There was more, and the police wrote it all down, but they already knew who the target was. The country house was in Granada, not Cajica, and the armored car was a Ford LTD, not a Mercedes. Still, only one colonel fit the information: Jaime Ramirez Gomez.

The informant continued. The pre-Cuco hit team, he said, had tried twice to kill the target. Once, outside a club in Cajica, they had aborted the hit because the colonel had too big an escort; the second time had been at his mother's house at Christmas, and the target had been surrounded by his relatives. Escobar, he said, wanted to kill the colonel but had no interest in murdering anyone else.

The informant said the new hit team had picked three places where they might best locate the colonel and kill him: across the street from the Paz de Rio Bakery on Avenida 68, on a highway overpass near the General Santander Police Academy, and at his mother's house.

The informant said he would be in regular contact with Cuco's people and would be glad to provide further information to the police. Anything else the police wanted, they should get in touch with him. And, oh yes, bring 400,000 pesos ($2,425).

Two days later the F-2 met with Police Lieutenant Colonel Teodoro Campo, the chief of the Anti-Narcotics Unit, and told him what the informant had said. Campo told the F-2 police to watch the Chía safe house and to wait for Colonel Ramirez to return from leave. He did not want to disturb Ramirez "until we are sure."

Jaime Ramirez had been officially relieved as Anti-Narcotics Unit police chief by Lieutenant Colonel Teodoro Campo Gomez on December 31, 1985. He took forty days' leave and returned to duty the second week in February. Ramirez always felt pretty good about himself and about life in general, but he was especially bouncy these days.

And why not? In the three years he had served as chief of the Anti-

Narcotics Unit, his men had seized twenty-seven tons of cocaine, arrested 7,941 men and 1,405 women, confiscated 2,783 trucks, 1,060 cars, 83 boats, and 116 airplanes. Fifty-four percent of all the cocaine seized in the world in 1985 was seized by his men. Ninety percent of Colombia's 1985 marijuana crop was destroyed by herbicide sprayed from his crop dusters.

His unit had been awarded best in the police in 1985, and Ramirez had been selected for general, moved ahead a class at the Superior War College, and slated for early promotion. At the beginning of 1986 he was undeniably the most famous narc in the world—a legend in his own country, revered by the DEA, sought for his counsel by police from Lima to La Paz to Washington.

Sought, too, by the Medellín cartel—which wanted him as much as it had wanted anyone else in its history. It was not surprising that Escobar ordered the hit. Escobar acted as if he kept a book on those who caused him pain. Every once in a while, it seemed, he took the book out of his pocket and examined the names he had written. And every once in a while he crossed one off: DAS Major Monroy Arenas, who had arrested him for dope in 1976; Rodrigo Lara Bonilla, who had told him off on the floor of Congress in 1983; Tulio Manuel Castro Gil, who had indicted him for murder in 1984.

Now it was Jaime Ramirez. Nobody had cost Escobar more money than Ramirez, and now Ramirez was going to pay. It would be a tough hit, maybe the toughest the cartel had ever attempted. The target was an outstanding professional lawman. He knew the traffickers wanted to kill him, would almost certainly find out about the plot, and would take extraordinary measures to protect himself. It was the kind of bald challenge that would appeal to Escobar. The cartel wouldn't dare go after Jaime Ramirez. Would it?

First Escobar contracted the job with his own hitmen. Then he farmed it out to the Ricardo Franco Brigade. Later he would give pieces of the contract to other members of the cartel, selling shares in vengeance. Gonzalo Rodriguez Gacha bought in, to get back for the millions he lost at Tranquilandia. Carlos Lehder also bought a piece. And he, probably more than any other member of the Medellín cartel, had reason to wish Ramirez dead.

In his final, superb year as chief of the narcotics police, Ramirez had hounded Lehder unmercifully. His detectives staked out airstrips and safe houses all across Colombia, questioned Lehder's friends and acquaintances, and meticulously developed a countrywide network of snitches and intelligence operatives.

Twice they almost got him. In March 1985 detectives reported that

Liliana Garcia Osorio, "Lili," a twenty-four-year-old party girl from Armenia, had left the town house that Lehder bought for her, had taken a commercial flight to Bogotá, and had climbed aboard a privately owned Bell JetRanger III helicopter and flown into the eastern *llanos*. Traveling with her was Verónica, the three-year-old daughter she had with Lehder.

Six weeks later, on April 26, several dozen Anti-Narcotics Unit police in two separate expeditions raided six sites in the *llanos* of Meta and Casanare provinces. They stayed five days, searched hundreds of square miles of jungle, and interviewed dozens of people. Yes, Lehder owned the property; yes, he had been here; but, no, he hadn't been around in a while. It was an old story: easy to seize labs, property, even cocaine, damn near impossible to sneak up on anyone.

But they made him suffer. At Finca La Gaitana on the Manacacias River in Meta, police found some bandoliers, a few walkie-talkies, and 355 kilos of cocaine buried in plastic tubs in the yard. And inside a nicely appointed white stucco house with a corrugated tin roof, they found $1,678,680 in cash, packed in cardboard rum boxes. La Gaitana had an airstrip, two airplanes, a couple of Toyota four-wheel-drive vehicles, a swimming pool, and space to sleep fifty people.

And some twenty miles away, at a rough-cut clapboard farmhouse, the police found Lehder's German passport, a pile of other documents, unlimited baby toys, and baby pictures. They also arrested ten people, including Liliana Garcia Osorio and Verónica Lehder. Lili was held for trial on charges of consorting with a known fugitive. She would do two years in Villavicencio and the Buen Pastor women's penitentiary in Bogotá.

After the April raids, Lehder moved into the forests on the eastern edge of Meta to another *finca* called La Abundancia. Ramirez's informants said Lehder was doing a lot of coke, lifting weights, and riding dirt bikes. Lehder also had no doubt that Ramirez was his chief tormentor, denouncing him in May in an "open letter" to the minister of defense. He complained of the treatment Lili and the other prisoners were receiving in Villavicencio and denounced the United States, "destined by providence to plague America with hunger and misery in the name of liberty."

Ramirez's men hit La Abundancia August 5, 1985. The helicopters got lost on the way and arrived a day late but still missed Lehder only by seconds. Two more captured girlfriends said he was last seen running toward the Rio Uva in his red underwear carrying a machine pistol at port arms.

The police stayed in the area eleven days. They found only sixty kilos of cocaine and no money, but the *finca* was chock full of useful documents, photographs, and other artifacts. Lehder had built a motorcycle repair shed and put two people to work in it. The house was unpainted clapboard with a tin roof, but roomy and comfortable. Lehder had a television (but nothing to watch), a couple of typewriters, a blender, and some stereo equipment. A book rack had an eclectic selection of Spanish and English titles: V. S. Naipaul's *The Return of Eva Perón* (Spanish); *Zen and the Art of Motorcycle Maintenance* (English); *Tai-Pan* (English); a German grammar; *In the National Interest* by Marvin Kalb and Ted Koppel (Spanish). The leather chair used by Lehder in the Spanish television interview was in the front yard.

The police also found a packet of letters indicating a long correspondence between Lehder and Pablo Salah, the Bogotá drug lawyer. Lehder's chief interest, not surprisingly, was to get out of the jungle, either through exile or by somehow resolving his legal problems.

Salah's replies—addressed "Dear Charlie"—were uniformly unctuous, patronizing, and painfully "hip" at the same time, like a middle-aged college professor suddenly trying to be a swinger. For all that, some of the advice was sound. On July 27 he told Lehder to keep his mouth shut: "All your problems began when you started with the politics. The trick is to make yourself dead, the phantom—no publicity so the gringos and Colombians forget you. . . . The important thing is not to die rich. The important thing is to live rich—like before."

In a later letter, Salah addressed Lehder's apparent intent to emigrate to Germany, explaining as to a moron the difference between East and West: "Watch out for Berlin. Berlin is in the middle of East Germany, Communist as if Bogotá were in the middle of Venezuela. Take care not to ride Pan Am, not to go to Berlin, not to enter American military bases or NATO bases."

Despite the lessons in geopolitics, Lehder in his more quixotic moments still entertained thoughts of a political comeback. At some point he apparently decided to enlist the help of the Soviet Union and drafted a letter to the Soviet embassy in Bogotá. It was addressed "Dear and Remembered Comrades" and opened with the thought that "rebellion against tyranny is the fiber and texture of our minds.

"What I know today, after many years of political and revolutionary experiences, after having become familiar with the brother governments of Cuba and Nicaragua, of the Bahamas and Belize, of Puerto Rico and Haiti, as well as all the countries of Latin America, as well as Central America, [is that] . . . their economic and social problems are caused by the imperialist gringo industrialists.'' He proposed an integrated Latin America, achieved through the ''eradication of gringo imperialism, headed by its para-military industrialists and international Judaism.''

Lehder suggested that he, as leader of the National Latin Movement, and ''your charismatic leader Gorvanache [cq]'' are ''making common cause'' in a revolution on behalf of ''those peoples enslaved by imperialism.''

La Abundancia was Ramirez's last try. He had failed to capture Lehder, but he had thrown Lehder's girlfriends in jail, seized his stash and his money, and run him ragged for more than a year. In September 1985 a photograph of Lehder, looking shaggier, hollow-eyed, and slightly crazed, circulated in Bogotá newsrooms purporting to show how he had joined the Indian guerrilla group Quintín Lamé under the nom de guerre ''Rambo.'' Lehder was nothing anymore. The reason was mostly Jaime Ramirez.

IN February 1986 Ramirez, his wife, Helena, and sons Jaime and Javier moved into their new quarters on the grounds of the General Santander Police Academy in Bogotá. As a senior colonel Ramirez was entitled to official housing, but security was also a concern. Ramirez had been a target for years, but now, as a student, he wouldn't have access to the daily flow of information that he'd had as a field officer. He needed extra protection, so he moved to General Santander. It was a standard maneuver by police officers with special security concerns, and many of his former associates had done the same thing. It was restrictive and often boring living on the base. But it was safe, at least for the family. Ramirez was going to have to drive to the War College each day.

Still, he wasn't particularly worried, even when he and Helena heard Campo's story. Cops had staked out the Chía safe house for a week after the informant had visited F-2 and had seen nothing untoward. The Renault was there, just as the informant had said, but so what? The worst thing that had happened was that the neighbors had seen the F-2 stakeout team taking pictures of the house and had called the police, which was quite embarrassing.

Ramirez only began to worry after he visited F-2, saw the informant, and asked him the famous Ramirez five or six questions. The answers made him visibly upset. ''This guy isn't lying,'' he told his family. ''This guy's telling the truth.''

Of particular interest were the two alleged assassination attempts that had already taken place. The first was an obvious reference to Ramirez's going-away party at the *Finca J. R.* near Cajica. Ramirez had no escort, but the generals and civilian brass at the party did, and there were hordes of bodyguards all over the place. The second incident clearly described his parents' Christmas Eve party. Late at night the entire family—brothers, sisters, aunts, uncles, children—had streamed into the front yard to watch a fireworks display. The idea that Escobar's torpedoes were hanging around filled Ramirez with dread.

He had to put the informant on the payroll, but F-2 could only spend 20,000 pesos ($121). Never mind, said Ramirez. He took the informant with him and drove to DEA headquarters to talk to Special Agent-in-Charge George Frangullie. The informant made his pitch, Frangullie nodded and handed over the money. The informant left for Medellín, promising to stay in touch.

JAIME Ramirez's life changed dramatically. For the first time in his career he could not hit back. He didn't have a command, didn't have access to unlimited intelligence, and couldn't make aggressive tactical moves of his own to keep his enemies off balance. He had always told his men that "you have to kick the drug traffickers in the nuts," and nobody was better at it than he was. Now he had to sit back and be dependent on other people. It was exasperating, worrisome, and frightening.

For the next eight months Ramirez drove to school and back and drove to police headquarters and back, and that was it. He rode in the LTD that the DEA had given him, carried a .38-caliber revolver and a MAC-10, and wore a bulletproof vest. His driver also had a .38 revolver, as did the police colonel who was going to school with Ramirez and who hitched an occasional ride. Both the driver and the other colonel knew Ramirez was under constant threat, but Ramirez didn't give them specifics. It wouldn't do them any good. The driver varied his route daily and took careful note of the ambush sites described by the informant. When possible, motorcycle police scouted the route before the LTD drove it.

The tension put a terrible strain on the family. Helena, an attractive woman seven years younger than Ramirez, was nervous by nature and extremely sensitive to her husband's moods. She had always worried about him and had occasionally been terrified—for instance, when the police had talked about transferring him to Medellín in 1984

—but this was different. She felt like a sitting duck, and she knew Jaime did, too. At times she was so nervous it made her sick.

The boys went to school every day in an armored bus, and everybody wore bulletproof vests on the rare occasions when the family went out to eat. Fortunately, young Jaime, "Jimy," was a lot like his father, calm, intelligent, confident way beyond his sixteen years. Jimy had learned to use the MAC-10, and he rode shotgun on family outings. In restaurants he kept the machine pistol on the floor between his legs.

Still, this was no way to live. Ramirez's own father, almost eighty, was asking after him, talking about how he kept dreaming that Jaime had died. Ramirez didn't dare visit him, but he called his brother Francisco, told him everything, and asked him to settle the old man down. "It will be impossible to avoid telling him about the danger," Ramirez said. "But minimize it."

During the week before Easter Sunday, Francisco and his wife, Lucero, prevailed upon Jaime and Helena to join them for a few days at a cabaña at the Club Militar—the first outing of any consequence either had had since they'd heard about the threat. Jaime was going stir crazy, fuming with rage and impatience: "I've always been the pursuer, and now they're pursuing me," he said. "I'm the one who puts people against the wall, not the other way around."

AT first the M-19 informant reported more or less regularly, giving police a fairly detailed description of Cuco's current movements. The news was not good. The hit team was now rumored to have unlimited explosives, rocket-propelled grenades and launchers, seven cars, a minivan, and a taxi. It was said that they were thinking of mining the *finca* in Granada and razing it to the ground with Ramirez inside.

Then, after a couple of months, the informant stopped calling, and the flow of news suddenly dried up. The police were extremely worried. They increased Ramirez's security and redoubled efforts to develop new information. But their regular snitches came up with nothing, and they couldn't make any progress with the original information. The Chía safe house was a dead end; nothing was happening there. The traitorous police lieutenant had not been found, and F-2 had finally concluded that he did not exist. Ramirez now had a noncommissioned officer, three patrolmen, and a motorcycle escort guarding him at all times.

In May the Anti-Narcotics Unit sent Captain Octavio Ernesto Mora

Jimenez to Medellín to head an intelligence group that would, among other things, check out the threats against Ramirez. An experienced officer, Mora had worked for Ramirez in the past and would report to him directly. It was understood that Mora would attempt to get close to Escobar's organization—a touchy assignment, but Mora had done similar jobs in the past.

Mora called Ramirez frequently. He had managed to make contact with relatives of Escobar. He confirmed that Cuco still held the contract—for twenty million pesos ($121,200), not twenty-five million—and that Escobar had sold pieces of it to Rodriquez Gacha and Lehder. His sources were hinting, however, that Escobar was thinking of pulling the contract or had already done so. Mora didn't know why this was contemplated, but he would keep checking.

By the way, Mora said, Escobar's people were telling him that Escobar wanted to meet with Ramirez, talk things over. Ramirez wasn't interested. This was just another variation on a theme he had been hearing for nearly four years. Get him in a room with Escobar, snap a couple of photos, and watch his career go straight down the toilet. Ramirez told Mora to tell Escobar that if he turned himself in, Ramirez would ensure that he got fair treatment.

And that was it. Escobar, ever hopeful, searched for a weakness in Ramirez's armor, and Ramirez fended off the advances as abruptly as possible. The news about the killing possibly being called off was seductive and seemed on the face of it to dovetail nicely with Escobar's alleged peace overtures. Still, Ramirez didn't put much stock in the exchange so far. Everything Ramirez knew about Escobar told him to keep his guard up.

This seemed to be a particularly wise course after Ramirez's caretaker in Granada reported later in May that suspicious characters had been hanging around the *finca*. There were four of them in all, said the man. The leader was muscular, curly-haired, and about five feet nine inches tall. One of his sidekicks was shorter and pale-faced. These two walked past the house one Thursday afternoon, left, and returned the next day with two friends in a red car. Neighbors told the caretaker that the car was a Renault. All four spent the afternoon walking back and forth, always keeping Ramirez's house in sight.

The caretaker saddled a horse and rode to Silvania, the next town, where he telephoned Ramirez from a booth. Then he got on a bus and traveled to the police academy. Ramirez questioned him, then showed him a mug book. The man identified the curly-haired fellow. Ramirez had never heard of him. Helena burst into tears.

"Easy, sweetie," Ramirez said. "Nothing's going to happen."

. . .

GENERALS school finished in August, and the class took a month-long field trip to Europe to visit other police departments and participate in seminars. Ramirez collected suitcases full of pamphlets and reports, returning to Bogotá brimming with new ideas about how to make his police force the best and most modern in the world.

Now he was marking time, waiting for his promotion at the end of the year and doing make-work at police headquarters. He often broke the tedium—and the tension—by working as a consultant. The Peruvian government invited him to give seminars in narcotics law enforcement, and the Bolivian government and the DEA asked him to participate in Operation Blast Furnace, busting labs in Bolivia's eastern Beni wilderness. In the Beni Ramirez was able to help locate a couple of labs belonging to Escobar; he watched with glee as the local police torched them. It was the first time he had been able to hit back in almost a year.

He went to Venezuela, Brazil, back to Peru, and then to the United States. He visited Washington and talked to old friends, among them Johnny Phelps, who now ran the cocaine desk at DEA headquarters. Phelps found Ramirez haggard, fidgety, and worried about his family. Phelps could sympathize. Police in general were among the most aggressive people on earth. They hated to feel helpless. Ramirez was more aggressive than most cops Phelps knew. This thing with Escobar was eating him up.

Ramirez finally got a break October 21, when word reached him that one Carlos Alberto Espinosa Osorio, more commonly known as Cuco, had been killed in a Medellín firefight. Captain Mora called and said it now appeared more likely that Escobar had pulled the contract on Ramirez. Cuco's demise also made it less likely that someone would try to kill Ramirez in the near future. Presumably whoever picked up the contract would have to repeat a lot of Cuco's research, if not start over altogether.

Ramirez liked this news so much that he called F-2 and asked that the department take back his bodyguards. He was feeling more secure, and there was no indication that any killers had been able to get close to the family. The Chía safe house had now been raided half a dozen times with no result, and a stakeout at Ramirez's *finca* had produced no further visits from the curly-haired man or his sidekicks. Mora called almost daily, and Ramirez was starting, finally, to relax. In a couple of months the ordeal would be over, and he would be back in harness.

On Thursday, November 13, 1986, Francisco Ramirez, knowing that things seemed to be looking up for his brother, invited him, Helena, and the boys to visit his and Lucero's *finca* for a family gathering the following Monday. It would be the last day of a three-day holiday weekend, and the drive for Jaime to Francisco's place in Sasaima, about thirty miles northwest of Bogotá, would be short and relatively risk-free. Jaime said he would think about it.

The next day at ten A.M. Ramirez received a call from Mora in Medellín. As Ramirez listened his face began to loosen, and he began to talk animatedly. He spoke for about ten minutes, then hung up.

"They've suspended the contract," he told Helena. Mora, he said, had researched further and had finally been able to confirm that Escobar was no longer interested in killing him—at least for the moment. He could take it easy. He did, however, have a lot more to tell Ramirez.

Ramirez told Mora he didn't want to talk any more over the phone, but Mora should come visit him. Fine, said Mora, when should I be there?

"Come Monday evening, about seven P.M.," Ramirez replied. "It looks like I'm going to be out of town for the weekend."

The Ramirezes left Bogotá Sunday afternoon. The DEA's armored Ford stayed in the garage, and the family rode in Ramirez's white Toyota minivan. Ramirez felt relatively safe for the first time in months. He didn't discount the danger altogether, but he knew he wouldn't be on the road for very long at a stretch, and he was confident there would be a lot of traffic because of the holiday. It would be hard to set up an ambush. And just in case, Jimy had the MAC-10 on the floor in the back of the Toyota.

The family stopped for lunch at a *finca* in Madrid just outside Bogotá, then drove northeast for about an hour to Villeta to spend the night at the house of a friend. At ten A.M. on Monday they climbed back into the Toyota and drove a half hour to Francisco's *finca* at Sasaima.

Everybody—parents, brothers, sisters, nieces, and nephews—was there, and Ramirez had a wonderful time. He was a gregarious man by nature, a kidder and a tall-tale teller who liked nothing better than to sit out on the lawn and chat with his family. It now looked as though he would become the police's chief of personnel, and he gushed with plans about how he would get all his favorite officers working for him again, how he would encourage beat cops and provincial commands to get interested in antinarcotics work. It was shop talk, but Francisco loved to hear it. Jaime seemed relaxed, which was good, Francisco thought. But had the threat really ended? Maybe Jaime just wanted so badly for it to be over that he pretended it no longer existed.

At 4:30 P.M. Ramirez pushed back his chair, refused another plate of Lucero's pig's knuckles, and summoned his family. Everybody would be driving back to Bogotá that evening. Better to get an early start.

As the Ramirezes pulled away, several other drivers parked haphazardly nearby started their engines and swung in behind the Toyota. Later, neighbors would remember that the cars and drivers had been hanging about for several hours. The neighbors would also remember that they didn't recognize any of the drivers or their cars. At the time, though, no one thought anything about it.

AT 5:43 P.M., November 17, 1986, the Ramirez Toyota started across a highway bridge over the Rio Bogotá separating Cundinamarca province from the capital. Traffic was heavy but manageable. The Ramirezes were moving steadily, albeit slowly, in the far right lane.

A little bit past the middle of the bridge a red Renault 18 came up along the Toyota's left side, as if to pass, then paused, matching the Toyota's speed. A MAC-10 machine pistol appeared in the Renault's passenger window. It bucked once and then coughed in a prolonged burst.

Ramirez, dead instantly from multiple gunshot wounds, slumped against the steering wheel. Helena, wounded slightly in the right knee, grabbed for the wheel and twisted it to the right, driving the Toyota into the side of the bridge, where it stalled against the curb. Javier was all right, knicked in the hand by a bullet, but Jimy was shot through both thighs and bleeding badly. Nonetheless, he fumbled in the darkness for the MAC-10. He had wrapped it in a blanket and stashed it out of sight to keep it away from his young cousins at Franciscos's house. Now, when he needed it, he couldn't find it.

The Renault pulled ahead and stopped in front of the van. The doors opened, and three men climbed out. They were all in their twenties, all well dressed and well groomed. Everybody remembered that. All three carried machine pistols. The driver remained in the Renault with the engine idling.

Two of the gunmen stood guard in front of the Renault and behind the Toyota. The third man walked to the driver's door of the Toyota, opened it, pulled the trigger of his MAC-10, and emptied his magazine into Jaime Ramirez.

Helena opened the Toyota's passenger door and slid to the ground.

Crouching and crawling, she edged to the back of the van, where she came face to face with one of the sentinels. "Please don't kill me," she said. The gunman looked at her, then turned away, climbed into the Renault, and drove off with his friends.

THE new year arrived, and Jaime Ramirez's classmates became generals. Helena Ramirez petitioned the government to grant Jaime a posthumous promotion. Her husband's superiors seconded her application, noting Ramirez's consistently outstanding performance. The letter moved up the chain of command, acquiring signatures and seals of approval.

On May 20, 1987, the Defense Ministry sent Helena a letter. Her husband's death unfortunately did not satisfy "the referenced norm," it said, in that it was not the result of "meritorious acts of service" or "acts of public order" or "reason of combat or international conflict." In other words, he had not been killed in action.

The ministry did not grant exceptions.

28.

THE CARTEL INDICTMENT

For a long time, U.S. Law enforcement had resisted the idea that any one group of Colombian cocaine traffickers controlled so much of the trade. In the 1970s the Colombian traffickers appearing in the United States were regarded as an amorphous wave of criminal entrepreneurs. In 1977 DEA agents in Medellín discovered the bookkeeping records of Griselda Blanco and began to learn of the ties among the traffickers they pursued. But the Colombians were merely lumped together under "the Medellín trafficking syndicate," a grab bag title that included Griselda Blanco, Pablo Escobar, and just about any other Colombian from Medellín. It was a shadow portrait, an outline without definition. No attempt was made to rank the traffickers, although even by the early 1980s Escobar, Ochoa, and Lehder always topped any informal list. The problem was that the three top traffickers were considered separately and not in concert. The 3,906-pound TAMPA seizure in Miami in 1982 demonstrated that the traffickers cooperated to an extent not previously believed possible. The TAMPA bust prompted the creation of Operation Fountainhead, a secret DEA program that used computers to try to break the codes on the kilo-sized cocaine packages. By 1983 Operation Fountainhead had traced dozens of cocaine shipments back to Jorge Ochoa. A pattern was emerging, a spiderweb of connections. Up to this point, Ochoa was merely referred to as either "a top echelon trafficker" or someone "well documented as the head of one of the largest cocaine smuggling organizations from Colombia," according to Fountainhead reports. The word "cartel" was introduced in 1983 in a Fountainhead analysis of the largest cocaine seizures in the United States: 1,254 pounds discovered in a van near Cleveland, Tennessee, on July 11, 1982, "was linked to the Medellín trafficking cartel under Operation

Southern Comfort''; codes on packages containing 652 pounds taken from an airplane in Dothan, Alabama, on March 15, 1983, "revealed that the cocaine originated from the Medellín trafficking cartel.'' The concept was taking form.

It wasn't until Tranquilandia, however, that the DEA analysts realized the scale of the Colombian cocaine trade. And it wasn't until later that year, when Barry Seal brought back the first evidence documenting how Escobar, Ochoa, and Lehder worked together, that the word "cartel" began to gain currency within DEA. When Barry Seal testified in Miami in the summer of 1985, he called the organization he worked for "the Jorge Ochoa cocaine cartel." That same year in debriefings with the DEA, Max Mermelstein referred to it as "the Medellín combine." The DEA itself made no attempt to single out the cartel at the apex of cocaine traffickers. They referred to "Colombian cocaine cartels," giving equal weight to the Medellín group and the Cali group run by Gilberto Rodriguez Orejuela and Jose Santacruz Londoño. Hundreds of cases and seizures and bits of intelligence information about Jorge Ochoa, Pablo Escobar, and Carlos Lehder were still disconnected, pieces of a huge picture yet to be assembled.

IN the summer of 1985 those pieces began to come together between the ninth and tenth floors of the U.S. Attorney's Office in downtown Miami. By then, law enforcement had made great strides against the cocaine trade in south Florida. The sustained heat of the increased DEA and Customs presence had driven the traffickers underground. Wild shoot-outs in shopping malls became a thing of the past. Centac 26, the DEA-Metro Dade police squad that targeted Colombian cocaine murders, methodically pursued the cocaine cowboys. El Loco, the balding gunman from the "turnpike shooting," got caught in Los Angeles in 1982. Paco Sepulveda, suspected but never charged in the Dadeland shooting, was finally arrested in New York City in 1983. And Griselda Blanco got nabbed in a DEA undercover operation in southern California in 1985. At the time she was living in a luxury town house in Irvine and supplying hundreds of kilos of cocaine each month to the ravenous Los Angeles market through her three young sons, Dixon, Osvaldo, and Wber.

American laws quickly adapted to the Colombian drug defendants. The low bonds that produced numerous bond jumpers in the Operation Swordfish money-laundering case led directly to a new federal law that allowed drug defendants to be held without bond in "pretrial detention.'' Money laundering became a federal crime. Sentences for Colombians convicted of drug crimes grew longer and longer.

Yet despite the arrests and advances in the United States, the center of the cocaine business, the Medellín cartel, remained intact, safely ensconced in its Colombian strongholds. And the cocaine poured in like never before. In one 15-day period in January 1985, police and federal drug agents in Florida seized 2,250 kilos of cocaine, more than they had in the first three months of 1984 and more than all the cocaine seized for the entire year of 1981. And 1985 proved to be the year of the crack epidemic, when the smoking of a crude form of cocaine base spread like wildfire through America's urban areas. By the end of the year cocaine seizures in south Florida topped twenty-five tons, more than double the previous record. The price kept dropping, from $35,000 a kilo down to $20,000, indicating that despite the seizures more cocaine was hitting the streets than ever before. Cocaine made the cover of *Newsweek* and *Time* magazines in the same week in February 1985. *Newsweek* even ran a sidebar with its cover story, "Colombia's Kings of Coke," naming Ochoa, Escobar, Lehder, Hernan Botero, Gilberto Rodriguez Orejuela, and Gonzalo Rodriguez Gacha. "Together they have become Colombia's cocaine overlords—a small tightknit clique of smugglers almost as rich and powerful as the Colombian government itself," the magazine story said. "To protect their extensive interests, a number have allegedly formed their own little cartel, buying as many opponents as they can, murdering some of those they can't."

Cocaine, the jet-set high, had metamorphosed into cocaine, the American middle-class phenomenon. It was in this period when cocaine use exploded in the United States that a small group of federal prosecutors in Miami prepared the way for the Medellín cartel's coming-out party.

In the stairwell of the U.S. Attorney's Office on the Miami River, Assistant U.S. Attorney Bob Dunlap bumped into Assistant U.S. Attorney Bob Martinez. Dunlap was prosecuting the Nicaragua case with Dick Gregorie, chief of the Major Narcotics Section. Martinez happened to be on his way up to talk to Gregorie. Dunlap was a repository for information on Colombian traffickers, one of the few people in the office who could keep all the names straight. He had been talking about "the Medellín cartel" for more than a year. Martinez was also obsessed with the cartel; he had handled the Frank Torres ether case that led to the discovery of Tranquilandia.

In the stairwell, Dunlap and Martinez began talking about their respective cases. The more they talked, the more it seemed they were working on different parts of the same, bigger case, a conspiracy involving the Ochoas, Escobar, Lehder, and others. Why not gather all the evidence involving these people and indict them as one criminal enterprise?

Martinez went up the stairwell and pitched the idea to Dick Gregorie.

"Why are we trying all these cases separately?" Martinez asked. "Why don't we do it as one big case? As one big RICO?"

RICO was the Racketeer-Influenced Corrupt Organizations Act, the tool that had been used so effectively for two decades against the Mafia. It allowed prosecutors to define an "enterprise," an organization put together to commit crimes. Once a RICO was established, any number of crimes could be pinned to the organization in a single court proceeding, and all the organization's assets could be seized.

Gregorie liked the idea. "Great," he said. "Let's do it."

The "cartel case," as it came to be known, was a volunteer project for Martinez, something he worked on in his spare time. Martinez was supposed to be handling corruption cases in the office, not drug cases. At thirty-two he was a product of the Georgetown Law Center and the Wharton School of Business. He had grown up in an upper-class Cuban family that had fled Fidel Castro's regime in 1960. He had been with the U.S. Attorney's Office for three years.

In late 1985 Martinez selected a federal grand jury and began presenting witnesses and evidence about the cartel's activities, a necessary first step toward putting together an indictment.

For help, Martinez turned to one of the brightest and most dogged DEA agents in Miami, a thirty-five-year-old woman who had grown up in a small town in Illinois. Carol Cooper had worked closely with Martinez on the Tranquilandia case. One of 201 women among the DEA's 2,630 special agents, "Coops" was organized and methodical. Her specialty was sifting through mountains of wiretap evidence and drawing the choice tidbits into a coherent case.

First Cooper pored over individual cases involving Escobar, Ochoa, and Lehder. Sorting through the Tranquilandia evidence in 1984 she had seen a pattern emerging. Now she worked to link all the cases, "to show the Colombians for what they really are." Cooper's job was made easier by lengthy briefings with Max Mermelstein, who served as the original source for most of the information about the cartel. It was Mermelstein who defined the scope and shape of the cartel's activities.

Like Martinez, Carol Cooper worked on the mammoth case in her free hours. The case wasn't a priority in the office. One reason was that all of the defendants were fugitives in Colombia; the indictment would produce no high-profile arrests. And then there was the fact that most of the defendants had already been indicted in the smaller cases. To some in the U.S. Attorney's Office in Miami, the whole exercise seemed like overkill.

But when Jorge Ochoa was released by Judge Pastrana in Cartagena in August 1986, the cartel case jumped onto the front burner. Gregorie and Martinez, enraged by the Ochoa affair, wanted to make a statement that would gain the attention of the world.

They discussed the case over dinner that night at La Choza, a Nicaraguan steak house on Key Biscayne. After dessert they went directly to Gregorie's nearby apartment to rough out a possible indictment.

Less than a week after Ochoa's release, Dick Gregorie, Bob Martinez, Carol Cooper, and Assistant U.S. Attorney Mark Schnapp, another staff member, met in a tenth-floor room at the U.S. Attorney's Office. The room was packed floor to ceiling with files and documents, including copies of the cartel records seized at Tranquilandia. The four people in the Ochoa War Room, as it was known, had much in common. They were all single workaholics who poured their lives into government service. For a week they worked fourteen-hour days, surviving on Chicken McNuggets and Kentucky Fried Chicken, in a cramped room full of trial transcripts, drug smugglers' ledgers, and DEA reports.

To build the indictment, they took Max Mermelstein's story about smuggling for Rafa Cardona and combined it with the Tranquilandia portion of the Frank Torres ether case. To this they added Barry Seal's Nicaragua indictment and Mermelstein's account of the plot to murder Seal. Most important, they used the indictment to describe, for the first time, how the cartel actually worked. The finished document brought a new organized crime phenomenon to the American consciousness. Count one began:

"From as early as 1978 to the date of the return of this indictment there existed an international criminal narcotics enterprise based in Medellín, Colombia, South America, known by various names, including 'The Medellín cartel' (hereinafter 'Cartel'), which consisted of controlling members of major international cocaine manufacturing and distribution organizations. . . . Through the Cartel, major cocaine organizations were able to pool resources, including raw materials, clandestine cocaine conversion laboratories, aircraft, vessels, transportation facilities, distribution networks, and cocaine to facilitate international narcotics trafficking.''

The cartel members met at "brokerage houses" in Medellín—private estates where drug lords dickered for pilots and lab service. The cartel maintained inventory control, corrupted officials of foreign governments, and carried out murders to "protect its business operations and enforce its mandates."

The indictment named the three Ochoa brothers, Pablo Escobar, Carlos Lehder, and Gonzalo Rodriguez Gacha as the cartel's leaders.

Finally, the indictment branded the cartel as the world's largest cocaine smuggling organization. The prosecutors who put the indictment together had no idea how much cocaine was involved until they stopped and added it all up. They astonished themselves: the cartel was charged with producing fifty-eight tons of cocaine between 1978 and 1985. Until the TAMPA seizure, no one had seen even a ton of cocaine in one place at one time. The cartel indictment was not just the largest cocaine case in U.S. history. It was larger than any previous case by a factor of seven.

And that was just what could be documented. The fifty-eight-ton figure represented only a part of the cartel's smuggled cocaine. Not all of the cases made against the cartel were included in the new indictment; doing that could take forever and produce a document too unwieldy to try in court. The cartel was too big to prosecute except in pieces. Fifty-eight tons was probably less than one-third of the cocaine that could be linked to Jorge Ochoa, Pablo Escobar, Rodriguez Gacha, and Carlos Lehder.

With the indictment drawn up, the final step was to present it to the federal grand jury and obtain formal action. The grand jury was expected to approve the indictment the same day it was presented on August 16, 1986. National television networks and selected influential newspapers were notified that something big was coming. A press conference was scheduled two hours after the grand jury finished. Everyone waited.

But the morning the indictment was to be returned, the press conference was canceled. Washington had called and instructed that the indictment be sealed. Word of the pending superindictment had somehow leaked to Colombia. Someone in the Colombian government, fearing another embarrassment on the heels of Jorge Ochoa's release, persuaded the State Department to talk to the Justice Department. And now the Justice Department had talked to the U.S. Attorney's Office in Miami.

Drug agents hastily called their sources at newspapers and television networks and coaxed them into killing stories that could have dominated front pages and evening news broadcasts. The opportunity to brand the Medellín cartel before the world didn't take place.

Still, there were indications that the cartel members were feeling the pressure.

In late October 1986, a little-known Miami criminal defense attorney flew to Colombia to meet Jorge and Fabio Ochoa at a three-thousand-acre ranch outside Cartagena. Bodyguards carrying machine guns and an ominous-looking leather satchel surrounded the Ochoas. Fabio wore a baseball cap and appeared about ten years younger than his age, which was twenty-nine.

Jorge Ochoa told the Miami attorney that he had been summoned because Ochoa wanted to see an American who could deliver a message to "the Americans."

The attorney had been to Colombia previously on the matter. That spring he had traveled to Bogotá at the invitation of one of his Colombian clients to discuss the extradition problems facing several major drug traffickers. In Bogotá, a Colombian woman attorney told him the twelve major traffickers who controlled 80 percent of the cocaine trade were willing to help stop the flow in return for amnesty from extradition.

The traffickers most anxious to negotiate for amnesty were Jorge Ochoa and Gilberto Rodriguez, who were then under arrest in Spain and awaiting the outcome of extradition proceedings. The Miami attorney was told that Ochoa and Rodriguez would eventually be sent to Colombia instead of the United States, but influencing the Spanish court was going to be expensive.

When the Miami attorney took the amnesty proposal to FBI agents in Miami six months later, Ochoa and Rodriguez were already in Colombia, and Ochoa, thanks to the Cartagena customs judge, was once again a free man. Despite this turn of events, the attorney told the agents that the traffickers were still eager to negotiate. The agents took the offer seriously enough to set up a meeting between the attorney and Dick Gregorie at the U.S. Attorney's Office. Gregorie listened to the attorney, found the idea preposterous, and gave it little further thought.

Now, in late October, just three weeks after the meeting with Gregorie, the Miami attorney faced the Ochoas for the first time.

Jorge Ochoa had summoned the attorney because he was upset with his own American lawyers. He screamed about having paid millions without getting satisfaction, including $2 million to an attorney who represented a friend of Ochoa who had been sentenced to twenty-five years. The only attorney he had ever trusted in Miami, Ochoa said, was a man who had been machine-gunned in his law office during the cocaine wars of the early 1980s.

Ochoa said he was "really mad" that he had been charged with the murder of Barry Seal. Although he personally hated Seal, he said that he and his brother Fabio were not Seal's murderers. He offered to provide a signed statement attesting to their innocence, to be delivered to the proper authorities in U.S. intelligence. Jorge Ochoa said he would not cooperate with the DEA. Their terms, he said, always ended up with people "compromised."

The Miami attorney returned to Cartagena for his flight home, but there he was told he had impressed the Ochoas and would be required to meet with them again in Medellín. Immediately. The attorney objected. Medellín was too dangerous. But in the end he went because he had little choice.

He resumed his discussion with Jorge Ochoa in "a rather ordinary house" up in the hills outside Medellín.

"I know what the U.S. wants," Ochoa said. "I'm not personally involved with the communists. There are people who are coming to our meeting who are, however."

Ochoa said they wanted to negotiate collectively with "the intelligence arm" of the United States government. They had certain information, Ochoa said, that could be of interest to U.S. national security.

While they waited for the others to arrive, Ochoa again complained that his various attorneys were cheating him despite the great fees he paid. He claimed to have more than one hundred attorneys on retainer. He confided that he was free now because he had paid $6 million to the judges who released him. The price outraged Ochoa.

Then a man in jungle garb and high boots sauntered in with a retinue of bodyguards. The man wore blue jeans and had a rifle slung over his shoulder. He introduced himself as Carlos Lehder. He struck the Miami attorney as handsome, with excellent English and the manner of a stone killer.

Another man entered after Lehder. He was introduced as "Escobar"—the Miami attorney didn't catch the first name. Lehder pointed to Escobar, who, though affable, spoke no English. Lehder said Escobar was their boss.

Lehder did the talking for all of them.

"We are here to open negotiations with the U.S. government," he said.

Lehder said he and the others had been forced to work with "the communists in the mountains," whom he described as a one-hundred-thousand-man army of Palestinians, Libyans, Peruvians, Argentinians, Ecuadorans, and Cubans. Lehder said they actually hated the communists and would give information about arms shipments and Cuban personnel in Colombia. Lehder also offered information about communist activities in Nicaragua, Cuba, Mexico, and Panama. He said he and Escobar had people in Nicaragua. (The Miami attorney had been told at the outset that Ochoa financed both contras and Sandinistas there.) Now Lehder proposed having their cartel operatives in Nicaragua gather intelligence for the United States for six months or so, and then, if everyone was satisfied, the cartel leaders would receive amnesty.

This was an immense irony: the cartel was offering the very thing Jorge Ochoa's lawyers had accused the U.S. government of trying to orchestrate earlier in the year during the Spanish extradition proceedings.

Now the cartel leaders wanted two or three U.S. agents—FBI, not DEA, they specified—to come to Colombia to hear their proposal in detail. Lehder pointed out that they had never harmed an American agent. They would guarantee the safety of any who came to hear them.

Then Jorge Ochoa gave the attorney a letter from his mother. Written in Spanish, it read:

By means of this letter, we give you complete authority to represent my three sons whose names are Fabio Ochoa, Juan David Ochoa, and Jorge Luis Ochoa, in negotiations with the government of the United States. It is necessary for you to prove their innocence in the United States.

The North American authorities have accused my three sons of many things which are not true. Several Colombian representatives have informed us that Colombian citizens cannot obtain a fair trial in the United States.

These allegations of discrimination against Colombians in the United States were mentioned in the Spanish courts during the case of my sons. We need your immediate reply.

Very Cordially,
Margot Vasquez de Ochoa

The attorney returned to Miami on October 28. Again he met with Dick Gregorie, who laughed at the offer to provide intelligence about

Colombian guerrillas in return for amnesty. Gregorie didn't care about Colombian guerrillas; he wanted more than anything to put the cartel leaders behind bars.

Nor did Gregorie think much of the cartel's proposal to get out of the business. He couldn't see giving absolute amnesty to the biggest drug dealers in the world based on their word that they wouldn't produce drugs anymore. Besides, it was virtually the same offer the cartel had made in Panama in 1984. It was unacceptable in any light.

Though Gregorie discredited the offer, he felt beholden to bring it to the attention of his boss, U.S. Attorney Leon Kellner. Kellner, who also didn't take the offer seriously, passed it along to Washington. There it died a quiet death. No one in the U.S. government wanted any part of the cartel's gambit.

THE cartel indictment was finally released November 18, the day after Jaime Ramirez's murder. In the United States its impact was muted. Most Americans knew nothing about Ramirez and had heard little about Colombia since Jorge Ochoa's release from jail. The public unveiling of the Medellín cartel thus rated about the same attention as any big drug indictment. It offered neither dramatic testimony nor big arrests, just a rather sketchy account of an enormous, illegal business operating with great secrecy out of a relatively unfamiliar foreign country. *The Miami Herald* and *The New York Times*, the two newspapers with the most extensive coverage of international cocaine trafficking, gave the story front-page treatment, but both featured it under a modest headline below the fold.

In Colombia the indictment caused a sensation, coming as the latest in a long line of outrages. Editors scrambled to get copies of an indictment that had taken all of Colombia's rotten eggs and tossed them into one basket. *El Espectador*, Colombia's second-largest newspaper, ran stories on the cartel indictment as a two-part *informe especial* ("special report") on December 5 and December 11, 1986. The special report team reviewed the indictment, but it also used the occasion for a deeper analysis of Colombia's cocaine traffic.

It was a common technique, developed over several years by individual Colombian news organizations when they wished to investigate drug trafficking without incurring the cartel's wrath. The cartel was much less likely to attack *El Espectador* if its reports displayed the information as though it all came directly from a U.S. federal court indictment. Reporters from Colombian news organizations were also often eager to pass information to U.S. colleagues in hopes it would be published in American newspapers or aired on American television. The Colombians then translated the U.S. reports and printed or aired "what the United States is saying about Colombia."

Still, reporting about the cartel on a regular basis was fraught with great danger and required uncommon courage. No one took these risks more readily than *El Espectador*. The *informe especial* team had not signed a major story on the cartel or its members in a couple of years, but the paper was nonetheless known for its categorical opposition to the traffickers. It had drawn special attention from Pablo Escobar since August 1983, when its front-page stories denounced "the Godfather's" first cocaine bust. Nothing had done greater damage to Escobar's budding political career than to have his police mug shot displayed prominently in Colombia's second-biggest newspaper.

In recent months *El Espectador*'s anticartel crusades were led by Editor-in-Chief Guillermo Cano Isaza, who wrote frequently on drugs in his editorial page column *Libreta de Apuntes* ("Notebook"). Cano, white-haired and distinguished, was sixty-one years old, a pillar of the Liberal party with impeccable patrician credentials. He had fought a long and lonely battle for stiffer laws against drug trafficking in Colombia. He was very disturbed when several respectable Colombians had recently attacked extradition and proposed legalization of the drug trade as a means to escape further violence.

"Legalize drug trafficking?" he asked rhetorically in a recent column. "That would be like legalizing and justifying all the collateral activities: money laundering, the assassination of Supreme Court justices, of cabinet ministers, of judges, and of so many other persons who by doing their duty have fallen victim to the narcotics traffickers and their hired killers."

On December 17, 1986, a Wednesday, Cano left work shortly after 7:30 P.M., as was his custom. He walked to his parking space, climbed into the driver's seat of his wine-red Subaru station wagon, and edged the car into traffic. The back of the Subaru was filled with brightly wrapped Christmas presents Cano had purchased during the lunch hour.

The newspaper offices were in the El Dorado district, on the western edge of Bogotá, near the airport and within a mile of *El Tiempo*, Colombia's biggest newspaper and *El Espectador*'s great rival. It was a sparsely populated industrial area, but it had a lot of traffic, and Avenida del Espectador, passing right in front of the paper, was a major commuter thoroughfare.

Cano's plan was to turn right coming out of the gate and scoot quickly to the far left lane so he could make a U-turn around a grassy median strip in the middle of the avenue. It was a tricky maneuver, but Cano did it five times a week. This night, however, Cano did not notice the motorcycle parked on the median on his left; or if he did, he paid it no mind. As he waited to make his U-turn, a young man climbed down from the motorcycle's rear seat, laid what looked like a musical instrument case on the ground, and opened it unhurriedly. From it he took a snub-nosed MAC-10 machine pistol. Then he stood up, walked quickly to the driver's window of the Subaru, and pulled the trigger. Cano died instantly.

29.

THE VIRGIN SMILES

The murder of Guillermo Cano Isaza stirred Colombia against the Medellín cartel like nothing since the killing 2½ years earlier of Rodrigo Lara Bonilla. Part of it was that Cano had been one of the two or three dozen most prominent men in Colombia. Presidents and ex-presidents were expected to be seen mourning him, and they were.

And part of it was that Cano was a newsman. Nothing enrages and terrifies reporters more than to have one of their own killed because of something written or broadcast. Any nobody is better positioned to make a stink about it.

On Thursday, the day after the killing, President Virgilio Barco led the funeral caravan that took Cano to a cemetery just outside Bogotá. Thousands of people lined the route to wave handkerchiefs and Colombian flags. News organizations recorded it all.

On Friday the Society of Journalists of Bogotá proclaimed a countrywide news blackout. Colombia's reporters, editors, and news technicians held "marches of silence" in Bogotá and other cities. Speeches paid tribute to the more than twenty newspeople murdered by the cartel in the previous four years.

For Barco the Cano murder was a challenge to act. His administration, like Betancur's before it, had been humiliated beyond endurance by the drug traffickers. First there was the Ochoa affair in Cartagena, a national disgrace that had once again made a mockery of the Colombian justice system. Then there was the Ramirez murder. And now, Cano. The Medellín cartel, it seemed, could get away with anything.

Law enforcement was demoralized. Barco was criticized in the U.S. Attorney's Office in Miami as a wimpy do-nothing and in the drawing rooms of Bogotá's most prominent citizens as an ineffectual bureaucrat. Voters in the street didn't care much for their new president, either. Unlike Betancur, Barco had no warmth and made few public appearances or statements. Colombians, like most people, wanted to see their leaders lead.

The time had come. Barco first issued a lengthy package of state of siege decrees, temporary but far-reaching. These allowed security forces to arrest and hold someone without showing cause for up to ten days. They also mandated prison terms of up to ten years for owning an illegal airstrip and up to eight years for illegal weapons possession. New motorcycle owners had to register with police within twenty-four hours of purchase. Sales of motorcycles bigger than 125 cc. were forbidden without special permission.

The government inaugurated both a Witness Protection Program and a reward system for people giving information to security forces. Finally, the government for the first time issued to law enforcement agencies a secret, most-wanted list of the 128 top drug traffickers in Colombia. The list included all the big names as well as fifty-six people currently sought by the United States for extradition.

After all this, Barco turned law enforcement loose in a full-scale crackdown and awaited results. This was his second antidrug offensive (the first had come after Ochoa's release) and Colombia's third since Lara Bonilla's death. Both of the earlier ones had made a lot of noise. There had been many arrests, some dope seizures, and some confiscated property, but few people ever seemed to go to prison, and the cartel never seemed to be damaged, not even in the slightest. The motorcycle registration gambit, for one, had been tried every couple of years since Griselda Blanco's assassins had invented motorcycle homicide. It was impossible to enforce.

Still, Barco didn't do badly. In the first three weeks after the decrees, police arrested 360 people, seized 243 kilos of cocaine, destroyed five labs, and confiscated more than four hundred weapons. They also crossed eight names off the most-wanted list, including two extraditables. The prize was Evaristo Porras, the Leticia gangster whose million-peso check allegedy ended up in Lara Bonilla's campaign war chest. Police busted him on the Caribbean resort island of San Andrés and held him for illegal weapons possession. Later in the year DAS detectives would privately name him, along with Gonzalo Rodriguez Gacha and Pablo Escobar, as a shareholder in the Cano plot, but by that time Porras had been quietly released for lack of evidence.

ONE significant way in which the post-Cano crackdown differed from earlier ones was in Barco's refusal to ignore guerrilla dealings with the drug traffickers. Barco's government had no enduring commitment to Belisario Betancur's Peace Process. The Barco guerrilla policy held that the FARC should disarm and rejoin the larger society. The FARC said disarmament was too dangerous, citing the three-hundred-plus Patriotic Union militants it said had been murdered by death squads.

The Barco government gave this view only limited credence, hinting that many of the murders resulted from a tawdry vendetta with the cartel. Administration officials said that FARC guerrillas and cartel middlemen in the *llanos* for several months had been kidnapping and killing each other over the guerrillas' rights to collect *gramaje* from the region's *campesino* coca growers. By early 1987 the *campesinos* were marching in the streets to protest the violence.

The FARC and the Patriotic Union, seeing the ugly propaganda turn this was taking, began denouncing the traffickers, focusing particular attention on Rodriguez Gacha, the emperor of Guaviare coca. Patriotic Union leader Braulio Herrera said Rodriguez Gacha had joined with "sectors of the armed forces, with ranchers, and also with some politicians to orchestrate plans of assassination against our people."

The crackdown's modest success put Colombia into a manic phase for four weeks, carrying through the Christmas holidays and into the new year. By now the traumas of Colombia's drug wars were capable of transforming even small triumphs or failures into earth-shaking events. After the horrors of 1986, the country was on a giddy upswing again. Bad guys were getting arrested; the police were seizing drugs; things looked pretty good for a change, even if it didn't last.

And it didn't. On January 13, 1987, word reached Bogotá that Colombian Ambassador to Hungary Enrique Parejo Gonzalez, the former justice minister who had successfully challenged the cartel for two hard years, had been accosted in a Budapest blizzard and shot five times in the face.

There was no question who was behind the shooting. Since Parejo's arrival in Budapest the previous August, he had received a stream of written death threats whose theme, repeated over and over, was, "You can run, but you can't hide." Here was the proof. The day of the shooting, Colombian news organizations received telephone calls from something called the Hernan Botero Command claiming responsibility for the attack. Botero was the first Colombian extradited under the 1979 treaty; his extradition order was the first of thirteen signed by Parejo. Parejo survived the attack, thanks to skillful Hungarian doctors who removed the bullets in two operations.

But Colombia badly needed a success.

. . .

NATIONAL Police Major William Lemus Lemus knew Carlos Lehder was near Medellín. He heard it on the street; he heard it from his snitches; he heard it everywhere; he practically smelled the man. Lemus had taken over in December 1986 as police chief in Rionegro, a town about thirty miles east of Medellín, and from the moment he arrived people told him the same story: Carlos Lehder was in town, up from his jungle hideaways to talk a little business with Pablo Escobar. Lehder wanted to set up a few cocaine labs around Medellín and was looking to make a joint venture with "the Godfather."

Escobar invited him for a visit, the story went, and put him up in a safe house in Rionegro. Lemus had been hunting him ever since. Following Guillermo Cano's murder, Lemus had been allowed to search anywhere he wanted and arrest damn near anyone who looked at him cross-eyed. And he still wasn't getting anywhere.

It wasn't the easiest part of Colombia to search. Rionegro was in the middle of the Andean piney woods that surrounded Medellín, beautiful country, wildflowers all over the place, crystal-clear mountain air redolent with resin and pine needles. But it was a semiwilderness, vast patches of forest interspersed with a few secondary roads, many of which led nowhere. Lemus thought Escobar had probably stashed Lehder in one of the chalets or A-frames the cartel had built in the mountains as weekend playhouses. But he didn't know which one it was or even which town it was in.

Around noon on February 3, 1987, the constable from Guarne, a town about twenty miles north of La Ceja, showed up with a *campesino* informant Lemus had assigned to chase a tip he had gotten about a chalet tucked deep in the back country. The *campesino* had been watching it, the constable said, and had noticed a "bunch of men" shouting, playing music, and generally raising hell for the last couple of days. The *campesino* said he had talked to the *finca*'s caretaker, who was disgusted with the mess the visitors were making and distressed about having to clean it up. Maybe, *mi Mayor*, the constable said, "you would come take a look?"

Why not?

Lemus and two young policemen cautiously approached the Guarne house at about four P.M. It was a two-story chalet, new, nicely painted, not particularly big. It had a small front lawn and one outbuilding off to the side. Lemus couldn't see the rear of the chalet, but the caretaker had assured him that it overlooked a deep, overgrown canyon with a small stream running far below. The far side of the canyon was a pine-covered hillside. Evergreens cloaked the rest of the house as well, making it invisible from the main highway. A tiny secondary road was the only obvious access.

Lemus and his men knelt in the trees for two hours, watching some sixteen men talk, laugh, and chat as they moved back and forth between the chalet and the yard. At six P.M. a short, blocky fellow came out the front door carrying a canvas chair. He walked to the lawn and sat down. It was Lehder. Lemus had seen him in Armenia in 1983 and knew him.

This presented a dilemma. Lemus had told his men they were hunting "guerrillas." Colombian security forces had fought guerrillas with great enthusiasm for twenty-five years, but they tended to want nothing to do with drug traffickers. The guerrillas were anonymous strangers; traffickers would kill a man's family if he messed with them. Lemus doubted whether either of his young troopers had the slightest idea whom they were looking at.

"Do you know that guy?" he whispered to the policeman closest to him.

"No, *mi Mayor,*" said the policeman. Lemus bent down so he could whisper Lehder's name in the man's ear. Then he caught himself. What good would that do? He kept his counsel.

Lemus and one of the troopers stayed in the woods watching the building. He sent the other policeman to the airport to look for reinforcements, especially a police special weapons team (GOES) stationed there for special assignments. The messenger returned shortly, bringing about thirty-six police, including the GOES men.

Lemus deployed his people on all four sides of the chalet. He particularly liked the hillside across the canyon because marksmen could shoot down on the house and even see what was going on in the front yard. He stationed a dozen men there, then put others in place to block off a couple of possible escape routes. He himself stayed in front with two snipers.

Then he settled down to wait. He had a couple of problems. Lehder had posted three sentries—in the front yard and on either side of the chalet. Every once in a while a sentry would duck into the house and be replaced by someone else. Everybody Lemus saw entering or leaving the chalet had a machine pistol. If there were only three of these, the police were okay. If there were sixteen, he and his people were going to be desperately outgunned.

The search warrant was the other problem. Even under state of siege measures Lemus couldn't go into the house before six A.M., and he had to have a warrant. He sent the Guarne constable off to get one, but the man didn't return until four A.M. The constable hadn't been able to find anybody to sign it, so he'd signed it himself. Was that all right? Sure, said Lemus.

It was cold and misty during the night, but at dawn the temperature rose rapidly as the sun began to burn away the fog. At 6:30 A.M. Lemus got a break: one of Lehder's sentries spotted one of the police snipers and stupidly fired a shot at him. The policeman returned fire, wounding the sentry, and the battle began. Now that the police had been attacked, Lemus didn't have to worry about serving the search warrant. His men could set fire to the chalet and burn it to the ground if they wanted.

But Lemus could see he wouldn't need to do that. Lehder's *pistoleros* had all gathered on the second floor and were shooting at the police hidden in the woods across the canyon. This was cover fire, Lemus concluded, so Lehder could sneak out the back door. He and his snipers had to get into the house as soon as possible, or Lehder was going to escape.

Lemus and his two snipers rushed the chalet, weapons drawn. Lemus flung open the front door and leaped through it, his revolver held with both hands at eye level. The second-floor gunfire, it turned out, was a diversion, not cover. While Lehder's men shot up the woods at the back of the house, Lehder himself raced for the front door and freedom. Instead, he found Lemus holding a pistol pointed right between his eyes.

"Little chief, don't shoot me," Lehder said.

"We aren't killers," Lemus replied. "Put your hands on your head and get down on the floor."

Lehder obeyed, reaching into his pocket as he knelt and flinging a huge wad of two-thousand-peso notes at Lemus's feet. "That's a million pesos [$4,500]," he said.

"Pick it up, señor," said Lemus. "You're going to need it for soft drinks."

"Do you want green instead?" Lehder asked. "How much?"

"No, I'm just doing my duty."

"Oh, little chief, what a *verraco* ['hot number'] you are," Lehder continued. "You're the most famous man in the world. You know those gringo sons of bitches want to hang me by the balls, and now you've got me. Too bad we didn't meet earlier."

Lemus soon had things sorted out. As he'd thought—and his prisoner confirmed—Lehder and his men had been near Rionegro in the town of La Ceja most of the time since they'd arrived from the *llanos*, barely managing to escape Lemus on a number of occasions. They had moved to Guarne a couple of days earlier and planned to go back to La Ceja as soon as Lemus left town, working on the principle that the police wouldn't immediately return to a place they had just searched. They were right, Lemus reflected.

Of more immediate importance to Lemus, it turned out that the sentries' three machine pistols were the only ones in the house. Lemus mustered everybody in the chalet's front room, searched them, and lined them up. He was starting to feel terrific. Really terrific.

"Gentlemen," he said to his own men, "I'd like to introduce you to Carlos Lehder."

Dead silence.

Lemus was undaunted. That was to be expected. He moved everyone into the yard and formed them up again for a collective mug shot. Working the camera himself, he made a motion with his free hand and said to no one in particular: "Where's the soccer ball? We're taking the team picture." Lehder's people laughed. Lemus snapped the photo.

At ten A.M. a pair of police vans picked up Lehder's sidemen for the hour-long trip to Medellín. Lemus followed with Lehder in his own car. Lehder was looking a little seedy from a big night of drinking, Lemus noticed, but he seemed to be in decent spirits, joking with women along the road and talking it up with Lemus.

At a roadside telephone booth Lemus called the Antioquia police chief to tell him what to expect. He was nearly breathless at this point, not believing his good fortune. What a coup!

"¡Mi Coronel, mi Coronel!" Lemus gushed. "We got him, we got him!"

"Yes, yes, calm down," the colonel answered. "You got who?"

"The Virgin has smiled on us," said Lemus. "We have captured Carlos Lehder."

Lemus's euphoria lasted until midafternoon. He moved Lehder into the police station with no difficulty, correctly figuring that all the reporters would be watching the vans. In the squad room Lemus got Lehder a drink of water and some lunch. Then about two P.M. an army Fourth Brigade helicopter landed in the yard, picked up the prisoner, and took him away. Shortly after that the chief of the National Police called Lemus to congratulate him. That done, he was advised to go back to Rionegro, pick up his stuff, and get the hell out of town as fast as he could.

At the Rionegro police station, the telephone had been ringing off the hook. Lemus's subordinates summarized the messages: "Lemus is dead''; "That son of a bitch''; "Who does he think he is?'' It was a good thing, his subordinates told him, that he didn't have a home telephone number yet, or people would have been talking with his wife. When was he leaving?

Lemus gathered his family, packed his bags, and flew to Bogotá for ten days. Then the U.S. embassy got him out of the country.

IN 1984 Jaime Ramirez had figured out that police could make big trouble for Carlos Lehder if they could catch him. Lehder's extradition case had been the only one treated by the Supreme Court in absentia, and the order had been signed by Belisario Betancur on May 8, 1984. This set of circumstances existed for no other drug defendant in Colombia. Lehder's case was wrapped up and signed off. Lehder had no further legal recourse. In theory he could be put aboard a plane and sent to the United States immediately.

Ramirez was right. The helicopter took Lehder to the airport in Rionegro, where a Colombian army C-130 waited to fly him to Bogotá. While this was happening, the Ministry of Defense was on the telephone to the U.S. embassy. If you want him, the ministry said, you can have him. Do you have a plane available?

The embassy did. Sitting on the tarmac at the El Dorado military terminal was a DEA Aerocommander turboprop en route to La Paz from the United States. The embassy called DEA Washington, and DEA Washington turned the plane around. The Aerocommander was not a big aircraft, and it would be a long, uncomfortable flight.

Lehder arrived in Bogotá about four P.M. and was hustled to the Aerocommander after minimum formalities. At one point the army brought a television camera to the runway to film an interview for its archives. Before the interview began, every soldier on camera covered his face with a black shroud.

The Aerocommander took off at 5:15 P.M. on February 4 with Lehder and two DEA agents aboard. The prisoner looked hung over and tired and wasn't particularly talkative. Tom Bigoness, one of the agents along for the ride, noted that Lehder spoke excellent English. Every once in a while the prisoner would sigh and confirm: "You got me now."

Lehder talked briefly about Detroit and his time in Danbury, but otherwise he was silent. In the middle of the night the plane stopped at the U.S. Naval Base at Guatanamo Bay, Cuba, to refuel. Everyone was ravenous, but the base was locked up tight, and the agents couldn't even get a soft drink. Bigoness and his DEA companion killed their appetites with cigarettes, but Lehder declined politely: "No, that's all right, I only smoke marijuana." At 1:15 A.M. on February 5, 1987, the Aerocommander landed in Tampa, Florida.

30.

"WITNESSES FROM HELL"

Three U.S. marshals brought Max Mermelstein into a Louisiana courtroom. Ordinarily parish deputies would be guarding the witness. The presence of federal marshals was an indication of Mermelstein's importance; even though he was testifying in a Louisiana murder trial, he was a federal informant. And the federal government was taking great care to protect its property.

The marshals kept their bodies close to Mermelstein and peered out into the spectators, who had already passed through two metal detectors. Mermelstein at forty-three looked like a stocky English professor gone to seed: long gray hair, white beard, blue blazer, loud shirt, no tie. He sat in the witness box and accepted a silenced MAC-10 machine pistol from the prosecutor, a petite but very dynamic dark-haired woman named Premila Burns. At thirty-seven, Prem Burns was the top homicide prosecutor in Baton Rouge.

"Mr. Mermelstein, would you look at these two exhibits before you marked State's 14 and State's 15, please?" she asked. State's 14 was the MAC-10; 15 was the silencer. "Have you ever seen previously either Exhibit 14 or 15?"

"Yes, I have," Mermelstein said calmly, his expression blank and unhurried.

As he testified, three men and their lawyers stared at him from the defense table. Miguel Velez—Carlos "Cumbamba" Arango was being tried under his alias—wore thick glasses and an aquamarine sweater. His thick black hair was combed straight back. The courtroom's four rows of neon lights made Cumbamba's pasty-white Antioquian complexion look corpselike. Cumbamba sometimes smiled at the bailiffs or his co-defendants, but more often his face hardened into a chilling squint. Bernardo Vasquez, wearing a brown sweater, stared about, seemingly unable to register the magnitude of the spectacle going on around him. Luis Carlos Quintero Cruz, the accused trigger man, wore glasses and a conservative gray business suit. He, too, looked on uncomprehendingly. Quintero Cruz, dark and Indian-looking, was distinctly different from the pale Antioquians. He understood no English, so he had to listen to the trial by translation. Cumbamba and Quintero Cruz did not change their clothes for the first two days of the trial. The three men sat at the defense table, staring across the blue velvet carpet toward Max Mermelstein.

Prem Burns had very deliberately handed Mermelstein the MAC-10 that had killed Barry Seal; she wanted each juror to handle it, too, to feel the weight of it and appreciate its deadly, alien quality. The weapon weighed 7.5 pounds and was 22 inches long; more than half of that length—11.5 inches—was taken up by the homemade silencer. This was no ordinary gun.

"Would you tell the jury the circumstances under when you first saw that?" Burns asked Mermelstein.

"Sometime in April or May of 1984, they were brought to my residence," Mermelstein said.

"By whom were they brought?" asked Burns.

"By Rafael Cardona," Mermelstein said.

"And why did he have that weapon with him?" Burns asked.

"To show me what he had just gotten," said Mermelstein. "That he had just gotten it. He wanted to show it to me."

"Was anything done with that weapon when it got to your residence?" Burns asked.

"He showed me the weapon and told me he wanted to test-fire it by the pool," Mermelstein said.

THE trial of Barry Seal's accused killers opened on April 6, 1987, more than a year after Seal's murder. It took place in the two-story Lake Charles federal building, which also housed the post office. Three of the six members of the Colombian hit team faced first-degree murder charges—Cumbamba, Quintero Cruz, and Vasquez. The state was seeking the death penalty—the electric chair at the Louisiana State Prison in Angola. A fourth, lesser member of the hit team was being tried separately. Evidence was lacking against the fifth and sixth men arrested, and they were simply deported to Colombia.

The trial had started out in Baton Rouge, but attorneys could not pick an impartial jury, so pervasive were knowledge and opinions about Barry Seal. So the trial was moved 170 miles west to the unlikely location of Lake Charles, Louisiana, an oil refinery town of about seventy-five thousand near the southeast Texas border. The town had once been a haven for Jean Lafitte, the pirate, a coincidence Barry Seal might have appreciated.

Lake Charles actively campaigned to host the Seal murder trial, winning out over New Orleans, Alexandria, and Jefferson Parish. The town fathers were glad to get what they saw as a needed economic boost and some national publicity. Jury selection began in an 8,400-seat livestock arena with dirt from the weekend horse show still on the floor. The stern Cajun judge sat at a makeshift bench adorned with red, white, and blue bunting. The Colombians arrived in a blue-and-white armored Louisiana State Police truck. More than a few people commented on the circus atmosphere.

"This case had been building up to the big top for the past year," said Miami defense attorney Richard Sharpstein, who was representing Cumbamba.

Sharpstein led the seven defense lawyers. He was a deeply tanned, aggressive Miami criminal attorney who made frequent objections in a style that was both smooth and disruptive to the prosecution. Sharpstein had performed something of a miracle in his last big drug case: he'd gotten Howard Hewett, the lead singer of the pop trio Shalamar, acquitted after DEA agents arrested Hewett and his girlfriend for allegedly selling a kilo of cocaine to an undercover agent in the Dadeland Mall parking lot. Now Sharpstein was being called upon to conjure up a similar feat against far greater odds.

The jury seated to hear the case consisted of ten women and two men, and that troubled Prem Burns. On death penalty cases, she preferred to have a predominantly male jury. Women jurors tended not to favor the death penalty. The jurors were sequestered, and they rode to their hotel in a yellow school bus outfitted with opaque windows.

Burns prosecuted the case with a particular passion. In twelve years as a prosecutor, Prem Burns had lost only three out of one hundred jury trials, and she had never lost a murder case. She was barely more than five feet tall with raven hair and a quick temper. Defense attorneys called her "the Black Widow." Burns got the case the day after Seal was shot. She had never even heard of the Medellín cartel, but as she learned of its power and reach, her desire to pursue the case grew into an obsession.

Federal officials wanted to try the defendants in federal court on charges of violating Seal's civil rights by killing him, which carried a possible life sentence—there is no federal statute or death penalty. But Burns and others in the East Baton Rouge District Attorney's Office had fought successfully to keep the case as a murder trial in state court, where the defendants would face the electric chair.

Burns had to overcome a sticky obstacle. The feds had let her know they had a witness who knew about the contract on Seal, but they steadfastly guarded his identity, refusing even to tell her his name. The mystery witness was so important that they wanted to preserve his anonymity and keep him from testifying at all at the Seal trial; instead the feds went behind Burns's back and tried to get Vasquez to take a plea bargain and "flip" against the other defendants, so the mystery witness would not have to testify. But Vasquez wouldn't accept the deal.

Finally Burns learned the identity of the mystery witness, whom she had taken to calling "MM," for mystery man. The initials turned out to be correct: the witness was Max Mermelstein. Al Winters and Dick Gregorie were concerned about Mermelstein making his first appearance in a state court without being guided and protected by one of the federal prosecutors who knew him best. They worried such a valuable witness could be ruined if he was mishandled on the stand and mauled by defense attorneys. But eventually Burns and others in Baton Rouge prevailed on the feds to let her use Mermelstein.

When the trial got under way in Lake Charles, Defense Attorney Richard Sharpstein's strategy was to hit hard on Seal's Machiavellian nature. "The man was too complex," Sharpstein said. "The man had many sides, not just two sides, right and wrong. Adler Barry Seal was a drug smuggler. He was a soldier of fortune, he was a mercenary. He was a man who would do what benefited Barry Seal. He was a man who understood the system. . . . He always found a back door out, and he always used it to benefit Barry Seal. He put bullets in his own head. I tell you the tale of Barry Seal will point in the direction of that, because he himself is responsible for where he is."

Max Mermelstein's testimony was devastating. Besides linking the MAC-10 to the cartel, he was able to identify Cumbamba. Sharpstein did his best to discredit the witness: "Max Mermelstein is a man who would make Barry Seal look like a midget." Mermelstein, he said, was "another Barry Seal, a clone, maybe even worse than Seal." But Mermelstein mesmerized the jury—he testified to arranging thirty-eight cocaine flights of 450 kilos apiece at a time when the record U.S. cocaine seizure stood at less than 400 kilos. The total amount he smuggled, Mermelstein said, was 50,000 kilos—as Sharpstein put it, about "twenty dump trucks" of cocaine.

"How much cash did you arrange to be taken out of the United States?" Sharpstein asked.

"Approximately three hundred million," Mermelstein said in his bland voice.

The jury gasped.

"You yourself arranged for approximately three hundred million dollars in illegal money to be taken out of the country?" Sharpstein asked.

"That is correct, sir," Mermelstein said.

Mermelstein testified in such a tranquil tone that Sharpstein asked him if he had taken Valium before coming to court. No, Mermelstein answered mildly.

The rest of the witnesses and the physical evidence were overwhelming. The fingerprints of Quintero Cruz, Vasquez, and Cumbamba were found in both the Buick—referred to in court as the "murder vehicle"—and the red Cadillac used for the getaway. A "neutron activation" test conducted after Cumbamba's arrest in Mississippi showed that he had handled a weapon that had been fired. And to top it off, Cumbamba had been arrested with the keys to the red Cadillac in his pocket. An expert matched Vasquez's handwriting to credit card receipts for hotel rooms and cars in New Orleans and Baton Rouge at the time of the murder. A car salesman identified Vasquez as the man who had bought the Buick for $6,500 in cash. A witness at the halfway house identified Velez as the driver of the Buick getaway car. Two other witnesses placed Quintero Cruz at the scene of the murder.

Burns took five weeks to present her case and put 118 witnesses on the stand. The defense called no witnesses. In closing arguments to the jury, Prem Burns justified using a witness like Max Mermelstein: "If you try the devil, you take your witnesses from hell."

PREM Burns pursued the death penalty. She waved the MAC-10 in front of the jury. "Why did they use a machine gun instead of walking up to Barry Seal and shooting him?" she asked. "Because this weapon was used to teach a lesson. Gangland style. To deter other snitches."

The jury took thirty minutes to decide in favor of life imprisonment.

Cumbamba, Vasquez, and Quintero Cruz listened to the decision without emotion. Three women on the jury sobbed.

Several weeks later the word went around that there was a seven-figure contract on the head of Max Mermelstein.

31.

THE FINAL OFFENSIVE

It began as a brief torrent of judicial activity, one of those incredibly complicated but apparently meaningless exercises in legal pedantry for which Latin America is unhappily notorious. The Colombian Supreme Court, reviewing one of several dozen challenges to the U.S.-Colombia extradition treaty, ruled on December 12, 1986, that the pact's enabling legislation was unconstitutional because it had been signed by an interim president and not by the president of Colombia himself.

The practical effect of the finding was immediate and dramatic. Suddenly the treaty was rendered useless; it could no longer be applied in Colombia because of what appeared to be a frivolous technicality.

The Supreme Court did, however, suggest a way out of the impasse: perhaps current President Virgilio Barco might want to "re-sign" the enabling legislation in his own name. On December 14 Barco did so; the treaty was back in force, and that, supposedly, was that. U.S. Ambassador Richard Gillespie commented that the United States was "pleased" at Barco's "decisiveness" in restoring the enabling legislation. "We at no time felt the treaty was inoperable," he said.

WHAT the United States ambassador saw as a momentary inconvenience was in fact the opening skirmish in a much larger and more important campaign: the Medellín cartel's final offensive against extradition.

For five years the cartel had battled the bilateral treaty with all the tools at its disposal. It had murdered more than thirty judges, including half the Supreme Court. It had put dozens of politicians on its payroll. It had bought enough publicity to portray the treaty as a violation of national sovereignty.

Nothing had worked—until now. On December 12 the cartel had finally found a loose thread. It had pulled a bit and sensed it could pull some more. By Christmas the cartel had filed nine new lawsuits challenging Barco's right to "re-sign" the enabling legislation. Barco, the suits charged, had either exceeded his authority or, at the very least, should be required to resubmit the enabling legislation to Congress for ratification.

Unlike the United States, the Colombian government had immediately understood that the treaty was in grave danger. For two days after the Supreme Court's initial finding, Barco consulted ex-presidents, legislators, and jurists as to what action he should take. The answers were fairly daunting. First, there was no quick legal fix he could make, nor was there anything he could do with state of siege or executive decree. Second, if he resubmitted the legislation, Congress would not pass it. Many lawmakers were already in the traffickers' pockets; many others were too scared to vote publicly for extradition.

That left the simple expedient of signing the measure again. It was an unprecedented action and perhaps unconstitutional. It would certainly be challenged, but it had at least an even chance of being sustained. Meanwhile it would buy some time. Maybe the government could find another, better mechanism. It was worth a try.

THE struggle that ensued was an exercise in quiet desperation. During it, Barco, the unsympathetic cipher who seemed always reluctant to take action, emerged as extradition's last champion. On the other side the cartel circled jackal-like, sensing that the treaty was badly wounded. The traffickers were anxious, finally, to make the kill.

In the middle, trapped by circumstances, was the Colombian Supreme Court. Before December 12 the justices—and especially those in the constitutional chamber—were receiving a steady diet of drug trafficker threats, both in the mail and on the telephone. The atmosphere was much the same as what had existed in the few months before the Palace of Justice attack. Now it was worse, of course, because the Palace of Justice murders had happened. Justices could see what might happen if they ignored the cartel's messages.

Then, after December 12, the threats stopped. The message was unmistakable. Hurt the cartel, suffer the consequences. Help the cartel, and the cartel lays off.

Still, there were plenty of battles left to be fought. The court had some advantages. Protection of the justices, for one, was better. Since the Palace of Justice affair the court had moved to temporary quarters in a narrow brick apartment building across the street from Bogotá's Hotel Tequendama, on the northern edge of the downtown area. The building was easily guarded and almost impregnable—like a medieval keep. All the justices now had twenty-four-hour bodyguards and moved about in police-escorted convoys.

But it was no way to live, especially for middle-aged and elderly jurists for whom membership on Colombia's highest court was supposed to be an honor to be enjoyed, not a horror to be dreaded. What sense did it make to spend a career scrambling to the top of the judicial heap only to have one's professional life submerged in a quotidian nightmare?

Besides the working conditions, the national ambience was horrible. The government had little confidence in the court's ability to do its job. The justices, for their part, had no confidence in the government's ability to protect them. The Colombian people by this time had little confidence in the integrity of either branch of government.

Finally, 1986 had been so bloody, so humiliating, and so full of failure, that the pendulum of political opinion had once again swung away from confrontation with the cartel and back to appeasement. The sense of hopelessness was such that important Colombians had begun to speak again of accommodation. In 1986 the spokesman was Samuel Buitrago Hurtado, president of the Council of State, a nonpartisan administrative agency charged with ruling on questions of governmental administration and procedure. His solution: legalize drug trafficking. His reasoning: "The drug business will cease to be profitable for the drug traffickers if it is legalized and if the Colombian state assumes total control not only of its sale, but also of its use."

In this fashion, presumably, two-bit gringo hoods seeking to buy a load could deal with an agent of the Colombian government instead of a member of the Medellín cartel. Buitrago had not thought about what legalized cocaine traffic would be like in a world where Colombia was the only country that had it.

Yet the fact that such views got a respectful airing was a testament to the degree of terror with which the cartel had infected the upper echelons of Colombia's bureaucracy. One assistant attorney general could insist that "threats are not a general fact of life" but admitted that "all you have to do is kill one or two, and you've got a climate of panic." An assistant interior minister stated the dilemma starkly: "These people have no problem whatsoever in killing a four-year-old child."

The final antiextradition offensive had barely begun when Guillermo Cano was killed. Then came the state of siege, the crackdown, the Parejo Gonzalez shooting, and, finally, the capture of Carlos Lehder. Two weeks after that, Colombian news organizations printed and broadcast stories based on a four-part series in *The Miami Herald* entitled "The Medellin Cartel, World's Deadliest Criminals." The reprint was the first venture in a cooperative campaign to report drug trafficking by sharing equally in the risk. Medellín's two dailies, *El Colombiano* and *El Mundo*, at first refused to print the *Herald*'s series, then finally ran it at the urging of colleagues.

THE Lehder capture, the news campaign, and, most of all, the image of a badly regarded government finally taking effective, aggressive action created an illusion of progress. Lehder's capture and extradition had provoked no significant cartel reprisals—almost unbelievable for an organization that derived its power from intimidation and fear. Either the cartel didn't care about Lehder, or it was on the run and couldn't afford to stop and take revenge.

There was a third possibility: the cartel had items on its agenda whose importance eclipsed the capture of Carlos Lehder. It could not afford to rock the boat while its grand strategy was unfolding.

AS the year progressed, the Supreme Court issued a series of findings that bit by bit cut away the government's maneuvering room. On February 17 the court refused to rule on seven pending extraditions while the question of the enabling legislation remained unresolved. On March 5 the court annulled as unconstitutional Barco's December state of siege decree giving the armed forces the power to judge drug traffickers. The ruling forced drug cases back into civilian courts, where they were virtually impossible to prosecute. Barco countered on March 11 by creating jobs for thirty-nine new special drug prosecutors and assigning them military protection.

The government appeared to get a break on May 1 when the Council of State—queried by Barco—issued its opinion that the extradition treaty was still in force and that the Supreme Court had to rule on pending cases. The court responded that no one had ever suggested that the treaty was invalid. The difficulty was that it could not be applied because the enabling legislation was no good.

Still, this was all fencing. The government was looking for a way to escape the trap the cartel was trying to spring. The Council of State had opened a window, but the Supreme Court wouldn't let the government climb out. This meant that in the end, the treaty would stand or fall on the question of whether Barco had been within his rights when he'd re-signed the enabling legislation in December. On May 28 the justices, meeting in plenum, emitted their finding: a 12–12 tie. They would have to hire a temporary "alternate justice" to break the impasse.

From that moment the treaty was finished. On paper the alternate justice stood a good chance of ruling on either side of the question. In practice the government never had a prayer. The Medellín cartel had succeeded in reducing the extradition treaty to a single finding by a single person. By 1987 this principle always worked in favor of the cartel. Years of murder and terrorism had taught Colombians the penalty for challenging the traffickers. If it was a question of one case, the cartel always picked on the judge, and the rest of the establishment—police, prosecutors, jailers—fell in line. Now the cartel had managed to do the same thing with extradition. It was unreasonable to suppose that one lawyer, working as a consultant on one case, could ignore cartel pressure in making his finding.

And so it proved. The court appointed three justices one by one from a pool of eminent lawyers assembled precisely for the purpose of breaking ties. One by one they recused themselves, citing conflict of interest. The fourth, Alfonso Suarez de Castro, also pronounced himself impeded, but the court refused to accept his excuse and ordered him to sit. He sat, and on June 25 he ruled that President Barco had acted unconstitutionally in re-signing the enabling legislation. By a vote of 13–12, the Supreme Court had hamstrung the extradition treaty. The Medellín cartel had won its biggest victory.

THE U.S. embassy issued a brave but ridiculous statement suggesting that the finding somehow did not mean what it meant: "No matter what, international treaties stand above internal decisions, and as such they must be obeyed."

Privately, however, one embassy official spoke of a "very bleak outlook" for drug enforcement now that extradition was no longer possible. The Colombian Justice Ministry lamented the disappearance of "a very valuable instrument" in the drug wars.

Others were much harsher: "It is the destruction of the nation's judicial system," said Conservative party leader Alvaro Gomez Hurtado, loser to Barco in the 1986 presidential elections. "The country should declare to the world that it has resolved not to have a Supreme

Court, that we cannot give it sufficient guarantees so it can find on the basis of law.''

The cartel, not surprisingly, was ecstatic. Writing to his Armenia followers from a U.S. jail on July 1, Carlos Lehder pronounced the day of the finding ''the happiest of my existence'' and expressed the fond but futile hope that he would soon be free because his extradition had been illegal. He apparently forgot that once he had appeared in the United States, nobody in the U.S. justice system cared how he got there.

Still, Lehder retained high spirits. In a later letter from Jacksonville he described how the long battle against extradition began ''with the burial of a Supreme Court who had sold out to imperialist interests.'' This letter was the clearest indication to date that the Palace of Justice attack had been a drug traffickers' job. As many Colombians already suspected, the cartel had begun its systematic dismemberment of the Supreme Court on the day of the palace takeover.

WITHOUT an extradition treaty, drug enforcement agents in the United States and Colombia had to count on the traffickers' arrest, trial, and conviction in Colombia. U.S. government and DEA officials had little faith that this would happen. This view was reinforced within thirty days of the Supreme Court ruling when a Cali judge acquitted Gilberto Rodriguez Orejuela of drug charges after a five-month trial. Rodriguez Orejuela, extradited from Spain in 1986 a couple of weeks before fellow prisoner Jorge Ochoa, had quietly bided his time in a Cali jail waiting for his trafficking case to be heard. The trial opened February 4 and was closed May 30 before amplifying evidence could be submitted by the United States.

In worse shape was Pablo Escobar, but ''the Godfather'' moved with characteristic efficiency to wipe out his pending charges. This time, however, he worked within the system. On July 22 three U.S.-inspired ''Requests for Provisional Arrest'' were dismissed as unenforceable. On August 9 newspapers discovered that a judge had withdrawn orders for the arrest of Escobar, Rodriguez Gacha, and Evaristo Porras in the murder of *El Espectador* editor Guillermo Cano. Three days later another judge dismissed the indictment against Escobar for the Lara Bonilla murder. The Cano judge cited lack of evidence; the Lara Bonilla judge cited improper methods of obtaining evidence. Interested policemen, of whom there were few, now had to look all the way back to the mid-1970s to find something on which to try Escobar. And in those cases the witnesses were all dead.

That left Jorge Ochoa as the only cartel fugitive with substantial legal difficulties. His two U.S. indictments would not cause him any problem, but all the maneuvering he had done in Spain in 1984 now came back to haunt him. He still had a twenty-month sentence to serve for bull smuggling and had broken his parole after his release on bond. Furthermore, his Medellín indictment for drug trafficking, copied from the Nicaragua case in Miami and filed in Colombia, was still alive. Neither case was a serious matter when set alongside the collection of homicides that had once confronted Escobar. But neither case was going to be dismissed on a technicality and forgotten. If Ochoa was caught, he was liable.

Barco did not give up after the Supreme Court finding. His new justice minister, Enrique Low Murtra, was a former member of the Council of State and a survivor of the Palace of Justice affair. He hated drug traffickers and made no secret of his, and Barco's, priorities. "The government wants to continue extraditing," Low Murtra told *El Tiempo* shortly after his appointment.

The problem was how to do it. Barco knew the easiest way would be to take the Supreme Court's advice and resubmit the old treaty's enabling legislation to Congress for passage. Barco's aides polled Congress and found what they suspected. No chance.

Quietly the government opened negotiations with the United States on possible new measures either to reinstate the crippled treaty, write a new one, or resurrect older pacts. Under consideration were a multilateral 1933 hemispheric agreement known as the "Montevideo Convention" and a bilateral 1888 agreement. Both documents in theory were applicable, but both would take a lot of work before they could be brought into play. In the latter part of the year the U.S. Justice Department began discussing all the possibilities with Low Murtra and Colombian Attorney General Carlos Mauro Hoyos. The cartel got wind of the talks and watched them closely.

By August the cartel could pronounce itself in better shape than it had been in in years. It had lost Lehder, true, but it had also defeated the extradition treaty through a combination of prolonged intimidation, canny legal maneuvering and, above all, patience. The cartel of the future, it seemed, would be more like the U.S. mafia—well-known, settled, and immensely powerful, but low profile and nonconfrontational.

Then in early August DAS announced it had solved the Guillermo Cano murder and broken up the Medellín murder gang that had held the contract. DAS described the gang, Los Priscos, as the "armed wing" of the Medellín cartel. Los Priscos included as many as fifty people between full-timers and subcontractors. It was led by two top echelon Medellín badmen, the brothers David Ricardo and Jose Roberto Prisco Lopera. David Ricardo had been described as "the number-one hired killer in Medellín" in an anonymous letter sent to Barco earlier in the year.

DAS attributed more than a dozen important cartel murders to Los Priscos but could link them solidly to only two: Cano and Supreme Court Justice Hernando Baquero Borda. On this pair, however, the DAS investigation was solid and impressive. Detectives had backtracked the gang through the Cano hit team's leader, Luis Eduardo Osorio Guizado, La Guaqua ("The Muskrat"). La Guaqua was dead, killed in a Medellín vendetta along with his top lieutenant, but DAS was able to bring the gang leaders under surveillance and follow a Prisco hit team when it arrived in Bogotá in early August to "score a goal," Medellín slang for murder. The gunmen spotted the DAS tail after two days, and detectives and Priscos shot it out late one night in the quiet residential streets of north Bogotá. DAS killed four gang members, including Jose Roberto Prisco.

DAS's description of Los Priscos was a bit folkloric, but for the first time someone had focused attention on the way the cartel did its dirty work. Whether it was Los Priscos or Los Quesitos, as in the Lara Bonilla assassination, or Los Magníficos or any of the other one-hundred-plus gangs that roamed the Colombian underworld, the method was the same, learned during the Griselda Blanco days and taught for years, it was rumored, in back alley homicide academies in Medellín's northern *barrios*. Cops called it "the Medellín signature": the MAC-10 machine pistol, the motorcycles, the sharp division of labor between planners and gunmen, the safe house, and the multiple cutouts. Lawmen could trace a cartel hit so far—and no farther.

DAS's exposé of Los Priscos hurt the cartel. Then Justice Minister Low Murtra did it further damage on November 12, charging that Gonzalo Rodriguez Gacha, working through a Prisco-like gang of thugs, had ordered the October murder of Patriotic Union leader Jaime Pardo Leal. The killing of Pardo Leal, a well-liked, forty-six-year-old Marxist lawyer and the Patriotic Union's 1986 presidential candidate, prompted a twenty-four-hour general strike, two days of riots, and general calls for Barco to take action against right-wing death squads.

Low Murtra said Pardo Leal had simply been caught like so many others in the middle of Rodriguez Gacha's turf war with the FARC guerrillas in Guaviare. No one doubted him. By late 1987 the Medellín cartel had ruined the FARC's reputation for all time. Colombia's proudest insurgents were now widely regarded as little more than a band of gangsters who had sold out to the cocaine barons.

32.

CITIZEN JORGE LUIS OCHOA

It was about 4:30 P.M. on November 21, 1987, when the traffic cop gestured to the driver of the white 1987 Porsche, indicating that he should pull over to the side of the road. It was a busy weekend afternoon, a Saturday, and the highway was filled with cars going to or coming from Cali, thirty miles to the west. The Porsche was outward bound, traveling to Pereira or Antioquia, perhaps, and, like any other car on the highway, it had to stop north of Palmira to pay tolls. The El Cerrito toll booths were a natural place for police to size up motorists, and that's what they were doing. Later, stories would surface suggesting that the Porsche was on the watch list, that the two policemen knew who was in it and had been stalking the driver for days. Another story—the police themselves pushed this one—said the roadblock was "routine," a precaution put into effect every weekend in hopes of catching the odd guerrilla transporting weapons. This explanation was ridiculous—no guerrilla would be transporting weapons in a brand-new white Porsche that in Colombia cost $260,000.

The policeman and his partner approached the driver's window and asked for some ID. It was never made clear whether they recognized the driver or what the driver ended up showing them. Whatever he said or did, it wasn't enough. The policemen told the driver that he, his woman passenger, and the Porsche would have to accompany them to Palmira. This did not sit well with the driver, who suggested something might be arranged, say, for 3,000 pesos ($12). The two officers demurred. Well, said the driver, how about 50,000 pesos ($200)? Really, the police said, don't make more trouble for yourself. How about 12 million pesos ($48,000)? No. Well, then, let's say 100 million pesos ($400,000).

The policemen wouldn't take the money. Neither man ever made any public statement about the incident, and their bosses, wisely, never released the officers' names. Maybe the two policemen were young idealists, or maybe they were like Major Lemus, Carlos Lehder's capturer, honest, ambitious cops who wanted to arrest bad guys and get ahead. Whatever their motives, there was no doubt they had trapped lightning in a bottle. The driver of the Porsche was Jorge Ochoa.

At traffic police headquarters in Palmira, Ochoa finally found some help. A woman lawyer for the Attorney General's Office, either by accident or by design, was on hand to greet the prisoner with a big hug and promises that everything would soon be made right. She got on the phone and started calling nearby military and police installations, looking for somebody to sign Ochoa out of jail. Saturday evenings weren't good for this sort of work, however, and the attorney couldn't find anyone willing to accept such a responsibility. Later the woman denied having done any of this, saying she was only concerned about alleged maltreatment of prisoners arrested on drug trafficking charges. The traffic police were unimpressed. They had seen her at work, and, anyway, who'd said anything about drug trafficking? The police were holding a warrant from a Cartagena Customs judge who said Ochoa had broken parole and jumped bail on a twenty-month bull-smuggling conviction.

The police booked Ochoa and put him in a holding cell, then sent him to the army's Codazzi Batallion on the outskirts of Palmira, where he spent the night and much of the next day in the stockade. At dusk Sunday a helicopter touched down at batallion headquarters, picked him up, and took him to a nearby airfield, where he was loaded aboard a Colombian air force C-130 Hercules and flown to Bogotá. He landed at seven P.M., to be greeted by a platoon of motorcycle policemen. They put him aboard an armored van. Then lights flashed, sirens shrieked, and the convoy dashed down the highway from El Dorado Airport, skirted the city, and headed north to the Brigade of Military Institutes, a huge military complex on the edge of the capital.

By nine P.M. Ochoa was safely locked away in a maximum security military prison, where he would stay while the Colombian government plotted its next move. The police and the armed forces had done their jobs. They had arrested Ochoa, moved him, and put him in a safe place. Now it was up to the government to figure out what to do.

OUTWARDLY the circumstances of Ochoa's arrest closely resembled those of the Lehder capture nine months earlier: the "chance enounter''; the lack of serious violence; the quick, capable action by the armed forces; the move to Bogotá.

Beyond these events, however, the two cases had nothing in common. Lehder's extradition was a done deal, signed off by President Belisario Betancur and simply waiting the day when somebody managed to catch him. Ochoa was doubly blessed—first, because he had a piddling sentence in Colombia to serve before any action whatsoever could be taken on his extradition, and second, and much more important, because the 1979 extradition treaty was effectively frozen. Not only was there no way to extradite him quickly, there wasn't even a working legal mechanism that would allow the government to initiate proceedings.

President Virgilio Barco knew all this but wasn't sure what action to take or even what action could be taken. The Colombian public, with its limited understanding of the nation's byzantine legal processes, expected Ochoa to be flown momentarily to Homestead Air Force Base in south Florida. The United States was publicly promulgating this view: "The president of Colombia could be courageous and greatly assist his country by throwing out Jorge Ochoa," said Miami DEA spokesman Jack Hook. "Once Jorge Ochoa arrives in the United States, he, like Carlos Lehder, will not be able to bribe, murder, or intimidate his way out of police custody."

In Colombia, of course, this was a real danger. Ochoa had already finessed his way out of jail once, and Colombian law enforcement had a long and terrible history of not being able to hold on to drug traffickers. The longer Colombia held Ochoa, the more difficult it would be to keep holding him.

The day after the arrest Barco met with a handful of his top advisers to discuss the government's options. The inner circle included Foreign Minister Julio Londoño Paredes, Justice Minister Enrique Low Murtra, and Attorney General Carlos Mauro Hoyos Jimenez. The meeting was held at Londoño's north Bogotá home and lasted all day Sunday, November 22.

In the end the government took the only short-term action possible, deciding to hold Ochoa on the old bull-smuggling charge—apparently good for twenty months in jail if necessary—while it tried to arrange his extradition. Low Murtra announced that Ochoa was being held "under the jurisdiction of the Cartagena Customs judge." The judge —successor to the ill-fated Fabio Pastrana Hoyos—revoked Ochoa's conditional liberty, citing parole violation. So far, so good.

To observe the machinations at close range and to offer suggestions, the U.S. government sent a six-member legal team from the

Departments of Justice and State to Bogotá immediately after Ochoa's arrest. Their brief was to urge Colombia to "find a mechanism" that would allow it to extradite Ochoa and other accused traffickers to the United States.

The team was nervous about the Colombians. Londoño in particular seemed deliberately obstructionist, anti-American, and bent on "slowing down and blocking any initiatives and prolonging problems," as one team superviser said later. The team felt the same way about Low Murtra, a curious position given the justice minister's hard-line statements on drug trafficking.

But the U.S. team saw him differently. He was another foot dragger, always looking for ways not to do something. The team knew he'd been threatened—who hadn't?—but now they felt that he'd been threatened more seriously and more specifically. He wasn't a Yankee hater like Londoño, but, he wasn't doing the U.S. cause any good.

For Barco, they had growing admiration. True, he'd started out like Betancur, ignoring the damage the cartel could do. But, also like Betancur, once the cartel had swatted him in the face a couple of times, he'd gotten mean. He was extradition's fastest friend now and had rapidly come to realize that the cartel was the scourge of Colombian institutions. He also knew that his administration could forget about any serious role in international affairs unless it did something about the Medellín cartel.

The one man in whom the U.S. team truly had confidence was Attorney General Hoyos, a low-key *paisa* from Medellín who had quietly moved his agency into the forefront of the drug wars. Hoyos was a fiftyish bachelor whose puckish smile belied a desperate shyness. He was never seen at parties and never hung around in Bogotá. He spent weekends with his mother and his fiancée at his *finca* outside Medellín, seemingly unaffected by the chaos tearing apart his hometown. Long before Ochoa's capture, representatives of the U.S. legal team had begun talks with Hoyos on how extradition might be restored. With Ochoa's capture the negotiations acquired greater urgency. Through it all, said one U.S. legal team member, Hoyos was "the one we trusted" and "the one who was serious."

THE cartel was serious, too, much more serious than it had been when Lehder was captured. Lehder had been an outsider, an English-speaking Quindio interloper who had been living in semiretirement when the police busted him. Ochoa was a different story. He was El Gordo, a main man, a *paisa,* the leading provider for the biggest crime family in Medellín, close personal friend and associate of Pablo Escobar. He must not be extradited.

The cartel reacted to Ochoa's capture almost immediately. A little more than twenty-four hours after the El Cerrito arrest—with Ochoa just settling into his new Bogotá jail cell and with Barco and his advisers locked away in the Londoño house—two vanloads of thugs, about twelve gunmen in all, stopped outside the Medellín home of Juan Gomez Martinez, editor of *El Colombiano,* the city's biggest daily newspaper.

One group banged on the front door. Gomez Martinez's son peeked outside, then warned his father that people were waiting to murder him. Gomez Martinez, watching television with his back to the door, flipped over his easy chair, crouched behind it, grabbed a pistol, and pulled the trigger.

The thugs returned the fire with gusto. Meanwhile, a second group, still riding in one of the vans, attempted to breach Gomez Martinez's defenses by crashing through the garage door. The van backed up and thumped repeatedly into the door, which turned out to be made of sheet steel. It bent but did not break.

Fifteen minutes of this was all the neighbors could take. "Hey, look!" yelled one man. "They're trying to kill Gomez Martinez. Let's do something!"

And then the whole neighborhood opened up. Ten years of near anarchy had taught the *paisas* how to take care of themselves and, when occasion required it, of their friends. Eventually somebody shot one of the gunmen, and the rest began to lose their enthusiasm. Taking their wounded comrade with them, they made an orderly withdrawal.

At first it seemed to be comic opera stuff. Then, an hour later, the gang's message arrived at news organizations. The idea, said the communiqué, had been to abduct Gomez Martinez briefly so the gang could deliver the message personally. Since that didn't work, here it was anyway.

The communiqué was addressed to Gomez Martinez, began "Respected sir," and proceeded with the stilted Antioqueño formality that Escobar had used during his troubles in Congress more than four years earlier:

"We have found out that the government is trying by whatever means possible to extradite citizen Jorge Luis Ochoa to the United States. For us, this constitutes the vilest of outrages."

The gang wanted Gomez Martinez to let the government know that "in case citizen Jorge Luis Ochoa is extradited to the United States, we will declare absolute and total war against this country's political leaders. We will execute out of hand the principal chieftains" of Colombia's main political parties, the communiqué said. It was signed "the Extraditables."

In Bogotá, far from the action, newspapers gave the communiqué and the attack on Gomez Martinez banner treatment. In Medellín, on the front lines, reaction was somewhat different. Gomez Martinez, in addition to his job as editor of *El Colombiano*, was the Conservative party candidate for mayor of Medellín. The Extraditables had assured him in the communiqué's last paragraph that the gang had "no political interests against your campaign," but Gomez Martinez was taking no chances. *El Colombiano* granted the assault on its editor's house six discreet paragraphs on page two below the TV schedule.

IF the government won the first battle for Ochoa by arresting and holding him, the cartel won the second, for after a few days it became clear that the prisoner would not—could not—be extradited to the United States without some reformulation of existing treaties.

This meant delay, and delay meant that Ochoa would have a chance to muster the high-priced legal strategy he would need to beat the rap yet again. He lost little time.

By the end of the first week he had six lawyers working for him, three of them former Supreme Court justices, including team leader Humberto Barrera. Within days the legal team had reactivated the long-moribund Medellín case that duplicated the 1984 Nicaragua trafficking charges against Ochoa. It was this document, lifted from public records in Miami, that had tipped the balance in Spain in favor of extraditing Ochoa to Colombia rather than the United States. Barrera judged the Medellín case could work again now, particularly since it looked as though the United States was going to try to get Ochoa with the so-called Montevideo Convention, which required that pending charges in the arresting country be cleaned up before extradition. Low Murtra had announced on November 23 that Colombia had issued a provisional arrest warrant against Ochoa—the first step in the extradition process under the now frozen 1979 treaty.

All of this was very confusing, as the defense attorneys meant it to be. While Ochoa languished at the Brigade of Military Institutions and, after a few weeks, at La Picota, Bogotá's maximum security civilian prison, Barrera and his team set about destroying the government's case against their client. The government watched closely at first, but as the Christmas season approached, officials began to let down their guard.

The U.S. legal team left Bogotá in mid-December, and the case against Ochoa immediately began to unravel. On December 17 Low Murtra withdrew the provisional arrest warrant outstanding against Ochoa, recognizing that it had no meaning in the absence of a working extradition treaty. An exultant Barrera called the ruling "a victory for international jurisprudence."

Sometime in the next ten days, members of the Ochoa team went to Medellín for talks with Judge Maria Cristina Cadavid, ostensibly investigating the Medellín case, and obtained her assurances that Ochoa's presence was not necessary. Later she would admit having also entertained a visit from Juan David and young Fabio Ochoa and Pablo Escobar, also accused in the case. She could find "no merit" in the charges against them.

Finally, on December 30 Barrera paid a call to Bogotá Criminal Court Judge Andrés Enrique Montañez. Ochoa had already served his bull-smuggling time, Barrera said, if the courts counted his jail stints in Spain, Cartagena, and Bogotá. Actually, he continued, Ochoa had served twenty-one months, not twenty, but we won't quibble. Barrera had sought to point this out to the judge in Cartagena, he said, but that judge was on vacation. Under Colombian law, Barrera continued, he was now entitled to present his case to any sitting judge. What exactly are we talking about? asked Montañez. We are talking about a writ of habeas corpus, Barrera replied. There are no arrest orders pending against my client. Montañez, without further preamble, signed the writ.

According to *Semana* magazine's minute-by-minute account, Ochoa's legal team showed up at La Picota at five P.M. on December 30 waving the writ and calling for Ochoa's release. Warden Alvaro Camacho stalled, then called for help from his boss, National Director of Prisons Guillermo Ferro. Unfortunately, Ferro said, he couldn't come immediately because he was at another prison trying to contain a mutiny, which, conveniently for Ochoa, had begun about an hour earlier.

Camacho stood fast for three hours, enduring a visit by Ochoa's sobbing wife: "Why are you being so arbitrary?" Ochoa's lawyers twice induced Camacho to order their client brought downstairs, which occasioned two confrontations with El Gordo himself: "What's going on, Mr. Warden?" At eight P.M. Camacho finally caved in, forced to let Ochoa go because he had no reason not to. Ochoa, wearing a blue flannel suit and carrying an overnight bag, left with his wife and his lawyers in a blue van. Soon he was on a charter airplane traveling to parts unknown to ring in the new year.

. . .

THE predictable, and by now standard, statements deploring the release of Ochoa were issued in Colombia and in the United States as
well. None of it did any good, of course. Ochoa was reported lying
low in Brazil, perhaps with Escobar helping him settle in.

But even though 1988 began with the government taking furious
action, the cartel continued to strike hard.

On January 18, in an apparent variation on the attempt to kidnap
Gomez Martinez, gunmen abducted Andrés Pastrana Gomez, Conservative party candidate for mayor of Bogotá, from his campaign headquarters. In initial communiqués the kidnappers presented themselves
as M-19 guerrillas, but M-19 denied having anything to do with the
crime. After a couple of days Pastrana's friends were pretty sure the
cartel had him. Pastrana, like Gomez Martinez in Medellín, was a
newsman—editor and anchorman of Bogotá's TV-Hoy—and a relatively outspoken opponent of drug trafficking.

A week later, right at dawn, Attorney General Hoyos bade his
fiancée good-bye and climbed into a chauffeured Mercedes for the
short ride to the Medellín Airport in Rionegro. He had spent the
weekend at his *finca* and, as usual, was taking the early Monday plane
to Bogotá to begin his work week.

Three carloads of gunmen ambushed Hoyos on the edge of the
airport just before seven A.M., spraying the limousine with machine-
gun bullets while a busload of commuters watched in shock. The
chauffeur and Hoyos's bodyguard died immediately. Hoyos, gravely
wounded and bleeding, was dragged from the limousine, packed into
one of the getaway vehicles, and driven away.

President Barco ordered the area around the ambush saturated with
police. At noon the searchers radioed headquarters. In looking for
Hoyos they had found and freed Pastrana, unharmed after a week in
a small farmhouse not five miles from the site of the Hoyos ambush.

Pastrana confirmed he had been held by the traffickers as part of a
campaign to dramatize cartel opposition to extradition. He was, he
thought, supposed to act as some kind of messenger, à la Gomez
Martinez. He said his captors told him they planned to kidnap others
for the same purpose, including Attorney General Hoyos.

They had botched the job, though. Around four P.M. an anonymous
caller representing "the Extraditables" told the police they could find
what was left of the attorney general in a field a couple of miles from
Pastrana's hiding place.

Hoyos was covered with blood. His spine had been shattered by a bullet in the ambush, and he had been paralyzed and perhaps dying even as he was dragged off. His attackers clearly did not want anyone to know this, for they had shot Hoyos eleven times in the face. Just to make sure.

"We have executed the attorney general, Mr. Carlos Mauro Hoyos, as a traitor and a sell-out," the caller had told the police. "Listen carefully: the war will go on. . . . "

33.

THE HENRY FORD OF COCAINE

Enormous publicity attended Carlos Lehder's capture and extradition. Never before had a cocaine trafficker of Lehder's stature been brought to the United States. The dramatic flight of the Aerocommander added to the excitement. For the first time American justice would be able to try one of the leaders of the Medellín cartel. DEA agents worldwide were told to be alert for possible retaliation. Everybody braced for the worst.

Federal agents with automatic weapons and pump shotguns ringed the Aerocommander as soon as it taxied to a halt on a remote runway at Tampa International Airport at two A.M. on February 5, 1987. In ten seconds Lehder was out of the plane and into a blue four-door sedan. The car sped with four others in a convoy to downtown Tampa, were Lehder was locked up in a small room at the federal courthouse.

When Lehder made his first appearance before a U.S. magistrate later that morning, he showed remarkable composure, smiling and grinning and speaking in precise, slightly accented English. What he said surprised everybody:

"I don't have any money."

"Is the information true?" asked Magistrate Elizabeth Jenkins.

"Yes, Your Honor," Lehder answered quietly. "Most of my assets are frozen by the government of Colombia."

Jenkins appointed a public defender to represent Lehder at his next court appearance—a hearing to determine whether he should be held without bond in Jacksonville, where he would face trial on the indictment brought against him in 1981. Lehder had been extradited solely on the Jacksonville charges, and those were the only ones on which he could be tried in the United States. If convicted, Lehder faced a maximum penalty of life without parole plus 135 years in prison.

LEHDER'S court appearance in Tampa occasioned his first meeting with U.S. Attorney Robert Merkle, who nearly four years earlier had flown to Bogotá to personally file for Lehder's extradition. To Merkle, Lehder appeared scruffy but in excellent physical condition, his muscles showing through his tight T-shirt. He also seemed unintimidated, which surprised Merkle.

If a federal prosecutor could have been designed to take on the Medellín cartel, he would have turned out to be Robert W. Merkle, the forty-three-year-old top law enforcement official in the Middle District of Florida. Merkle was an imposing 245 pounds and had been a running back at Notre Dame. His hair was blond and close-cropped, his face extraordinarily ruddy. As a county prosecutor, Merkle had gone after public corruption with a zeal that earned him the nickname "Mad Dog." As U.S. attorney, he had even taken on Florida Governor Bob Martinez in a bribery trial involving a Tampa political fixer. Martinez was not charged, but he had to take the stand and face withering questions from Merkle. Nine of the twelve jurors told a *Miami Herald* reporter that they didn't believe the governor's denials.

The "Mad Dog" tag misrepresented Merkle in many ways. He was aggressive, but he was also a brilliant trial tactician with a mind so quick his arguments often jumped ahead of the defense attorneys' responses. Out of the courtroom he was a family man with nine kids and a fondness for singing and playing the guitar. He earned $70,000 a year, a pittance compared with what he could have made in private practice. But he was a man consumed by his job. He was not humble about his abilities, and mediocre minds drew his scorn. Now Bob Merkle set his sights on Carlos Lehder.

At the Tampa hearing, Merkle insisted that Lehder be immediately detained without bond, saying there had been death threats against judges.

"That's a lie!" Lehder shouted.

"He has said if he was caught, he would kill a federal judge a week until he is freed," said Assistant U.S. Attorney Ernst Mueller, Merkle's deputy.

After the hearing, U.S. marshals whisked Lehder away under the gaze of a rooftop sharpshooter. Lehder was flown to a military base near Jacksonville and put in solitary confinement. His exact whereabouts were kept secret, even from his court-appointed attorneys.

Lehder's hearing in Jacksonville on February 9 drew the same un-precedented security measures as the one in Tampa. The metal detectors were so sensitive that many spectators had to remove their shoes because the nails set off an alarm. A bomb-sniffing dog roamed the courthouse corridors. Parking was banned on the four streets adjacent to the courthouse.

Lehder said he couldn't get access to money to hire a lawyer right away because the Colombian government had frozen his assets. Merkle noted that he wore a Rolex watch: "Are you aware that that watch is worth approximately six thousand dollars?"

"No," Lehder answered.

At the hearing, Lehder's public defender, Rosemary Cakmis, accused Pablo Escobar of setting up Lehder.

"Your Honor, we understand that he was turned in to the police by an underworld figure, Pablo Escobar," Cakmis said. She did not elaborate.

The judge ordered Lehder held without bond for the duration of his trial. Things got worse for Lehder before the day was over. The IRS filed a $70 million lien against him, estimating that he had earned $300 million smuggling cocaine in 1979 and 1980 alone.

Lehder was then taken to the federal maximum security prison in Marion, Illinois. This was the best gauge yet of the fear Lehder provoked in American law enforcement. Marion is the most secure federal prison in the country, the modern-day equivalent of Alcatraz. It made Lehder's previous federal home, the prison in Danbury, look like a summer camp. Marion's inmates are drawn from prisoners "who demonstrate an inability to function" in federal maximum security prisons, according to the Justice Department's prison policy manual. In other words, Marion is for the hardest of the hard-core. For 3½ years Marion had been under a "lockdown"—all 350 of its inmates confined to their seven-by-eight-foot cells for twenty-three hours a day. Carlos Lehder was one of the few pretrial detainees in the history of Marion.

From Marion Lehder was moved to the federal prison in Talladega, Alabama, to make it easier for his lawyers to visit. Again he was kept in total isolation. At Talladega a mentally ill prisoner bunked near Lehder "spent much of the night and day yelling and emitting unintelligible guttural sounds," Lehder's attorneys later complained. "Lehder was unable to sleep day or night because of the incessant noise." Next Lehder was moved to the maximum security prison in Atlanta, again to bring him closer to his lawyers. He was kept in isolation on a floor of otherwise empty cells. The floors underneath him housed

1,800 Cuban prisoners from the Mariel boatlift. These Marielitos also kept him awake. "Primal screams punctuate the air minute by minute, and from time to time the din is so pervasive that one cannot hear himself think," his lawyers complained.

Eleven days after Lehder's court-appointed attorney claimed that Pablo Escobar fingered her client, a curious letter appeared in the offices of Colombia's leading newspapers. It was from Escobar in hiding.

Escobar admitted to "personal quarrels with Lehder on several occasions, but these would not lead me to perform such a low and cowardly act as to betray him to the authorities." Escobar complained that Lehder's lawyer's remarks were part of a "plan to attack my moral and personal integrity."

Carlos Lehder did not intend to put his future in the hands of court-appointed attorneys. His emissaries began courting some of the best legal talent in Miami. Speculation in legal circles set the fee as high as $2.5 million, or thirty times Bob Merkle's yearly salary. Surprisingly, several top Miami drug lawyers declined the case. They feared a new federal law, the Money Laundering Control Act, which made it a crime for an attorney to accept a fee from illegal sources. The law was as yet untested, but the thought of what Merkle might do with it gave plenty of lawyers pause.

Eventually, though, Lehder wound up with two top Miami defense attorneys, Ed Shohat and Jose Quiñon. Shohat had defended many big Colombian drug cases in Miami, including the one involving Hernan Botero. Colleagues described him as "a lawyer's lawyer—competent, ethical, and very meticulous." He was extremely bright, analytical, witty, and aggressive in the courtroom, the perfect foil for Bob Merkle. He would make most of the arguments in court. Quiñon, a former state prosecutor, was a Cuban-American who could speak Spanish with his client. Quiñon did things in a courtroom with a supernal ease and was noted for his rapport with juries and witnesses.

Delays kept pushing the trial date back, from late spring to early fall. Then a curious thing happened during a day-long pretrial hearing in May 1987. Lehder's attorneys were arguing to get him transferred from Atlanta to the federal Metropolitan Correctional Center south of Miami, when Merkle unveiled a surprise: Carlos Lehder had sent a letter to Vice President George Bush offering to cooperate in return for immunity. Merkle said the letter "got to the White House," but he couldn't release its contents because a magistrate had ordered it sealed. He said he thought the letter frivolous and added that Bush's staff "didn't take it seriously, either." Merkle had no intention of making any deal with Lehder. After the hearing, Lehder's attorneys denied that he wanted to turn informant.

"It is absolutely false beyond any doubt that Carlos Lehder is co-operating," Quiñon said, adding, "This letter is to some degree the product of his solitary confinement."

But the letter made headlines in the next day's *Miami Herald*: AC-CUSED COLOMBIAN DRUG CHIEF'S OFFER TO COOPERATE DESCRIBED AS FRIVOLOUS. In the basement of the federal detention center in North Dade, George Jung read the story with disgust. It brought back the feelings of betrayal that he had harbored against Lehder for years. The FBI had contacted Jung in prison in 1986 with a proposal that he travel to Colombia and lure Lehder into a trap. Jung was willing, but unknown to the FBI he had his own plan for Lehder when they met: he intended to finally exact his revenge and try to kill his former partner. But before the plan could be implemented, Lehder was captured in Colombia. Jung was approached to testify, but he refused. He didn't want to be a snitch. (Jung was sitting in a federal jail cell, sentenced to fifteen years in prison for importing three hundred kilos of cocaine into the United States.) Now, if Lehder was going to start telling on his fellow smugglers, well, then Jung had a few things to tell, too. He called the FBI and later sat down to write a detailed letter about Carlos Lehder.

BY the time Carlos Lehder's trial finally opened on November 17, 1987, Merkle had amassed an enormous case that stretched from Dan-bury in 1974 to Medellín in 1985. Merkle's strategy was audacious. He had charted a course far beyond the charges listed in the Jackson-ville indictment, which only covered smuggling acts committed be-tween 1978 and 1980. Merkle planned to lay out Lehder's career as one big conspiracy to flood the United States with cocaine. The pros-ecutor sought to present the big picture of the Medellín cartel for the first time in an American courtroom.

Merkle's opening argument was appropriately grandiose:

"This case will take you back in time to 1974, and forward over the course of many years in which Carlos Lehder pursued a singular dream, a singular vision, to be the king of cocaine transportation," Merkle said, adding later, "He was to cocaine transportation what Henry Ford was to automobiles. . . .

"He saw America as a decadent society. He saw cocaine as the wave of the future in the United States, reeling from Watergate and Vietnam, particularly susceptible to the seductive allure of cocaine."

The next day, when it was Lehder's attorneys' turn, they called their client "Joe Lehder" and said he was just a cocky young Colombian kid set up by American marijuana smugglers.

"This case comes down to Joe versus the United States government," Ed Shohat said. "The conviction of Joe Lehder has become a cause célèbre like nothing seen in law enforcement."

Shohat said Lehder went to Norman's Cay to develop the island into a resort haven and befriended Ed Ward. When the DEA caught up with Ward, Shohat said, Ward lied about Lehder to get off.

"Joe Lehder was his own worst enemy," Shohat said. "He was a young, wealthy, brash Colombian, flamboyant to say the least. He did things that left him wide open for Ward's plans. . . . He confronted the DEA with his mouth."

For Carlos Lehder, the trial in Jacksonville must have seemed like one long nightmare version of *This Is Your Life*. Ed Ward had agreed to testify against Lehder back in 1981, never figuring he would have to make good on his promise. Now he was the key witness against Lehder. And after Lehder's arrest nine months earlier, witnesses from his past started coming out of the woodwork. George Jung's letter got the prosecution's attention, and he would be the first witness. Steve Yakovac surfaced, working as a foreign car mechanic in Fort Lauderdale. He, too, wrote a letter and was now set to testify. A number of Lehder's Norman's Cay cohorts rose like the dead from federal prison cells around the country. Richard Blankenship, a former naval aviator in World War II turned drug smuggler for Lehder, wanted to testify after reading in the newspaper that Lehder had threatened to kill American judges. "I'm an American convict," Blankenship said. "Mr. Lehder, no one, by threats to this country, is going to intimidate me." Long-buried secrets emerged in the Jacksonville courtroom. Eben Mann, a Continental Airlines pilot, testified he once flew loads for Lehder nine years earlier. Russ O'Hara, a California disc jockey who now did antidrug public service ads for his station, testified that he, too, had worked for Lehder. Walter Cronkite, now retired from his CBS anchor chair, was subpoenaed to testify about being run off Norman's Cay nearly a decade ago.

Jung took the stand first, recounting the whole story, beginning in Danbury and going through Norman's Cay to his last telephone call with Lehder in 1985. A small man with lanky brown hair and a heavily lined face, Jung at forty-five looked old and dissipated, the ravages of cocaine showing in his face. He had made and lost a fortune in cocaine, $10 million by his own count. He had lost his freedom. Now he testified like a man who had nothing left to lose. He smiled often while he spoke, finally feasting on the revenge that had eluded him for so many years.

"You could compare it to somebody at school taking your lunch money," Jung said in his Boston accent.

While Jung was on the stand, Merkle brought Barry Kane into the courtroom; Kane, the successful Massachusetts lawyer, had refused to testify for the government. Merkle had subpoenaed Kane so Jung could identify the silver-haired man in the $700 suit as the pilot who had flown Carlos Lehder's first big cocaine load.

Winny Polly, who had carried Carlos Lehder's suitcases with cocaine from Antigua to the United States, followed Jung. Polly was a hostile witness who had tried to meet with Lehder's lawyers before testifying to relay the message to Carlos that she did not want to take the stand against him.

"I held Mr. Lehder in the utmost respect and awe," Polly testified.

Under Merkle's questioning, she admitted to becoming a cocaine dealer for Lehder and then an addict, shooting cocaine into her veins.

Saddled with a cocaine habit and a longing for Lehder, Polly flew to Medellín to be near him and his family.

"Everybody's looking for love out there," she told Merkle.

Ed Ward was the key prosecution witness, spending a week on the stand. While Ward recounted his long tale of smuggling for Lehder on Norman's Cay, Carlos Lehder often shook his head in disgust.

Lehder at thirty-eight still retained some of his boyish good looks, but he had heavy bags under his eyes and the lack of sunlight made him deathly pale. With his neatly trimmed hair and tailored suits, he looked like a young banker sitting at the defense table next to Jose Quiñon. During testimony he rhythmically tapped his right hand against the table, sucked on candy, smiled at reporters whose faces he had become familiar with, and jotted notes into a spiral notebook with a felt-tip pen. Three U.S. marshals always sat directly behind him. Occasionally the static from their earpieces disturbed the courtroom quiet. Once the trial got started, efforts were undertaken to make the security less obvious. The only time a weapon could be glimpsed in the courtroom was when a marshal sat and crossed his legs, lifting his pants to reveal an ankle holster. After a while the press coverage dwindled down until only three reporters remained in the courtroom.

As court finished each day, the marshals took Lehder to a fifth-floor holding cell down a hallway and around the corner from the courtroom. The room had a nineteen-inch remote-control color television and a private bathroom. Lehder was allowed to make unlimited phone calls to anywhere within the United States and to order any food he wanted at any time during the day. For exercise, he had twenty-five-pound dumbbells, a treadmill, a stationary bicycle, and a small trampoline.

In the final week of the trial, Lehder could look out the window of his holding cell and gaze at a blue-and-red sign on a thirty-story glass skyscraper: "Southern Bell Says No to Drugs."

34.

NATIONAL SECURITY

On February 5, 1988, U.S. Attorney Leon Kellner announced a twelve-count federal indictment charging Panama's General Manuel Antonio Noriega with drug-related crimes dating back to 1982. "In plain language," Kellner told reporters in Miami, "what he did is utilize his position to sell the country of Panama to the traffickers." In addition to Noriega, the indictment listed fourteen other defendants, among them Pablo Escobar and his cousin Gustavo Gaviria. Jorge and young Fabio Ochoa were also named but not charged. Noriega, the indictment said, provided safe haven for cartel members, permitted them to set up a cocaine lab in Panama, helped them ship cocaine to the United States, and helped them obtain ether and acetone for their lab operations.

"Manuel Antonio Noriega and trusted associates were able to assure drug traffickers that Panamanian military, Customs, and law enforcement personnel would not interfere with their operations in Panama as long as substantial fees were paid to Manuel Antonio Noriega." If convicted on all charges, Noriega faced 145 years in prison and fines totaling $1.145 million.

THE federal grand jury had worked on the Noriega case for months, and the indictment had long been expected. Nonetheless Kellner's announcement had enormous political significance. Noriega had been Panama's de facto head of government since he took over leadership of the Panama Defense Forces in 1983. For most of that time he had also been a fast friend of the United States, capably fulfilling the only requirement that any U.S. government had ever had for any Panamanian leader: security for the Panama Canal. To that end the United

States demanded that Panama have a pro-American, stable political regime that did not object to having ten thousand U.S. military personnel permanently stationed in bases straddling the canal. So long as this formula was maintained, the United States seemingly overlooked all other sins.

The Miami indictment made it clear that the deal was off, but at first it was difficult to see why. The litany of conspiracies and racketeering outlined in the indictment included several items not generally known: Noriega's deals with Escobar at the end of 1982; the meeting in Havana to resolve the Darién misunderstanding; several specific cases in which Noriega was alleged either to have accepted cartel kickbacks or to have provided logistical support for cartel loads.

But Noriega's other supposed transgressions concerned incidents that had been public knowledge for years: the Darién lab; the cartel's presence in Panama following the Lara Bonilla assassination; the INAIR drug shipment; the death of Rubén Dario Paredes Jimenez in Medellín in March 1986. For news reporters and other knowledgeable observers working in the region, Noriega's inviolability had been manifest at least since 1984. The United States had always looked the other way. Why not now?

What had happened was that Noriega had broken the unwritten agreement: he could no longer guarantee Panama's political stability by 1988. Domestic opposition had grown out of control. During 1987 Panamanian police had put down several noisy and violent anti-Noriega demonstrations, and by 1988 the consensus in Panama was that Noriega was a politically corrupt drug dealer and a thief. Three weeks before the indictment, U.S. Secretary of State George Shultz said publicly that Noriega should "step back" from power. His usefulness as the guardian of U.S. interests in Panama was fast disappearing.

The Panama indictment touched an important nerve in the United States, sweeping aside years of controversy over U.S. policy in Central America. Drug trafficking had become such a compelling issue that conservative Republicans and liberal Democrats came together in an almost unanimous—and unprecedented—congressional condemnation of Noriega. Drug trafficking had become so politically important in the United States that it could no longer be ignored or shunted to the margin of international diplomacy. By 1988 the activities of the Medellín cartel were important enough to affect the way the U.S. government managed its national security interests.

Pablo Escobar, who had striven so hard for so long to be a politically important person, finally saw his dream come true in a way he could never have imagined or wanted. Noriega's indictment gave Escobar and the cartel more U.S. publicity than they had ever had. On February 15 *Newsweek* magazine published a cover story entitled "Drugs, Money and Death"; on March 7 *Time* featured "The Drug Thugs." Both magazines had Noriega on the cover. In mid-March, 48 percent of the respondents to a CBS News–*New York Times* poll said drug traffic was the most important international problem facing the United States, eclipsing Central America (22 percent) and arms control (13 percent). Democratic party presidential hopeful Jesse Jackson made drug trafficking the top item on his foreign policy agenda.

Just as important, the Panama indictment had suddenly and sharply limited U.S. policy options in at least one country where the United States had important and enduring interests. Before the indictment the United States was impatient with Noriega, hoping that he would leave power, trying to coax him to depart. After the indictment the United States was committed to Noriega's overthrow. The United States publicly and in a very messy way had accused one of its one-time favorite dictators of drug trafficking in collusion with the Medellín cartel. Unlike rigged elections and institutional corruption, the indictment could not be swept aside and ignored.

FIRST in February and again in April 1988, a U.S. Senate Foreign Relations subcommittee heard testimony on Panama and Central America from a swarm of witnesses that included former U.S. diplomats and military officers, former Noriega confidants, and flipped drug dealers and money launderers. "Stopping drug trafficking into the United States has been a secondary U.S. foreign policy objective," said Democratic Senator John Kerry, chairman of the hearings. "It has been sacrificed repeatedly for other political goals."

Several of the drug defendants-turned-informants said that the U.S.-backed contra rebels had at times used cartel money to finance their war against Nicaragua's Sandinista government. Although the allegations were unproved, contra involvement with the cartel was a legitimate question. Over the years the traffickers had done business with the FARC, the M-19, and half a dozen other Colombian guerrilla groups. There was no reason to think they wouldn't do the same thing with the contras. It was clear that the cartel had no politics. Governments tied to the cartel included Panama, Nicaragua, Cuba, and the Bahamas. Drug-corrupted police and public officials came from almost every nation in the hemisphere. Cocaine had corrupted both the Colombian guerrillas and government officials opposing them.

The Medellín cartel was marching across Central America, infecting governments far more readily than communism ever had. The hearings in Congress demonstrated that the United States had no coherent policy that examined the effects of drug trafficking on important questions of U.S. national security. Before the Panama indictment, the Reagan administration had noticed the Medellín cartel only once, during the Nicaragua case. The administration had sacrificed a groundbreaking drug investigation on that occasion and now, four years later, had to confront the same group of criminals in Panama. Now those criminals had put in jeopardy one of the most important U.S. bilateral relationships in Latin America.

THE many strands of the Medellín cartel story came together at the end of the Carlos Lehder trial. U.S. Attorney Robert Merkle presented the testimony of 115 prosecution witnesses over seven months. Several of the witnesses alleged that Lehder had paid off Bahamian officials; Gorman Bannister said his father, Everette, was receiving $100,000 a month from Lehder and giving it to his friend, Prime Minister Lynden O. Pindling. By the end of the trial Merkle's office was directing a grand jury investigation of Pindling.

Perhaps most damaging of all the testimony were the radio and television interviews Lehder gave in Colombia. These were among the last pieces of evidence presented to the jury. In a famous interview with Bogotá's Radio Caracól on June 28, 1983, Lehder said he would not deny helping out Colombia's smuggling "bonanza."

"That was our obligation, to bring the dollars back to our people however we could," Lehder said. "So then, that is it. It can be called Mafia, it can be called syndicate, it can be called a bonanza, it can be called whatever you like, but the truth is that it is a fact, and it is out in the open. In other words, Colombia would not be able to deny that it was the world's foremost producer of marijuana and cocaine."

Lehder blamed the drug problem on the United States, "where there are forty million marijuana smokers and twenty-five million cocaine consumers. . . . What I ask that they do is help the Colombian drug addict that they themselves corrupted. And that they help to combat drug addiction existing in Colombia. . . . "

The tapes were extraordinary. They displayed Carlos Lehder in all his colors: the facile mind, the ardent nationalist, the hardworking entrepreneur who had caught the big wave of his time. Most remarkable, they showed a cocaine kingpin trying to explain himself with something approaching honesty. He was, he said on the tapes, a victim of the environment, just "a poor Colombian peasant who has made something of himself." It was as if Al Capone were rationalizing his bootlegging on national television. And Lehder's description of Norman's Cay jibed with every informant's account of Lehder's dream: to provide a means to go beyond the suitcase smuggling of cocaine. But Lehder's tapes, though damning, did not amount to a confession. He always skirted the issue of his own guilt.

"I have never transported, uhh—drugs," he said. "It is just that my lands, the flexibility afforded by their location being two hundred miles from the United States, provided the opportunity for the Colombians, who were being trapped like flies over there with little suitcases and with little boxes, of going in there, by means of a different system, a different means, a different platform."

After Merkle finished presenting his case, Lehder's defense attorneys made a surprise announcement: they would rest their case without calling any witnesses. They would finish with the closing argument of Lehder's chief attorney, Ed Shohat.

The arguments for both sides began May 10, 1988. By coincidence it was national "Just Say No to Drugs" week. Also that day, a full-page ad paid by the Bahamian government ran in *The Miami Herald* and *The New York Times*. Titled "Setting the Record Straight," the ad extolled the Bahamas' war against drug trafficking and belittled the corruption allegations against Pindling.

"No new evidence with the slightest credibility has been forthcoming," the ad said. "Yet we have been besieged with allegations which are eight and nine years old."

Merkle had one and one-half days to make his closing argument. Then Shohat would speak. Merkle would be allowed to make a rebuttal, then the case would go to the jury.

In his argument, Merkle decided to hammer away at two themes he saw develop during the trial: the complicity of Americans in the rise of Carlos Lehder and the destructive nature of cocaine, which mirrored the desire to destroy in Lehder's own nature. In the smaller drama of the courtroom, cocaine had destroyed everyone it touched: George Jung, Winny Polly, Ed Ward, and, finally, Carlos Lehder himself. As Merkle saw it, the trial of Carlos Lehder was a reckoning, for both Lehder and the American people.

"Carlos Lehder and Henry Ford had a lot in common," Merkle began. "Henry Ford perfected the mass transportation of automobiles for the American consumer. Carlos Lehder perfected the mass transportation of cocaine for the American consumer. From there, the differences between the two men become marked. Mr. Ford sought to better the American consumer's way of life. Mr. Lehder sought to destroy the American consumer's way of life."

Merkle attacked the defense's portrayal of Lehder as a legitimate businessman, holding up a MAC-10. Would a legitimate businessman use such a weapon to protect his property?

Merkle described the witnesses against Lehder as "human wreckage" that bore the scars of their cocaine use. "You have seen tragedy upon tragedy come into this courtroom," Merkle said. "They were at war with society, together with Mr. Lehder. He's still at war. He hasn't stopped. . . . A trail of bribery, corruption, violence, and personal debasement has been created and fostered by Mr. Lehder with the help of those witnesses, and that wreckage exists in Colombia, the Bahamas, and the United States."

"That wreckage is the legacy of Mr. Lehder's children. That wreckage in Colombia and the Bahamas and the United States is an open wound, and that wound will not be healed by vengeance. That wound will only be healed by justice and truth and reconciliation."

At this point Merkle held up a coke spoon. He pointed out that one spoon of cocaine is equal to 1/30 of a gram. Carlos Lehder, Merkle pointed out, brought in eighteen million grams. Cut to 50 percent purity, that amounted to more than one billion snorts.

"Mr. Lehder was an opportunity waiting to meet another opportunity—the U.S. demand for drugs," Merkle said. He dismissed the idea that Lehder was an organizational genius. "His strength, ladies and gentlemen, was he was able to capitalize on the weakness of others . . . the disenchanted, the rogues, the crippled. He bought, charmed, or pushed aside all obstacles. He's finally come to a situation where he can't do that."

Shohat followed Merkle to the podium. As he had throughout the trial, he attacked the credibility of the prosecution witnesses. Where Merkle almost whispered, Shohat shouted at the jury. He gestured, he flailed, he became apoplectic with outrage on behalf of his client.

"This was a case in which the government brought into this courtroom twenty-nine bought witnesses," Shohat said, referring to the various plea bargains handed out to some in return for their testimony.

Then it was Merkle's turn again. At the very end of his rebuttal argument his tone changed, becoming circumspect, even gentle.

"Mr. Shohat yesterday told you I would have you believe that Mr. Lehder was the cause of America's drug problem. No, I do not suggest that. In fact, I suggest just the contrary.

"The striking side of this case, the striking story in this case, is that America, a substantial portion of America, has been an active partner with Mr. Lehder. While it is true, as Mr. Lehder told you on his own tapes, tragically, that his acts were motivated by hatred and bitterness against the United States, it is also true that all of Mr. Lehder's money and all of his guns and all of his power could not force American pilots to fly for him; could not force American businessmen to sell property to him; could not force aircraft salesmen to sell planes for cash; could not force victims of Mr. Lehder's crimes to inject cocaine into their arms, such as Winny Polly did, or to snort it up their noses.

"The story of this case is the story of an absence of love, an absence of responsibility, a fleeing from responsibility by the witnesses in this case and by Mr. Lehder.

"So your verdict is an act of reconciliation with truth, an act of reconciliation with the past. You have a duty and you have a privilege of returning a true verdict in this case, a duty which you must not shirk and you must not fear.

"Thank you."

Following Merkle's rebuttal, Judge Melton ordered the jury sequestered during their deliberations. After the jury had exited the courtroom, Carlos Lehder turned to the reporters in the spectator sections and held up a handwritten sign: "Just Say No to Racism."

THE Lehder jury did not reach a verdict after the first day of deliberation—or the second or the third. Finally, on the fourth day, they asked to have the tapes of Carlos Lehder's Colombian television interviews replayed for them.

The two tapes provide a portrait in miniature of Carlos Lehder defending himself, equivocating, rationalizing, smiling, and trying to place the blame elsewhere. It was as if Carlos Lehder were answering directly the final arguments of Bob Merkle. The interviews also showed a mind dissolving on cocaine.

First came the 1983 interview that Lehder gave the day after his Radio Caracól interview. He was dressed in a sport coat and turtleneck, his hair neatly trimmed in a shag.

The interviewer asked, "Any country, any nation, is based upon moral principles and, well, of course, that includes Colombia. Uhh—don't you think that those moral principles are more important than getting money?"

"The end justifies the means," Lehder said. "In order to get my country ahead, and those people that are—that were being persecuted, uh—the truth is that I'll hang my misgivings at the door before going into the house and then pick them up on the way out."

Next the jury watched the tape of the interview in the jungle in February 1985. Lehder sat on his thronelike chair, hair down to his shoulders. He was guarded by armed men wearing masks. There was a marked change in Lehder from the earlier interview. In contrast with the well-spoken businessman of two years earlier, he rambled and spoke in an agitated, frenetic manner.

"Cocaine has become and marijuana has become a revolutionary weapon in the struggle against North American imperialism," Lehder ranted. "Stimulants from Colombia are the Achilles' heel of imperialism. That's why the persecution against us is not legal, it is political."

He continued: "The drug phenomenon was brought into Colombia by U.S. imperialism via the Peace Corps. Nowadays the demand for drugs in the United States is such—right?—that the countries which produce it, such as Colombia—right?—play a truly minor role compared to the commercialization and the consumption incurred in the United States."

But his sloganeering failed to convince the young Colombian woman who interviewed him.

"Where did you get so much money if not from drug trafficking?" she asked.

"Very well, I, ever since I was very young, I went to the United States, I worked, I studied, right? Eventually, I was charged with marijuana conspiracy, I was placed in jail for two years," Lehder said.

"Was that true?" the interviewer asked.

"That was not true!" Lehder said. "I was a hippie, right? I smoked, of course. I was an adventurer, hey! But I was no trafficker. So then, in the jail in the United States . . . we were chained, like dogs, from the waist, right? Transported in trucks, uh, buses, let's say, from the penitentiaries, from Miami to New York and back again. That was, it was something horrible to see over five hundred Colombians—this was ten or twelve years ago, imprisoned, by imperialism."

"You didn't answer my question about where you got so much money if it was not from drug trafficking?" the interviewer asked.

"I, I am a pilot, right?" Lehder said. "And a very expensive one."

He smiled cryptically.

After forty-two hours of deliberations over seven days, the jury announced that it had reached a verdict at 11:10 A.M. on May 19. All parties assembled in the courtroom. Everyone seemed to be holding their breath when the verdict was announced.

Carlos Lehder was guilty on all counts. He looked down, showing no emotion. In the audience, his brother, Guillermo, was also stoical. His aunt wept. Three women on the jury also wept.

Afterward a very drained Ed Shohat attacked the jury's verdict as another indication that the drug war had eroded the constitutional rights of individuals. Saddest of all, he said, the verdict accomplished nothing.

"Until we take the problem out of the schoolyard, you can put all the Carlos Lehders you want in prison," Shohat said, "but the problem is it doesn't work. What have we accomplished? Do we have one gram of drugs less available to us because of this prosecution?"

Bob Merkle also held a press conference. Smiling broadly for the first time in a week, he strode up to the television cameras and said, "In the immortal words of James Brown, I feel good. This is a victory for the good guys, and by the good guys I mean the American people."

The verdict, he said, "reflects to people in other nations that we are a nation of laws and will not tolerate the violence of drug traffickers."

The verdict also meant the Medellín cartel had "nowhere to run, nowhere to hide. . . . I'm always an optimist. I think their days are numbered."

Someone asked what would be the effect on the drug trade.

"The war on drugs is not measured in terms of the amount of drugs that's seized," Merkle said. "It's a war of the human spirit . . . the real issue is will. The will of the American people versus the will of the cartel."

Merkle said the Medellín cartel would eventually be destroyed by its own penchant for violence. The rest, he said, was up to the American people.

"Carlos Lehder was an opportunity waiting to encounter an opportunity," Merkle said. "Carlos Lehder was in a very real sense the product of a lot of failures on this side, the American side.

"The Carlos Lehders of the world are going to have a narrower and narrower opportunity to wreak their crimes on this country. Carlos Lehder or anybody who takes his place can't put a gun to America's head and force it to take cocaine."

EPILOGUE

Carlos Lehder's sentencing took place on July 20, 1988. Lehder was allowed to speak to U.S. District Judge Howell Melton before the sentence was handed down. But it was a different Carlos Lehder from the one who had sat through the seven-month trial. Gone was the clean-shaven "businessman." Now he sported a full beard and mustache. He spoke in English for twenty-eight minutes without notes.

"I feel like an Indian in a white man's court," said Lehder. He called himself a political prisoner victimized by an ambitious federal prosecutor. He described his trial as "twenty-nine confessed criminals against one Latin. . . . Witnesses that never had a second underwear claimed they made millions from Lehder. . . . I was kidnapped from my own country with the complicity of some Colombia police officers. . . . I was flown against my will to this country. It's a far worse crime than any of these allegations.

"I am also against drug abuse. But I am also against kidnapping and extradition. This trial is illegal."

Then Judge Melton spoke.

"The truth of the matter is your main goal was to make money, and you did so at the expense of others," Melton said. "Your conspiracy burned a path of destruction and despair from the coca fields of South America to the streets and byways of this country. Accordingly, Mr. Lehder, the sentence I impose on you today is meant to be a message for drug smugglers who control large organizations for importers of cocaine and for street pushers.

"This sentence is a signal that our country will do everything in its power and within the laws to battle the drug problem that threatens the very fabric of our society."

Then he sentenced Lehder to the maximu   without parole plus 135 years.

PABLO Escobar also fell on hard times in 1988. A little before dawn January 13, a gigantic car bomb exploded outside the Monaco Building, a fancy eight-story apartment house owned by "the Godfather" in the upper-crust El Poblado section of Medellín. The bomb killed two night watchmen, dug a thirteen-foot-deep hole in the street, broke windows in dozens of nearby buildings, exploded water mains, and cracked the Monaco's concrete facade for its entire length. Escobar's wife, Victoria Eugenia, and his twelve-year-old son were sleeping in the Monaco's penthouse apartment when the bomb went off. They escaped in a Renault within five minutes of the blast. Escobar was not at home.

The Monaco explosion was the showcase event in the so-called War of the Cartels, a 1988 struggle for cocaine markets, power, and hegemony between Pablo Escobar and the "Cali cartel" led by Gilberto Rodriguez Orejuela and Jose Santacruz Londoño. Escobar originally blamed the DEA for the Monaco bombing, then decided that the Cali group was trying a power play to eliminate him and take over his networks. Still later he determined that he had a traitor within his own organization and began a ruthless housecleaning.

At the same time, the Colombian army mounted an Antioquia-wide manhunt and twice nearly captured Escobar. When the army failed to pursue the Cali traffickers with the same vigor, Escobar—according to some sources—once again decided that Cali was cooperating with the government in a vendetta against the Medellín cartel. He responded the only way he knew: by September 1988, the army reported eighty people murdered in the War between the Cartels. More than sixty were from Cali.

WHATEVER Escobar's problem, it was clear by early 1988 that Jorge Luis Ochoa did not share it. After his holiday departure from La Picota, Ochoa dropped from view. U.S. law enforcement received reports he had "stepped back" from everyday operations of his vast cocaine empire because his high profile made it almost impossible for him to work effectively in Colombia. Other sources, however, said Ochoa simply reverted to character. When the army's crackdown came, Escobar, as usual, attacked everything that stood in his way. Ochoa, also as usual, hunkered down.

Those who believed in the War of the Cartels blamed the Cali group for fingering Ochoa at the El Cerrito tollbooth in November 1987 and for murdering some higher-ups in his organization. Despite these provocations, however, most sources agreed that neither Ochoa nor his father, Fabio, nor his brothers Juan David and young Fabio were participating in the alleged vendetta.

LIKE Ochoa, Jose Gonzalo Rodriguez Gacha also had no axes to grind with Cali. Both U.S. and Colombian law enforcement agreed that 1988 was "the Mexican's" biggest and most profitable year. With Escobar occupied with gang war and Ochoa out of the picture, Rodriguez Gacha stepped from his colleagues' shadow to lead the Medellín cartel in an aggressive expansion into the southwestern United States and Europe.

U.S. lawmen also received reports that in the late spring of 1988 Rodriguez Gacha traveled to New York City in a bid to take over the Cali group's longtime distribution network there. His bigfooting in the New York City borough of Queens, some lawmen said, triggered a summer-long New York version of the War of the Cartels among local cocaine and crack dealers.

Others, however, maintained that Rodriguez Gacha was instrumental in reasonably successful efforts to mend fences between Escobar and Cali. The Queens venture, these sources contended, was simply a business deal—and Rodriguez Gacha, before anything else, was a businessman. In 1988 he joined Escobar and Ochoa for the first time in *Forbes* magazine's list of the world's billionaires.

ON November 30, 1987, DEA agents and U.S. marshals fanned out over Florida and seized $20 million in property allegedly owned by Pablo Escobar, Gustavo Gaviria, and Juan David Ochoa. Agents seized an $8 million apartment complex and a $1 million luxury estate in Miami Beach, both of which Escobar purchased in his own name in 1981 and later transferred to Panamanian corporations. The agents also seized Juan David's horse ranch in central Florida along with thirty-nine of his prize *caballos de paso* walking horses.

At the time of the seizures, the officers of the Panamanian corporations that held the Escobar properties included Escobar's wife and sister, Victoria Eugenia Henao de Escobar and Alba Marina Escobar. The two women did not appear in federal court in Miami to fight forfeiture claims.

. . .

GILBERTO Rodriguez Orejuela remained Cali's first lord of cocaine and recovered his early 1980s position as an immensely powerful—if no longer particularly well respected—businessman and entrepreneur. Escobar, it was rumored, thought Rodriguez Orejuela had cut a deal with the DEA to win his freedom, another reason for the War of the Cartels. And on August 18, 1988, arsonists torched the biggest Medellín outlet of Rodriguez Orejuela's Drogas Le Rebaja chain of drugstores. Despite these insults and provocations, Rodriguez did not respond.

JOSE Santacruz Londoño emerged in 1988 as the most visible member of the Cali group, the apparent manager of its cocaine interests both in the United States and Cali. It was Santacruz's ten-year-old Queens distribution network that Rodriguez Gacha allegedly targeted for takeover. Many lawmen in both United States and Colombia agree that if there really is a War of the Cartels, Santacruz will probably fight the Cali side of it.

RAFAEL Cardona Salazar was gunned down inside his antique car dealership outside Medellín on December 4, 1987, just three days after *The Miami Herald* printed a lengthy account of his relationship with Max Mermelstein. Cardona, thirty-five, died in a spray of automatic weapons fire by assassins who also killed his twenty-eight-year-old secretary. Later, Colombian police speculated the Cardona murder was a Cali job, the first killing in the War of the Cartels. The case remains unsolved.

BOB Merkle did not attend the sentencing of Carlos Lehder. Five weeks after Lehder's May 19, 1988, conviction, Merkle resigned as U.S. attorney for the Middle District of Florida to run for the Republican nomination to the U.S. Senate.

Starting late with scant campaign funds, Merkle trailed his opponent, Republican Congressman Connie Mack III, throughout the nine-week race. Mack, grandson of the legendary Philadelphia Athletics baseball manager, enjoyed the endorsement of President Reagan and the support of Florida's Republican party establishment. Mack spent $37,000 of his campaign funds to bring in Oliver North, who by then had been indicted in the Iran-contra scandal, to speak at campaign stops. Mack refused to debate Merkle, who took to appearing with a life-size cardboard poster of Mack and posing his own questions to the opponent.

On September 5 Mack crushed Merkle in the Republican primary with 62 percent of the vote, 399,022 to 247,336.

GEORGE Jung was rewarded for his testimony in the Lehder trial with a Rule 35 hearing before a federal judge in Fort Lauderdale in September 1988. His fifteen-year sentence was reduced to time served. While he was in prison, Jung wrote a book about his exploits in the drug trade called *Grazing in the Grass Until the Snow Came*. He now says his only regret is that he told Carlos Lehder about his California connection. "I'm just sorry I got screwed out of my $200 million," he said in a recent interview. But he is proud that his ten-year-old daughter participates in the "Just Say No to Drugs" program. He still thinks often of his former partner. "I know that he's going to come after me," Jung said. "He has the money, and money is power."

DOUG Driver, the DEA agent who was the lead investigator in the Carlos Lehder case, received the Justice Department's highest honor, the Attorney General's Award for Exceptional Service, during a ceremony in Washington in August 1988. Attorney General Edwin Meese praised the forty-one-year-old agent for "unrelenting pursuit of every aspect of the Medellín cartel." Ten years had passed since Driver began the investigation that eventually led to Lehder.

STANFORD Bardwell resigned as U.S. attorney for the Middle District of Louisiana only a few months after the murder of Barry Seal. Bardwell took a job as deputy general counsel with the Department of Energy in Washington. He said his leaving had nothing to do with the handling of the Barry Seal matter.

FRANK Polozola remained a federal district court judge in Baton Rouge. He has never spoken publicly on the Seal case, refusing all requests from the media for comment.

. . .

JOHN Camp, the WBRZ-TV reporter who produced the *Uncle Sam Wants You* documentary on Seal, won a Sigma Delta Chi Distinguished Service Award, widely considered the highest honor in journalism after the Pulitzer Prize, for his reporting on Seal. The next year, Camp won a second Distinguished Service Award for his reporting on the state of Louisiana's penchant for settling million-dollar law suits. He remains convinced that Barry Seal had a genuine change of heart after years of smuggling and did not engage in drug trafficking after he became a DEA informant.

ON October 5, 1986, eight months after Barry Seal's murder, the C-123K cargo plane once used by Seal to fly cocaine out of Nicaragua was shot down as it carried arms to contra rebels fighting inside Nicaragua. The Sandinistas captured the lone survivor of the flight, Eugene Hasenfus. Within months the flight was exposed as a CIA-supported resupply mission in violation of congressional prohibitions, one of a series of revelations that culminated in November 1986 with the disclosure by Attorney General Meese that money from arms sold secretly to the Iranians had been illegally funneled to the contras. In the ensuing media frenzy, convicted drug dealers in south Florida claimed they had participated in the secret contra resupply network trading arms for drugs. The claims were never substantiated, but speculation emerged in some quarters that Seal was part of this network and his mission to Nicaragua was a CIA-led effort to frame the Sandinistas. No evidence has yet emerged that Seal's mission was anything but a legitimate DEA operation compromised by Reagan administration officials seeking to score a propaganda coup against the Sandinistas at a time when Congress was debating contra aid.

WITHIN a year after Seal's death, Jake Jacobsen, the lead investigator on the Barry Seal case, left the DEA to return to the U.S. Customs Service. In the summer of 1988 he testified before the House Judiciary Committee's Subcommittee on Crime, speaking behind a screen to conceal his identity. Jacobsen said that the DEA in Miami had refused a request from the CIA to release the photos Seal had taken of Escobar and a Nicaraguan official loading Seal's plane with cocaine in Nicaragua. "The CIA at Langley wanted to release them to the press," Jacobsen said. "We were in the middle of the most significant investigation of my career. We had a chance to get together all the cartel members." Ron Caffrey, former head of the DEA's cocaine desk, and Frank Monastero, former DEA assistant administrator, also testified. Asked why the DEA had not investigated the leak that destroyed the Seal mission, Monastero said the decision to leak may have been made at "a very high place" in government. "There may have been a conscious decision to disclose the information to the press. If that were the case, there would be no need to investigate," Monastero said. Dewey Clarridge, the CIA official who had been briefed about Seal's mission along with Oliver North, refused to testify before the subcommittee. Clarridge had been head of the CIA's Central American task force at the time of the Seal mission. North, who at the time was under indictment for his role in the Iran-contra affair, also refused to testify.

BOB Martinez left the U.S. Attorney's Office in Miami in 1986 to return to private practice.

CAROL Cooper was promoted in 1987, becoming one of the three women supervisors among the DEA's more than 2,500 agents.

DESPITE overwhelming support from the prosecutors working under him, Dick Gregorie was passed over when a replacement was picked for the outgoing U.S. attorney in Miami in 1988. He remained in the office as chief assistant U.S. attorney.

AFTER testifying at the Barry Seal murder trial, Max Mermelstein went on to appear at the trial of two Colombians accused of laundering $21 million for the cartel in Miami. Although Mermelstein had never met the Colombians and had no connection with the case, he was allowed to testify as an expert witness on the cartel. Holding a classroom pointer and referring to a chalkboard, Mermelstein interpreted figures and names found on the cartel accounting ledgers seized by agents. The two defendants were convicted.

Six months later, Customs and FBI agents rounded up the ring of pilots and powerboaters that had served as Mermelstein's cocaine transporters. The agents arrested fourteen people, including the promoter of the Gran Prix of Palm Beach. The ring was charged with using what Customs agents called "the most sophisticated methods we've yet seen" to import more than ten tons of cocaine for the Medellín cartel.

Along with sixteen of his relatives, Mermelstein was enrolled in the federal Witness Protection Program. He now lives under a new identity in a remote area in the United States.

LEWIS Tambs began a new assignment as U.S. ambassador to Costa Rica in July 1985. In 1986 the U.S. Attorney's Office in Miami investigated rumors that the anti-Sandinista contra rebels had picked up a Medellín cartel contract to murder Tambs. Tambs was never harmed, but he was forced to resign in January 1987, when he was named as having helped U.S. National Security Council aide Oliver North set up an illicit contra resupply network in Costa Rica. Testifying before Congress in May 1987, Tambs said he had reported his actions to his boss, Assistant Secretary of State Elliot Abrams, at the time they occurred. Abrams later denied knowledge of Tambs's activities. After his testimony Tambs returned to his history professorship at Arizona State University.

JOHNNY Phelps was head of the DEA's Cocaine Investigations Section in Washington for about a year. In late 1985 he took a new assignment as head of the Office of International Programs. He stayed for two years and in early 1988 moved to Miami, Florida, as the DEA's associate special agent-in-charge. He remained one of the DEA's most highly regarded officials.

ERROL Chavez left Colombia in 1983 to spend eight months with a DEA street group in Houston, Texas. Then he was promoted to group supervisor and sent to New York City, where he spent two years pursuing Albanian heroin traffickers. In March 1987 he was transferred to the DEA's Cocaine Investigations Section in Washington. In 1988 he was assigned full-time to gather and evaluate intelligence on the Medellín cartel and to make cases against its members.

AFTER closing the DEA's Medellín bureau, Mike Vigil took over as resident agent-in-charge in Barranquilla on Colombia's Caribbean coast. In October 1986 he was transferred to Miami and promoted to group supervisor. Like many of his colleagues, he remained in contact with events in Colombia by talking by telephone to friends in Colombia law enforcement.

AFTER surrendering the sash of office to Virgilio Barco in 1986, Belisario Bentancur retired from public life to write occasional newspaper columns and to pursue an active, behind-the-scenes role in the Social Conservative party (the word "Social" was added to the party's name in 1987). In mid-1988 he still traveled in an escorted armored car and had a twenty-four-hour-a-day security force guarding his modest north Bogotá home.

LESS than three weeks after a cartel killer shot him in the face in Budapest, Enrique Parejo Gonzalez was elected chairman of the thirty-second United Nations Commission on Narcotics Drugs. The Foreign Ministry reassigned him to Prague as ambassador to Czechoslovakia. Parejo continued to espouse a hard line, both abroad and in Colombia. In late 1987 he appeared heavily escorted in Medellín, where he gave a speech and departed unmolested.

FOUR months after the cartel's gunmen tried unsuccessfully to kidnap him, Juan Gomez Martinez, editor of Medellín's venerable *El Colombiano* newspaper, was elected mayor of the hemisphere's most violent city. He promised to "look for a dialogue" with the cocaine traffickers, but by August 1988 he admitted that the alleged War of the Cartels had practically made the city unliveable. In 1988 Medellín was averaging nine murders a day.

COLOMBIAN National Police Major William Lemus Lemus left Colombia within ten days of having captured Carlos Lehder. He was given diplomatic status as a "police attaché" and put in a makework job in a foreign city. Trying to live on a police major's salary augmented by a small stipend, Lemus in mid-1988 was reported having financial difficulties. The Colombian government was not contemplating bringing him home at any time soon, and Lemus was unhappy. Instead of fame, promotion, and success, his capture of Carlos Lehder had put William Lemus in a prison of his own.

. . .

ROBERTO Suarez Gomez, Bolivia's Black Swan, made the mistake of airing his views too publicly and too often. Fed up with his antigovernment speeches on radio and television, Bolivian police in July 1988 trekked through the northeastern Beni jungles to surprise and arrest him at his hacienda. He was sent to a La Paz jail to serve a fifteen-year sentence for drug trafficking.

GENERAL Manuel Antonio Noriega, the cartel's friend in Panama, teetered and nearly fell from power in March 1988 when widespread street demonstrations were accompanied by a wave of strikes and an attempted coup d'état by some of Noriega's own officers. Noriega took quick action to shore up his power within the army, then rebuffed countless attempts of U.S. diplomats to negotiate his departure. Late in 1988 Noriega was solidly in control, but Panama, crippled by months of economic slowdown and stagnation, was falling apart around him. His survival was by no means assured.

LYNDEN Pindling was reelected to his sixth consecutive term in July 1987 and has been prime minister of the Bahamas since 1967. Pindling and the Progressive Liberal party he heads have held power in the Bahamas ever since the island nation was granted independence from Great Britain in 1973. A federal grand jury investigation of Pindling continued in Orlando supervised by the office of the U.S. attorney for the Middle District of Florida in the summer of 1988. After *The Miami Herald* and *The Washington Post* printed stories on the investigation, the White House announced that future indictments of foreign leaders would have to be approved by the president, a marked change from the Justice Department procedure that led to the indictment of General Noriega. By the fall of 1988, with Bob Merkle gone, the Pindling grand jury was said to have foundered.

NOTES

Chapter 1: DADELAND

PAGE 9 They left a loaded 9-mm Browning automatic pistol. Carl Hiaasen and Al Messerschmidt, "The Cocaine Wars," *Rolling Stone,* 20 September, 1979, pp. 82–82.

PAGE 10 One leveled a silenced .380 Beretta automatic. Philip Ward, "U.S. Implicates Smuggler in '79 Dadeland Shoot-Out," *The Miami Herald,* 21 May, 1984, p. 1B.

PAGE 10 Morgan Perkins, an eighteen-year-old. Edna Buchanan, "Assassins Open Fire in Store," *The Miami Herald,* 12 July, 1979, p. 1A.

PAGE 10 Another man in the cab spied Perkins. Hearings before the U.S. Senate Permanent Subcommittee on Investigations, "Organized Crime and the Use of Violence," 2 and 5 May, 1980.

PAGE 11 Oh, shit, here we go again. Interviews with Al Singleton, 9 June and 30 December, 1987. Singleton, who later went on to investigate the Dadeland killings as part of a federal task force, Centac 26, provided both a personal account of what he saw on the day of the killings and details contained in the official police report.

PAGE 11 The operative theory involved a rivalry. Carl Hiaasen and Al Messerschmidt, "Shoot-Out at the Cocaine Corral," *The Miami Herald,* 8 July, 1979, p. 1A.

PAGE 13 Less than three months before the Dadeland shooting. Allen Levy and Rick Hirsch, "Gun Battle Shatters South Dade Noon Hour," *The Miami Herald,* 24 April, 1979, p. 1B.

PAGE 13 Less than a month after the shooting. Carl Hiaasen and Al Messerschmidt, "El Loco, Commando in Cocaine Wars Specializes in Getting Away," *The Miami Herald,* 22 July, 1979, p. 1B.

PAGE 13 Al Singleton turned south at the Palmetto Expressway. Singleton interviews with authors.

PAGE 15 The killers had planned to escape. Edna Buchanan, "Death Machine Drove Killers to the Scene," *The Miami Herald,* 12 July, 1987.

PAGE 15 Since Jimenez was hit in the face. Edna Buchanan, "Killers Got to Drug Chief First," *The Miami Herald,* 14 July, 1979.

PAGE 15 His death was believed to be retaliation. Kate Wheeler, "Killings Believed Part of Drug Feud," *The Miami Herald,* 29 May, 1979.

PAGE 15 The theory went that Panello feared Jimenez's wrath. This is based on various sources, including confidential interviews with present and former Metro-Dade homicide detectives, DEA agents, and a 1987 prison interview with Rafael Leon "Amilcar" Rodriguez, a notorious killer of the cocaine cowboy era in south Florida.

Chapter 2: THE NEW BREED

PAGE 18 By the middle of the 1980s. By 1986 U.S. law enforcement regularly affirmed that the Medellín cartel controlled 80 percent of the cocaine entering the United States. See, however, Mario Arango Jaramillo and Jorge Child Velez, *Los Condenados de la Coca*, Editorial J. M. Arango, Medellín, 1985, p. 99, which reprints the cartel's famous 1984 letter to President Belisario Betancur saying its members controlled "between 70 and 80 percent" of all the cocaine produced in Colombia. Based on cartel production records seized at Tranquilandia and a six-month study of cocaine seizures in the United States, the authors determined that the cartel easily produced and distributed more than 50 percent of U.S. cocaine by the mid-1980s.

PAGE 19 The first Colombian cocaine trafficker. Authors' interview with a knowledgeable DEA agent who asked not to be identified, 24 September, 1987; official law enforcement documents made available to the authors in Miami by sources who did not wish to be identified.

PAGE 19 Blanco was short. Metro-Dade Homicide Section Memorandum, "Colombian Activities Intelligence Information," 6 March, 1981.

PAGE 20 At first glance the city. Material on setting and geography of the city gathered during a visit by the authors in December 1986; see also James J. Parsons, *Antioqueño Colonization in Western Colombia*, rev. ed., Berkeley, CA: University of California Press, 1968, for the historical geography of Antioquia; Agustín Jaramillo Londoño's *Testamento del Paisa*, Medellín: Agustin Jaramillo Londoño, seventh ed., 1986, is a fine introduction to *paisa* customs and folklore.

PAGE 21 This was where Colombia's. Information on Chilean cocaine traffic comes mainly from the authors' interview with DEA agent Charlie Cecil, 24 September, 1987, who worked in Chile in the early 1970s. Cecil also provided a large cache of newspaper clippings and documents detailing the Chilean industry and the early days in Colombia. The principal Chile-based trafficker was Adolfo Tobias Sobosky, captured by Pinochet's police in the Pacific coast city of Arica, the center of the Chilean cocaine business, and sent to New York, where he was arrested. The Chilean newspaper *La Tercera de la Hora*, 13 November, 1973, reported Sobosky subsequently named some twenty other Chilean traffickers who were later arrested and deported.

PAGE 22 From the beginning. Cecil interviews, Cecil documents. The first notorious Colombian cocaine trafficker was Benjamin Herrera Zuleta, "the Black Pope." He was first arrested in June 1973 at Miami Airport with a kilo of cocaine. Paroled from federal prison in 1975, he dropped out of site in 1980. On December 15, 1987, DEA agents arrested him outside Fort Lauderdale, Florida, on a Las Vegas, Nevada, cocaine trafficking warrant. See Guy Gugliotta " 'Black Pope' of Cocaine Is Captured in Davie," *The Miami Herald*, 16 December, 1987, p. 1A.

PAGE 24 In studying Griselda Blanco. The descriptive word "floater" is from authors' interview with a DEA intelligence source who asked not to be identified, 29 July, 1987.

PAGE 24 One of the rising newcomers. The daily newspaper *El Espectador*, Bogotá, 25 August, 1983, reprints 1976 DAS story describing Escobar as a "mule."

PAGE 24 And Escobar looked like nothing. Physical description of Escobar from confidential Colombian narcotics police documents examined by the authors 28 August, 1987.

PAGE 24 Escobar was born December 1, 1949. Details of early career from authors' interviews with Colombian narcotics police sources who asked not to be identified, December 1986.

PAGE 25 After high school. Authors' interview with DEA agent Errol Chavez, 2 December, 1987.

PAGE 25 Escobar's first known. *El Espectador*, 25 August, 1983; see also Fabio Castillo, *Los Jinetes de la Cocaina*, Documentos Periodisticos, Bogotá, 1987, pp. 54–65.

PAGE 25 Ochoa was the second. *Semana* magazine, Bogotá, 1 December, 1987; authors' interview with DEA agent Errol Chavez, 28–29 July, 1987; authors' interview with a DEA intelligence source who asked not to be identified, 27 July, 1987.

PAGE 26 Ochoa went to Miami. DEA 6 report, "Controlled Delivery of Approximately 60 Lbs. of Cocaine," 19 October, 1977. Ochoa was in Miami officially as secretary and director of the SEA-8 Trading Corp., 7403 N.W. 7th St. At the time, Ochoa lived in Miami at 8600 S.W. 67th Ave., Apt. 914.

PAGE 27 "Jorge Ochoa is currently residing in Medellín." DEA 6 report, "Requested Information on Fabio Restrepo," 31 July, 1978.

Chapter 3: THE DREAM OF DANBURY

PAGE 29 Lehder found himself bunked next to George Jung. Testimony of George Jung, United States of America v. Carlos Lehder Rivas, United States District Court, Middle District of Florida, 17–19 November, 1987. Authors' interviews with George Jung, August 1988.

PAGE 31 As soon as he reached Medellín. Testimony of Frank Shea, U.S. v. Lehder, 13–14 April, 1988.

PAGE 33 Winny was so smitten with Carlos. Testimony of Winny Polly, U.S. v. Lehder, 23 November, 1987.

PAGE 34 Jung told Kane that he and Carlos Lehder. Jung testimony. Barry Kane has never been charged with a crime. Jung identified him as the man who flew Carlos Lehder's first cocaine load at the Lehder trial in November 1987. Kane refused a request for an interview by the authors.

PAGE 35 He and five thousand other inmates. Description of prison based on the testimony of Stephen Yakovac, U.S. v. Lehder, 14–16 December, 1987.

PAGE 35 Stephen Yakovac was a onetime auto mechanic. Yakovac testimony.

PAGE 36 Out of prison, Lehder called George Jung. Jung testimony and interviews.

Chapter 4: THE BAHAMAS PIPELINE

PAGE 42 The dream of smuggling cocaine. Jung testimony, U.S. v. Lehder, 17–19 November, 1987.

PAGE 43 He was consuming five to eight grams a day. Jung interviews, August 1988.

PAGE 43 *1987 Yachtsmans' Guide to the Bahamas*, p. 284. Testimony of Charles Kehm, former island manager of Norman's Cay, U.S. v. Lehder, 9–10 December, 1987.

PAGE 44 Beckwith demanded the money be counted. Testimony of Charles Beckwith, U.S. v. Lehder, 17 December, 1987.

PAGE 44 Later that year Lehder appeared. Testimony of Guardian Trust accountant Graham Cooper, U.S. v. Lehder, 13 April, 1988.

PAGE 45 CBS News anchorman Walter Cronkite. Testimony of Walter Cronkite, U.S. v. Lehder. Interview with Cronkite, 28 January, 1988.

PAGE 45 Philip Kniskern, who owned three vacation villas. Testimony of Philip Kniskern, U.S. *v.* Lehder, 17 December, 1987.

PAGE 45 Richard Novak, a college professor who leased a diving business. Testimony of Richard Novak, Bahamian Royal Commission of Inquiry report, December 1984. The three-member Royal Commission was appointed by the governor-general of the Bahamas in November 1983 to investigate allegations of drug corruption in the islands made in a September 5, 1983, broadcast by NBC News reporter Brian Ross and producer Ira Silverman. From November 1983 to December 1984, the commission heard testimony from more than five hundred witnesses on a number of drug-related matters, including Lehder's operations on Norman's Cay.

PAGE 46 One of those ordered off Norman's Cay was Charles Kehm. Testimony of Charles Kehm, U.S. *v.* Lehder, 9–10 December, 1987.

PAGE 46 The hairdresser knew a hulking marijuana pilot. Testimony at U.S. *v.* Lehder of John Finley Robinson, 7–8 December, 1987, and Russ O'Hara, 9 December, 1987.

PAGE 47 "I couldn't speak," Yakovac wrote. Diary of Steven Yakovac, U.S. *v.* Lehder. Yakovac's diary was discovered in the possession of his ex-wife, now living in the northwestern United States, in 1987.

PAGE 47 Lehder was returning to Colombia. Testimony of Yakovac, U.S. *v.* Lehder.

PAGE 50 As Carlos Lehder's business boomed in the Bahamas. Jung interview, August 1988.

PAGE 51 A few months later, a forty-nine-year-old Nassau businessman. Testimony of Norman Solomon, U.S. *v.* Lehder, 2 February, 1988. Royal Commission testimony, 1984. Interview with Michael Whiteley, " 'Curious' Englishman Made Drug Rumor Fact," *The Jacksonville Times-Union*, 7 February, 1981.

Chapter 5: THE KING OF COCAINE TRANSPORTATION

PAGE 53 Ward was an ex-marine. Testimony of Edward Hayes Ward, U.S. *v.* Lehder, 19–21, 25–27, 28, January, and 9–10 February, 1988.

PAGE 53 The Ward gang set about flying 1,200-pound loads of marijuana. Ward testimony at Royal Commission of Inquiry, 1984.

PAGE 54 One day a neighbor kid. Laura Griffin and Larry Hand, "Lehder Connection to Jacksonville Began in Late '70s," *The Jacksonville Times-Union*, 15 February, 1987, p. 1A.

PAGE 54 The DEA became interested after one of Greg Von Eberstein's brothers paid cash out of a paper bag. Interview with DEA special agent Doug Driver, 19 May, 1988.

PAGE 54 He thought he had come up with a foolproof way to smuggle. Testimony of Emilie "Lassie" Ward, U.S. *v.* Lehder, 14–16 March, 1988.

PAGE 54 Ward was worried that Lehder would think. Ed Ward testimony.

PAGE 55 In late August 1978, Greg Von Eberstein brought. Lassie Ward testimony.

PAGE 55 On September 6, 1978, eight of them had a meeting. This account is based on the testimony of Ed Ward, Charles Gregory Von Eberstein, 8–10 March, 1988, and Leverette Merrill Francis, 29 February and 1 March, 1988.

PAGE 56 Ward, the straight-arrow ex-marine, was getting. Lassie Ward testimony.

PAGE 57 As the Wards left Jacksonville. Michael Whitely, "Indictment Details Drug Case Charges," *The Jacksonville Times-Union*, 9 February, 1981, p. 1B.

PAGE 57 On the afternoon of September 13, 1979, Ed Ward took off. This account of the raid is based on Ed and Lassie Ward's testimony at the Lehder trial and the Royal Commission report, pp. 43–45, 115–123.

PAGE 60 Lehder offered to sell his entire operation. Ad appeared in *The Miami Herald,* October 1979.

PAGE 60 In the wake of the raid, the ad was strange enough. Arnold Markowitz, "Resort Island and Mystery up for Sale," *The Miami Herald,* 19 October, 1979, p. 1A; Markowitz, "Drug Fugitive Owns Mysterious Norman's Cay," *The Miami Herald,* 24 October, 1979, p. 7D.

PAGE 61 The Bahamas in 1979 was a nation for sale. Carl Hiaasen and Jim McGee, "A Nation for Sale," six-day series in *The Miami Herald,* 23–28 September, 1984.

PAGE 62 A DEA informant later said Bowe. Testimony of Tom Harney, U.S. *v.* Lehder, 12–13 January, 1988.

PAGE 62 Another informant eventually charged. Testimony of George Baron, U.S. *v.* Lehder, 11, 16–17 February, 1988.

PAGE 62 Lehder gave the money to Bowe. Testimony of Gorman Bannister, U.S. *v.* Lehder, 24 February, 1988.

PAGE 62 Mysterious things continued to happen near Norman's Cay. Al Messerschmidt, "Man Slain: Sea Mystery Investigated," *The Miami Herald,* 2 August, 1980; Messerschmidt, "Blood, Signs of Damage Deepen Mystery at Sea," *The Miami Herald,* 3 August, 1980; Carl Hiaasen, "Bloody Cruise in the Bahamas, Mystery Shrouds Couple's Fate," *The Miami Herald,* 1 September, 1980, p. 1A.

PAGE 62 Lehder had sent out his armed German bodyguards. Baron testimony.

PAGE 63 He told one of the smugglers. Harney testimony.

PAGE 63 Jung wanted to distribute cocaine. Jung testimony and interviews.

PAGE 64 He retained the services of Nigel Bowe. Ed and Lassie Ward testimony. Bowe was later indicted on cocaine trafficking charges in the United States in 1985. A U.S. request for his extradition from the Bahamas had wended its way through several appeals in Bahamian courts and fallen before the Privy Council in London by late 1988.

PAGE 65 Gail Von Eberstein told her husband. Gregory Von Eberstein testimony.

PAGE 65 It was clearly time to go. John Finley Robinson testimony.

PAGE 66 Lehder told the pilot he was running a very successful operation. Testimony of Jack Devoe, U.S. *v.* Lehder, 30–31 March, 1988.

PAGE 66 Lehder's symbolic public shower of money on the Bahamas. Royal Commission report, p. 46.

Chapter 6: MIAMI 1982

PAGE 67 In 1979 the Federal Reserve Bank of Miami reported a $5.5 billion cash surplus. Andy Rosenblatt, "Operation Draws Dollars from Drug Business," *The Miami Herald,* 9 April, 1981, p. 1A.

PAGE 68 Early that year Greenback agents searched the Landmark Bank branch. Mary Voboril, "Plot Bared to Launder Drug Cash," *The Miami Herald,* 11 February, 1981, pp. 1B, 2B.

PAGE 68 Three weeks later the agents raided two Miami banks. Andy Rosenblatt, "Feds Raid Two Miami Banks in Drug-Money Investigation," *The Miami Herald,* 28 February, 1981, pp. 1A, 13A.

PAGE 68 Kattan, forty-six, drove a Chevy Citation. Anders Gyllenhaal, "Drug Funds and S. Florida's 'Al Capone,' " *The Miami Herald,* 24 May, 1981, pp. 1A, 12A.

PAGE 69 Nobody followed the trails up the pyramid of the cocaine trade. Interviews with Assistant U.S Attorney Dick Gregorie and former Assistant U.S. Attorney Bob Dunlop, April 1988.

PAGE 70 Opposing the government's lawyers was an armada. Carl Hiaasen, "The Drug Lawyers," *The Miami Herald*'s Tropic Magazine, 28 June, 1981, p. 22.

PAGE 71 A vigorous leader who projected a can-do image. Interviews with Assistant U.S. Attorney Mark Schnapp and former Assistant U.S. Attorney Roberto Martinez, July 6, 1987.

PAGE 71 The three Customs inspectors had no idea. Account of the TAMPA bust is based on interviews with Vann Capps, Jerry Dranghon, Mark Schnapp, and Robert Dunlop in 1986, 1987, and 1988.

PAGE 71 Inspector Tony Knapik pushed a short screwdriver. Fred Grimm and Richard Wallace, "3,600 Pounds of Cocaine Seized at Airport," *The Miami Herald*, 10 March, 1982, p. 1A.

PAGE 72 The kilos were wrapped in yellow plastic. Grimm and Wallace, *The Miami Herald*, 10 March, 1982.

PAGE 73 The DEA determined the cocaine represented. Interviews with confidential sources.

Chapter 7: JOHNNY PHELPS

PAGE 74 Johnny Phelps arrived. Authors' interviews with Johnny Phelps, 30 July, 21 December, 1987.

PAGE 77 The traffickers were career criminals. For general background on Colombia and La Violencia, see Mario Arrubla et al, *Colombia, Hoy*, 4a. edicion, Siglo Veinte Editores, Bogotá, 1979.

PAGE 78 Phelps's resident agent. Authors' interviews with DEA agent Errol Chavez, 28–29 July, 1987.

PAGE 81 What Chavez didn't know. Authors' interviews with Phelps and Chavez.

PAGE 81 Phelps needed some way. Authors' interviews with Phelps.

PAGE 81 Neither man was badly hurt. Authors' interviews with Chavez and DEA agent Herb Williams, August 1987. The phrase "takes care of business" is Williams's. Details of the agents' kidnapping from hearings of the President's Commission on Organized Crime, "Organized Crime and Cocaine Trafficking," 27–29 November, 1984.

PAGE 81 The heat was Johnny Phelps. Authors' interviews with Errol Chavez.

Chapter 8: THE CARTEL'S GOLDEN AGE

PAGE 82 On April 18, 1981, just before Johnny Phelps arrived. Details of Hacienda Veracruz meeting from the United States of America v. Pablo Escobar Gaviria, et al, United States District Court, Southern District of Florida, 18 November, 1986.

PAGE 83 The realignment in Colombia. Authors' interviews with DEA agent Errol Chavez, 27–28 July, 1987.

PAGE 84 The few who wouldn't go along. Authors' interviews with Errol Chavez. On decline and fall of Griselda Blanco, see also the daily newspaper *El Tiempo*, Bogotá, 28 September, 1980; also *El Tiempo*, 21 September, 1981.

PAGE 84 Escobar and the rest of Los Pablos. Property records from Broward and Dade counties; see also *The Miami Herald*, 4 December, 1987.

PAGE 84 Jorge Ochoa's father had left. Authors' interviews with Errol Chavez.

PAGE 86 Among those living it up. Details of Carlos Lehder's return to Colombia from authors' visit to Armenia and interviews there with Leonel Cabezas Linz, Liliana Garcia Osorio, Javier Rivas, and other sources who asked not to be identified, 9–10 November, 1987. Hereinafter described as "Armenia interviews." See also George Stein, "Cocaine Kingpin Flees Colombia," *The Miami Herald*, 18 September, 1983, p. 1A, and Guy Gugliotta, "Hometown Is Still Spellbound by Lehder," *The Miami Herald*, 16 November, 1987, p. 1A.

PAGE 86 In November 1978. Best account of the airplane affair from Jorge Eliecer Orozco, *Lehder . . . El Hombre*, Bogotá: Plaza & Janes Editora, 1987, pp. 26–62.

PAGE 87 Lehder himself began. Armenia interviews.

PAGE 88 "I worked in restaurants." Armenia interviews, remembered by Leonel Cabezas.

PAGE 88 Lehder's presence in Armenia. Armenia interviews.

PAGE 88 It was only a question of time. Armenia interviews. For a detailed account of the kidnapping, see Orozco, Lehder, *El Hombre*, pp. 128–131.

PAGE 89 As Lehder told the story. Armenia interviews, remembered by Leonel Cabezas.

PAGE 89 Soon they had them. For background on M-19, see Patrica Lara, *Siembra Vientos y Recogerás Tempestades*, Bogotá: Planeta, 1982.

Chapter 9: MAS

PAGE 91 The small airplane. For details on the beginnings of MAS, see Fabio Castillo, *Los Jinetes de la Cocaina*, Bogotá: Editorial Documentos Periodisticos, 1987, pp. 111–114.

PAGE 91 The leaflet, dated December 3, 1981. MAS communiqué dated 3 December, 1981. MAS's drug trafficking origins from the authors' interviews with DEA agent Errol Chavez, 27–28 July, 1987, the resident agent in Medellín at the time, and with Fabio Castillo, 25 August, 1987, a journalist who worked as a publicist for the Colombian attorney general during the attorney general's investigation of MAS in 1982–83. For a summary of the early debate concerning MAS, see Agence France Presse dispatch reprinted in the daily newspaper, *El Colombiano*, Medellín, 22 January,1982. Colombian Justice Minister Rodrigo Lara Bonilla on the floor of Congress August 17, 1983, accused Pablo Escobar of being a MAS founder, *El Espectador*, 17 August, 1983. Finally, in a 1983 interview with Bogotá's Radio Caracól, Carlos Lehder admitted his MAS affiliation: "Kidnap victims have to protect their interests."

PAGE 92 Kidnappings among traffickers. Authors' interview with Errol Chavez; authors' interview with a special antiterrorism prosecutor who asked not to be identified, October 1986.

PAGE 92 The Lehder kidnapping was not. Interview with Errol Chavez.

PAGE 93 After the communiqué was written. Interview with Fabio Castillo.

PAGE 93 But before the new feeling. MAS's exploits from newspapers *El Colombiano* and *El Tiempo*.

PAGE 93 It also became clear. Interview with Chavez.

PAGE 94 In all, police. MAS communiqué, 6 February, 1982.

PAGE 94 In fact, the Ochoas did negotiate. Police report related by Chavez; talks in Panama described by Panamanian government source who asked not to be identified, July 1987; details of the talks confirmed and amplified by Jose Blandón in an interview with Andrés Oppenheimer of *The Miami Herald*, 16 December, 1987.

PAGE 94 Sources familiar with the negotiations. Blandón to Oppenheimer; details of

Noriega dealings with the cartel provided in indictment unsealed in U.S. District Court, Southern District of Florida, 5 February, 1988. See also Stephen Hedges, "U.S.: Noriega Sold out Panama," *The Miami Herald*, 6 February, 1988, p. 1A, and testimony of Jose Blandón 2 February, 1988, and 9 February, 1988, before the Senate Foreign Relations Committee.

PAGE 95 For the DEA's Errol Chavez. Interview with Chavez.

PAGE 96 In Colombia, authorities either weren't catching on. Official U.S. law enforcement documents made available to the authors by sources who did not wish to be identified.

PAGE 97 Pablo Escobar was known. Chavez interview.

PAGE 97 A corps of publicists. From an undated issue of *Medellín Cívico*, 1983.

PAGE 97 The campaign's culmination. See "Un Robin Hood Paisa," *Semana,* 19 April, 1983.

Chapter 10: THE COLONEL AND THE AMBASSADOR

PAGE 99 Belisario Betancur won election. Betancur's goals and original assessment of drug trafficking taken from authors' interview with former Colombian Foreign Minister Augusto Ramirez Ocampo, 26 August, 1987.

PAGE 99 Carlos Lehder, who a few months before. Armenia interviews, remembered by Leonel Cabezas.

PAGE 99 The United States and Colombia. See U.S. Senate, Treaty Document No. 97–8, "Extradition Treaty with the Republic of Colombia," U.S. Government Printing Office, Washington, D.C., 1981.

PAGE 99 Things began to change. Analysis of extradition treaty from authors' interviews with Johnny Phelps, 30 July, 21 December, 1987.

PAGE 100 Betancur's "philosophical opposition." Authors' interviews with Ramirez Ocampo.

PAGE 100 "In December National Police Colonel Jaime Ramirez Gomez. Background on Jaime Ramirez comes from authors' interviews with Phelps; with the U.S. State Department's former Colombia Narcotics Assistance Unit chief Caesar Bernal, 28 July, 1987; with former (DEA) Special Agent-in-Charge for Colombia George C. Frangullie, 16 June, 1987; with Ramirez's brother, Francisco Ramirez Gomez, 17 June, 1987; with Ramirez's wife, Helena de Ramirez, 21 and 30 August, 1987; with former members of his Anti-Narcotics Unit who asked not to be identified, 22 August 1987; and with Ramirez himself on two occasions, August and December 1984.

PAGE 101 Ramirez's passion was information. Remembered by former members of the Anti-Narcotics Unit.

PAGE 101 Ramirez's people thought. Remembered by former members of the Anti-Narcotics Unit.

PAGE 101 Ramirez got along famously. Authors' interview with George C. Frangullie.

PAGE 102 Ramirez then began interviewing. Authors' interviews with Francisco Ramirez Gomez.

PAGE 102 Next, the cartel tried to flatter him. Interview with Francisco Ramirez Gomez.

PAGE 102 And then the approaches. Interviews with former members of the Anti-Narcotics Unit.

PAGE 103 In April 1983 U.S. Ambassador Lewis Tambs. Authors' interview with Lewis Tambs, 19 December, 1987; assessments of Tambs's personality, effectiveness in Colombia, from interviews with Phelps and interview with former Colombian Foreign Minister Ramirez Ocampo.

PAGE 103 Tambs would always be emphatically anticommunist. Clark's words remembered by Tambs.

PAGE 105 The FARC had been in existence. Estimates of FARC strength from authors' interviews in 1982, 1983, and 1984 with Colombian army intelligence sources who asked not to be identified. In 1983 Tambs was literally the only person in the country talking about "narco-guerrillas." For an excellent primer on the origins and history of the FARC, see Carlos Arango Z., *FARC: Veinte Anos, de Marquetalia a La Uribe*, Bogotá: Ediciones Aurora, 1984.

PAGE 106 Lara Bonilla was thirty-five. Assessment of Lara Bonilla's naiveté and lack of support from Betancur from authors' interviews with Phelps, Tambs, and Francisco Ramirez Gomez.

Chapter 11: HOT MONEY

PAGE 108 Jairo Ortega began his speech slowly. The August 17, 1983, editions of *El Tiempo* and *El Espectador* give excellent blow-by-blow accounts of the famous interchange.

PAGE 109 Lara Bonilla was in trouble. Assessment of Lara Bonilla's lack of preparation from authors' interviews with Johnny Phelps, Lewis Tambs, and Francisco Ramirez Gomez.

PAGE 110 Escobar, recognizing what was at stake. *El Tiempo*, 18 August, 1983.

PAGE 110 Evaristo Porras also contributed. *El Espectador*, 18 August, 1983.

PAGE 110 And the battle was joined. *El Espectador*, 18 August, 1983.

PAGE 110 Escobar asked for an investigation. Knowledgeable judicial sources consulted by the authors in Bogotá in October 1986 asserted that Lara Bonilla almost certainly received the Porras check. It is almost equally probable that he never had the slightest idea who Porras was or whom he represented. Porras in 1989 remained a major second-echelon cartel chieftain based in Leticia.

PAGE 110 The drug lords were extremely exposed. Description of the Medellín scene from interviews with DEA agent Errol Chavez, 28–29 July, 1987, and his successor, Mike Vigil, 16 July, 1987.

PAGE 111 But perhaps his greatest accomplishment. The institutional involvement of the Medellín Catholic Church with the cartel is impossible to assess accurately. The links of Lopera and Cuartas with Escobar, however, are well documented and created a scandal at the time. See the May 15, 1983, edition of Escobar's newspaper, *Medellín Cívico*, for a glimpse of the publicity surrounding the affair. Also well documented are Lopez Trujillo's rage and his vendetta against the Colombian journalistic establishment. See, for instance, Maria Jimena Duzán's "Lo Santo-fimio de Lopez Trujillo," in *El Espectador*, 21 September, 1983, and the church's response, "Cuando las Víboras Son Periodistas." in *El Colombiano,* 28 September, 1983.

PAGE 112 Outside of working hours. Details of Escobar's life at Hacienda Los Napoles from *Semana* magazine, 19 April, 1983; authors' interviews with Colombian journalists who visited the farm.

PAGE 112 The Ochoas were not nearly as splashy. Authors' interviews with Colombian journalists who had visited La Loma, December 1986; authors' interviews with federal informant Max Mermelstein, 27 November, 1987.

PAGE 113 In Armenia, Carlos Lehder's influence. Armenia interviews. 9–10 November, 1987.

PAGE 113 On March 11, 1983. Details of National Latin Movement from authors' interviews with co-founder Leonel Cabezas, 9–10 November, 1987.

PAGE 114 The movement pitched an ultranationalist. Remembered by Leonel Cabezas. Also, Radio Caracól interview, July 1983.

PAGE 114 Four months after the formation. Interviews with Robert Merkle, April 1988.

PAGE 115 Lehder's shamelessness, like Escobar's. Armenia interviews; Radio Caracól interview.

PAGE 115 But bravado wouldn't be enough. Authors' interviews with Colombian journalists who asked not to be identified, December 1986.

PAGE 116 Then, on September 2, 1983. Quoted in *Semana*, March 1984.

PAGE 116 On August 25 the Bogotá newspaper. *El Espectador*, August 25; confiscation of the newspaper in Medellín asserted in interviews with Colombian journalists, confirmed in authors' interviews with Errol Chavez.

PAGE 116 In early September Lara Bonilla. Details provided in authors' interviews with Francisco Ramirez Gomez, June 17, 1987.

PAGE 117 On September 11, Escobar severed his connection. Quoted in *El Tiempo*, 12 September, 1983.

PAGE 117 So Lara Bonilla kept pushing. *El Tiempo*, 26 September, 1983.

PAGE 118 For Escobar this was the last straw. *El Tiempo*, 21 January, 1984.

Chapter 12: THE ETHER TRAIL

PAGE 119 On February 9, 1984, the Medellín cartel gathered. U.S. *v.* Pablo Escobar, November 1986.

PAGE 119 A vast complex of laboratories. Records seized at Tranquilandia raid.

PAGE 120 The process of making cocaine. This account of the cocaine production process is based on a number of sources: *The Coke Book: The Complete Reference to the Use and Abuses of Cocaine*, Bookmark Books Inc., 1984; Frank Monastero, "Recommendations for the regulation of selected chemicals and controlled substance analogs," September 1985, a report that appeared in "America's Habit: Drug Abuse, Drug Trafficking and Organized Crime," the President's Commission on Organized Crime, March 1986; Joel L. Phillips and Ronald D. Wynne, Ph.D, *Cocaine, the Mystique and the Reality*, New York: Avon Books, 1980, pp. 119–121; B. J. Plasket and Ed Quillen, *The White Stuff*, New York: Dell Publishing Co., Inc., 1985, pp. 75–93; Robert Sabbag, *Snowblind*, New York: The Bobbs-Merrill Company, Inc., 1976, pp. 68–88.

PAGE 122 Johnny Phelps and his men knew most. Conduct and development of the study from authors' interview with Johnny Phelps, 30 July, 1987.

PAGE 122 Phelps's study, code-named Operation Steeple. From 108-page report, "Operation Steeple: The Illicit Precursor Market in Colombia," by DEA intelligence analyst Brian R. Stickney, Bogotá, Colombia, 14 December, 1981.

PAGE 124 On November 22, 1983, Frank Torres walked into J. T. Baker. Affidavit of DEA Special Agent Carol Cooper in United States of America *v.* Francisco Javier Torres Sierra, United States District Court, Southern District of Florida, 1985; "Little Man Led to Big Drug Bust, DEA Tracked Drums of Ether to Colombian 'Grandfather Lab,' " *The Miami Herald*, 3 December, 1987, p. 1A.

PAGE 125 Four days after Schabilion's call. DEA report.

PAGE 126 Torres was married and had two daughters. Carol Cooper interview, June 1987.

PAGE 126 About the size of cigarette packs. Interviews with several law enforcement sources, first appeared in *The Miami Herald*, 3 December, 1987.

PAGE 126 On March 4, 1984, Herb Williams. Based on DEA report, March 4, 1984.

PAGE 127 Johnny Phelps waited a day. Authors' interview with Phelps. Conversations remembered by Phelps.

PAGE 128 Ramirez looked at Phelps's mark. Thoughts related by Ramirez to his brother, Francisco, related to the authors by Francisco in interview, June 17, 1987.

Chapter 13: TRANQUILANDIA

PAGE 129 At 9:20 A.M. on March 10, 1984. Details from the official Anti-Narcotics Unit police reports on the Tranquilandia raid examined by the authors on 29 and 31 August, 1987. Hereafter described as "Tranquilandia papers"; authors' interview with DEA agent Ron Pettingill, January 1988.

PAGE 129 Jaime Ramirez had moved. Authors' interview with Francisco Ramirez Gomez, June 17, 1987.

PAGE 129 Phelps picked Pettingill. Authors' interview with Johnny Phelps, 30 July, 1987.

PAGE 130 On March 9 the Colombian. Tranquilandia papers.

PAGE 130 Now it was well past noon. Authors' interview with Pettingill.

PAGE 131 At the edge of the jungle. Authors' interview with Phelps.

PAGE 131 Back at the landing site. Tranquilandia papers.

PAGE 131 The next day in Bogotá. Authors' interview with Francisco Ramirez Gomez.

PAGE 132 Ramirez arrived at Tranquilandia. Tranquilandia papers.

PAGE 133 Pettingill reluctantly flew back. Interview with Pettingill.

PAGE 133 And so they were. Tranquilandia papers.

PAGE 133 It was also March 17. Details of the FARC camp from the authors' 1984 interviews with Johnny Phelps. See also Guy Gugliotta, "Colombia's Drug Runners, Guerrillas: Friends or Foes?" *The Miami Herald*, 22 May, 1984, p. 1A.

PAGE 134 For Phelps and Ramirez. Interviews with Phelps.

PAGE 135 As for Ramirez, before Tranquilandia. Interview with Francisco Ramirez Gomez.

PAGE 135 The army, for its part. Tranquilandia is what gave the concept "narco-guerrillas" its first serious jolt of credibility. Concept of *gramaje* described in "Analisis de Documentos No. 028," May 1982, an excerpt of a Colombian army intelligence analysis of the FARC Sixth Conference Final Document.

PAGE 135 Like the army, Ambassador Tambs. Authors' interview with Lewis Tambs, 19 December, 1987; authors' interview with former Colombian Foreign Minister Augusto Ramirez Ocampo, 26 August, 1987.

PAGE 135 Colombia still wasn't ready. Arenas quoted in Guy Gugliotta, "Colombia's Drug Runners, Guerrillas: Friends or Foes?" *The Miami Herald*, 22 May, 1984, p. 1A.

PAGE 136 Phelps and Ramirez had only a passing interest. Tranquilandia papers.

Chapter 14: THE WHITE MERCEDES

PAGE 138 Justice Minister Lara Bonilla's nerves. Authors' interview with Johnny Phelps, 21 December, 1987.

PAGE 138 And Lara Bonilla didn't stop there. Authors' interview with Francisco Ramirez Gomez, 17 June, 1987.

PAGE 139 And on March 26, with the cartel. *El Tiempo,* 27 March, 1984.

PAGE 139 It was this last remark. Authors' interview with Phelps.

PAGE 140 Meanwhile, in Medellín, it was obvious. Authors' interview with DEA agent Mike Vigil, 16 July, 1987.

PAGE 140 It was in August 1983. Authors' interviews with Department of Administrative Security (DAS) detectives who asked that their names not be used, 21, 24, and 25 August, 1987. Hereafter described as "DAS interviews."

PAGE 141 Tambs and Phelps, under no illusions. Authors' interview with Lewis Tambs, 19 December, 1987.

PAGE 141 Sometime soon after the Tranquilandia raid. Details of the Lara Bonilla plot from DAS interviews and DAS documents examined by the authors; outline of the plot and most of the description and details, however, from a superb, unsigned cooperative reprise and investigative report published by Colombia's journalists, one version available as "El Asesinato de Lara Bonilla," *El Tiempo*, 11 August, 1987. Hereafter described as "journalists' report."

PAGE 142 At ten A.M., April 30, 1984. Authors' interview with Lewis Tambs.

PAGE 143 At seven P.M. on April 30. Journalists' report; see also Guy Gugliotta, "Cabinet Minister's Murder Galvanizes Colombian Outrage," *The Miami Herald*, 6 May, 1984, p. 29A.

PAGE 144 Belisario Betancur and the Colombian cabinet. Authors' interview with former Colombian Foreign Minister Augusto Ramirez Ocampo, 26 August, 1987.

PAGE 144 Lara Bonilla's body, in a closed coffin. Details of services, funeral, from authors' interview with Tambs.

Chapter 15: BARRY SEAL

PAGE 145 A month after the fall of Tranquilandia. Seal's testimony in the Bustamante case.

PAGE 146 Born and raised in Baton Rouge, Louisiana, Barry Seal. The description of Barry Seal is based on interviews with John Camp, Debbie Seal, Ben Seal, Lewis Unglesby, and Tom Sclafani and on "Fatal Judgement," a three-part series by Jeff Leen, *The Miami Herald*, 11, 12, and 13 October, 1986.

PAGE 147 Seal began to fly cocaine for the Ochoas in 1981. Interview with Ernst "Jake" Jacobsen, 1986.

PAGE 147 Ultimately he created a system that was nearly fail-safe. Seal described his smuggling methods in testimony before the President's Commission on Organized Crime, October 1985.

PAGE 148 Seal once bumped into a Louisiana State Police agent. Jacobsen interview, September 1986.

PAGE 148 When Seal finally got caught. Interview with Randy Beasley, September 1986.

PAGE 148 His name and several of his aliases: George Stein, "DEA's Airline for Drugs Delivers with a Cargo of 84 Indictments," *The Miami Herald*, 23 March, 1983, p. 1A.

PAGE 148 He promised big things. Beasley interview.

PAGE 149 He refused even to see Seal. Interview with Stanford Bardwell, 10 October, 1986.

PAGE 149 All during this time, Seal had managed. Seal testimony in Bustamante case.

PAGE 149 The task force's DEA liaison. Interview with DEA agent Ken Kennedy, who was at the time acting as liaison to NNBIS, July 1987. Kennedy, whose experience lay in fighting heroin in New York City, was unfamiliar with the Colombian names Seal mentioned. Kennedy sent Seal to DEA agent Frank White on the cocaine desk at headquarters. White, a veteran of the south Florida cocaine wars, immediately saw Seal's value.

PAGE 150 Jacobsen knew that Seal was big time. Jacobsen interview.

PAGE 150 Seal said he had worked for the Ochoas since 1981. DEA reports.

PAGE 151 Ochoa asked Seal how his friend William Roger Reeves was. Seal testimony.

PAGE 152 Ochoa outlined the mission. DEA reports.

PAGE 153 Entitled "Notes to Meditate on (Ponder)." The ten-page cartel manual was seized from a safety deposit box in October 1985 after Marquez was arrested. The manual was entered into evidence at the trial of Bustamante, Bates, and Marquez.

PAGE 153 Marquez was pleased that Seal. DEA reports.

PAGE 155 On May 20 Seal met the cartel leaders. Seal testimony.

PAGE 155 About five miles outside the city. DEA reports.

PAGE 157 A frantic Seal was now behind bars. Interview with Thomas Sclafani, September 1986.

Chapter 16: THE NICARAGUA DEAL

PAGE 158 As soon as Barry Seal got out of jail. Seal testimony.

PAGE 160 They spent the next three days with Lehder. DEA reports.

PAGE 160 Seal and Camp were jailed overnight. Seal testimony.

PAGE 161 A couple of days later Vaughan visited. *El Nuevo Diario*, "EPS explica sobre disparos a avioneta," 5 June, 1984. The article was entered into evidence at the Bustamante trial.

PAGE 161 Pablo Escobar told Seal. DEA reports.

PAGE 161 Seal suggested they buy a military cargo plane. Seal testimony.

PAGE 162 By now the CIA had signed on to the Seal mission. DEA reports.

PAGE 162 Back in Miami three days later. Transcripts of tapes entered into evidence at the Bustamante trial, Tape Number F, 24 June, 1984.

PAGE 163 Seal took off from Key West. DEA reports.

PAGE 163 The two men talked in Lito's car. Seal testimony.

PAGE 164 The DEA had hit on a daring plan. DEA reports.

PAGE 164 One of the surveillance agents did a play-by-play. Interview with DEA Special Agent-in-Charge Peter Gruden, July 1986.

PAGE 164 A bystander who had seen the accident. Florida Highway Patrol accident report.

PAGE 164 At 2 A.M. that night Seal got a call. Seal testimony.

PAGE 165 Seal said yes, then called Vaughan. Tape transcripts. Tape Number G, 5 July, 1984.

PAGE 166 Seal called Escobar directly. Tape transcripts, Tape Number K, 15 July, 1984.

PAGE 166 A little later, Seal got an angry call. Seal testimony.

PAGE 167 Joura wanted Seal to fly the Bolivian cocaine base. Testimony of Robert Joura at Seal's Rule 35 hearing.

PAGE 167 The DEA was poised for what might. Material from North's notebooks and

Ron Caffrey's testimony about his briefings of North and Dewey Clarridge came out of hearings conducted by the House Judiciary Committee's Subcommittee on crime in the summer of 1988.

PAGE 168 A day later, Army Lieutenant General Paul Gorman. Peter Slevin, "U.S. Details Alleged Sandinista Drug Role," *The Miami Herald*, 19 July, 1984, p. 1A.

PAGE 168 Joura got even more troubling news. Joura testimony at Rule 35 hearing.

PAGE 168 Lito produced a driver's license. DEA reports.

PAGE 168 Nicaragua denied the charges. Slevin, "U.S. Details Alleged Sandinista Drug Role," *The Miami Herald*, 19 July, 1984, p. 1A.

PAGE 169 Politics grabbed the headlines. Joel Brinkley, "U.S. Accuses Managua of Role in Cocaine Traffic," *The New York Times*, 19 July, 1984, p. 6A.

Chapter 17: CRACKDOWN

PAGE 170 In addition, drug trafficking. Authors' interview with former Colombian Foreign Minister Augusto Ramirez Ocampo, 26 August, 1987.

PAGE 171 In Medellín police raided. Authors' interview with DEA agent Mike Vigil, 16 July, 1987.

PAGE 171 Police also invaded Escobar's. *The Miami Herald*, 10 February, 1987.

PAGE 171 More important, however, the cartel had. Details of cartel's 1984 relationship with Noriega described by Panamanian government source who asked not to be identified, July 1987; see also Guy Gugliotta, "Scandals Hint at Panama Role in Drug Trade," *The Miami Herald*, 3 September, 1984, p. 1A; Jose Blandón interview with Andrés Oppenheimer of *The Miami Herald*, 16 December, 1987; Sam Dillon and Andrés Oppenheimer, "Smuggling Enriched Noriega," *The Miami Herald*, 30 January, 1988, p. 1A; U.S. District Court, Southern District of Florida indictment, unsealed February 5, 1988; *The Miami Herald*, 6 February, 1988, p. 1A; testimony of Jose Blandón 2 February, 1988, and 9 February, 1988 before the Senate Foreign Relations Committee.

PAGE 172 The cartel wanted a truce. Authors' interview with Alfonso Lopez Michelsen, 18 June, 1987.

PAGE 174 The success of this strategy. Blandón to Oppenheimer, 16 December, 1987; Blandón Senate testimony.

PAGE 175 Jimenez Gomez left Bogotá. The entire document is reproduced in Mario Arango Jaramillo and Jorge Child Velez, *Los Condenados de la Coca*, Editorial J. M. Arango, Medellín, 1985, pp. 94–105. On the manifesto's effects in Colombia, see David Marcus and Nery Ynclan, "Colombia's Drug Kings Want a Deal," *The Miami Herald*, 23 July, 1984, p. 1A.

PAGE 176 The cartel members heard nothing. On the INAIR affair, see Gugliotta, "Scandals Hint at Panama Role in Drug Trade," *The Miami Herald*, 3 September, 1984, p. 1A, and Jeff Leen, "Witness Links Noriega to Drugs," *The Miami Herald*, 17 September, 1987, p. 1A.

PAGE 177 For Lewis Tambs and Johnny Phelps. Assessments made in authors' interviews with Johnny Phelps, 21 December, 1987, and Lewis Tambs, 19 December, 1987.

PAGE 178 And on August 14, Bogotá. *El Espectador*, 14 August, 1984.

PAGE 178 The case against Escobar. Authors' interview with Francisco Ramirez Gomez, 17 June, 1987.

PAGE 179 Ramirez felt there was no way. Authors' interview with Francisco Ramirez Gomez.

PAGE 179 Ramirez began to stalk his quarry. Information on Anti-Narcotics Unit efforts to capture Lehder in 1984–85 generally from reports in confidential Colombian law enforcement files examined by the authors 28 August, 1987, hereafter described as the "Lehder papers." "Open letter" dated 24 July, 1984; *Semana*, March 1984.

PAGE 179 In early 1984 Lehder had tried. Lehder papers.

PAGE 180 Finally, in February 1985. From a transcript of the television interview obtained by the authors, March 1988.

Chapter 18: DRAWDOWN

PAGE 182 Furthermore, police only picked up. Assessment of effects of the crackdown from the authors' interview with U.S. embassy officials, December 1984; See also Guy Gugliotta, "Colombian Drug Dealers Retaliate for Crackdown," *The Miami Herald*, 10 December, 1984, p. 2A.

PAGE 182 Phelps was one of the first. Authors' interviews with Johnny Phelps, 21 December, 1987.

PAGE 182 The traffickers, hunkered down. *Semana*, April 1984.

PAGE 183 Suddenly Colombia was a much more dangerous place. Authors' interview with former Colombian Foreign Minister Augusto Ramirez Ocampo, 26 August, 1987.

PAGE 183 Lewis Tambs had begun to notice. Authors' interview with Lewis Tambs, 19 December, 1987.

PAGE 184 In the immediate aftermath of the Lara Bonilla assassination. Authors' interview with DEA agent Mike Vigil, 16 July, 1987.

PAGE 184 A secret police memo dated. Anti-Narcotics Unit intelligence report dated 22 August, 1984.

PAGE 185 As if to drive this point home. The kidnapping was impossible to confirm. The official Escobar account holds that the old man was kidnapped October 8, 1984, and released twenty-four days later. Newspapers received no details of the "kidnapping" until the elder Escobar was already freed.

PAGE 185 Escobar's money was everywhere. From a confidential letter dictated by Castro Gil and handwritten by a companion outside a Medellín courthouse, 23 October, 1984, and submitted to the Department of Administrative Security (DAS).

PAGE 185 The Lara Bonilla assassination. Authors' interview with Phelps.

PAGE 185 Vigil's security. Authors' interview with Vigil.

PAGE 186 At first they brought widespread condemnation. Liberal Senator Ernesto Samper quoted in David Marcus and Nery Ynclan, "Colombia's Drug Kings Want a Deal," *The Miami Herald*, 23 July, 1984, p. 1A.

PAGE 186 "I told them I would deliver their note." Quoted in *El Espectador*, 5 July, 1984.

PAGE 187 Betancur, prodded to make a statement. Quoted in Marcus and Ynclan, *The Miami Herald*, 23 July, 1984, p. 1A.

PAGE 187 Yet Betancur did not convince. Quoted in Marcus and Ynclan, *The Miami Herald*, 23 July, 1984, p. 1A.

PAGE 187 In addition, on July 9 Pablo Escobar. Radio Caracól broadcast transcript, 9 July, 1984.

PAGE 187 Shortly after midyear. From confidential Anti-Narcotics Unit police intelligence documents examined by the authors, 29 and 31 August, 1987.

PAGE 188 It was the guerrillas who finally. Authors' interview with Vigil.

PAGE 188 At the same time, Tambs. Interview with Tambs.

Chapter 19: THE AUDIENCIA

PAGE 190 By the fall of 1984. Most of material concerning Ochoa's and Rodriguez's life in Madrid comes from the Spanish Judicial Police's Arrest Report, Direccíon General de la Policia, RS 14.791/9, Madrid, 21 November, 1984.

PAGE 191 At the end of August. Authors' interview with DEA agent James Kibble, February 1988.

PAGE 191 The judicial police told the DEA. Judicial Police Arrest Report, 21 November, 1984.

PAGE 192 The Spaniards seemed cooperative. Authors' interviews with Kibble and with DEA agent William Mockler, February 1988.

PAGE 194 Such sentiments had a certain resonance. See the Madrid daily *Liberacíon*, 30 November, 1984, for presentation of the case. See the daily newspaper *El País*, Madrid, 6 June, 1985, for a summary of the Nicaragua debate.

PAGE 194 Kibble later described the allegations. Interview with Kibble.

PAGE 194 At the outset of the Ochoa case. Descriptions of U.S thinking regarding the Ochoa case and analysis of how the case developed are from the authors' interviews with two U.S. State Department lawyers assigned to follow the matter. The lawyers, interviewed in February 1988, asked not to be identified. Hereafter described as "lawyers' interviews."

PAGE 195 In Spain the integrity of the courts. Changing descriptions of the defendants in news stories can be easily noted by studying story display in *El País* over the first year of their incarceration.

PAGE 196 Also pure cartel was an April 2, 1985, story. *El País*, 2 April, 1985; Mockler's problems described by Mockler in interviews with the authors.

PAGE 196 One Ochoa lawyer denounced. Lawyers' interviews. Quotes as remembered by the lawyers.

PAGE 196 The prosecution could not match. EFE dispatch printed in *El País*, 8 June, 1985.

PAGE 196 The cases against Ochoa and Rodriguez. Lawyers' interviews.

PAGE 198 The judges closed the hearing. Finding quoted in *El País*, 26 September, 1985.

PAGE 198 But it was not the last word. Finding quoted in *El País*, 22 January 1985.

Chapter 20: *UNCLE SAM WANTS YOU*

PAGE 200 Yet despite the fact that Seal. This account of Seal's troubles with federal officials in the Middle District of Louisiana is largely based on "Fatal Judgement," a three-part series on Seal by Jeff Leen in *The Miami Herald*, 12–14 October, 1986; *Uncle Sam Wants You*, an hour-long documentary on Seal by John Camp that aired on WBRZ in Baton Rouge, 20 November, 1984; and *Murder of a Witness*, an hour-long documentary by Camp that aired on WBRZ in February 1986. In addition, the account is augmented by interviews with John Camp, former Baton Rouge U.S. Attorney Stanford Bardwell, Seal lawyer Lewis Unglesby, Chief Assistant U.S. Attorney Dick Gregorie in Miami, Organized Crime Strike Force prosecutor Al Winters in New Orleans, former DEA agent Ernst Jacobsen, former DEA Special Agent-in-Charge Peter Gruden in Miami, Debbie Seal, and Ben Seal. Officials with the Louisiana State Police refused interview requests by the authors in 1986.

PAGE 201 The U.S. Attorney's Office in Miami. Interviews with Stanford Bardwell, 10 October, 1986, and Dick Gregorie, April 1988.

PAGE 201 Sclafani figured the Louisiana feds. Interview with Thomas Sclafani, September 1986.
PAGE 202 The Louisiana State Police believed Seal. Interviews with Jacobsen, Sclafani, Camp, and Unglesby.
PAGE 202 Webb claimed the state police told him. In an interview on *Uncle Sam Wants You*.
PAGE 202 Camp was skeptical at first. Interviews with Camp, September 1986, and *Murder of a Witness*.
PAGE 202 So Gregorie called Winters. Interviews with Gregorie and Winters, September 1986.
PAGE 203 He was a sharp Baton Rouge lawyer. Unglesby interview, September 1986.
PAGE 203 He learned that his client was a witness. Sclafani interview, September 1986.
PAGE 203 Bardwell and Winters left happy. Interviews with Bardwell, 10 October, 1986, and Winters in September and October 1986.
PAGE 203 Seal agreed to plead guilty. Letter to judge, "Re United States *v.* Adler B. Seal," 19 November, 1984. The plea agreement, written on U.S Department of Justice stationery, is signed by Seal, Thomas Sclafani, Stanford Bardwell, and Albert J. Winters. In the document, Seal agrees to plead guilty to two counts: conspiracy to possess two hundred kilograms of cocaine and causing a financial institution to not file currency transaction reports.
PAGE 204 On November 20, Camp's documentary. From *Uncle Sam Wants You*.

Chapter 21: MAX

PAGE 207 Shortly after the program aired. DEA sources.
PAGE 207 A few days later Max Mermelstein. Based on testimony of Max Mermelstein in State of Louisiana *v.* Miguel Velez, et al, 29 April, 1987; and interview with Mermelstein, 27 November, 1987. The authors interviewed Mermelstein, who is hidden in the federal Witness Protection Program, for more than three hours by telephone while a U.S. marshal monitored the call to prevent information leaking about Mermelstein's whereabouts. The interview, which took place in a bare-walled room at the federal courthouse in downtown Miami, was the first public account by an insider in the Medellín cartel.
PAGES 327–329 He told Max it was necessary. Interview with Mermelstein, 27 November, 1987.
PAGE 210 After they dumped the body. Antonio Arles Vargas, Metro-Dade Homicide Case 335213-Y. Vargas's body was discovered Christmas Day in a field near an apartment complex. Cause of death: "Multiple gunshot wounds to the head and torso from a .38- or .357-caliber weapon," Permanent Subcommittee on Investigations, "Organized Crime and Use of Violence," 2 and 5 May, 1980, p. 503.
PAGE 210 "Basically, from that point on. Mermelstein testimony.
PAGE 211 Back in Miami, Mermelstein coordinated. U.S. *v.* Escobar, November 1986. This document is also known as "the Medellín Cartel Indictment."
PAGE 211 All the big traffickers were at Rafa's party. Mermelstein interview.
PAGE 212 Acting on Rafa's authority, Max. United States of America *v.* Michael O. Munday, et al, United States District Court, Southern District of Florida, 4 November, 1987.
PAGE 212 When the cocaine came into Miami. Mermelstein interview.
PAGE 214 Soon Blanco had amassed a $1.8 million debt. United States of America *v.*

Griselda Blanco de Trujillo, United States District Court, Southern District of Florida, 26 September 1986, p. 5. In a DEA debriefing, Mermelstein said the Blancos had Marta Ochoa killed. The murder of Marta Ochoa, Jorge Ochoa's first cousin, is filed under Metro-Dade Homicide No. 181899-E, 17 May, 1984. It remains an open case.
PAGE 214 But Marta Ochoa's father came to Miami. Mermelstein interview.
PAGE 214 Cumbamba carried a black attaché case. Mermelstein testimony.

Chapter 22: FLIPPING

PAGE 215 Max Mermelstein had never killed anybody. Mermelstein testimony.
PAGE 215 The prisoners arrived aboard a Colombian C-130 cargo plane. Marc Fisher, "Colombia Starts Drug Extraditions," *The Miami Herald,* 6 January, 1985, p. 1B.
PAGE 215 Hernan Botero Moreno was a soccer team owner. Mary Voboril, *The Miami Herald,* 11 February, 1981.
PAGE 215 In late January 1985 Mermelstein and an associate. Mermelstein testimony.
PAGE 217 It almost appeared to them that Max sighed with relief. Kim Murphy, "One Man's Word Against World's Most Dangerous Cocaine Cartel," The *Los Angeles Times,* 6 July, 1987.
PAGE 217 A few days earlier Rafa had told Max. Mermelstein DEA debriefing.
PAGE 217 Mermelstein and Rafael Cardona had been indicted in Los Angeles. United States of America *v.* Max Mermelstein, Rafael Antonio Salazar Cardona, et al, U.S. District Court, Middle District of California, October 1984.
PAGE 218 "In the language of *The Godfather.*" Murphy, *Los Angeles Times,* 6 July, 1987.
PAGE 218 Mermelstein didn't spill his guts. Gregorie interviews.
PAGE 219 It was the biggest cocaine bust in the history of Nevada. Don Campbell testimony at Seal's Rule 35 hearing, 24 October, 1985.
PAGE 219 The money was for protecting drug shipments. Liz Balmaseda, "Remote Islands' Top Officials Held in Drug Smuggling Plot," *The Miami Herald,* 6 March, 1985, p. 1A.
PAGE 220 For the first fifty days he was kept. U.S. *v.* Adler Berriman Seal, "Sealed Motion for Reduction of Sentence," October 1985.
PAGE 220 The Medellín cartel incensed him. Interviews with Dick Gregorie.
PAGE 221 Seal's performance drew grudging praise. Brian Duffy, "Case of Mumps Complicates Turks Trial," *The Miami Herald,* 18 July, 1985, p. 1B.
PAGE 221 In his opening argument, Gregorie called. U.S.A. *v.* Bustamante.
PAGE 221 The story of the trial's opening. Brian Duffy, "U.S. Prosecutors: Sandinistas Linked to Coke Cartel," *The Miami Herald,* 31 July, 1985, p. 2B.
PAGE 221 One of the things Max Mermelstein told the DEA. Mermelstein debriefing.
PAGE 221 The plot could have been lifted from a bad thriller. Jeff Leen, "Prisoners Air Escape Plot Foiled," *The Miami Herald,* 18 November, 1985, p. 1B.

Chapter 23: "THIS IS DOUBLE-CROSS"

PAGE 224 In fact, it was merely the formal execution. See plea agreement description, note for p. 203.
PAGE 224 Once again it was John Camp. John Camp, *Murder of a Witness.*
PAGE 226 So it came as no surprise. The hearing, on a motion to reduce Seal's sentence, took place October 24, 1985, before Judge Norman C. Roettger, Jr.
PAGE 227 When Seal appeared December 20, 1985. United States of America *v.* Adler

Berriman Seal, United States District Court, Middle District of Louisiana, sentencing proceedings, 20 December, 1985.

PAGE 229 The trap was ready to spring. Unglesby interview.

PAGE 231 On January 23, the day before the hearing. Sclafani interview. This account reflects Sclafani's recollection of what Judge Polozola said. The judge has refused to be interviewed about the Seal case.

PAGE 232 The next morning Gregorie called Winters. This account of the collapse of the Seal negotiations is based on interviews with Sclafani, Winters, and Gregorie originally published by Jeff Leen in "Court Issued Deadly 'Lesson,' Legal Tug of War Cast Federal Witness' Fate," *The Miami Herald,* 13 October, 1986.

PAGE 233 Characteristically, he gave a telephone interview. John Semien, "Seal Pleads Guilty, Questions Sentence," The *Baton Rouge Morning Advocate,* 23 January, 1986, p. 1A.

Chapter 24: THE HALFWAY HOUSE

PAGE 234 No one expected Barry Seal to remain for long. Interview with Al Winters.

PAGE 234 Gregorie said it was no use. Interview with Dick Gregorie.

PAGE 234 Seal told Jake Jacobsen. Interview with Jake Jacobsen.

PAGE 234 Cumbamba had taken over Max Mermelstein's contract. Documents filed in State of Louisiana *v.* Miguel Velez, et al, also known as the "Seal murder case."

PAGE 235 After Seal had been in the halfway house for fifteen days. This account of Seal's last days in the halfway house is based on court documents and testimony filed in the Seal murder case.

PAGE 236 Seal spent much of his time. John Semien, *The Baton Rouge Morning Advocate,* 19 February, 1986.

PAGE 236 The morning mail brought more bad news. Interview with Debbie Seal, September 1986.

PAGE 236 Just before six that evening. Interview with Bill Lambeth, September 1986.

PAGE 236 He drove right past the parked gray Buick. This account of the shooting is based on a visit to the halfway house parking lot and an interview with Salvation Army Major Bennie Lewis, September 1986.

PAGE 236 Even through the silencer the shooting sounded loud. Testimony of Bennie Lewis, Seal murder case.

PAGE 236 Three bullets hit Seal in the left side of the head. The description of the paths of the bullets first appeared in *The Miami Herald* on October 14, 1986, and was derived from the autopsy report of Seal placed in the court file.

PAGE 237 At 6:04 P.M., John Camp was in the WBRZ newsroom. Interview with Camp, September 1986.

PAGE 237 When Lambeth in Phoenix got tired of waiting. Interview with Lambeth, September 1986.

PAGE 237 Debbie Seal called over there. Interview with Debbie Seal, October 1986.

PAGE 237 The next day U.S. Attorney Stanford Bardwell. Account taken from transcript of press conference aired on *Murder of a Witness.*

PAGE 238 In the pandemonium after the killing. FBI reports in Seal murder case.

PAGE 238 They were laughing. Testimony of East Baton Rouge Sheriff's Deputy Brent Bonnette, Seal murder trial.

PAGE 239 The cab had hit a deer. Steve Wheeler, "Cabbie Recalls Ride with Suspect in Seal Murder," The *Baton Rouge State Times,* 23 February, 1986, p. 1A.

PAGE 239 The family put a telephone pager. Interview with Debbie Seal, September 1986.

PAGE 239 The bosses in Washington let Jacobsen and Joura know. Interview with Ken Kennedy, July 1987.

PAGE 240 Four months after Barry Seal's death. Interview with Dick Gregorie, April 1988.

PAGE 240 Winters told Max that the murder weapon. Winters interview in the *Los Angeles Times,* 6 July, 1987.

Chapter 25: PALACE OF JUSTICE

PAGE 241 One day in August 1985. Authors' interview with María Cristina de Patiño, October 1986. See also Guy Gugliotta, "Threats Try Colombia's Drug Judges," *The Miami Herald,* 26 October, 1986, p. 1A.

PAGE 243 In the early days of Colombia's. Material on judges' lives, pay, threats, attitudes, and so on from authors' interviews with judges and prosecutors at Paloquemao Court House, Bogotá, October 1986. All attorneys asked not to be identified. Hereafter described as "Paloquemao interviews."

PAGE 244 When none of this worked. Judicial employees union sources listed thirty judges killed between 1980–86, apart from Supreme Court justices, but were unable to tell whether all were murdered by drug traffickers. Although no accurate count existed, by mid-1988 the cartel had almost certainly murdered fifty judges.

PAGE 244 On July 23, 1985, five gunmen. Authors' interviews with detectives from the Colombian Department of Administrative Security (DAS), 24 August, 1987. Escobar is the prime suspect in the Castro Gil killing.

PAGE 245 This was an old story. The uproar that attended the treatment of the extradited prisoners described in authors' interview with former Foreign Minister Augusto Ramirez Ocampo, 26 August, 1987.

PAGE 245 So the cartel did what it could. Escobar quoted in Sam Dillon, "Drug Lords Are Blamed in Colombian Killing," *The Miami Herald,* 14 September, 1985, p. 1A.

PAGE 246 But the Betancur administration. Parejo quoted in Dillon, *The Miami Herald,* 14 September, 1985, p. 1A.

PAGE 246 Three ambassadors were. Authors' interviews with Ramirez Ocampo, 26 August, 1987.

PAGE 247 At 11:40 A.M., about thirty-five M-19 guerrillas. Despite its polemics, the most comprehensive collection of basic information, documents, and accounts relating to the Palace of Justice affair can be found in Manuel Vicente Peña Gomez, *Las Dos Tomas,* 2nd ed., Bogotá: Fundación Ciudad Abierta, January 1987.

PAGE 247 Yesid Reyes Alvarado, a young lawyer. Authors' interview with Yesid Reyes Alvarado, 27 August, 1987.

PAGE 248 Down the hall from Alfonso Reyes. Authors' interview with Humberto Murcia Ballen, October 1986.

PAGE 250 Belisario Betancur's presidency never recovered. During the rest of his presidency, Betancur never resolved the question of negotiations; the official explanation given for the guards' withdrawal was that they had only been assigned temporarily during a state visit by French President François Mitterrand that had ended November 4. Three years after the seizure neither issue had been resolved to the judiciary's satisfaction.

Chapter 26: BETANCUR AT TWILIGHT

PAGE 251 Betancur was double-damned. Author's interview with former Colombian Foreign Minister Augusto Ramirez Ocampo, 26 August, 1987. Ramirez Ocampo confirmed that from the day he was inaugurated until the day he left office, the Peace Process remained the cornerstone of Betancur's administration.

PAGE 251 Apparently Betancur still thought. Public acceptance of the "narco-guerrilla" concept grew gradually. Because of the FARC's pivotal role in the Peace Process, the Betancur administration discouraged open debate on the matter. This changed with the arrival of his successor, Virgilio Barco, in 1986. The "FARC-Narc" relationship described in the text was first discussed in detail with the authors in a January 1987 interview with a high-level Barco administration official who asked not to be identified.

PAGE 252 The criminal justice system was a joke. Quoted in an undated 1986 news release issued by the National Association of Functionaries and Employees of the Judicial Branch.

PAGE 253 The cartel had murdered one. The justices' despair related to the authors in an October 1986 interview with a former justice who asked not to be identified.

PAGE 253 By the end of 1986 Colombia. Ten Colombians, two U.S. citizens, and a West German.

PAGE 254 The year opened with a vendetta. *El Espectador,* 29 March, 1986.

PAGE 254 On March 19, several weeks after. U.S. District Court, Southern District of Florida, indictment unsealed February 5, 1988; see also Sam Dillon, "Son of Ex-Panama Defense Chief Snatched," *The Miami Herald,* 25 March, 1986, p. 6A.

PAGE 254 This sort of ugly intrigue. On violence in 1985–86, see Guy Gugliotta, "Life Cheap, Death Easy in Lawless Colombia," *The Miami Herald,* 5 October, 1986, p. 1A.

PAGE 255 In 1986 Medellín eclipsed these figures. See the daily newspaper *El Mundo,* Medellín, 9 December, 1986, p. 1A.

PAGE 255 Law enforcement in the city. Authors' interviews with detectives of Colombia's Department of Administrative Security (DAS), 24 August, 1987.

PAGE 255 On January 31 the court agreed. *El País,* Madrid, 13 February, 1986, describes the February 12 finding and summarizes the case to date in reasonably coherent fashion.

PAGE 255 The U.S. request looked sadly deficient. Assessment made by two U.S. State Department lawyers assigned to the case and interviewed by the authors in February 1988. The lawyers asked not to be identified.

PAGE 256 Furthermore Barco, like Betancur. See, for example, *Colombia Today,* vol. 21, no. 6, a newsletter in English published by the Colombia Information Service, a Colombia lobby in Washington. The newsletter introduces Barco and gives his views on fifteen different subjects. Drug trafficking is not among them.

PAGE 257 On July 16 Luis Roberto Camacho. One high-level Barco administration source who asked not to be identified told the authors in January 1987 that fewer than a half-dozen people knew that Parejo was leaving Colombia until the day he actually departed.

PAGE 257 In Cali the widespread lawlessness. See Gugliotta, *The Miami Herald,* 5 October, 1986, p. 1A.

PAGE 257 On July 13, 1986, after twenty months. Old Fabio quoted in *El Tiempo,* 14 July, 1986.

PAGE 258 The Spanish Audiencia Nacional. Quoted in *El País,* 26 March, 1986.

PAGE 259 Parejo Gonzales had reason to worry. See, for instance, *El Espectador*, 9 January, 1988, which prints a photocopy of the document. According to *El Espectador*, the document was seized by the Colombian army's IV Brigade (Medellín) on February 7, 1987, during a house search. Arrested at the time was Mauricio Isaza Ochoa, described as a relative of Jorge Luis Ochoa. In all, the document detailed payments of 318.3 million pesos ($1.6 million) in Cartagena, Bogotá, Medellín, and to someone or some entity described only as "Garces." Efforts to contact Judge Fabio Pastrana Hoyos at the time the document was leaked proved unsuccessful.

Chapter 27: THE RAMIREZ CONTRACT

PAGE 260 On January 25, 1986, a middle-aged man. Basic outline of the original plot described in a confidential police intelligence memorandum undated but probably submitted at the end of January 1986. Hereafter described as "police memorandum." Most details on the plot, however, come from National Police Inspector General Alfonso Gomez Garcia's report on the death of Jaime Ramirez. A copy of this confidential report was examined by the authors in late 1987. Hereafter described as "inspector general's report."

PAGE 261 Two days later the F-2. Authors' interview with Helena de Ramirez, 30 August, 1987.

PAGE 261 Jaime Ramirez had been officially relieved. Ramirez's sense of well-being described during authors' interview with Francisco Ramirez Gomez, 17 June, 1987.

PAGE 262 First Escobar contracted the job. Authors' interview with Francisco Ramirez Gomez.

PAGE 262 In his final, superb year. Information on Anti-Narcotics Unit efforts to capture Lehder in 1984–85 generally from reports in confidential Colombian law enforcement files examined by the authors 28 August, 1987, hereafter described as the "Lehder papers."

PAGE 262 Twice they almost got him. Information regarding Liliana Garcia from the Lehder papers and from the authors' visit to Armenia 9–10 November, 1987, and conversations with Garcia at that time.

PAGE 263 Six weeks later, on April 26. Lehder papers.

PAGE 264 Salah's replies—addressed "Dear." Salah correspondence contained in Lehder papers.

PAGE 264 Despite the lessons in. Letter to the Soviets contained in Lehder papers.

PAGE 265 In February 1986 Ramirez, his wife, Helena. Authors' interview with Helena de Ramirez.

PAGE 265 Still, he wasn't particularly worried. Interview with Francisco Ramirez Gomez; police memorandum.

PAGE 265 Ramirez visited F-2. Remembered by Francisco Ramirez Gomez.

PAGE 266 He had to put the informant. Authors' interview with DEA agent George C. Frangullie, 16 June, 1987.

PAGE 266 Jaime Ramirez's life changed. Interview with Francisco Ramirez Gomez.

PAGE 266 For the next eight months. Inspector general's report.

PAGE 266 The tension put a terrible strain. Interview with Helena de Ramirez.

PAGE 267 Still, this was no way to live. Interview with Francisco Ramirez Gomez.

PAGE 267 In May the Anti-Narcotics Unit. Inspector general's report; interview with Francisco Ramirez Gomez.

PAGE 268 This seemed to be a particularly wise course. Inspector general's report; interview with Helena de Ramirez.

PAGE 269 Generals school finished in August. Interview with Francisco Ramirez Gomez; authors' interview with Johnny Phelps, 21 December, 1987.

PAGE 270 The next day at ten A.M. Ramirez. Conversation remembered by Helena de Ramirez.

PAGE 270 Everybody—parents, brothers. Interview with Francisco Ramirez Gomez.

PAGE 271 As the Ramirezes pulled away. Inspector general's report; interview with Francisco Ramirez Gomez.

PAGE 271 At 5:43 P.M., November 17, 1986. Inspector general's report; interview with Helena de Ramirez.

PAGE 272 The new year arrived. Letters quoted in full in inspector general's report.

Chapter 28: THE CARTEL INDICTMENT

PAGE 273 In 1977 DEA agents in Medellín. Interview with DEA agent Charles Cecil.

PAGE 273 The TAMPA bust prompted. Interviews with several confidential law enforcement sources.

PAGE 273 By 1983 Operation Fountainhead had traced dozens. From a 1983 Fountainhead database report.

PAGE 274 At the time she was living. Interview with DEA agent Bob Palumbo, 1986.

PAGE 275 In one 15-day period in January 1985. Jeff Leen, "Cocaine Seizures Soaring," *The Miami Herald,* 10 February, 1985, p. 1B.

PAGE 275 Cocaine made the cover of *Newsweek* and *Time* magazines. See *Newsweek,* "Cocaine: The Evil Empire," 25 February, 1985, pp. 14–23, and "Colombia's Kings of Coke," pp. 19–22; and *Time,* "Fighting the Cocaine Wars," 25 February, 1985, pp. 26–33.

PAGE 275 In the stairwell of the U.S. Attorney's Office. The account of how the cartel indictment came about is based on more than a dozen interviews with Dick Gregorie, Roberto Martinez, Robert Dunlop, Mark Schnapp, and Carol Cooper in 1987 and 1988.

PAGE 277 Count one began. United States of America *v.* Pablo Escobar Gaviria, et al., 18 November, 1986.

PAGE 282 *The Miami Herald* and *The New York Times.* Jeff Leen, "5 Colombian Drug Lords Are Indicted, Cartel Called No. 1 Trafficker," *The Miami Herald,* 19 November, 1986, p. 1A.

PAGE 282 In Colombia the indictment. *El Espectador,* 5 and 11 December, 1986.

PAGE 282 It was a common technique. Nevertheless by 1988 most of the members of *El Espectador*'s Informe Especial team, their counterparts from *El Tiempo,* and more than a dozen others of Colombia's finest journalists were living outside the country because of threats.

PAGE 283 "Legalize drug trafficking?" *El Espectador,* 5 December, 1986.

PAGE 283 On December 17, 1986, a Wednesday. *El Espectador,* 18 December, 1986.

Chapter 29: THE VIRGIN SMILES

PAGE 285 For Barco the Cano murder was. For details of the post-Cano crackdown see Guy Gugliotta, "After Murder, Colombia Leans on Drug Lords," *The Miami Herald,* 11 January, 1987, p. 1A.

PAGE 286 Still, Barco didn't do badly. Authors' interviews with detectives of Colombia's Department of Administrative Security (DAS), 24 August, 1987.

PAGE 286 One significant way in which. Barco's feelings regarding the Peace Process and guerrillas from the authors' interviews with Patriotic Union leader Jaime Pardo Leal, October 1986, and with a high-level Barco administration official who asked not to be identifed, January 1987.

PAGE 287 The FARC and the Patriotic Union. Herrera quoted in *El Tiempo,* 13 November, 1987.

PAGE 287 And it didn't. On January 13, 1987. Material on Parejo Gonzalez shooting from *El Tiempo,* 14 January, 1987, and *El Espectador,* 14 January, 1987.

PAGE 287 There was no question. Threats against Parejo related to authors by DAS detectives, 24 August, 1987. Comando Hernan Botero letter shown to the authors by friends at *El Tiempo* who asked not to be identified.

PAGE 288 National Police Major William. Most of the account of the capture of Carlos Lehder was related to the authors by a Colombian law enforcement source who asked not to be identified. He was interviewed 31 July, 1987. This material was augmented during the authors' interview 16 July, 1987, with DEA agent Mike Vigil, who had spoken at length with Lemus.

PAGE 292 In 1984 Jaime Ramirez had figured out. Material on the politics, diplomacy, and logistics of the Lehder capture from the authors' interview with a high-level DEA source who asked not to be identified, 27 July, 1987.

PAGE 292 Lehder arrived in Bogotá. Material on the trip to Florida from authors' interview with DEA agent Tom Bigoness, 22 June, 1987.

Chapter 30: "WITNESSES FROM HELL"

PAGE 294 Three U.S. marshals brought Max Mermelstein. Jeff Leen, "Tale of Intrigue Spun in Seal Trial, Testimony Paints Vivid Picture of Cartel," *The Miami Herald,* 11 May, 1987, p. 1A. The observations in this chapter are based on four days of reporting by Leen in Lake Charles.

PAGE 295 Prem Burns had very deliberately. Interview with Prem Burns, April 1988.

PAGE 296 Sharpstein had performed something of a miracle. Jeff Leen, "Singer's Drug Arrest Stuns Friends," *The Miami Herald,* 13 January 1986, p. 1B.

PAGE 296 On death penalty cases, she preferred. Interview with Prem Burns.

PAGE 297 Max Mermelstein's testimony was devastating. Mermelstein testimony, State of Louisiana *v.* Miguel Velez, Bernardo Antonio Vasquez, and Luis Carlos Quintero Cruz, 29 April, 1987.

Chapter 31: THE FINAL OFFENSIVE

PAGE 300 It began as a brief torrent. For a summary of the early sparring on extradition, see "Colombia Resurrects Extradition Treaty," *The Miami Herald,* 16 December 1986, p. 15A.

PAGE 300 The Supreme Court did, however. Authors' interview with U.S. Ambassador Richard Gillespie, January 1987.

PAGE 301 Unlike the United States. Barco's discussions with prominent Colombians confirmed in authors' interview with former President Misael Pastrana, January 1987.

PAGE 301 In the middle, trapped by circumstances. The desperation and disillusionment of the Supreme Court and easing off after the December 12 ruling described in the authors' interview with a highly placed juridical source who asked not to be identified, August 1987.

PAGE 302 Finally, 1986 had been so bloody. Buitrago quoted in *El Espectador*, 2 December, 1986.

PAGE 302 Yet the fact that. Authors' interview with Assistant Attorney General Fernando Navas Talero, 27 August, 1987. Authors' interview with an assistant interior minister who asked not to be identified, August 1987.

PAGE 303 The final antiextradition. See *The Miami Herald*, 8–11 February, 1987. The joint publishing campaign was put into effect January 14, the day after former Justice Minister Enrique Parejo Gonzalez was shot in Budapest.

PAGE 303 As the year progressed. For a chronology of these events, see *El Tiempo*, 13 June, 1987.

PAGE 304 The U.S. embassy issued. Quoted in Bradley Graham, "Extradition Law Voided in Colombia," *The Washington Post*, 28 June, 1987.

PAGE 304 Privately, however, one embassy official. Interview with DEA Special Agent-in-Charge George C. Frangullie, 25 August, 1987.

PAGE 304 Others were much harsher. Gomez quoted in daily newspaper *El Siglo*, Bogotá, 26 August, 1987.

PAGE 305 The cartel, not surprisingly. Letter from Lehder to Leonel Cabezas Linz in Armenia, Colombia, 1 July, 1987.

PAGE 305 Still, Lehder retained high spirits. Letter from Lehder to Cabezas, no date.

PAGE 305 Without an extradition treaty. Description of the tortuous course of the Rodriguez Orejuela case comes from authors' August 1987 interviews with a DEA agent and a Colombian prosecutor both of whom asked not to be identified.

PAGE 305 In worse shape was Pablo Escobar. Assessment of the cartel members' legal situation from authors' interview with a high-level official of the Colombian Department of Administrative Security (DAS), 21 August, 1987.

PAGE 306 Barco did not give up. Low Murtra's interview in *El Tiempo*, 8 November, 1987.

PAGE 306 Then in early August DAS. Material on Los Priscos from the authors' interviews with a high-level DAS official, 8 November, 1987, and with DAS detectives, 24 August, 1987.

PAGE 307 DAS's exposé of Los Priscos hurt the cartel. For Low Murtra's statement on Rodriguez Gacha and the Pardo Leal affair, see *El Tiempo* and *El Espectador*, 13 November, 1987. For analysis of the narco-guerrilla phenomenon, see Guy Gugliotta, "Fight between Rebels, Traffickers, Bleeds Colombia," *The Miami Herald*, 14 November, 1987, p 17A.

Chapter 32: CITIZEN JORGE LUIS OCHOA

PAGE 309 It was about 4:30 P.M. For basic information on the facts of Ochoa's arrest, see *El Tiempo* and *El Espectador*, November 22, 1987, and Jeff Leen and Guy Gugliotta, "Colombian Drug Lord Arrested," *The Miami Herald*, 22 November, 1987, p. 1A.

PAGE 310 Outwardly the circumstances of Ochoa's arrest. The best analysis of the government's plight appears in *Semana*, 1 December, 1987.

PAGE 311 President Virgilio Barco. Jack Hook interviewed by the authors, 21 November, 1987.

PAGE 311 The day after the arrest. Meeting and nature of the discussion confirmed to the authors by people who attended but did not wish to be identified by name, 22 November, 1987.

PAGE 311 In the end the government. Low Murtra quoted in *El Tiempo,* 23 November, 1987.

PAGE 311 To observe the machinations. Authors' interviews with members of the team, February 1988. Hereafter identified as "legal team."

PAGE 313 The cartel reacted to Ochoa's capture. See *El Tiempo,* 24 November, 1987, for an account of the Gomez Martinez incident, reprint of the communiqué.

PAGE 314 If the government won the first battle. See *El Tiempo,* 24 November, 1987, for an account of the initial sparring. Analysis is from authors' interviews with the legal team.

PAGE 315 The U.S. legal team left. Interviews with legal team. Barrera quoted in *El Tiempo,* 18 December, 1987.

PAGE 315 Sometime in the next ten days. Interviews with legal team; authors' interview with Humberto Barrera, 31 December, 1987.

PAGE 315 Finally, on December 30 Barrera. Authors' interview with Barrera.

PAGE 315 According to *Semana* magazine's. *Semana,* 12 January, 1988; interview with Barrera.

PAGE 316 The predictable, and by now standard. Authors' interview with DEA agent Errol Chavez, January 1988.

PAGE 316 On January 18, in an apparent. Authors' interviews with close friends of Pastrana who asked not to be identified, January 1988. The Pastrana family believed it was a cartel kidnapping by the second day.

PAGE 316 A week later, right at dawn. Details of the Hoyos murder, telephone call, *Semana,* 2 February, 1988; analysis of motives in both Hoyos and Pastrana kidnappings from authors' interviews with friends of Pastrana, February 1988.

Chapter 33: THE HENRY FORD OF COCAINE

PAGE 318 Federal agents with automatic weapons. Sydney P. Freedberg, "Drug King Goes to Court, Millionaire Gets Public Defender," *The Miami Herald,* 6 February, 1987.

PAGE 319 To Merkle, Lehder appeared scruffy. Robert Merkle interview. 17 April, 1988.

PAGE 319 Nine of the twelve jurors told. Joel Achenbach, "Showdown at Credibility Gap," *The Miami Herald's Tropic* magazine, 29 March, 1987, p. 12.

PAGE 320 Lehder's hearing in Jacksonville. Ron Word, "Tight Security for Court Appearance," Associated Press, 9 February, 1987.

PAGE 321 Speculation in legal circles. Rosalind Resnick, "1987 Was the Year Professionals Danced on an Ethical High Wire," *The Miami Herald,* 28 December, 1987, p. 15BM.

PAGE 321 Colleagues described him as "a lawyer's lawyer." Rosalind Resnick, "Black Sheep, Big Money," *The Miami Herald,* 19 April, 1987, p. 1F.

PAGE 321 Merkle said the letter. Joan Fleischman, "Accused Colombian Drug Chief's Offer to Cooperate Described as Frivolous," *The Miami Herald,* 6 May, 1987, p. 6A.

PAGE 322 In the basement of the federal detention center. Interview with Jung, August 1988.

PAGE 322 Merkle planned to lay out Lehder's career. Jeff Leen, "Lehder Aspired to

Be 'Coke King,' Prosecutor Portrays Him as Father of Modern Drug Smuggling," *The Miami Herald,* 17 November, 1987, p. 1A.

PAGE 323 Long-buried secrets emerged. Jeff Leen, "Greedy Pals Aided Drug Boss, Prosecutor: Lehder Sought Moral Destruction of U.S.," *The Miami Herald,* 31 January, 1981, p. 1A.

PAGE 324 Lehder at thirty-eight still retained. Description of Lehder based on the reporting of Jeff Leen, who attended four weeks of the Lehder trial for *The Miami Herald.*

PAGE 325 In the final week of the trial. Ron Word, Associated Press, May 1988.

Chapter 34: NATIONAL SECURITY

PAGE 326 On February 5, 1988, U.S. Attorney Leon Kellner. U.S. District Court, Southern District of Florida, indictment unsealed February 5, 1988; Kellner quoted in Stephen J. Hedges, "U.S.: Noriega Sold Out Panama," *The Miami Herald,* 6 February, 1988, p. 1A.

PAGE 327 But Noriega's other supposed transgressions. See, for instance, Guy Gugliotta, "Scandals Hint at Panama Role in Drug Trade," *The Miami Herald,* 3 September, 1984, p. 1A. During 1984, the Drug Enforcement Administration refused repeated attempts by the authors and other reporters to discuss allegations of drug trafficking in Panama.

PAGE 327 Pablo Escobar, who had striven. See *Newsweek,* 15 February, 1988; *Time,* 7 March, 1988; *The New York Times,* 10 April, 1988.

PAGE 328 "Stopping drug trafficking. Kerry quoted in Andrés Oppenheimer, "U.S. Urged to Step Up Drug Fight," *The Miami Herald,* 14 February, 1988, p. 1A.

PAGE 329 By the end of the trial Merkle's office was directing. Jeff Leen, "Bahamian Leader Targeted in Bribery Probe, Sources Say," *The Miami Herald,* 30 April, 1988, p. 8A.

PAGE 334 Afterward a very drained Ed Shohat. Jeff Leen, "Cocaine Czar Lehder Guilty, Colombian Trafficker Could Face Life Term for Shipping Drugs," *The Miami Herald,* 20 May, 1988, p. 1A.

ACKNOWLEDGMENTS

The authors conducted more than three hundred interviews during the three and one half years of research that went into this book. Some of those interviewed, like Colonel Jaime Ramirez and Jaime Pardo Leal, have died in the drug wars. Others are in hiding or living in exile, pursued by the traffickers because of what they have written, said, or testified to in court. Many friends in Colombia and the United States at their own request shall not be named here. They know who they are, and they know the debt that is owed them.

Special thanks are due to Colombian news organizations and especially to individual reporters who helped make a difficult and dangerous story comprehensible to outsiders. Their knowledge and assistance were indispensable.

Special thanks are also due to James Savage, the investigations editor of *The Miami Herald,* who was deeply involved in the conception and execution of a ten-part series that appeared originally in the *Herald* and later became the basis for this book. The authors would also like to thank Janet Chusmir, executive editor of the *Herald,* and Pete Weitzel, the paper's managing editor, for granting the authors leaves of absence and the right to use material that had originally appeared in the *Herald.* City Editor John Brecher and Foreign Editor Mark Seibel were also very gracious in committing their resources to this project. Finally, Rick Ovelmen, the *Herald's* general counsel, read the manuscript with a keen eye and provided sage advice.

This book could not have been written without substantial cooperation from the people who fight the drug war, particularly those in the U.S. Drug Enforcement Administration, whose diligence and effort at an often thankless task receive too little notice. The authors would like to thank in particular Jack Lawn, the administrator of the DEA, and several of those under his command: William Alden, Charlie Cecil, Errol Chavez, Carol Cooper, Con Daugherty, Robert Feldkamp, George Frangullie, Larry Galina, Jack Hook, Jake Jacobsen,

James Kibble, William Mockler, Johnny Phelps, Mike Vigil, and Billy Yout.

We cannot name everyone who helped us; what follows is only a partial list. We thank Caesar Bernal, John Camp, Fabio Castillo, Candace Cunningham, Carlson Daniel, Liz Donovan, Ruthie Golden, Dick Gregorie, Gonzalo Guillen, Carl Hiaasen, Rose Klayman, Bob Levinson, Roberto Martinez, Lynn Medford, Gay Nemeti, Francisco Ramirez Gomez, Carla Anne Robbins, Timothy Ross, Enrique Santos Castillo, Mark Schnapp, Tom Sclafani, Al Singleton, Lewis Tambs, Gray Thomas, Alfonso Torres Robles, and Ron Word.

INDEX